Office 2010 Just the Steps™ FOR DUMMIES®

by Elaine Marmel

Office 2010 Just the Steps™ For Dummies®

Published by
Wiley Publishing, Inc.
111 River Street
Hoboken, NJ 07030-5774

www.wiley.com

Published by Wiley Publishing, Inc., Indianapolis, Indiana

Published simultaneously in Canada

For general information on our other products and services, please contact our Customer Care Department within the U.S. at 877-762-2974, outside the U.S. at 317-572-3993, or fax 317-572-4002.

For technical support, please visit www.wiley.com/techsupport.

Wiley also publishes its books in a variety of electronic formats. Some content that appears in print may not be available in electronic books.

Library of Congress Control Number: 2010924566

ISBN: 978-0-470-53219-5

Manufactured in the United States of America

10 9 8 7 6 5 4 3 2 1

About the Author

Elaine Marmel is President of Marmel Enterprises, LLC, an organization that specializes in technical writing and software training. Elaine has an MBA from Cornell University and worked on projects to build financial management systems for New York City and Washington, D.C. This prior experience provided the foundation for Marmel Enterprises, LLC to help small businesses manage the project of implementing a computerized accounting system.

Elaine left her native Chicago for the warmer climes of Arizona (by way of Cincinnati, OH; Jerusalem, Israel; Ithaca, NY; Washington, D.C.; and Tampa, FL) where she basks in the sun with her PC; her dog, Josh; and her cats, Cato, Watson, and Buddy; and sings barbershop harmony with the 2006 International Championship Scottsdale Chorus.

Elaine spends most of her time writing; she has authored and co-authored more than 50 books about Microsoft Project, QuickBooks, Peachtree, Quicken for Windows, Quicken for DOS, Microsoft Excel, Microsoft Word for Windows, Microsoft Word for the Mac, Windows 98, 1-2-3 for Windows, and Lotus Notes. From 1994 to 2006, she also was the contributing editor to monthly publications *Peachtree Extra* and *QuickBooks Extra*.

Dedication

To Polly Thompson, a fun client who has become a good friend and who inspired much of the content in the Outlook section. I sure hope this book helps you!

Author's Acknowledgments

Because a book is not just the work of the author, I'd like to acknowledge and thank all the folks who made this book possible. Thanks to Kyle Looper for the opportunity to write this book. Thank you, Lisa Bucki, for making sure I "told no lies." Thank you, Teresa Artman, for making sure I was understandable. And, Blair Pottenger, you made my life so easy and writing the book such a pleasure with your top-notch management of all the players involved in this book.

Publisher's Acknowledgments

We're proud of this book; please send us your comments at http://dummies.custhelp.com. For other comments, please contact our Customer Care Department within the U.S. at 877-762-2974, outside the U.S. at 317-572-3993, or fax 317-572-4002.

Some of the people who helped bring this book to market include the following:

Acquisitions and Editorial

Project Editor: Blair J. Pottenger

Acquisitions Editor: Kyle Looper

Senior Copy Editor: Teresa Artman

Technical Editor: Lisa Bucki

Editorial Manager: Kevin Kirschner

Editorial Assistant: Amanda Graham

Sr. Editorial Assistant: Cherie Case

Cartoons: Rich Tennant (www.the5thwave.com)

Composition Services

Project Coordinator: Sheree Montgomery

Layout and Graphics: Claudia Bell, Carl Byers, Joyce Haughey, Ronald G. Terry

Proofreaders: Jacqui Brownstein

Indexer: BIM Indexing & Proofreading Services

Publishing and Editorial for Technology Dummies

Richard Swadley, Vice President and Executive Group Publisher

Andy Cummings, Vice President and Publisher

Mary Bednarek, Executive Acquisitions Director

Mary C. Corder, Editorial Director

Publishing for Consumer Dummies

Diane Graves Steele, Vice President and Publisher

Composition Services

Debbie Stailey, Director of Composition Services

Contents at a Glance

Introduction

You probably bought this book because you're focused on "getting the job done." You probably already know why you want to do something, but you want a refresher on how to do something. Rather than wade through a book that contains both the how and the why, use *Microsoft Office 2010 Just the Steps For Dummies* to quickly find the steps you need to accomplish tasks in Word, Excel, PowerPoint, or Outlook — and move on.

About This Book

Several software programs sport the "Office 2010" moniker. In addition, Microsoft Office 2010 is available in several editions, and each edition includes a different set of software programs. For example, most editions include Word and Excel, but you won't find Microsoft Office Access 2010 in every edition of Office 2010. Because Word, Excel, PowerPoint, and Outlook are among the most widely used Office programs, this book focuses on these four applications.

In addition to presenting steps to accomplish a wide variety of tasks within these powerful products, there is also a section that helps you use these products together. For example, you can create mailing labels using your Outlook contacts, but you need to use both Word and Outlook — and possibly Excel, too — to get those labels. This book is all about getting productive with Office 2010 right away. As the title suggests, here are the steps — *just the steps* — that you need to do many common Office 2010 tasks.

Why You Need This Book

You can't wait weeks to master Office 2010. You use these applications daily to prepare reports, spreadsheets, presentations, and get your e-mail. You have to figure out these products quickly. When you hit a bump in the road and you need a quick answer to get you moving again, open this book; it's full of quick, clear steps that keep your learning in high gear.

Conventions used in this book

- When you have to type something in a text box, I put it in **bold** type.
- For menu commands, I use the ⇨ symbol to separate menu items. For example, choose Tools⇨Options. The ⇨ symbol just means "Open the Tools menu and then click Options."
- Points of interest in some figures are circled. The text tells you what to look for, and the circle makes it easy to find.

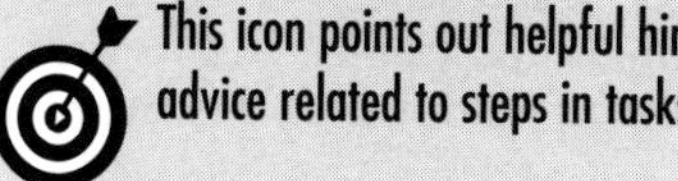
This icon points out helpful hints or advice related to steps in tasks.

How This Book Is Organized

This book is conveniently divided into several handy parts.

Part I: Word

In this part, you cover everything from typing text into a document, formatting text, saving and opening documents, creating tables and columns, and printing.

Part II: Excel

When it comes to crunching numbers, nothing beats Excel. In this part, you see how to build a spreadsheet, work with formulas, format worksheets and manage workbooks, work with various Excel tools, create charts, and print Excel information.

Part III: PowerPoint

When it comes to sharing information, presentations are one of the most powerful tools that you can use. In PowerPoint, you can create presentations that pack a punch that gets your audience's attention. In this section, see how to create and edit a presentation; add objects, art, animations, and themes to your slides; create audience handouts; and set up and run a slide show.

Part IV: Outlook

Outlook is the most widely used e-mail client on the planet, but it's so much more than just a way to collect e-mail. In Outlook, you can store contacts, set up meetings and appointments, manage where you're supposed to be at any particular time, and keep track of the things you need to accomplish. This part helps you use Outlook well beyond just collecting and answering e-mail.

Part V: Using Office Products Together

It never fails; you start building a table in Word, only to realize that the analysis of the table data would be sooooo much easier if you had the table information in Excel. Or, you *really* need the gorgeous chart you just created in Excel to appear in your PowerPoint presentation. Yes, you can easily get information from one product into another, this part shows you how. The first chapter in this section, Chapter 25, covers features that are common to all Office programs — like the Ribbon and the Quick Access Toolbar (and more). Mail merging is included this section because although Word actually does the merging, the information typically needs to be merged (such as the mailing list information) to come from Excel or Outlook. And finally, this section covers the concept of working with Office 2010 documents in a group environment, where you have many people reviewing documents and making comments.

Get Ready To . . .

Whether you need to get started editing a Word document, create a formula in Excel, add animation to a PowerPoint presentation, or manage your Outlook contacts, just browse this book, pick a task, and jump in. Office 2010 can be your best friend if you know how to use it, and the tasks covered in this book will help you quickly master the things you need to do.

Part I
Word

"They won't let me through security until I remove the bullets from my Word document."

Handling Document Files

1

Use Microsoft Office Word 2010, the gold standard of word processor applications, to create and edit documents, such as letters and reports. To keep copies of your work, you save the documents you create. If you need to make a change to a document you created earlier and then saved and closed, you open the document. You also open documents other people may give you if you want to read or edit those documents.

With Word 2010 open, when you open a document created in Word 97–2007, Word opens the document in Compatibility Mode, enabling only those features available in the version used to create the document. To incorporate features available in Word 2010, you can convert the document from a `.doc` to a `.docx` file (and I show you how).

This first chapter helps you familiarize yourself with the Word screen and get started working with documents. In this chapter, you

- Open, explore, and close the Word window.
- Enter text and move around a Word document.
- Save a document.
- Set options that specify the folder where you want to save your documents.
- Start a new document and open an existing document.
- Convert a Word 97–2007 document to Word 2010 format.

Get ready to . . .

Open and Explore Word

1. Choose Start➪All Programs➪Microsoft Office➪Microsoft Word 2010 to open a blank, new document in Word. Figure 1-1 and the table here help you identify the major parts of the Word window.

Location	Item
1	Quick Access Toolbar (QAT)
2	Title bar
3	Ribbon
4	Document area
5	Status bar

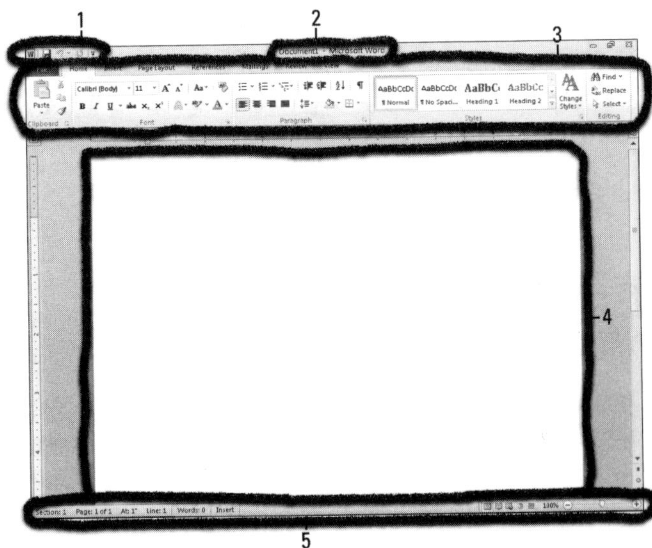

Figure 1-1

The Ribbon appears between the default placement of the Quick Access Toolbar and the title bar and above the document area. Both the Ribbon and the Quick Access Toolbar appear at all times in Word.

You can change the appearance of the Ribbon, the Quick Access Toolbar, and the Status bar; see Chapter 25 for details.

2. Close any document by clicking the X in the upper-right corner of its screen. Close Word by clicking the File tab and then clicking Exit in Backstage view that appears.

Enter Text in a Document

1. In an open Word document, click in the document area.
2. Type text. As you type, Word displays characters to the left of the *insertion point,* which is the vertical black bar shown in Figure 1-2.

You don't need to press Enter at the end of a line because Word automatically wraps text to the next line. Press Enter only to start a new paragraph.

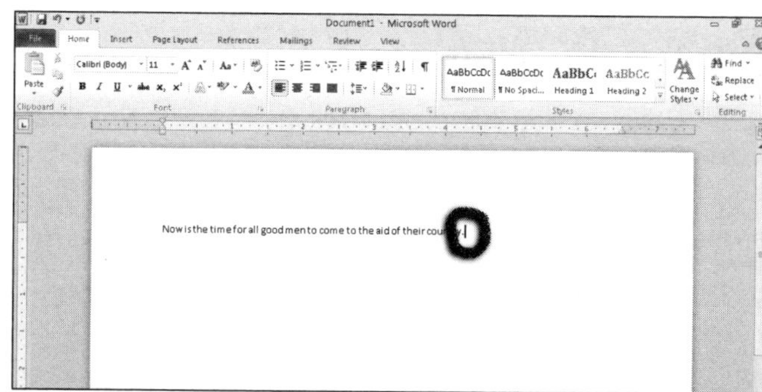

Figure 1-2

Move Around in the Document Area

The insertion point marks the location where text appears when you type. You can move to other locations in the document using any of the following keystrokes:

Press	*To Move*
Any arrow key	One character in the direction of the arrow key
Ctrl+↑ or Ctrl+↓	Up or down one paragraph
Page Up or Page Down	One screen up or down
Home or End	To the beginning or the end of the current line
Ctrl+Home or Ctrl+End	To the beginning or the end of the document

Save a Document

1. Click the File tab. From Backstage view that appears, choose Save As.
2. In the Save As dialog box that appears (see Figure 1-3), navigate to the folder where you want to save the document.
3. Type a name for the document in the File Name field. To down-save in Word 97–2003 format (`.doc`), choose that format from the Save As Type list.
4. Click Save, and Word saves the document. The name of the document appears in the title bar. To save subsequent changes to the document, you can click the Save button on the Quick Access Toolbar.

The Save button looks like an old-time computer floppy disk.

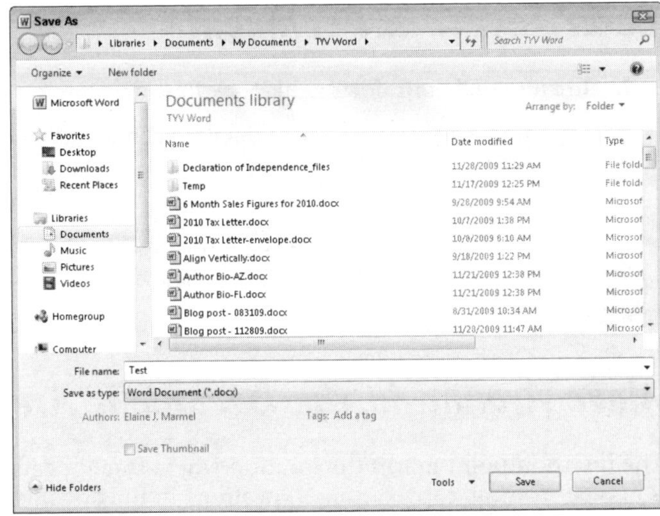

Figure 1-3

Set Options for Saving Documents

1. Click the File tab; from BackStage view that appears, choose Options.
2. In the Word Options dialog box that appears, click Save (left side of the dialog box) to display options you can apply to all documents you save (see Figure 1-4), including the folder where you save your documents and the format for all Word documents. You also can set *AutoRecover* preferences, which Word uses to help you recover unsaved work if Word closes prematurely.
3. Click OK to save your selections.

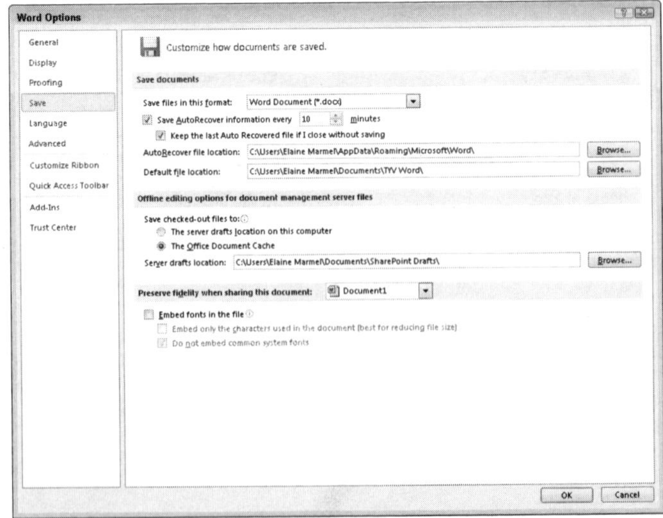

Figure 1-4

Start a New Document

1. Click the File tab; from Backstage view that appears, choose New (see Figure 1-5).
2. In the New dialog box that appears, click a template (from the Available Templates list on the left); the right side displays a preview of the template you select.
3. Click Create below the preview; a new document appears onscreen.

A template contains predefined settings and styles — such as how text and headings look — which helps you avoid re-creating them each time you need them. You can use a template you make or one you find at Office.com.

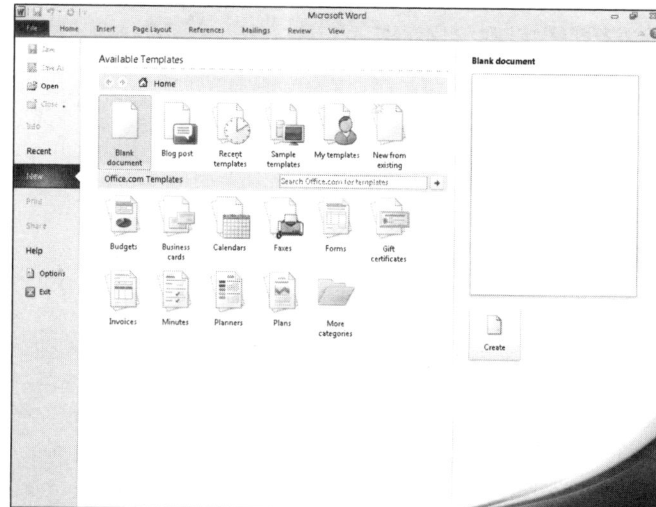

Figure 1-5

Open a Document

1. Click the File tab; from Backstage view that appears, choose Open. To view documents you opened recently, choose Recent from Backstage view.
2. In the Open dialog box that appears (see Figure 1-6), navigate to the folder containing the document you want to open and then click the document. You can choose a document created in a prior version of Word.
3. Click Open. The document you selected appears onscreen in Word, ready for you to edit.

When you finish working with a document, save it; then, click the X in the upper-right corner to remove it from the Word screen.

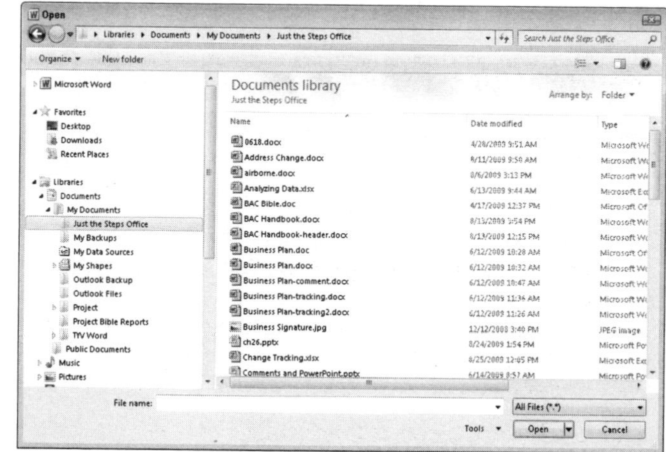

Figure 1-6

Convert a Prior Version Document to a Word 2010 Document

1. Using the steps in "Open a Document" earlier in this chapter, open a document created in an earlier version of Word; the title bar indicates that Word opened the document in Compatibility Mode (see Figure 1-7).
2. Click the File tab; in Backstage view, choose Convert. Word displays a message indicating you're about to convert the current document to a Word 2010 document (see Figure 1-8).
3. Click OK. `Compatibility Mode` disappears from the Word title bar, but Word doesn't save the document.
4. Click the Save button on the Quick Access Toolbar. By default, Word replaces the older version of the document, using the name assigned to the older version of the document. If the older version was a Word 97–2003 document, Word 2010 changes the extension from `.doc` to `.docx`.

Converting a document replaces the original unless you supply a new name. To supply a new name, click the File tab and choose Save As.

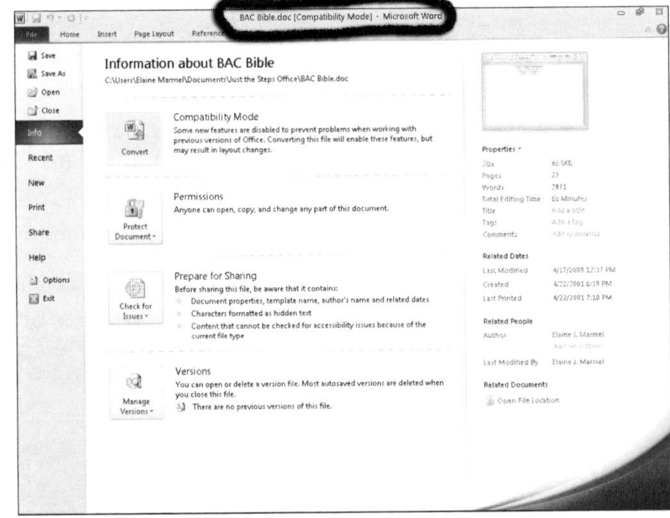

Figure 1-7

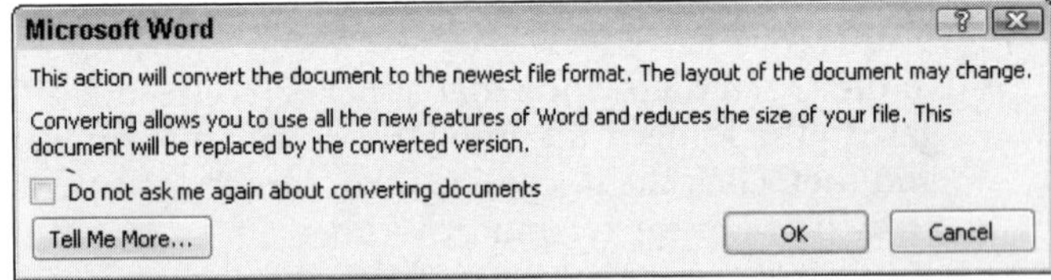

Figure 1-8

Exploring the Basics of Editing

Chapter 2

You'll devote much of the time you spend in a Word document to editing that document. Whether you're editing text, paragraphs, or pages, I devoted separate chapters in this book to each category because you take different actions, depending on the type of editing you need to do.

However, all types of editing share some common characteristics and actions, and this chapter focuses on those basic editing techniques you'll need.

In this chapter, you

- Insert additional text and replace existing text.
- Work with Insert and Overtype modes.
- Delete text and undo changes.
- Select text so that you can move or copy it.
- Use the Office Clipboard to copy several blocks of text in one copy operation.
- Mark your place in a document so that you can return to that location.
- Insert blank lines in a document.
- View your document in different ways.

Get ready to . . .

Insert Additional Text

1. Click the location in the document where you want to insert text (see Figure 2-1). The insertion point flashes where you clicked.

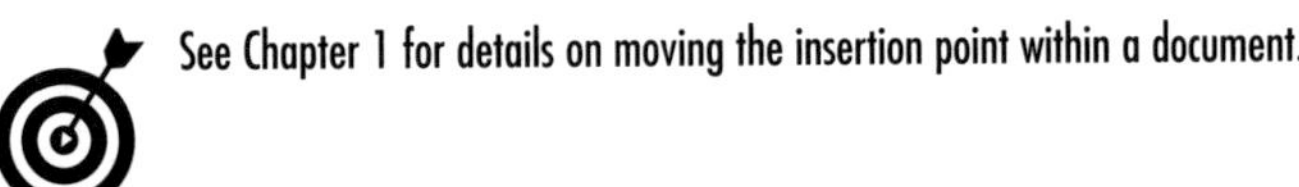

See Chapter 1 for details on moving the insertion point within a document.

2. Type the text you want to insert. Word inserts the text to the left of the insertion point and moves existing text to the right (see Figure 2-2).

By default, Word functions in Insert mode, adding any text you type without overwriting existing text.

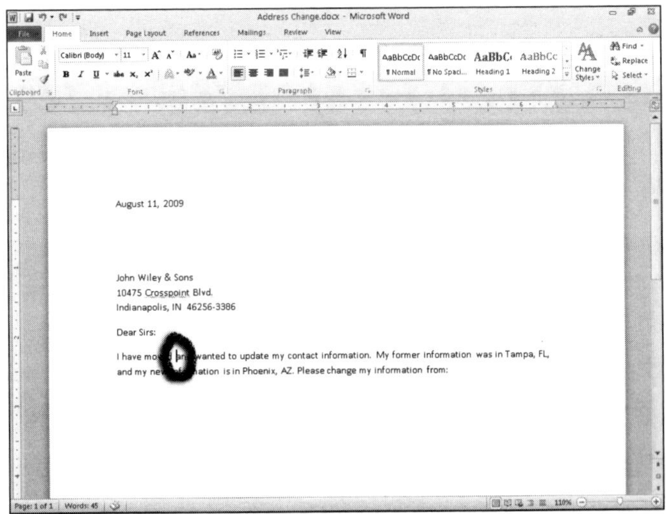

Figure 2-1

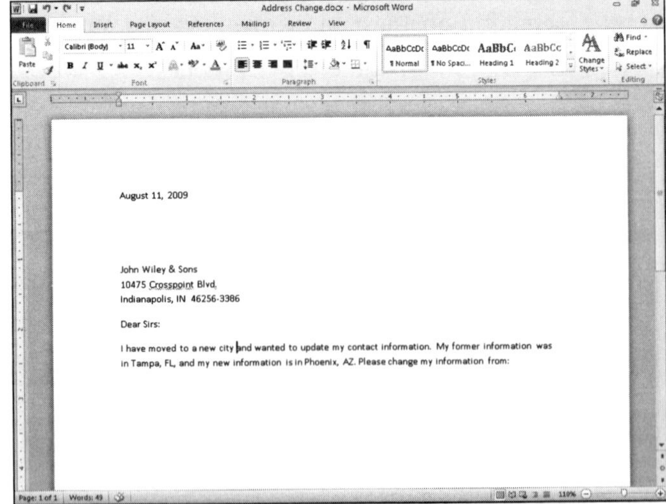

Figure 2-2

Insert Text by Replacing Existing Text

1. Select the text you want to replace with new text. See "Selecting Text" later in this chapter for details on how to select text.
2. Type the new text. Word replaces the selected text with the new text you type (see Figure 2-3).

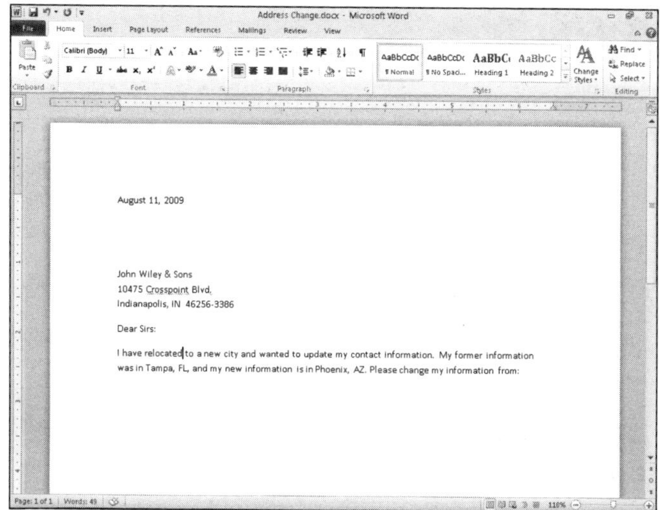

Figure 2-3

Switch between Insert and Overtype Modes

1. Right-click the status bar and choose Overtype to display the Insert/Overtype indicator on the status bar (see Figure 2-4).
2. Click anywhere in the document area to close the Customize Status Bar menu.

Clicking Overtype doesn't switch Word to Overtype mode; instead, it displays the indicator on the status bar that you can use to switch between modes.

3. Click the indicator to switch between Overtype and Insert mode. In Overtype mode, Word replaces existing text to the right of the insertion point, character for character. In Insert mode, Word adds to existing text.
4. Position the insertion point where you want to replace existing text; then type the new text.

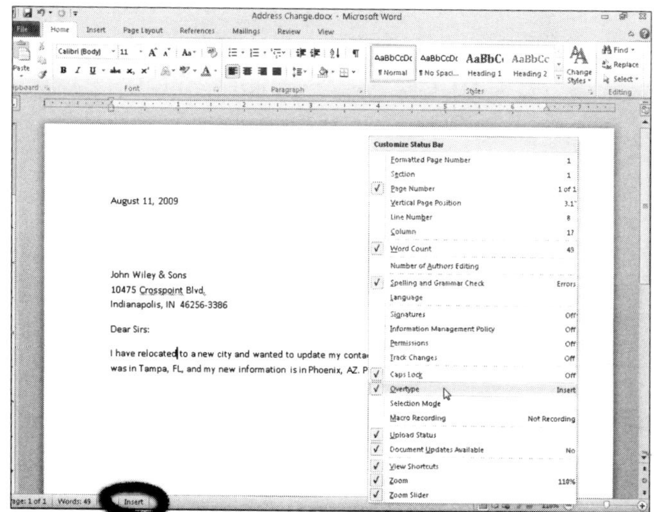

Figure 2-4

Delete Text

1. Click immediately to the right of the character you want to delete (see Figure 2-5).

2. Press the Backspace key on the keyboard. Word deletes one character to the left of the insertion point each time you press the Backspace key.

To delete the character to the right of the insertion point, press the Delete key on the keyboard.

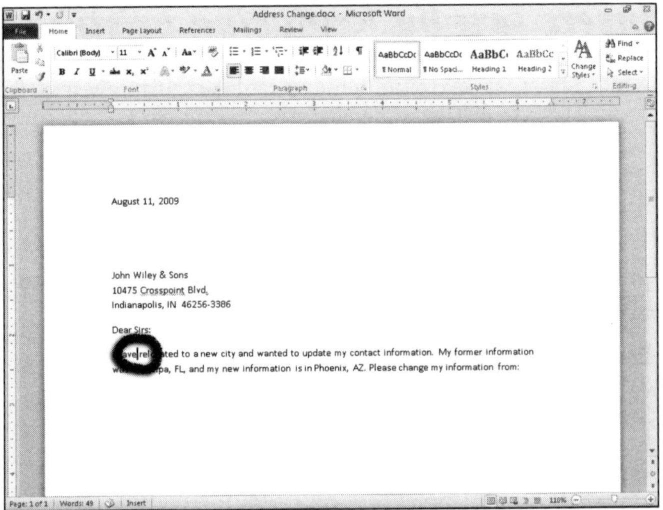

Figure 2-5

Undo Changes

1. Click the Undo button on the Quick Access Toolbar. Word removes the effects of your last action (see Figure 2-6).

2. Click Undo repeatedly to remove the effects of your actions in the reverse order that you took them.

Click the Redo button (to the right of the Undo button) to reinstate an action removed by clicking Undo.

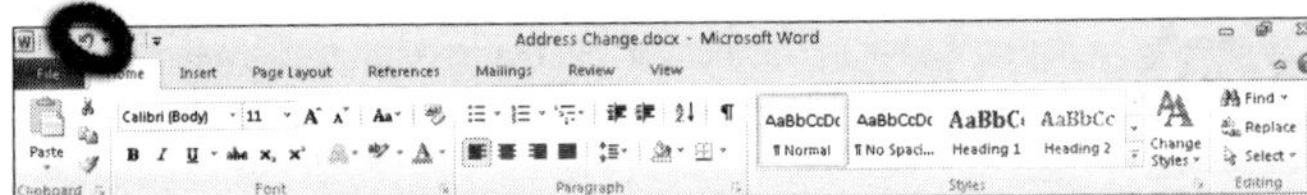

Figure 2-6

Select Text

1. Place the insertion point to the left of the first character you want to select (see Figure 2-7).
2. Drag to the right and down over the text you want to select (see Figure 2-8). When you release the mouse button, Word highlights the selection and displays the Mini Toolbar, which initially appears transparent, but, as you move the mouse pointer over it, the Mini Toolbar solidifies. You can use the Mini Toolbar or ignore it.

You can select using the keyboard; press and hold the Shift key while you press an arrow key.

To cancel a selection, you can press any arrow key on your keyboard or click anywhere onscreen.

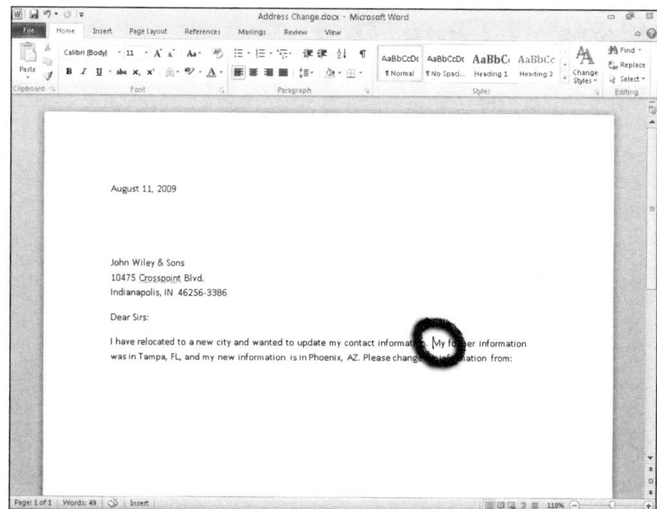

Figure 2-7

Use the following shortcuts to make some common selections:

To Select This	Do This
A word	Double-click the word.
Contiguous words	Click at the beginning of the first word; then press Ctrl+Shift+→.
Noncontiguous words	Double-click the first word; then press Ctrl while you double-click each subsequent word.
A sentence	Press Ctrl and click anywhere in the sentence.
The entire document	Press Ctrl+A.

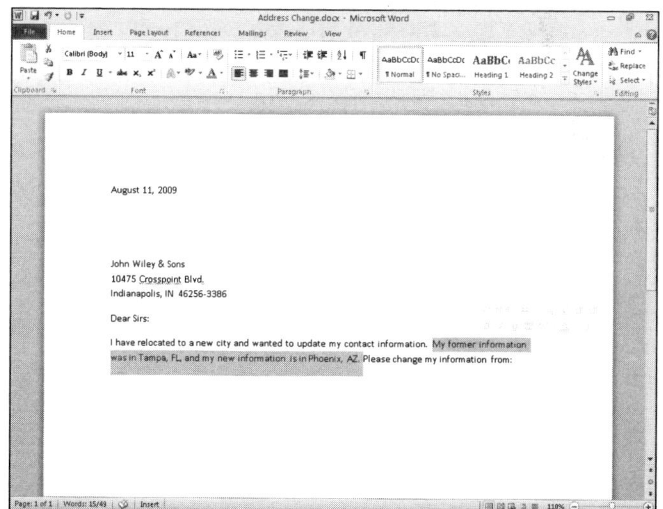

Figure 2-8

Move or Copy Text

1. Select the text you want to move or copy; then click the Home tab.
2. Click the Cut button to move text or the Copy button to copy text.
3. Place the insertion point where you want the text to appear.
4. Click the Paste button (see Figure 2-9).

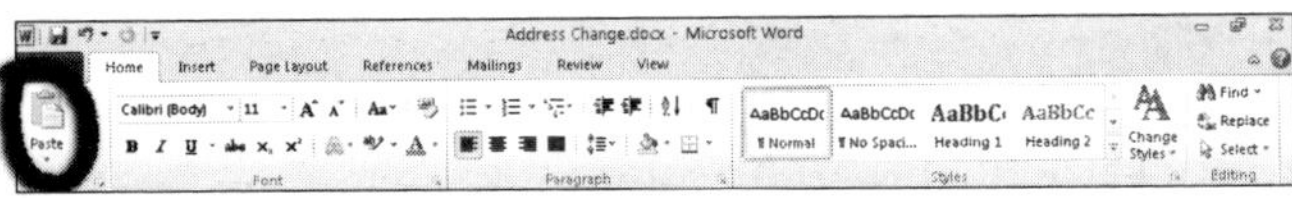

Figure 2-9

Copy Blocks of Text

1. On the Home tab, click the Dialog Box Launcher button (arrow, bottom right) of the Clipboard group to display the Clipboard pane.
2. Select text; then click the Copy or Cut buttons. The selected text appears on the Clipboard (see Figure 2-10). Repeat this step for each block of text you want to cut or copy.
3. In the document, click where you want to place one of the selections from the Clipboard.
4. In the Clipboard pane, click the item you want to paste.
5. Repeat Steps 3 and 4 for each selection.
6. When you finish pasting, click the X in the Clipboard pane to close it.

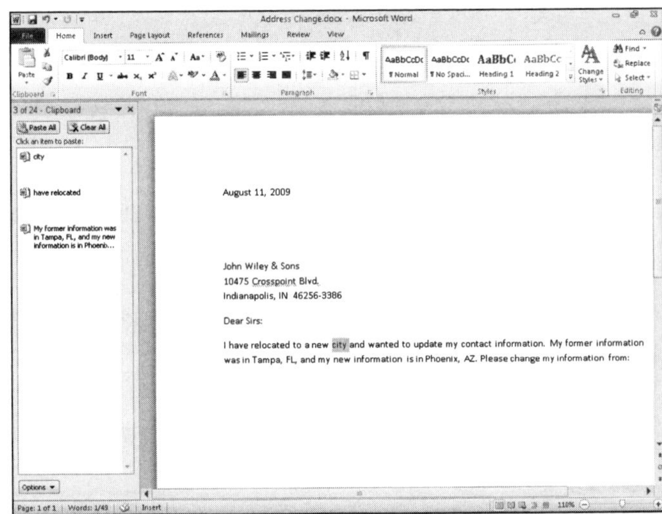

Figure 2-10

Mark Your Place in a Document

1. Click the location you want to mark. You can select text to mark the location but that isn't necessary.
2. Click the Insert tab.
3. In the Links group, click Bookmark (see Figure 2-11).
4. In the Bookmark dialog box that appears (see Figure 2-12), type a single-word name for the bookmark.
5. Click Add. Word saves the bookmark and closes the Bookmark dialog box.

You can display bookmarks in your document. Click the File tab and then click Options. In the Word Options dialog box that appears, click Advanced on the left. Then, in the Show Document Content section, select the Show Bookmarks check box and click OK. A bookmark that doesn't contain text looks like a light gray capital I. If a bookmark contains text, Word surrounds the text with brackets ([ ]).

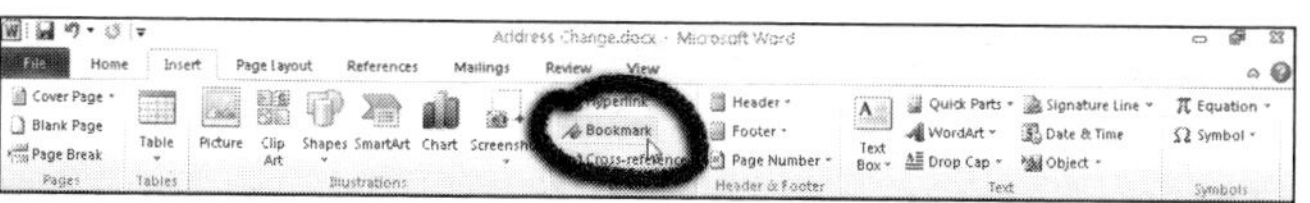

Figure 2-11

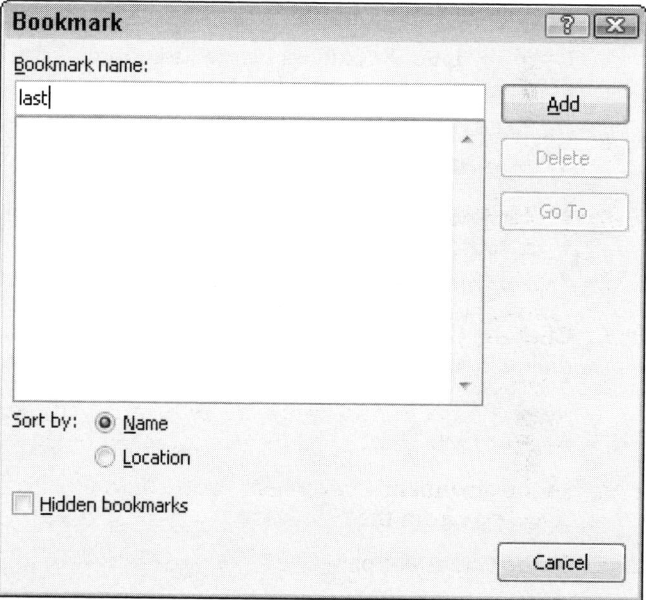

Figure 2-12

Find a Marked Place in a Document

1. Press F5 on the keyboard to display the Go To tab of the Find and Replace dialog box (see Figure 2-13).
2. Choose Bookmark from the Go To What list.
3. Open the Enter Bookmark Name drop-down list (click the down-arrow) and select a bookmark.
4. Click the Go To button. Word moves the insertion point to the bookmark (see Figure 2-14).

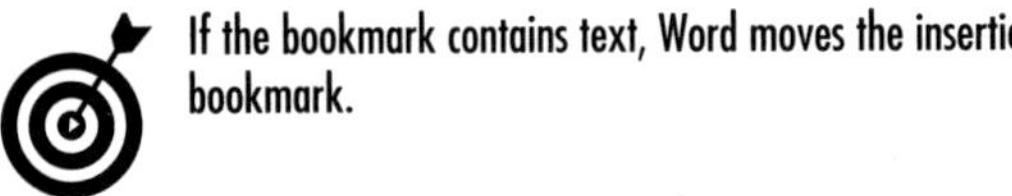

If the bookmark contains text, Word moves the insertion point to the beginning of the bookmark.

5. Click the Close button to close the Find and Replace dialog box.

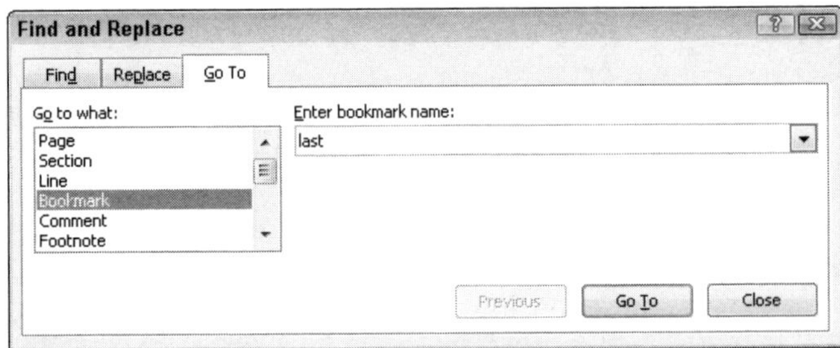

Figure 2-13

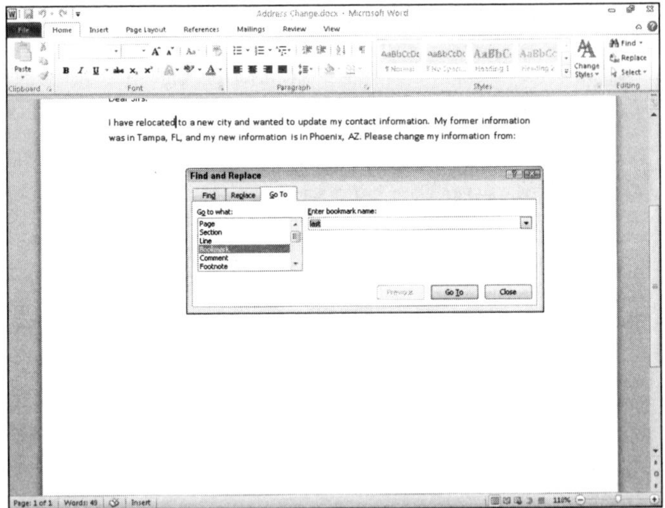

Figure 2-14

Start a New Paragraph

1. Place the insertion point where you want to start a new paragraph.
2. Press Enter. Word inserts a paragraph mark at the end of the line. You can display paragraph marks (¶; pilcrow characters, which look like a backward P) (see Figure 2-15) by clicking the Show/Hide button in the Paragraph group on the Home tab.
3. Press Enter for each blank line you want to insert.

Word stores paragraph formatting in paragraph marks. When you start a new paragraph, you can change the new paragraph's formatting without affecting the preceding paragraph's formatting. See Chapter 5 for details on paragraph formatting and displaying formatting marks.

Figure 2-15

Insert a Line Break

1. Place the insertion point where you want to start a new line.
2. Press Shift+Enter. Word inserts a line break, also called a *soft return,* like the one shown in Figure 2-16 after the word "Sons."
3. Press Shift+Enter for each blank line you want to insert.

Lines separated by line breaks are still considered part of the same paragraph; therefore, paragraph formatting applies to all lines, even when separated by line breaks.

Figure 2-16

Switch Document Views

1. Click the View tab.
2. From the Document Views group, select a view.

You also can click a View shortcut button at the right edge of the status bar.

- In *Print Layout view,* shown in Figure 2-17, Word displays the document as it will print.
- In *Draft view,* Word displays placeholders for page breaks and reveals information that won't print, such as the style assigned to each paragraph (see Figure 2-18).

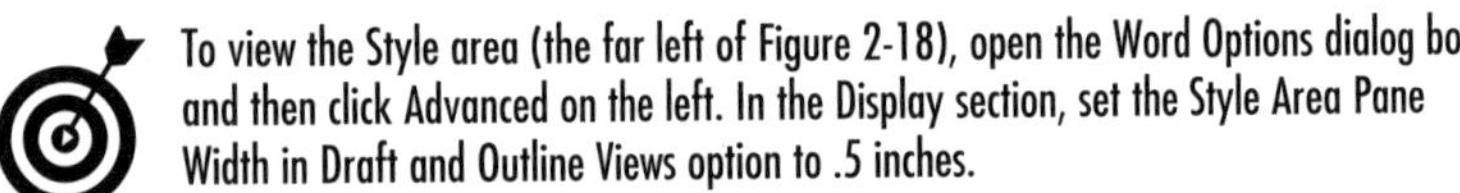

To view the Style area (the far left of Figure 2-18), open the Word Options dialog box and then click Advanced on the left. In the Display section, set the Style Area Pane Width in Draft and Outline Views option to .5 inches.

- Use *Web Layout view* when you are designing a Web page.
- *Outline view* focuses on a document's organization, indenting text styled using headings based on the heading number. You can easily move or copy all text associated with a single heading.
- By removing the Ribbon and the Quick Access Toolbar as well as other screen elements, *Full Screen Reading view* aims to minimize eye strain when you read a document onscreen. To return to the previous view, click Close in the upper-right corner of the screen.

Figure 2-17

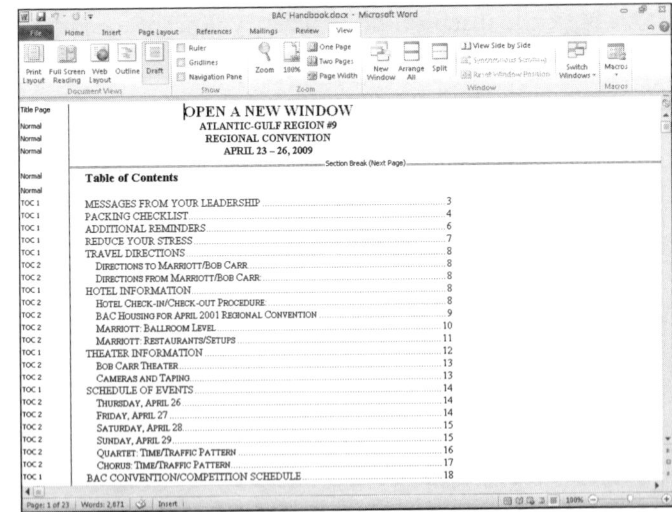

Figure 2-18

Proofing Documents

Proofing a document is essential, especially if others will be reviewing your document. Nothing destroys credibility more quickly than a document filled with spelling errors or grammar mistakes. And, sometimes, you might have known how to spell a word, but that evil keyboard just jumped right up and misspelled it for you. Word contains tools that help you give a professional look and feel to your document even if spelling and grammar aren't your specialty or your keyboard is particularly uncooperative.

In this chapter, you discover how to

- Find and replace text.
- Automatically correct typing mistakes and check spelling and grammar.
- Insert frequently used phrases.
- Use the Word Thesaurus.

Chapter

3

Get ready to . . .

Find Text

1. Place the insertion point in the document where you want to begin to search.
2. Click the Home tab. From the Editing group, click the Find button. The Navigation pane appears (see Figure 3-1).

Depending on the screen resolution you use, you might see only the Editing button, which you click to open a drop-down list of commands that includes the Find button.

3. Click in the Search Document box and type the text for which you want to search.
4. To search for text, press Enter. Word displays a list of occurrences in the Navigation pane and selects the first instance of that text in the document (see Figure 3-2).
5. Click any occurrence to navigate to it. To start a new search, click the X beside the Search Document box.

Use the other tabs in the Navigation pane to browse the headings and pages in your document.

6. Click the X in the upper-right corner of the Navigation pane to close it.

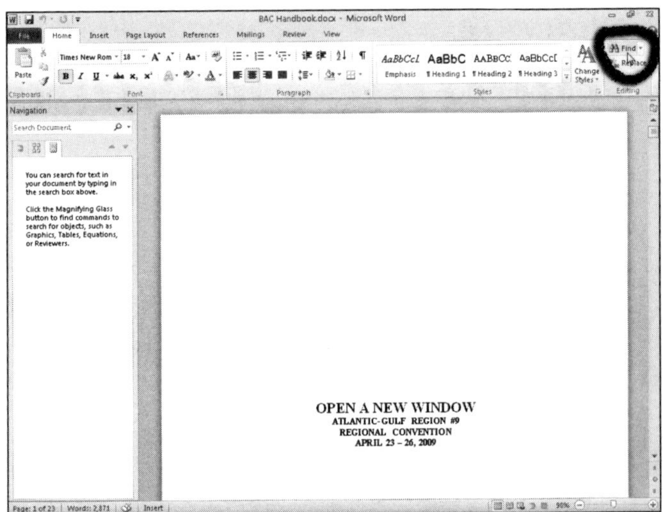

Figure 3-1

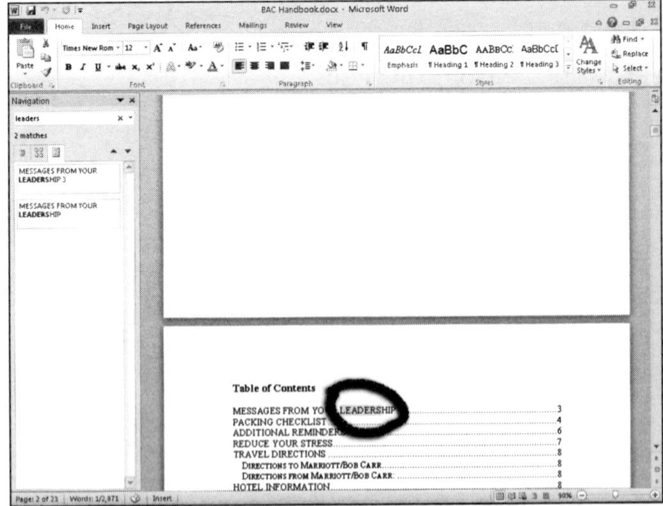

Figure 3-2

Replace Text

1. Click the Home tab. From the Editing group, click Replace to display the Find and Replace dialog box. If necessary, click the Editing button to select Replace.
2. In the Find What field, type the text for which you want to search (see Figure 3-3).
3. In the Replace With field, type the text you want to substitute.
4. Click the Replace button. Word finds the first occurrence of the text you typed in the Find What field, replaces it with the text you provided in the Replace With field, and looks for the next occurrence. If Word finds additional occurrences, it highlights each occurrence, letting you replace that occurrence if appropriate. When Word finds no additional occurrences of the phrase for which you searched, Work displays a message to that effect (see Figure 3-4).

Click the More button to set search options or to search for formatting (such as boldface) or special characters (such as tabs).

5. Click the Close button.

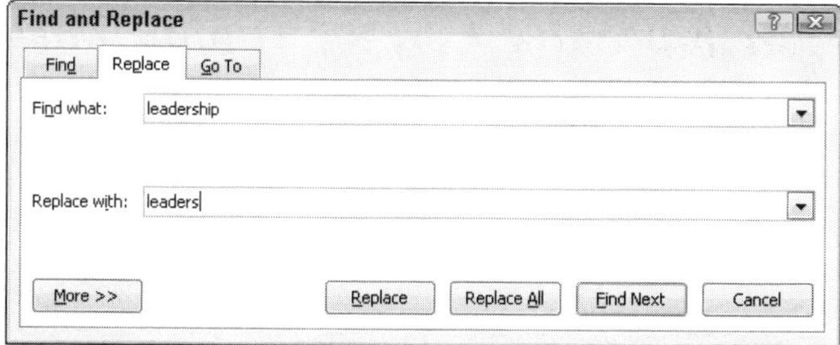

Figure 3-3

Figure 3-4

Automatically Correct Typing Mistakes

You can add words you commonly mistype to the list of words corrected automatically by Word using these steps:

1. Click the File tab. In the Backstage view that appears, choose Options (see Figure 3-5).

2. In the Word Options dialog box that appears, click Proofing on the left.

3. Click the AutoCorrect Options button (see Figure 3-6) to display the AutoCorrect dialog box.

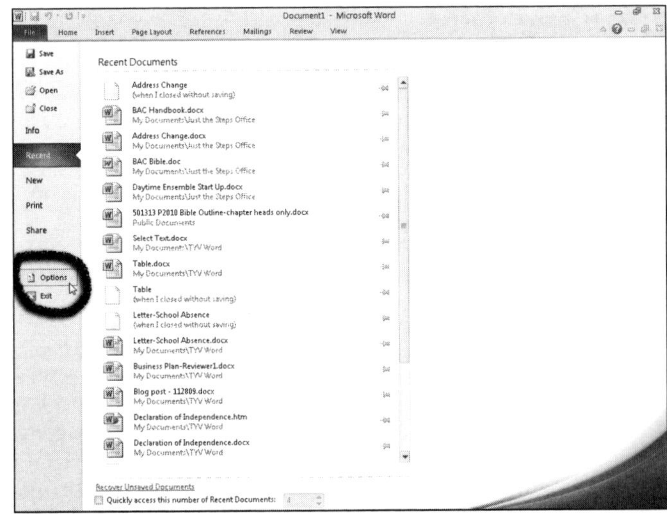

Figure 3-5

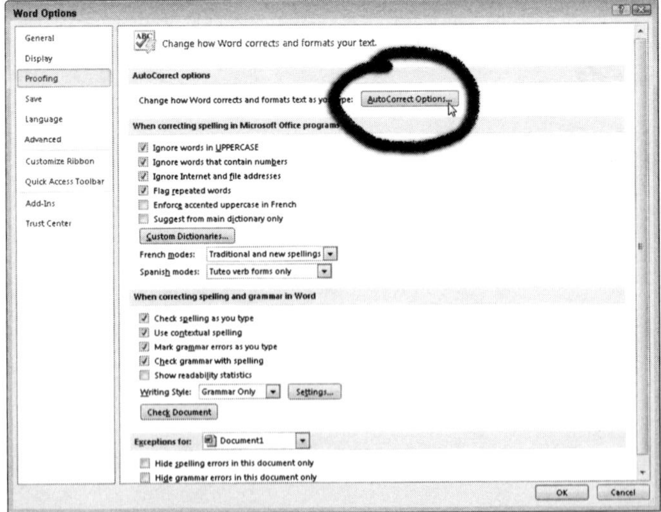

Figure 3-6

4. Click in the Replace field and type the word you typically mistype or misspell (see Figure 3-7).
5. Click in the With field and type the correct version of the word or phrase (see Figure 3-8).
6. Click the Add button to add the entry to the list of entries you want Word to correct automatically.
7. Repeat Steps 4–6 for each automatic correction you want to add.
8. Click OK twice to close the AutoCorrect dialog box and then the Word Options dialog box. Now when you mistype the word or phrase you just added to the AutoCorrect dialog box, Word automatically replaces your typing with the corrected version.

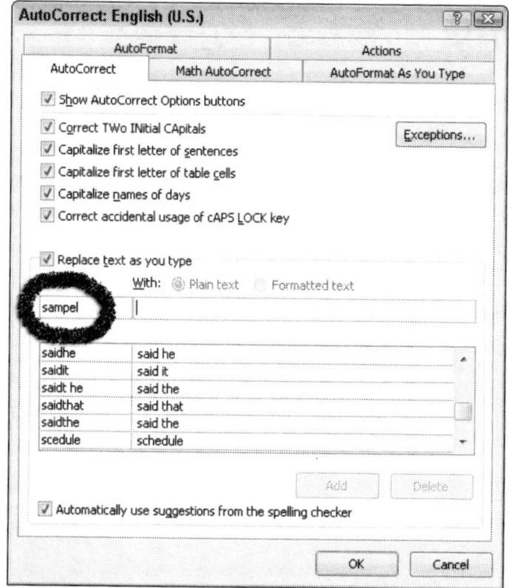

Figure 3-7

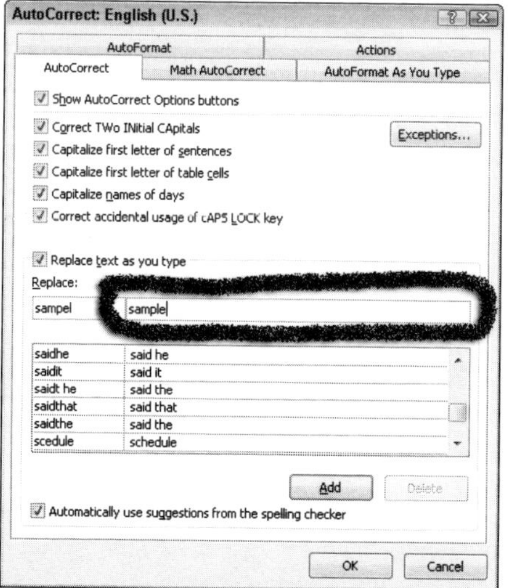

Figure 3-8

Create a Quick Part Entry to Insert Frequently Used Phrases

1. Type the text that you want to store, including all formatting that should appear each time you insert the entry.
2. Select the text you typed (see Figure 3-9).
3. Click the Insert tab.
4. From the Text group, click Quick Parts.
5. Click Save Selection to Quick Part Gallery (see Figure 3-10).

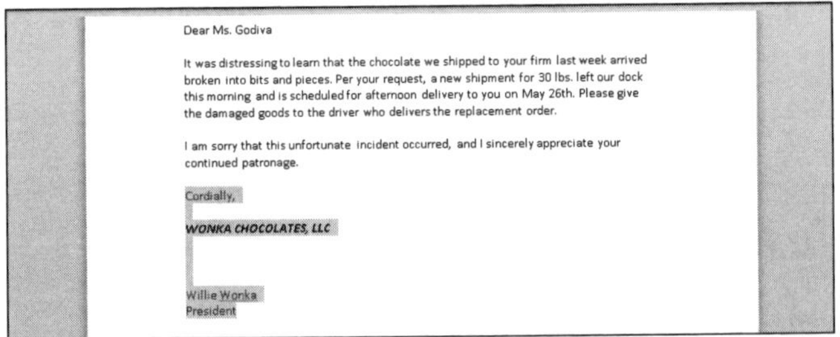

Figure 3-9

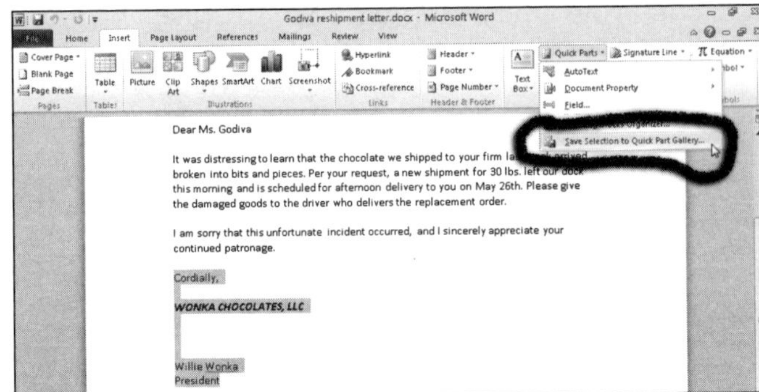

Figure 3-10

6. In the Create New Building Block dialog box that appears, type a single-word name in the Name field to identify the Quick Part entry (see Figure 3-11).
7. Click OK to store the entry on the Quick Parts Gallery.

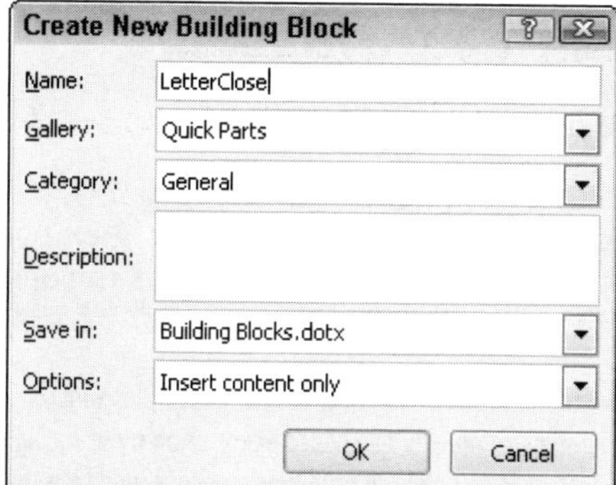

Figure 3-11

Insert a Quick Part Entry

1. Place the insertion point where you want the Quick Part entry to appear.
2. Click the Insert tab.
3. From the Text group, click Quick Parts to the display the Quick Part Gallery, which contains all building blocks defined as Quick Parts (see Figure 3-12).
4. Click the entry, and Word inserts the Quick Part entry into your document.

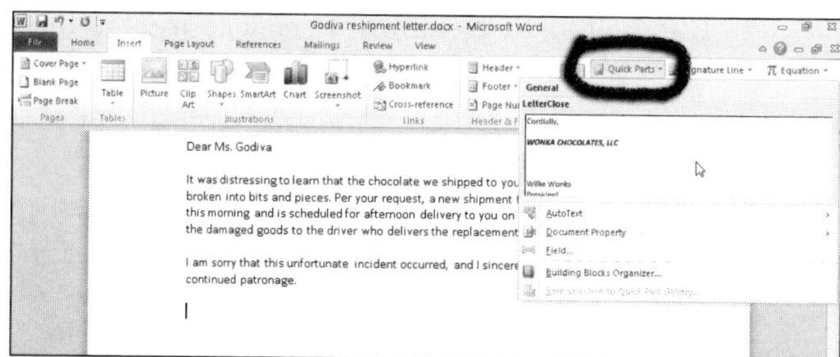

Figure 3-12

Check Spelling and Grammar

1. Click the Review tab.

2. From the Proofing group, click the Spelling & Grammar button (see Figure 3-13). Word selects the first spelling or grammar mistake in your document and displays the Spelling and Grammar window (see Figure 3-14).

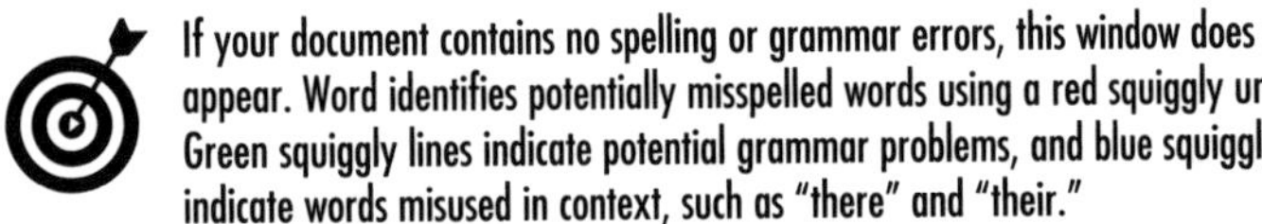

If your document contains no spelling or grammar errors, this window does not appear. Word identifies potentially misspelled words using a red squiggly underline. Green squiggly lines indicate potential grammar problems, and blue squiggly lines indicate words misused in context, such as "there" and "their."

   - The spelling or grammar mistake appears in the field at the top of the Spelling and Grammar dialog box.
   - Possible ways to correct the error appear in the Suggestions list.

3. If you see a suggestion you want to use, highlight it and then click the Change button. If you click the Ignore Once or the Ignore All button, Word leaves the selected word or phrase unchanged.

4. Word moves to the next spelling or grammar mistake. Repeat Step 3 for each spelling or grammar mistake.

5. When Word finds no more spelling or grammar mistakes, a message box appears to indicate that Word has finished checking the document. Click OK.

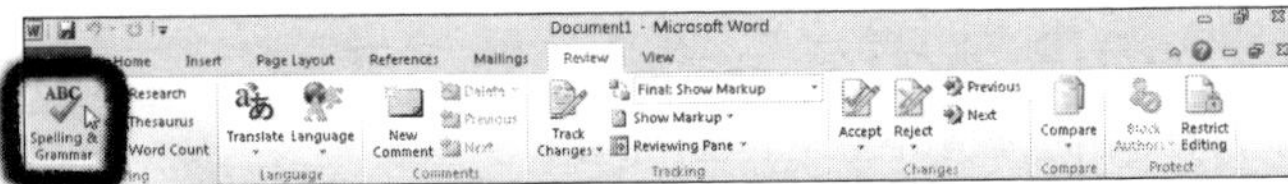

Figure 3-13

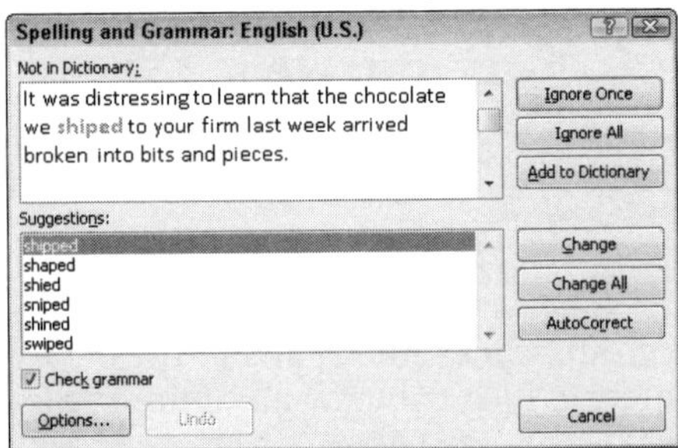

Figure 3-14

Disable Automatic Grammar and Spell Checking

1. Click the File tab. In the Backstage view that appears, click Options (see Figure 3-15).
2. In the Word Options dialog box that appears, click Proofing left side of the dialog box.
3. In the When Correcting Spelling and Grammar in Word section, clear the Check Spelling as You Type check box to disable automatic spell checking (see Figure 3-16).
4. In the same section, clear the Mark Grammar Errors as You Type check box to disable automatic grammar checking.
5. Click OK, and Word no longer identifies the spelling and grammar errors in your document by underlining them using red and green wavy lines, respectively.

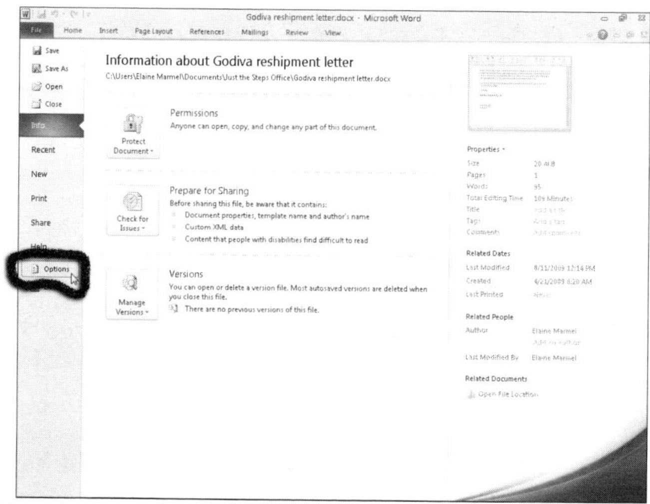

Figure 3-15

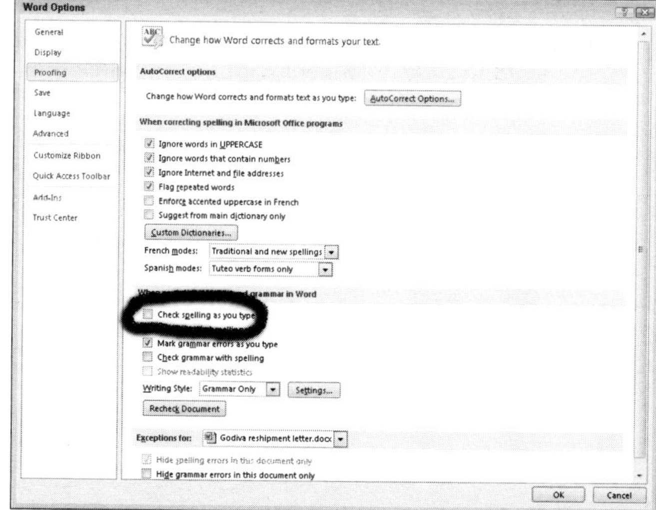

Figure 3-16

Use the Thesaurus to Find a Synonym or an Antonym

1. Click anywhere in the word for which you want to find a substitute or an opposite.
2. Click the Review tab.
3. From the Proofing group, click the Thesaurus button (see Figure 3-17). Word displays the Research pane; the word you selected appears in the Search For field at the top, and a list of words with similar meanings appears below (see Figure 3-18).
   - Word lists bold words, along with their part of speech — noun, verb, adjective — that have a similar meaning to the word you selected. Each word below a bold word is a synonym for the bold word.
4. Point the mouse at the word you want to use in your document to display a drop-down arrow.
5. Click the drop-down arrow and click Insert. Word replaces the word in your document with the one appearing in the Research task pane.
6. Click the X in the Research pane to close it.

Figure 3-17

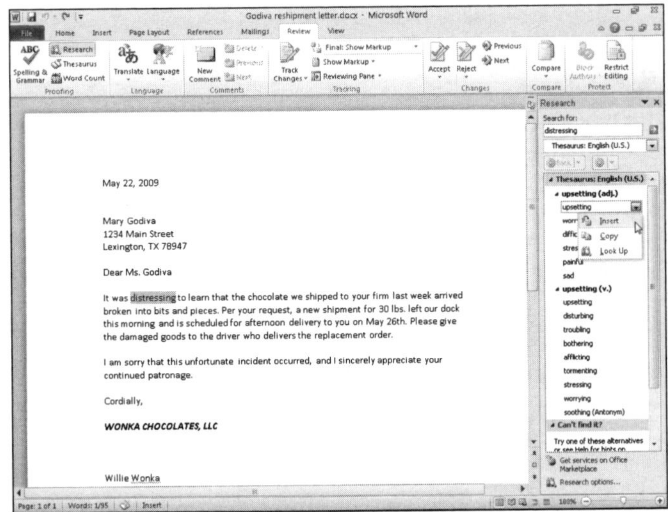

Figure 3-18

Focusing on Text

Of course your document is made up of text, so this chapter title might seem slightly odd — but here is the reason. In this chapter, I focus on the types of editing changes you can make that affect just the text in your document — not the paragraphs or the pages. For example, you might add boldface or italics to a word or phrase; this type of change affects only a word or a phrase and typically doesn't affect an entire paragraph or a page. Changing the case of text affects individual words, as does changing the font face, size, and color you use for text. Word also contains a feature that you can use to apply highlighting to selected words — similar to how you use a yellow or pink highlighter — to emphasis a concept.

In this chapter, you

- Change the case of text: say, from lowercase to uppercase.
- Make modifications to the font you select, both temporarily and permanently.
- Apply font enhancements, such as boldface or italics.
- Work with colors for text.
- Copy formatting applied to one portion of text to another portion of text.

Chapter

4

Get ready to . . .

Change Text Case

1. Select the text you want to change.
2. Click the Home tab.
3. From the Font group, click the Change Case button to display a drop-down menu of choices to help you quickly and easily change the case of any text you've already typed to any of the following (see Figure 4-1):
   - *Sentence case* capitalizes the first letter of the selected text and displays all other text in lowercase letters.
   - *lowercase* displays all selected text in lowercase letters.
   - *UPPERCASE* displays all selected text in uppercase letters.
   - *Capitalize Each Word* capitalizes the first letter of each word in the selected phrase.
   - *tOGGLE cASE* swaps all letters in the current select to the opposite case; this option is particularly useful if you accidentally pressed the Caps Lock key and typed a fairly long phrase.
4. Select an option, and Word changes the case of the selection to match your choice (see Figure 4-2).

You can quickly toggle between these choices using the keyboard; select the text and press F3 repeatedly.

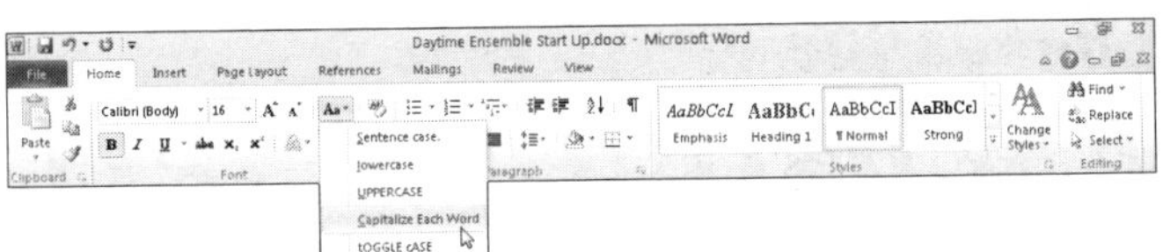

Figure 4-1

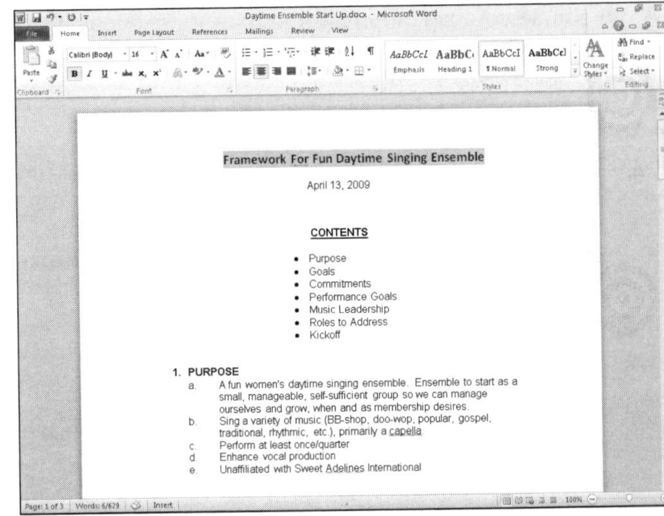

Figure 4-2

Change the Font

1. Select the text you want to change.
2. Click the Home tab.
3. Click the drop-down arrow in the Font list box to display all available fonts (see Figure 4-3).

Word's Live Preview feature displays the selected text in each font as you move your mouse pointer through the list.

4. Click a font. Word changes the selected text so that it appears in the font you selected (see Figure 4-4).

You can change the size of text by using the same basic method. Select the text you want to change and click the drop-down arrow for the Font Size list box, which appears immediately to the right of the Font list box. Word's Live Preview feature also displays a preview of the selected text in each size as you move your mouse pointer through the list. Each time you click the Grow Font and Shrink Font buttons, which appear immediately to the right of the Font Size list box, Word respectively increases and decreases font size by one choice in the Font Size list box.

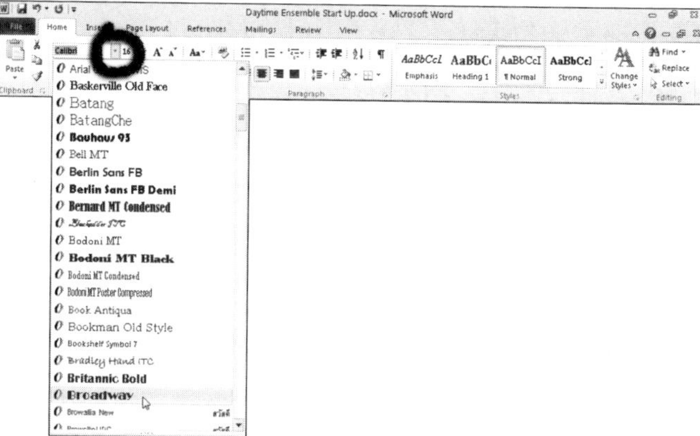

Figure 4-3

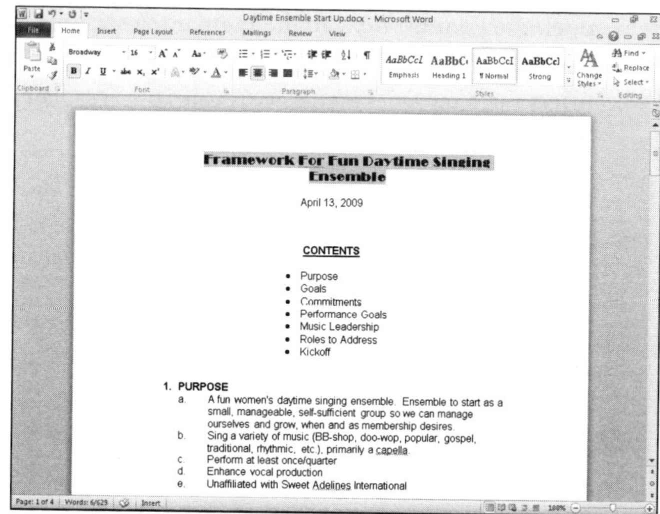

Figure 4-4

Select a New Default Font for All New Documents

1. Click the Home tab.
2. From the Styles group, right-click the Normal style and choose Modify from the menu that appears (see Figure 4-5).

Word displays each style as a white square in the Styles group; the top of the square displays sample text in the format of the style, and the name of the style appears below the sample text. If you don't see the Normal style, click the scroll buttons beside the styles or click the More button below the scroll buttons to display the Style palette. Read more about working with Styles in Chapter 5.

3. In the Modify Style dialog box that appears (see Figure 4-6), open the Font list box (in the Formatting section) to select a new font, and use the Font Size list box to set the font's size.
4. Select the New Documents Based on This Template radio button.
5. Click OK.

When you start a new document using the same template as the open document uses, Word sets the default font in the new document to the font and font size that you selected in Steps 3 and 4.

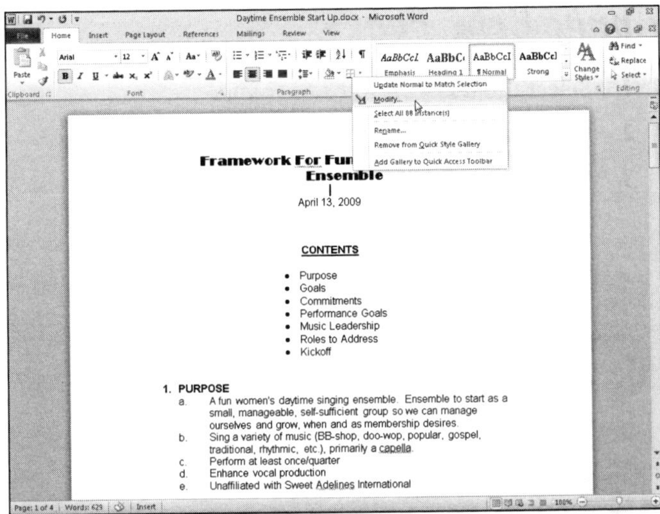

Figure 4-5

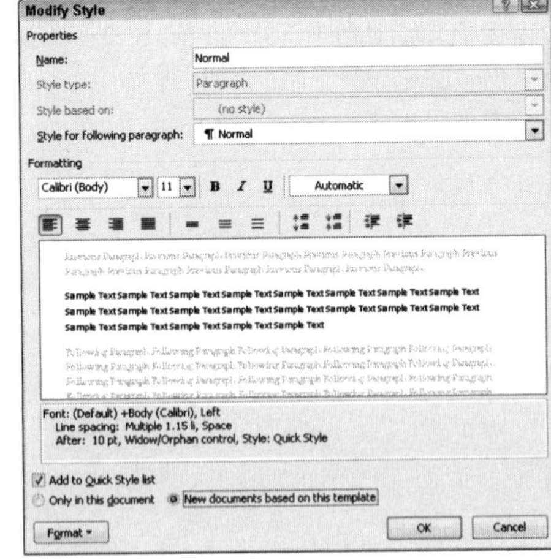

Figure 4-6

Apply Bold, Italics, or Underline

1. Select the text you want to change.
2. Click the Home tab.
3. From the Font group, click the Bold, Italics, and Underline buttons to apply the type of emphasis you want for the selected text (see Figure 4-7). Word applies the emphasis to the selected text (see Figure 4-8).

To emphasize a single word, don't bother to select it; place the mouse pointer anywhere in the word and click the appropriate button. You also can press Ctrl+B to apply boldface, Ctrl+I to apply italics, and Ctrl+U to apply underlining.

To specify a line style for underlining, click the down arrow beside the Underline button.

To remove any form of emphasis, repeat these steps.

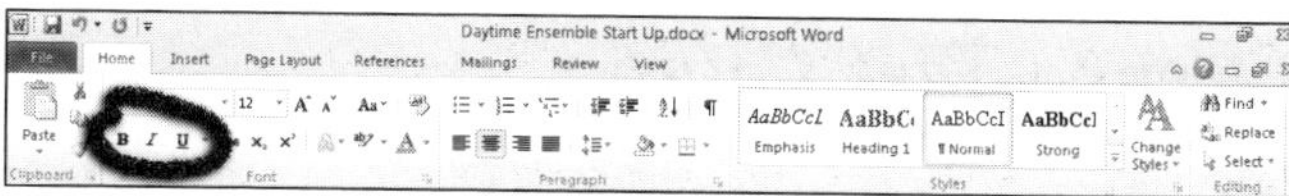

Figure 4-7

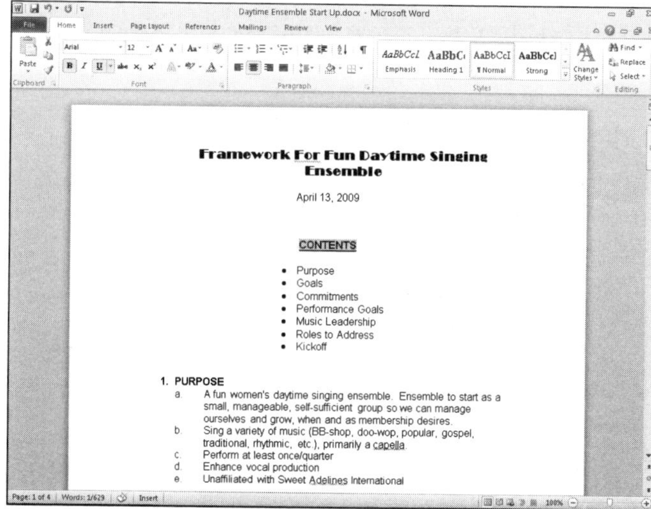

Figure 4-8

Change Text Color

1. Select the text you want to change.
2. Click the Home tab.
3. Click the down arrow beside the Font Color button (see Figure 4-9). Word displays the Font Color palette.

Word's Live Preview feature displays a preview of the selected text in each color as you move your mouse pointer over the colors in the Font Color palette.

4. Click a new color for the selected text. Word changes the color of the selected text's font to match the color you chose (see Figure 4-10).

Using a font color other than black is effective only when displaying the text onscreen or using a color printer.

To return the text to its default color, repeat these steps but in Step 4, click Automatic.

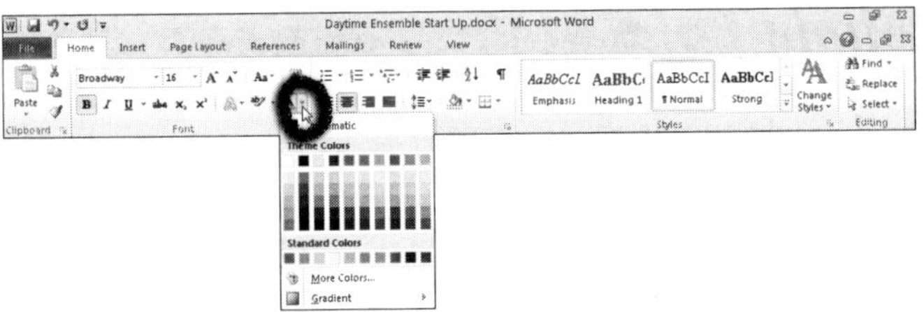

Figure 4-9

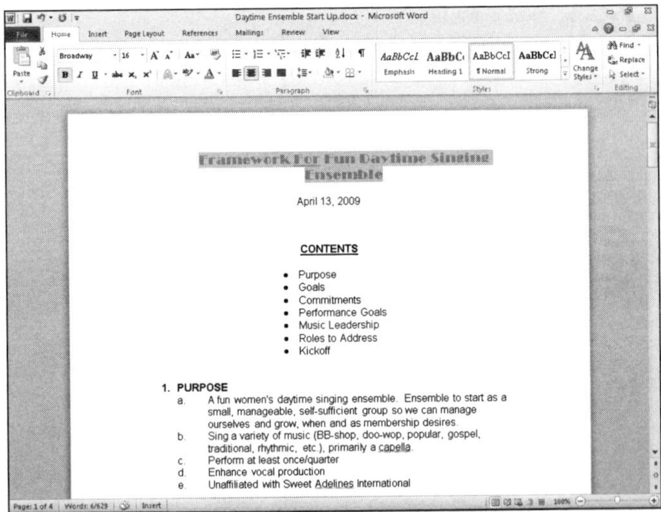

Figure 4-10

Highlight Text with Color

1. Select the text you want to highlight.
2. Click the Home tab.
3. Click the down arrow beside the Text Highlight Color button (see Figure 4-11). Word displays a palette of colors.

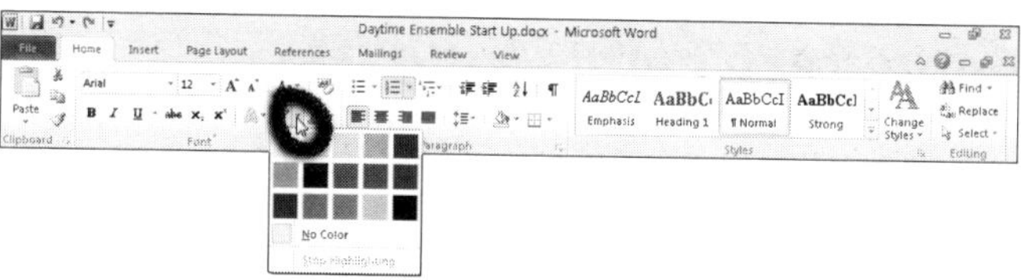

Figure 4-11

> Word's Live Preview feature displays a preview of the selected text highlighted in each color as you move your mouse pointer over the colors in the palette.

4. Click a color in which to highlight the selected text. Word cancels the selection of the text and displays the selected text highlighted in the color you chose (see Figure 4-12).

> Using a highlight color is effective only when displaying the text onscreen or using a color printer.

> To return the text to its default color, repeat these steps but in Step 4, click No Color.

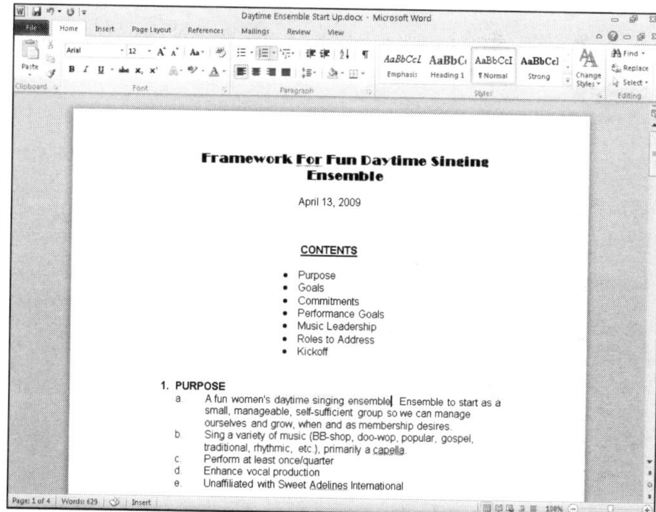

Figure 4-12

Copy Text Formatting

1. Select the text containing the formatting you want to copy.
2. Click the Home tab.
3. From the Clipboard group, click the Format Painter button (see Figure 4-13).

Figure 4-13

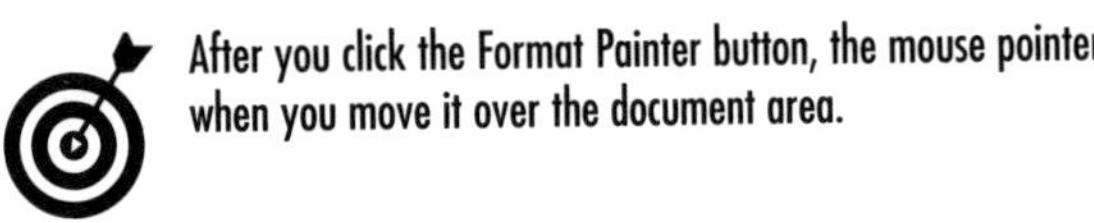

After you click the Format Painter button, the mouse pointer changes to a paint brush when you move it over the document area.

4. Click the word or select the text to which you want to copy the formatting. Word copies the formatting of the text you selected in Step 1, including paragraph formatting (such as indention), to the word you clicked or the phrase you selected in this step (see Figure 4-14).

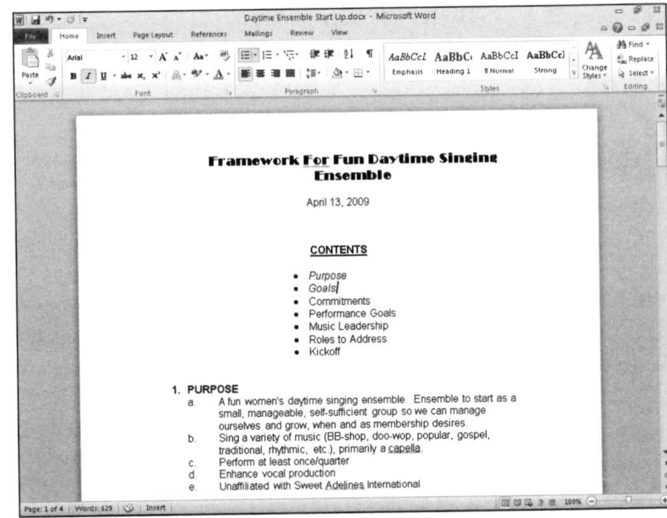

Figure 4-14

If you want to copy the formatting to several noncontiguous locations, complete Steps 1 and 2. Then, in Step 3, double-click the Format Painter button. Click each word or drag to select each phrase until you have copied the formatting as many times as necessary. Then, click the Format Painter button once to indicate that you no longer want to copy formatting.

Formatting Paragraphs

When you format paragraphs, you affect the appearance of a paragraph of words instead of affecting individual words within the paragraph. For example, you can align all the text in a paragraph on the left margin, on the right margin, centered between margins, or justified so that all words align on both the left and right margins. Tab settings, indentions, line spacing also affect an entire paragraph of words. In fact, spacing between paragraphs also affects an entire paragraph of words. Bulleted and numbered lists are forms of paragraph formatting.

You also can create styles in Word that store a collection of text and paragraph formatting, making it easy for you to assign a set of formats to a paragraph of text. In this chapter, you

- Display paragraph formatting information.
- Align text, set tabs, and indent paragraphs.
- Set line spacing within and between paragraphs.
- Create bulleted or numbered lists.
- Work with styles.

Chapter

5

Get ready to . . .

Display Formatting Information

1. Open any document (see Figure 5-1).
2. Click the Home tab.
3. From the Paragraph group, click the Show/Hide (¶) icon (see Figure 5-2) to display all formatting marks in your document.
   - *Spaces* look like single dots between words, such as the one between Fun and Daytime in Figure 5-2; they appear each time you press the spacebar.
   - *Paragraph marks* look like backward capital P's and appear each time you press the Enter key; the icon after Ensemble in Figure 5-2 is a paragraph mark.
   - *Line breaks,* such as those separating the lines in the Contents list of Figure 5-2, appear when you press Shift+Enter; they represent the end of line but not the end of a paragraph. Lines separated by line breaks share the formatting applied to the paragraph.
   - *Tabs* appear as arrows; in Figure 5-2, a Tab appears between the number 1 and the word Purpose.

Word stores all formatting you apply in each paragraph's paragraph mark. If you ever run into a corrupted document, try copying the entire document *except* the last paragraph mark to a new document. To select the entire document without the last paragraph mark, press Ctrl+A and then press Shift+←.

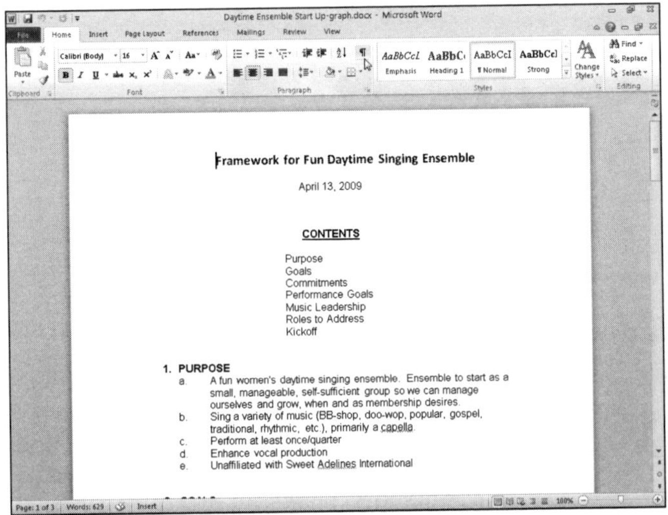

Figure 5-1

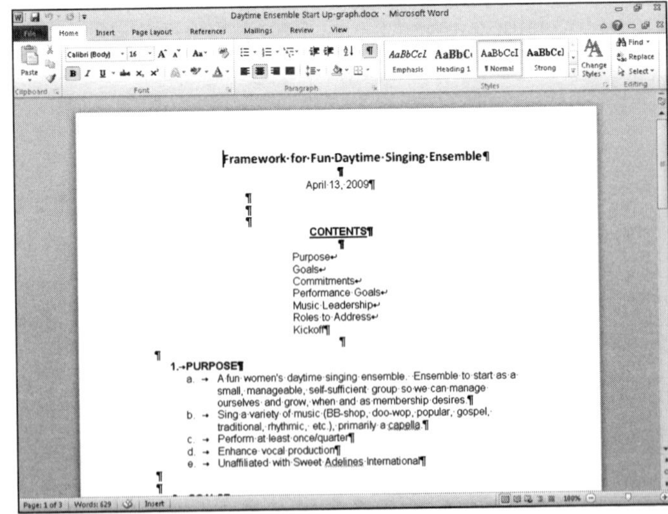

Figure 5-2

Hide and Display Rulers

1. Click the View tab (see Figure 5-3).
2. To hide rulers, From the Show group, remove the check beside the Ruler check box. To display rulers, in the Show group, select the Ruler check box.

   When you display rulers, they appear below the Ribbon and on the left side of your document (see Figure 5-4). When you hide rulers, the area below the Ribbon and on the left side of your document is blank (refer to Figure 5-3).

You can use these rulers to, for example, help you identify the position of the insertion point or to set tabs in a paragraph.

You can also hide or display the rulers by using the View Ruler icon that appears just above the vertical scroll bar on the right side of the Word window.

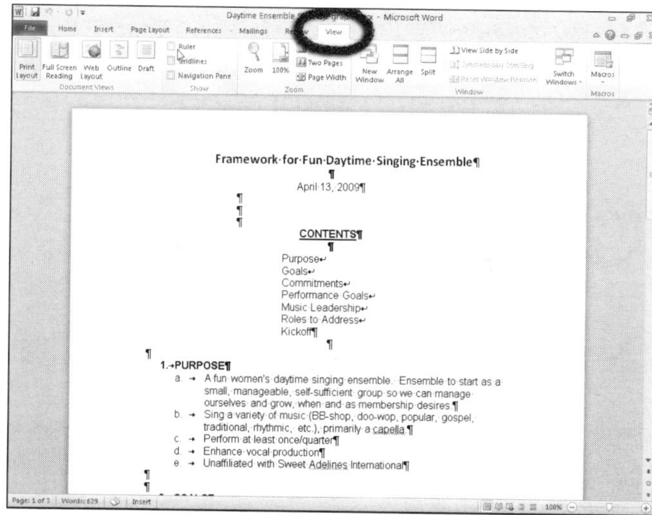

Figure 5-3

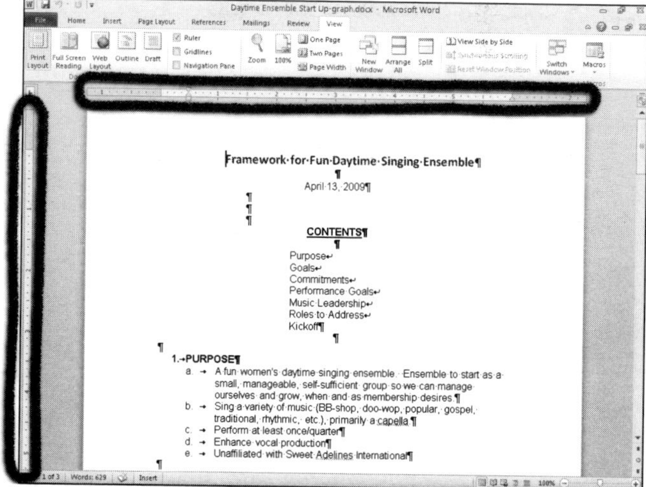

Figure 5-4

Align Text

1. Select the paragraph containing the text you want to align (see Figure 5-5).

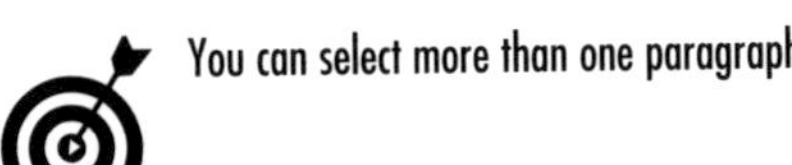

You can select more than one paragraph.

2. Click the Home tab.
3. From the Paragraph group, select an alignment button. In Figure 5-6, I justified the selected paragraphs.

When you justify a paragraph, Word pads the spacing between words in the paragraphs so that the text in those paragraphs aligns on both the left and right margins.

You can align text on the left margin, on the right margin, centered between both margins, or justified between both margins.

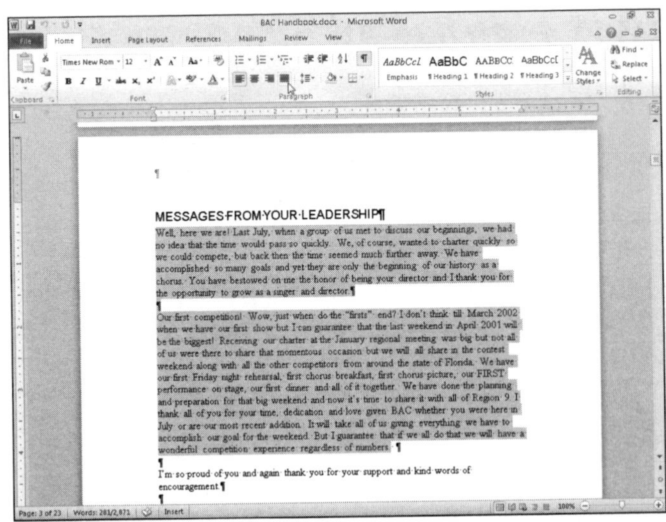

Figure 5-5

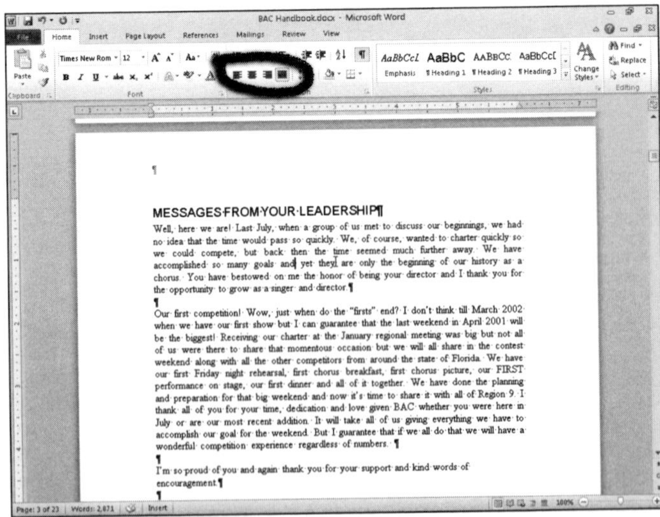

Figure 5-6

Work with Tabs

1. Click the icon above the left vertical ruler until it represents the type of tab you want to add. See the table to determine the type of tab you want to add.

Type of Tab	Purpose
	Text you type starts at the left edge of a Left tab and extends to the right.
	Text you type centers around a Center tab, with some characters appearing on the left side of the tab and some on the right.
	Text you type starts at the right edge of a Right tab and extends to the left.
	Text you type starts at the right edge of a Decimal tab and extends to the left until you press the period; then text extends to the right.
	At the location where you place a Bar tab, Word displays a vertical bar and then displays text extending to the right.

Tabs apply only to the paragraph containing the insertion point. To apply tabs to multiple paragraphs, select them before you create the tab.

2. Click the horizontal ruler where you want the tab to appear. Word displays the type of tab you chose at the location you clicked. In Figure 5-7, I placed a tab of each type at the 2-inch mark on each line and then pressed Tab and typed text so that you can see the effects of each type of tab.

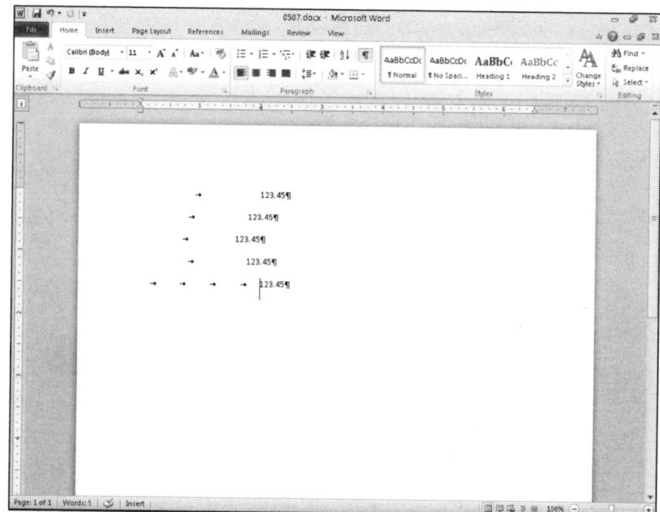

Figure 5-7

To move a tab, drag it to a new location on the horizontal ruler. To delete a tab, drag it off the ruler.

Indent Paragraphs

1. Click in the paragraph for which you want to adjust indentation.
2. Click the Home tab.
3. From the Paragraph group, click the dialog box launcher icon (see Figure 5-8).
4. In the Indentation section of the Paragraph dialog box that appears (see Figure 5-9), you can
   - *Use the Left and Right fields and spinner controls* to control the amount, in inches, that Word indents the paragraph from the document's margins.
   - *From the Special drop-down list box,* select a hanging indentation or a first line indentation; then set the amount from the By field and its spinner control.

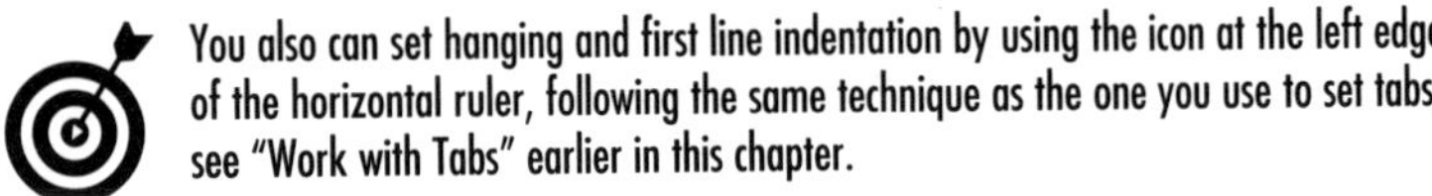

You also can set hanging and first line indentation by using the icon at the left edge of the horizontal ruler, following the same technique as the one you use to set tabs; see "Work with Tabs" earlier in this chapter.

5. Click OK to close the Paragraph dialog box and apply the settings.

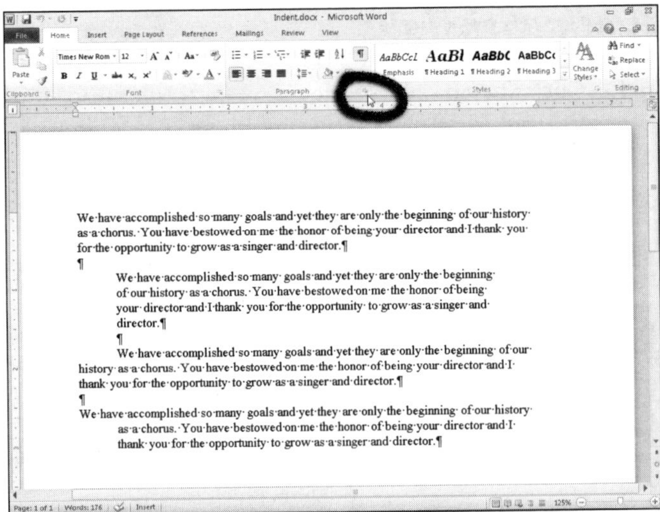

Figure 5-8

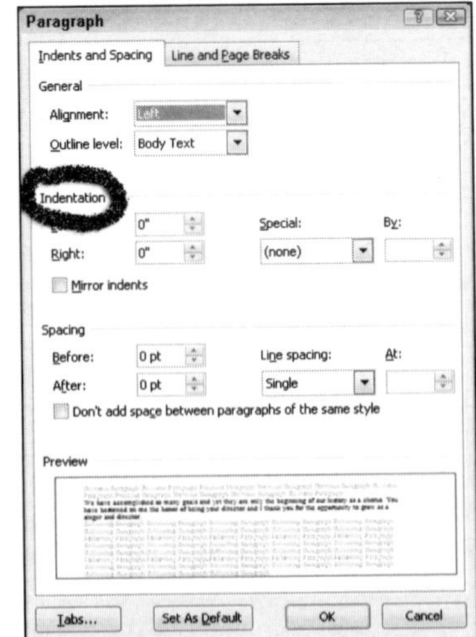

Figure 5-9

Add a Border to a Paragraph

1. Select the text that you want to surround with a border.
2. Click the Home tab.
3. From the Paragraph group, click the drop-down arrow of the Borders button (see Figure 5-10).
4. Choose Borders and Shading, at the bottom of the menu.
5. In the Borders and Shading dialog box that appears (see Figure 5-11), click the Borders tab (if it's not already showing).
6. Click in the Setting section to select a type of border.
7. Click in the Style list to select the style for the border line.
8. Use the Color drop-down list box to select a color for the border line.
9. Use the Width drop-down list box to select a thickness for the border line.
10. Click OK. Word displays a border around the selected text.

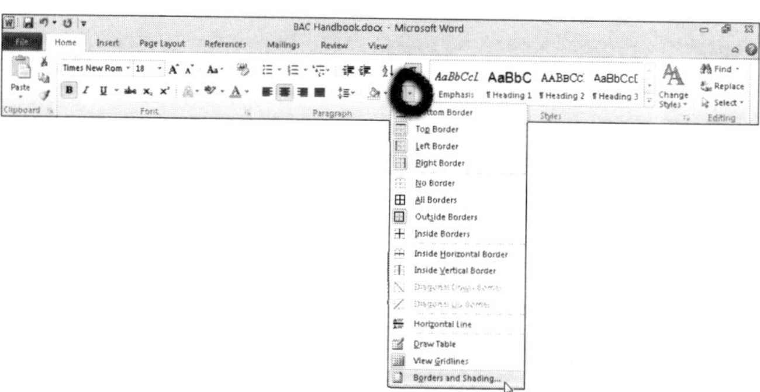

Figure 5-10

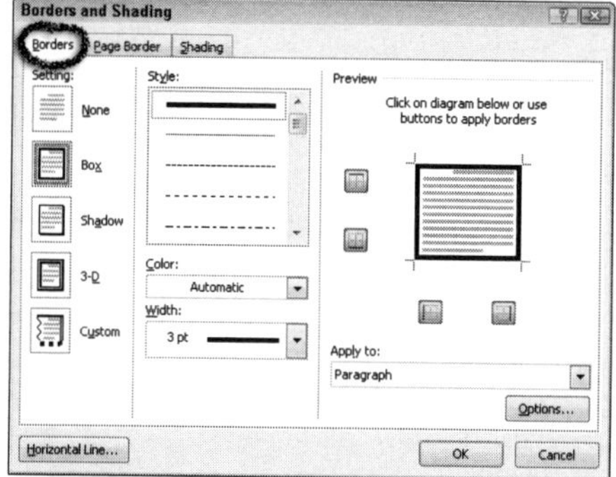

Figure 5-11

Set Line Spacing within a Paragraph

1. Click in the paragraph or select the paragraphs for which you want to set line spacing and click the Home tab.
2. From the Paragraph group, click the Line and Paragraph Spacing button (see Figure 5-12).
3. Click a number to represent the amount of space Word places between the selected lines of text.
   - 1.0 represents single spacing and was the default in Word 97–2003.
   - 1.15 is the default spacing in Word 2007 and later.
   - 1.5 places one-half of a blank line between lines of text.
   - 2 represents double spacing, placing one blank line between lines of text.
   - 2.5 and 3 add one and one-half and two blank lines, respectively.

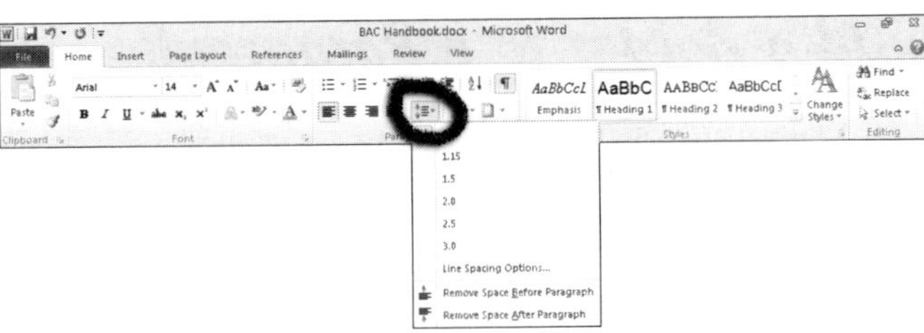

Figure 5-12

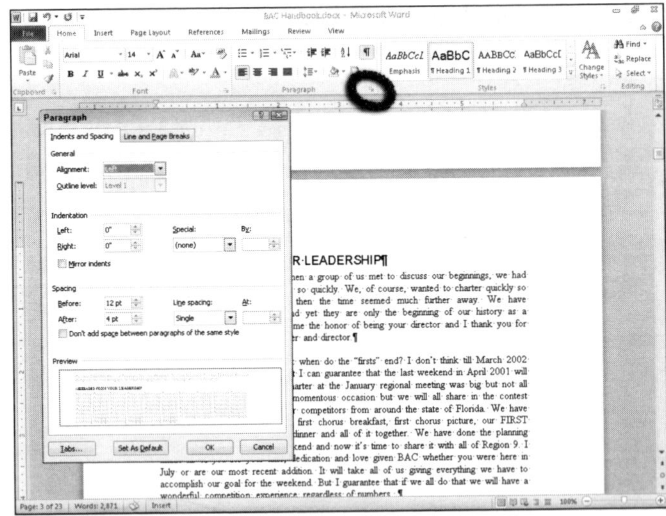

Figure 5-13

Set Line Spacing between Paragraphs

1. Click in the paragraph or select the paragraphs between which you want to define spacing and click the Home tab.
2. In the lower-right corner of the Paragraph group, click the dialog box launcher to display the Paragraph dialog box (see Figure 5-13).
3. In the Spacing section, click the spinner arrows to increase or decrease the space before or after the selected paragraph.

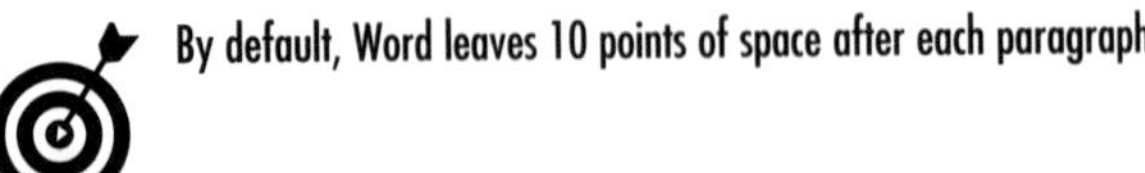

By default, Word leaves 10 points of space after each paragraph.

4. Click OK.

Create a Bulleted or Numbered List

1. Click the Home tab.
2. From the Paragraph group, click either the Bullets button or the Numbering button (see Figure 5-14). Word automatically starts a list (see Figure 5-15).

Press the down arrow beside either button to select a bullet or numbering format.

3. Type a list item and press Enter.
4. Repeat Step 3 until you finish typing your list.
5. To stop entering items in the list, press Enter twice.

You can create a bulleted or numbered list from existing text by selecting that text and then performing Steps 1 and 2.

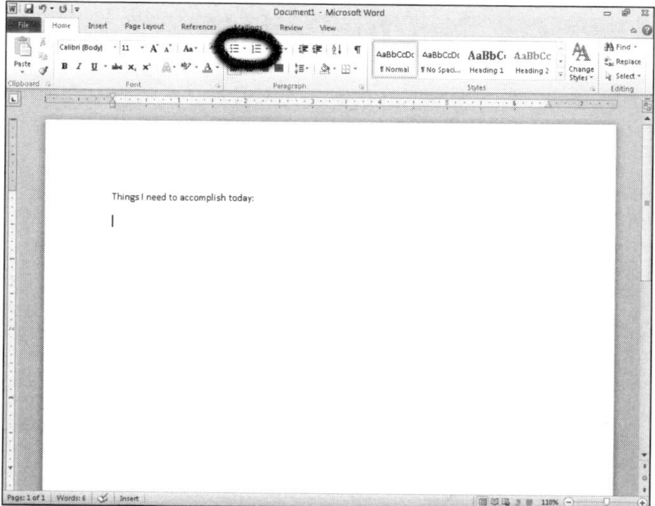

Figure 5-14

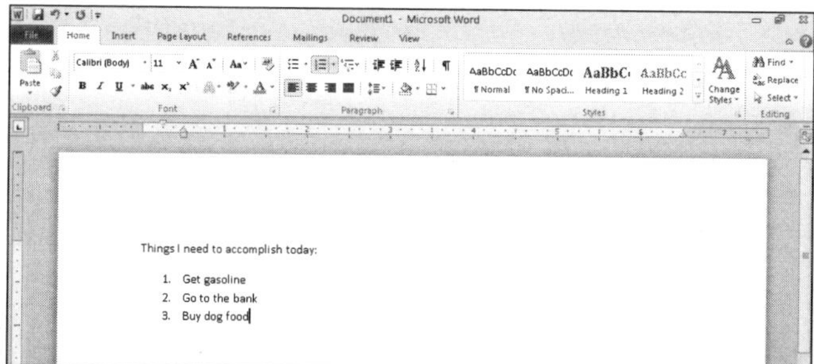

Figure 5-15

Create a Multilevel List

1. Place the insertion point at the location where you want to start the multilevel list.
2. Click the Home tab.
3. From the Paragraph group, click the Multilevel List button to display the available list formats (see Figure 5-16).
4. Select a list format, and Word applies the format to the line containing the insertion point (see Figure 5-17).
5. Type a list item and press Enter.
    - *To indent an item,* press Tab.
    - *To outdent an item,* press Shift+Tab.
    - *To stop entering items in the list,* press Enter twice.

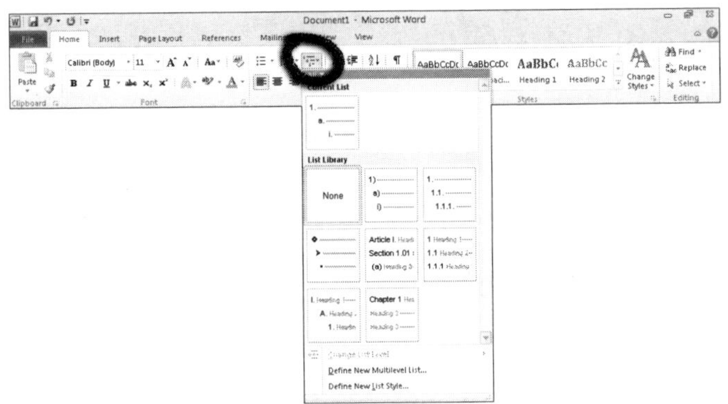

Figure 5-16

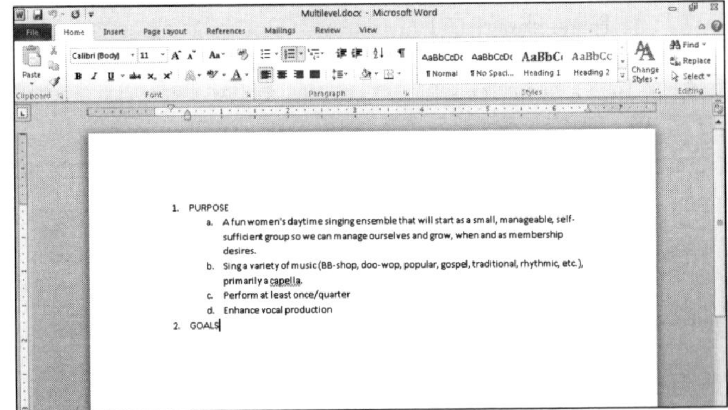

Figure 5-17

Format with Styles

1. Click in the paragraph or select the text to which you want to apply formatting.
2. Click the Home tab.
3. From the Styles group, click the scroll arrows to view available Quick Styles or click the More button (see Figure 5-18) Word displays the Quick Styles gallery (see Figure 5-19).

Styles are predefined sets of formatting that can include font, paragraph, list, and border and shading information. The top of each white square in the Quick Styles Gallery shows the type of formatting stored in the style; the bottom of each square identifies the name of the style. As you move the mouse pointer over each style, Live Preview shows you the way the selected text would look in each style.

4. Click a style to apply it to the selected text.

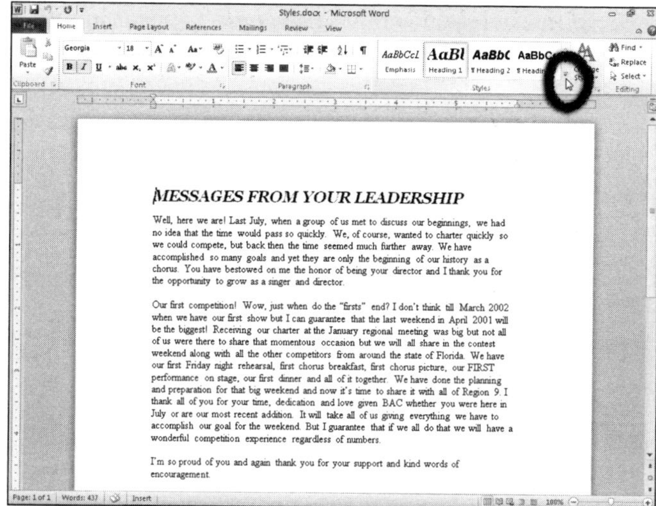

Figure 5-18

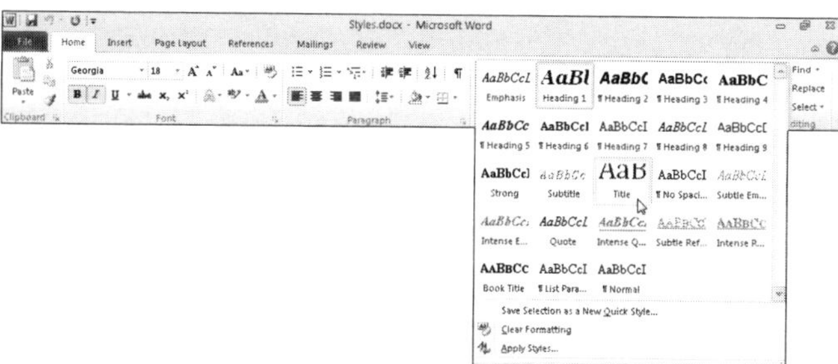

Figure 5-19

5. If the style you want to use doesn't appear in the Quick Styles gallery, click Apply Styles at the bottom of the Quick Styles gallery.
6. From the Apply Styles dialog box that appears (see Figure 5-20), use the Style Name drop-down list box to select a style. Or, click the Styles button (with the two capital As) to display the Styles pane, shown in Figure 5-21. The Styles pane displays styles using the formatting assigned to them.
7. Click a style, and Word applies the style to the paragraph containing the insertion point or to the selected text.
8. Click the X in the upper right corner of the Apply Styles dialog box and the Styles pane to close them.

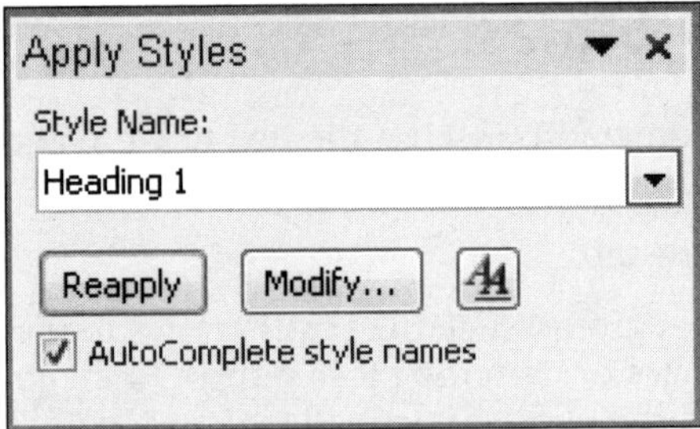

Figure 5-20

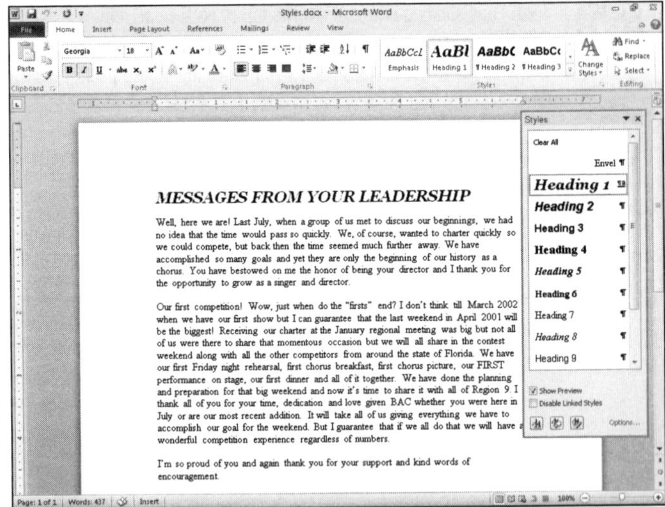

Figure 5-21

Switch All Text of One Style to a Different Style

1. Select text or click in a paragraph that uses formatting that you want to change.
2. Click the Home tab.
3. From the Styles group, click the dialog box launcher. Word displays the Styles pane, highlighting the style associated with the selected text or the paragraph containing the insertion point. In Figure 5-22, the insertion point appears in a paragraph that uses the Normal style.

Point the mouse at any style to display its formatting information.

4. In the Styles pane, move the mouse pointer over the selected style, and a drop-down arrow appears. Click the drop down-arrow and choose Select All Instance(s). Word selects all text in your document formatted using the selected style.
5. Click the style you want to apply to all selected text. Word changes all selected text to the style you selected. Notice that the Styles pane in Figure 5-23 shows the selected style as List Paragraph.
6. Click the X in the upper right corner of the Styles pane to close it.

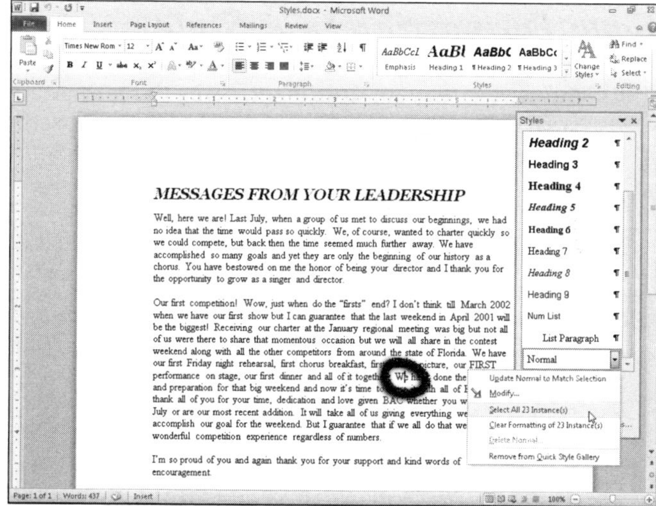

Figure 5-22

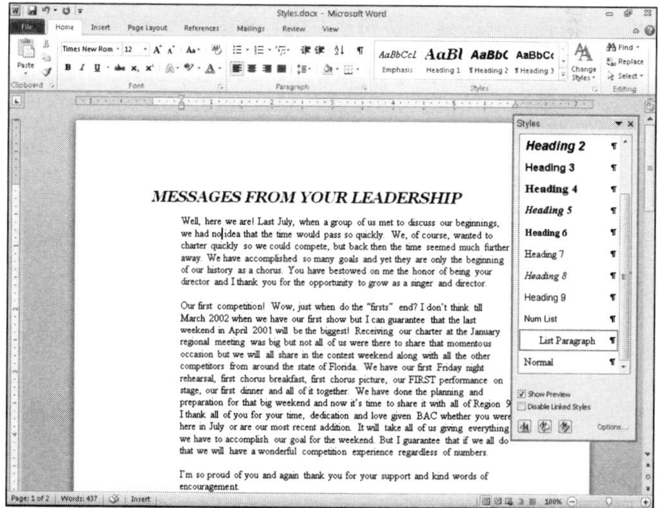

Figure 5-23

Save Formatting in a Style

1. Format text in your document, using the formatting you want to save, and then select that text or place the insertion point there.
2. Click the Home tab.
3. From the Styles group, below the scroll bars, click the More icon. The Quick Style gallery appears (see Figure 5-24).
4. Choose Save Selection as a New Quick Style. The Create New Style from Formatting dialog box appears (see Figure 5-25).
5. Type a name for the style and then click the Modify button to display additional options you can set (see Figure 5-26):
   - *Select the style* that Word should assign to the paragraph that follows a paragraph that uses the style you are creating.
   - *Select the font formatting, paragraph alignment, spacing, and indentation options* for the style.
   - *Make your style available in new documents* based on the current template; use the options at the bottom of the dialog box.
6. Click OK to close all dialog boxes.

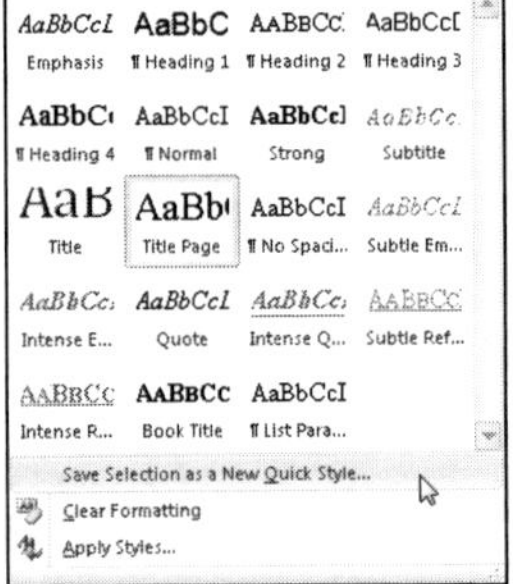

Figure 5-24

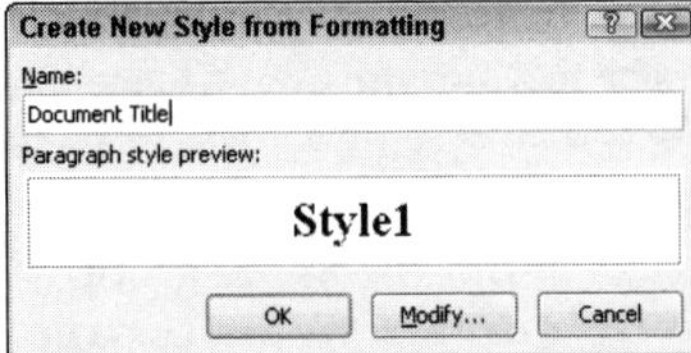

Figure 5-25

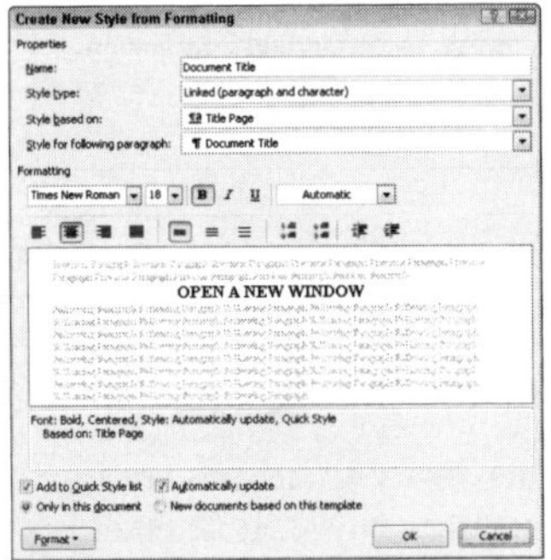

Figure 5-26

Managing Pages and Printing

As you work with Word documents, some of the editing and formatting you do affects entire pages rather than characters and words or paragraphs. When you format pages, you affect the appearance of text on a page. For example, changing page margins affects the amount of text that will fit on a page. You can take a variety of actions to specify what actually appears on a page.

This chapter focuses on the actions you can take to change the appearance of pages in your document and print your document. In this chapter, you

- Change page margins and orientation.
- Insert page and section breaks.
- Work with headers and footers.
- Handle special pagination situations such as controlling widows and orphans.
- Work with tabular and newspaper columns.
- Preview document and print it.

6

Get ready to . . .

Change Margins

1. Click anywhere in the document or section for which you want to change margins.
2. Click the Page Layout tab.
3. From the Page Setup group, click the Margins button.

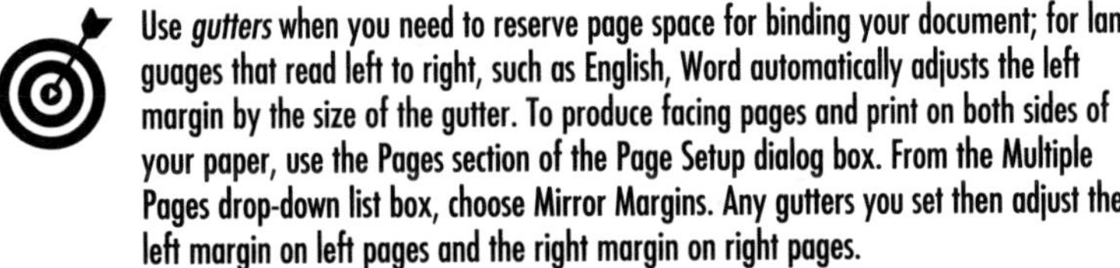

If the margin settings you want to use appear in the Margins Gallery, click that choice and skip the rest of these steps.

4. In the Margins gallery that appears (see Figure 6-1), click Custom Margins (at the bottom).
5. On the Margins tab of the Page Setup dialog box that appears (see Figure 6-2), type a new margin setting in any or all of the fields in the Margins section.

Use *gutters* when you need to reserve page space for binding your document; for languages that read left to right, such as English, Word automatically adjusts the left margin by the size of the gutter. To produce facing pages and print on both sides of your paper, use the Pages section of the Page Setup dialog box. From the Multiple Pages drop-down list box, choose Mirror Margins. Any gutters you set then adjust the left margin on left pages and the right margin on right pages.

6. Click OK. Word saves your changes.

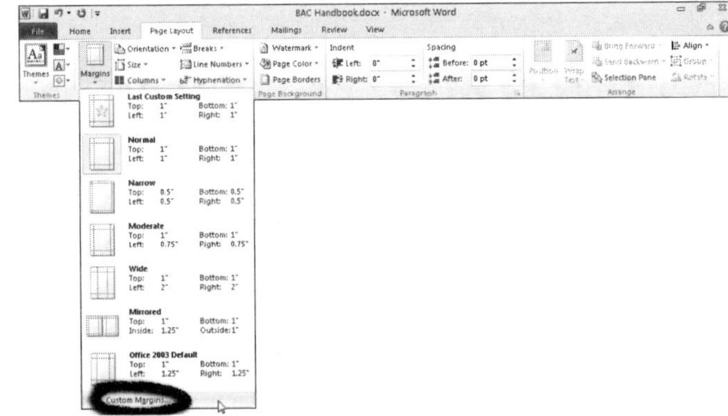

Figure 6-1

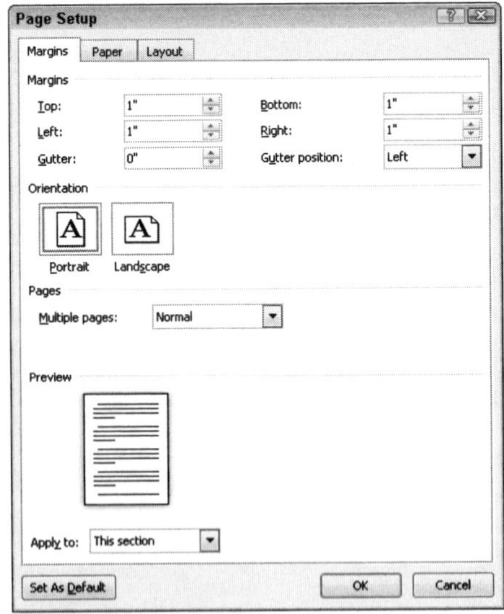

Figure 6-2

Change Page Orientation

1. Click the Page Layout tab.
2. From the Page Setup group, click the Orientation button and then select Portrait or Landscape (see Figure 6-3).

Portrait orientation sets up the page with the long side running vertically, while Landscape orientation sets up the page with the long side running horizontally. Changes to orientation affect your entire document unless you break the document into sections and set the orientation for each section.

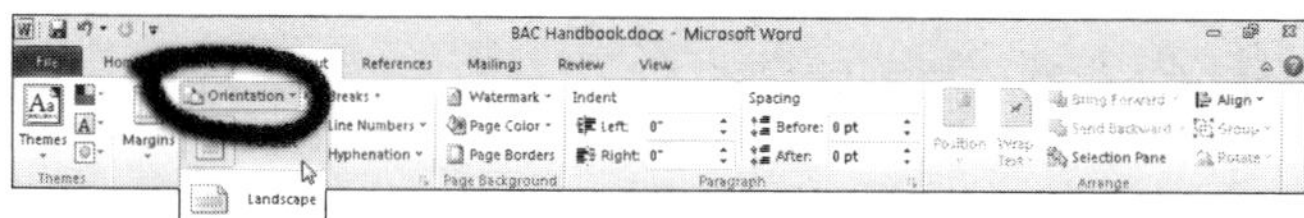

Figure 6-3

Insert a Page Break

1. Place the insertion point at the location in the document where you want the current page to end and the next page to begin.
2. Click the Page Layout tab.
3. From the Page Setup group, click the Breaks button.
4. From the Break gallery that appears, select Page (see Figure 6-4).

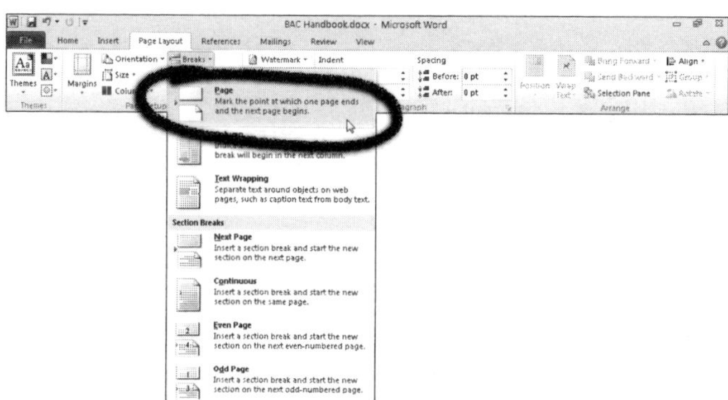

Figure 6-4

You can also press Ctrl+Enter to insert a page break.

Insert a Section Break

1. Click in the location where you want to start a new section in your document.
2. Click the Page Layout tab.
3. From the Page Setup group, click the Breaks button.
4. In the Break gallery that appears (see Figure 6-5), click an option to select the type of section break you want to insert. (See table for details on each type of break.)

Insert a section break in a document to use, for example, different margins, headers, footers, or vertical page alignment in different portions of your document. You can remove a section break by displaying the document in Draft mode; the section break appears as a line. Click the section break line and then press the Del(ete) key on your keyboard.

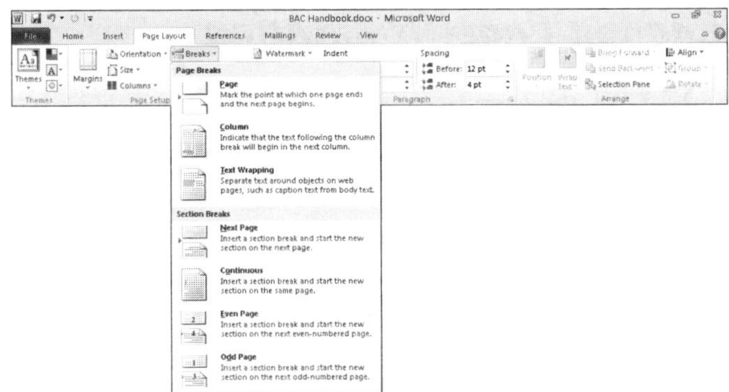

Figure 6-5

Section Break Type	Function
Next Page	Word inserts a section break and displays subsequent text on a new page.
Continuous	Word inserts a section break but displays subsequent text on the same page.
Even Page	Word starts the new section on the next even page. If you insert the break on an odd page, Word leaves the odd page blank.
Odd Page	Word starts the new section on the next even page. If you insert the break on an even page, Word leaves the even page blank.

Add a Header or Footer

1. Click the Insert tab.
2. From the Header & Footer group, click the Header button or the Footer button.

> This example shows you how to create a footer, but the steps are the same when you create a header.

3. In the appropriate gallery that appears (see Figure 6-6), click a header or footer style. The text in your document appears dimmed, the insertion point appears in the Header or Footer field, and the Header & Footer Tools Design tab appears on the Ribbon (see Figure 6-7).
4. If the header or footer you selected contains a prompt for information, click it to select it.
5. Type; when you finish, click outside the prompt.

> You can apply boldface, italics, underlining, and other character formatting the same way that you apply them in the body of a document. The Header area and the Footer area each contain two predefined tabs: one center tab and one right-aligned tab.

6. Click the Close Header and Footer button on the Ribbon.

> You can zoom out to view the header or footer on multiple pages of your document.

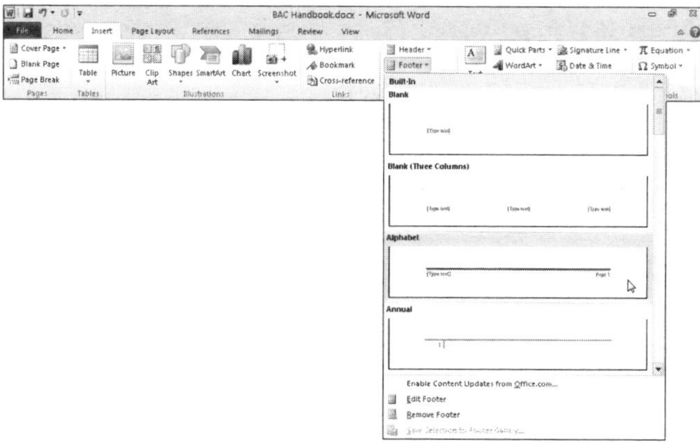

Figure 6-6

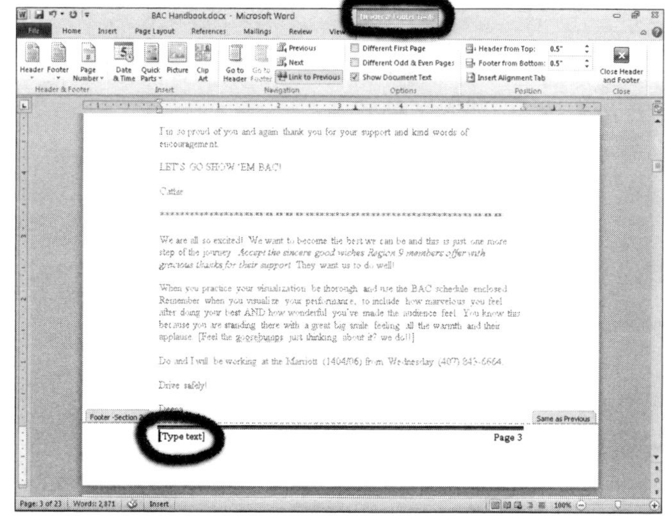

Figure 6-7

Use Different Headers or Footers within a Document

1. Using the steps in the previous task, "Add a Header or Footer," create a header or footer for the document. The header or footer you create appears on every page.
2. Using the steps in "Insert a Section Break" earlier in this chapter, insert section breaks to separate sections that will display different headers or footers.
3. Press Ctrl+Home to position the insertion point at the beginning of the document.
4. Click the Insert tab.
5. From the Header & Footer group, click the Header button. The Header gallery appears (see Figure 6-8).

This example uses headers, but you can use the steps when working with footers, substituting Footer for Header.

6. In the Header gallery that appears, click Edit Header to display header text and the Header & Footer Tools Design tab (see Figure 6-9).

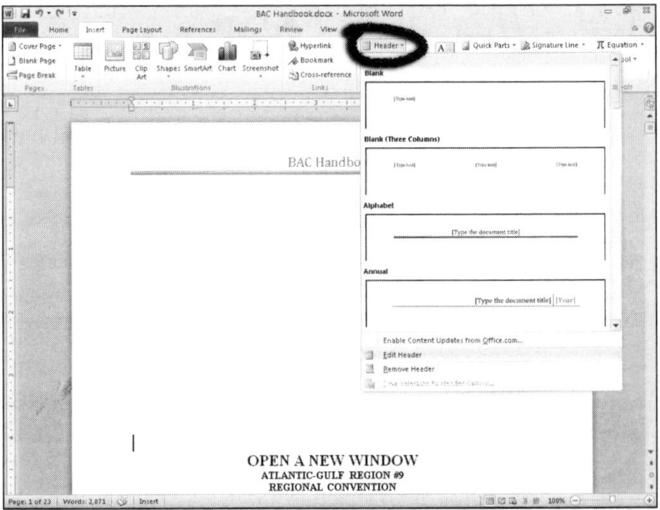

Figure 6-8

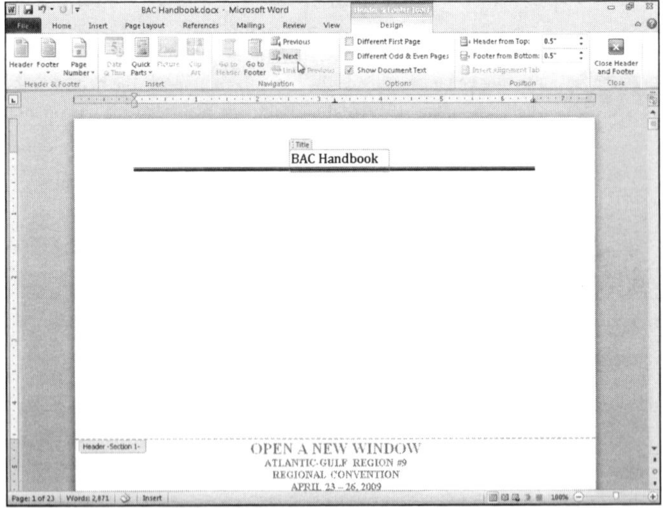

Figure 6-9

7. Click Next. Word moves the insertion point into the header of the next section and identifies the header or footer as Same as Previous (see Figure 6-10).

8. Click Link to Previous (in the Navigation group) to unlink the headers of the two sections. Word removes the Same as Previous marking from the header (see Figure 6-11).

9. Repeat these steps for each section for which you want a different header.

10. Using the Previous Section and Next Section buttons in the Navigation group of the Head & Footer Tools tab, you can display each section's header and edit it.

To remove a header from a particular section, display that section's header. Then, click the Header & Footer Tools tab; in the Header & Footer group, click Header. Choose Remove Header from the Header Gallery that appears. Word removes the header for the selected section.

11. Click the Close Header and Footer button.

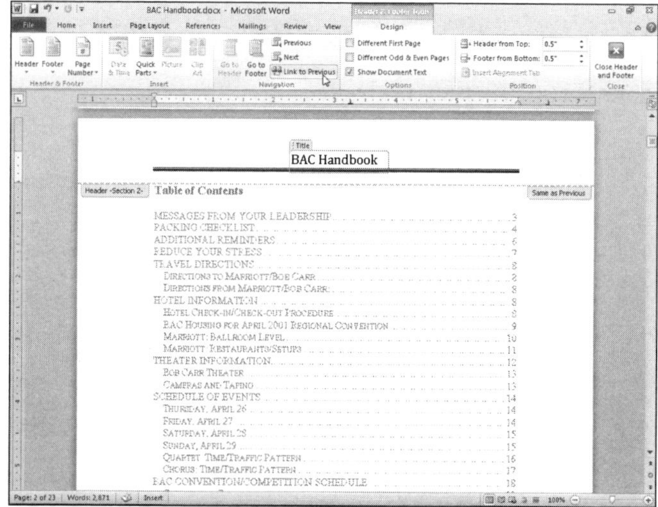

Figure 6-10

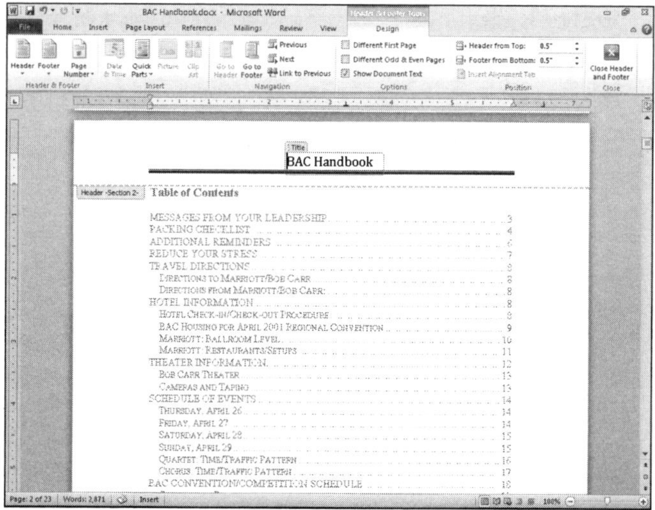

Figure 6-11

Control Text Flow and Pagination

1. Select the text you want to keep together.
2. Click the Page Layout tab.
3. From the Paragraph group, click the dialog box launcher.
4. In the Paragraph dialog box that appears, click the Line and Page Breaks tab (see Figure 6-12).
5. Use the options in the Pagination section to control page breaks. (See the table for an explanation of each option.)

Option	Function
Widow/Orphan Control	Ensures that at least two lines of a paragraph appear at either the bottom or the top of a page.
Keep with Next	Prevents a page break from occurring between selected paragraphs.
Keep Lines Together	Prevents a page break from occurring in the middle of the selected paragraph.
Page Break Before	Inserts a page break before the paragraph containing the insertion point.

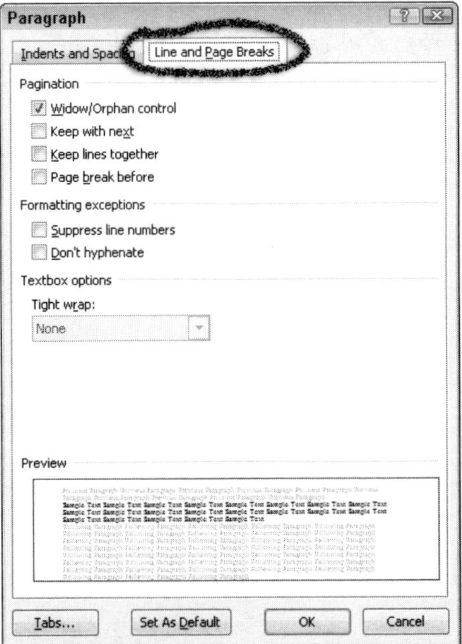

Figure 6-12

Add Document Page Numbers

1. Click the Insert tab.
2. From the Header & Footer group, click the Page Number button.
3. From the list of choices that appears, select Top of Page or Bottom of Page to display a gallery of choices for the page number format (see Figure 6-13).

If you select Current Position, you'll also see a gallery of page number–formatting choices; Word will insert the page number wherever the insertion point is positioned.

4. Select a format, and Word inserts the current page number, formatted as you chose, in a header or a footer (see Figure 6-14).
5. Click the Close Header and Footer button on the Ribbon to continue editing your document.

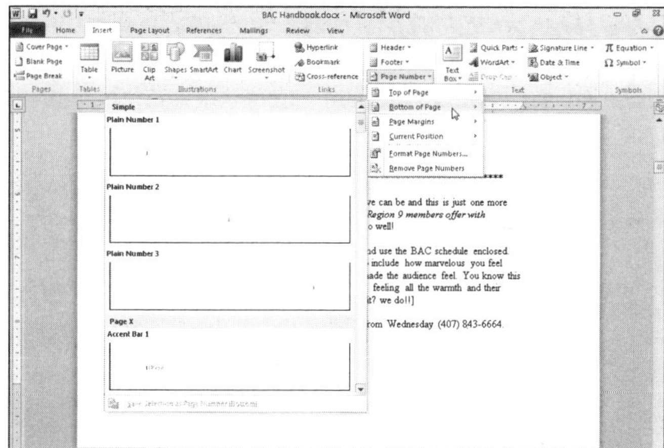

Figure 6-13

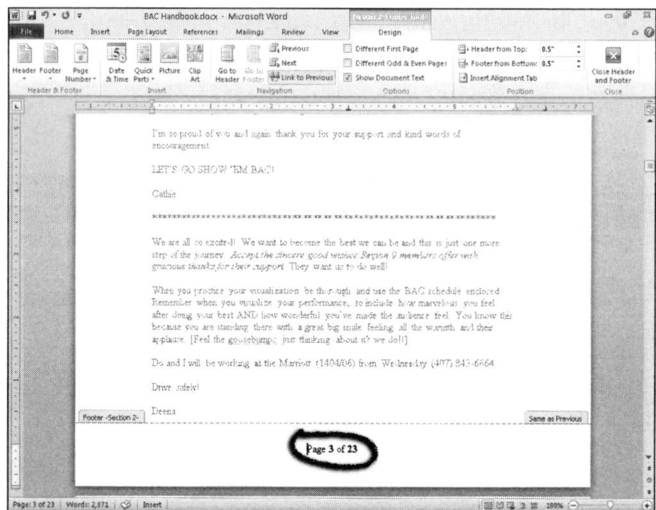

Figure 6-14

Create a Table

1. Click in your document where you want the table to appear.
2. Click the Insert tab.
3. From the Tables group, click the Table button to display a table grid.
4. Move the mouse pointer across the squares that represent the number of rows and columns you want in your table. Live Preview draws a sample of the table onscreen (see Figure 6-15).
5. Click the square representing the lower-right corner of your table. The table appears in your document, with the insertion point in the table. The Table Tools tab appears on the Ribbon, consisting of a Design tab and a Layout tab (see Figure 6-16).
6. Click in the table cell where you want to enter information.
7. Type the information; if necessary, Word expands the row size to accommodate the text. Press the Tab key to move the insertion point to the next cell.

Word automatically adds rows to the table when you press Tab while the insertion point appears in the last cell. To insert rows in other locations or columns, click the Layout tab under Table Tools and use the buttons in the Rows & Columns section.

8. Click outside the table to resume working with other document text.

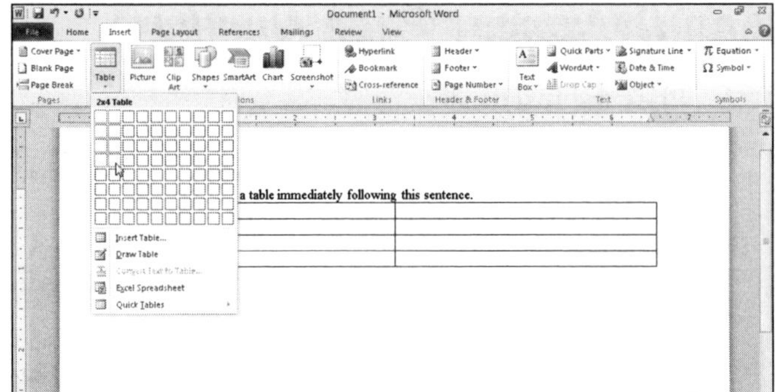

Figure 6-15

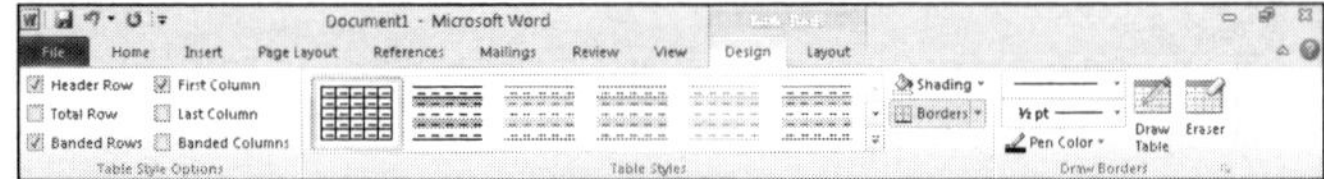

Figure 6-16

Create Newspaper Columns

1. Place the insertion point at the location in the document where you want to begin working in newspaper-style columns or select the text you want to convert to newspaper-style columns.
2. Click the Page Layout tab.
3. From the Page Setup group, click the Columns button.
4. Click More Columns (see Figure 6-17).

If you make a selection from the Columns Gallery, Word formats your entire document using your selection.

5. From the Columns dialog box that appears (see Figure 6-18), use choices in the Presets section to select the number of columns you want.
6. Optionally, you can
   - *Select the Line Between check box* to add a line between columns.
   - *Use the settings in the Width and Spacing section* to change the width of each column and the spacing between columns.
7. Use the Apply To drop-down list box to apply columns to your entire document or to the text that appears below the insertion point.
8. Click OK to set up the columns.

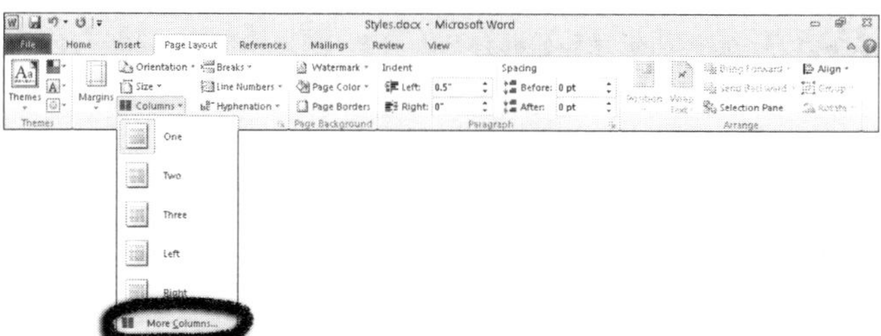

Figure 6-17

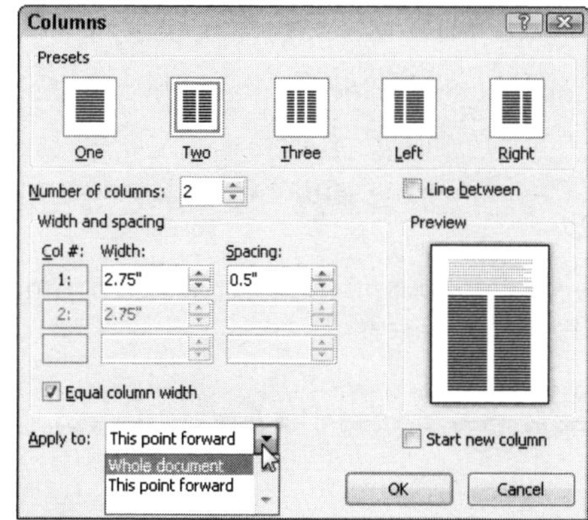

Figure 6-18

Preview a Document Before Printing

1. Click the View tab.
2. From the Document Views group, click Print Layout. Your document appears onscreen as it will print.
3. From the Zoom group, you can
   - *Click One Page* to view an entire page at one time; see Figure 6-19.
   - *Click Two Pages* to view two pages at a time; see Figure 6-20.
   - *Click the Zoom button* to open a dialog box and set a custom zoom level.
   - *Click the 100% button* to display your document at 100% zoom level.
   - *Click the Page Width button* to zoom your document so that it fills the document area.

You can edit your document regardless of the Zoom level you select.

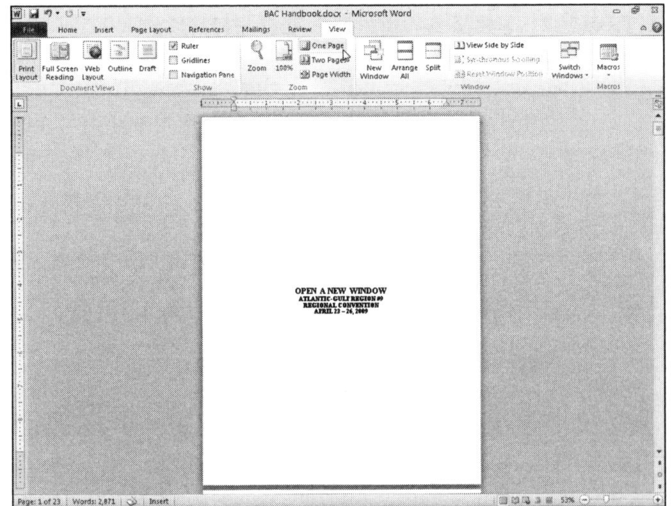

Figure 6-19

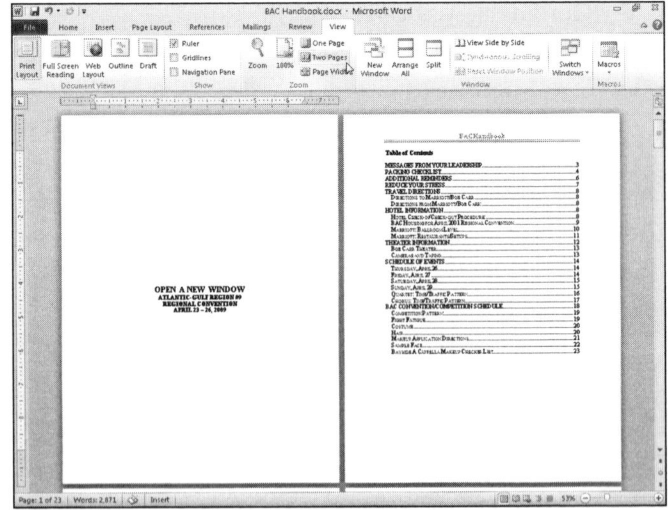

Figure 6-20

Print a Document

1. Click the File tab. From the Backstage view that appears, click Print (see Figure 6-21). A preview of your document as it will print appears on the right. You can use the arrows below the preview to page through your document.

You cannot edit this preview of your document, but you can use the Zoom tools in the lower-right corner to change the size of the preview or place the mouse pointer over the document and click to magnify an area of the page.

2. In the Copies field, identify the number of copies to print.
3. If you want to use a printer other than the Windows default printer, use the Printer section to find and select a printer.
4. In the Settings section, you can print all pages of the document or specify the pages of the document that you want to print. You can print selected pages by typing the page numbers in the Pages field, as shown in Figure 6-22.

Click the button above the Pages field to select from some standard choices, such as Current Page or All. You also can opt to print document properties, such as the styles you used.

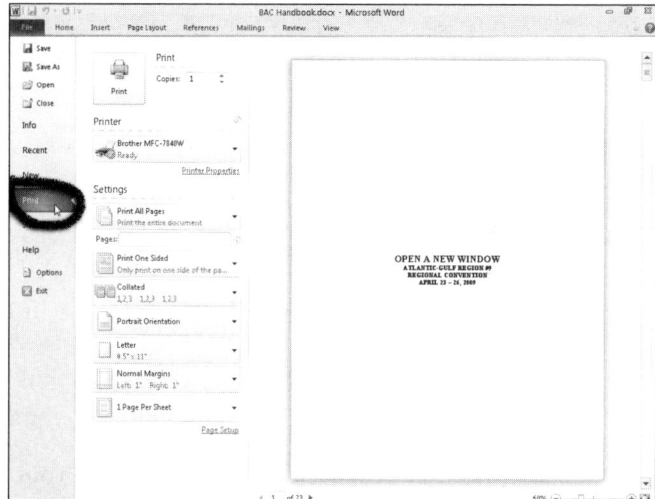

Figure 6-21

Figure 6-22

5. In the Settings section, you also can

   - *Print on one side or both sides of the page.*
   - *Print multiple copies collated or uncollated.*

If you print two copies of a document and choose to collate, all pages of the first copy will print before all pages of the second copy prints. If you print two copies of a document and choose not to collate, both copies of Page 1 print, followed by both copies of Page 2, both copies of Page 3, and so on.

   - *Select an orientation for your document.* Choose from Portrait or Landscape. See "Change Page Orientation" earlier in this chapter for more information on orientation.
   - *Select a paper size.* Click the third button from the bottom (see Figure 6-23) and scroll through the list. The height and width of each paper size appear below your selection.
   - *Change document margins.* Clicking the second button from the bottom. For each set of margins, Word displays top, bottom, left and right margin settings.
   - *Specify the number of pages you want to print on each sheet of paper.* Click the last button (see Figure 6-24).

6. Click the Print button at the top of the list of printer options to print your document using your selected settings.

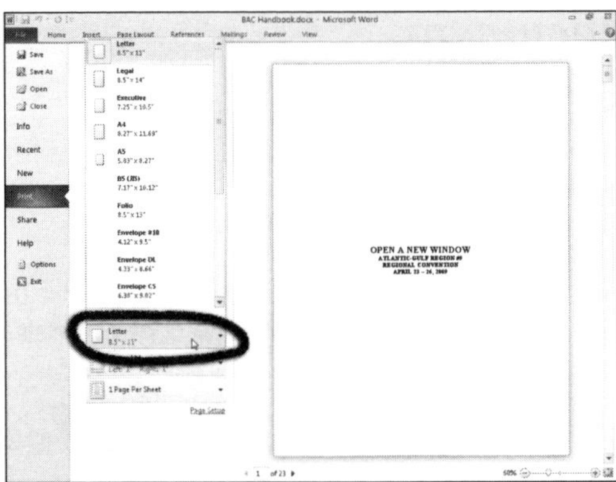

Figure 6-23

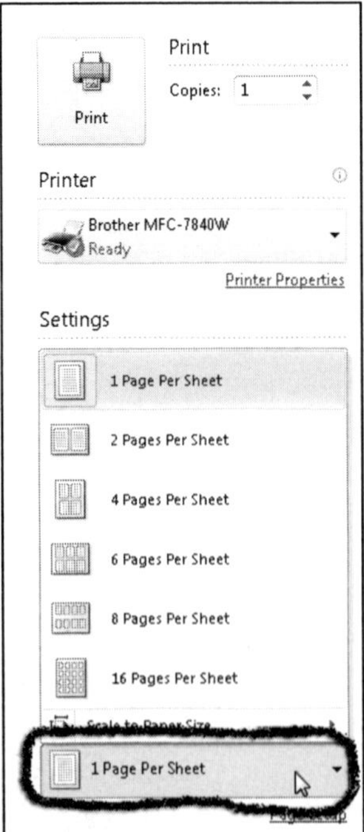

Figure 6-24

Part II
Excel

Chapter 7: Getting Started with Excel 69

Chapter 8: Working with Excel Formulas 83

Chapter 9: Formatting Worksheets 93

Chapter 10: Managing Workbooks 103

Chapter 11: Using Excel Tools 113

Chapter 12: Creating Charts in Excel 127

Chapter 13: Printing in Excel.................139

Getting Started with Excel

Chapter 7

Excel is like a giant accountant ledger sheet comprising a grid made up of columns and rows. Each intersection of a row and column is a *cell.* A single worksheet contains 16,374 columns across the top (stretching from column A to column XFD) and many rows down (from 1 to 1,048,576). That's more than 17 *billion* cells in a single worksheet. A cell address is the description of the intersection of a column and a row, such as D23 or AB205.

In those cells, you typically enter three types of data:

- **Labels,** which are traditionally descriptive pieces of information, such as names, months, or other identifying statistics. Labels usually include alphabetic characters.
- **Values,** which are generally raw numbers or dates.
- **Formulas,** which are instructions for Excel to perform calculations.

In this chapter, I show you how open Excel and enter basic spreadsheet data. I also show you how to

- Open, save, and delete files.
- Move around and select spreadsheet cells.
- Copy or move cell data.

Get ready to . . .

Open and Explore Excel

1. Choose Start⇨All Programs ⇨Microsoft Office ⇨Microsoft Excel 2010. The Microsoft Excel program begins with a new, blank workbook displayed like the one shown in Figure 7-1, ready for you to enter data.

2. Click the File tab to open Backstage view, which displays a list of options.

Click the Back button to close the Backstage view if you don't want to make a selection at this time.

3. Pause your mouse over any of the three icons above to the File tab. By default, this toolbar — the *Quick Access Toolbar* — includes the Save, Undo, and Redo functions.

4. When you click any Ribbon tab (the task-oriented portions of the Ribbon), features relevant to the tab appears. The tabs are broken into subsections called *groups*. For example, the Home tab includes the Clipboard, Font, Alignment, Number, Styles, Cells, and Editing groups.

Additional contextual tabs appear when they are useful for the current task.

5. On the Home tab, in the Styles group, clicking the Format as Table button makes a gallery of table styles appears. (Click the arrow again to close the gallery.)

6. On the Home tab, clicking the dialog box launcher on the bottom-right corner of the group opens a related dialog box (see Figure 7-2). In this example, clicking the dialog box launcher in the Font group, opens the Format Cells dialog box.

7. To close Excel, click the File tab; from Backstage view that appears, choose Exit.

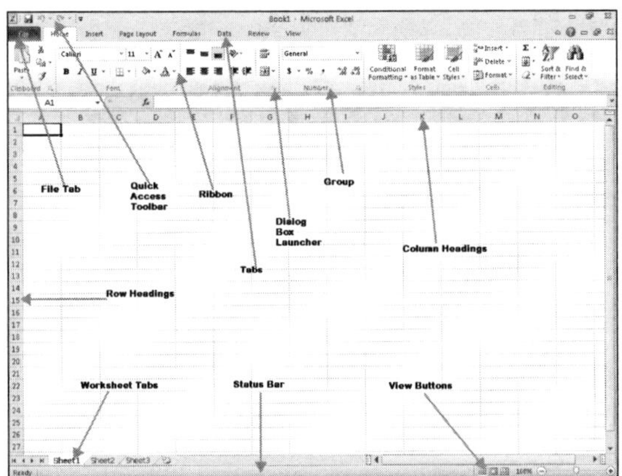

Figure 7-1

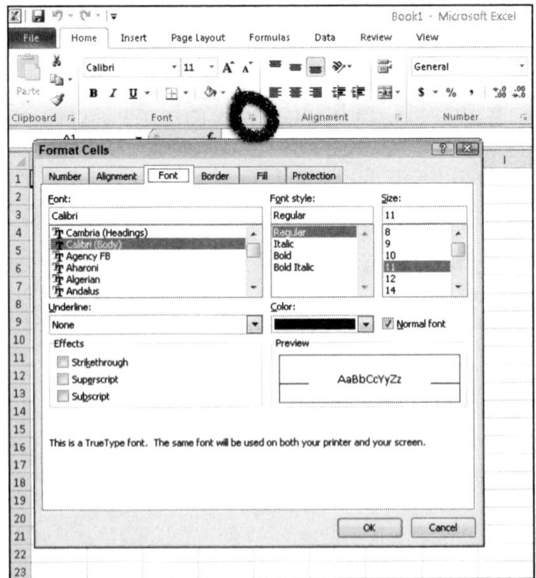

Figure 7-2

Create a New Excel File

1. Click the File tab; from Backstage view that appears, click New. On the left side, available templates appear; the right side displays a preview of the selected template (see Figure 7-3).

A template contains predefined settings, and optionally, data.

2. Click Blank Workbook.
3. Click the Create button. Excel creates a blank workbook for you.

Optionally, press Ctrl+N to create a new workbook without opening the New Workbook options.

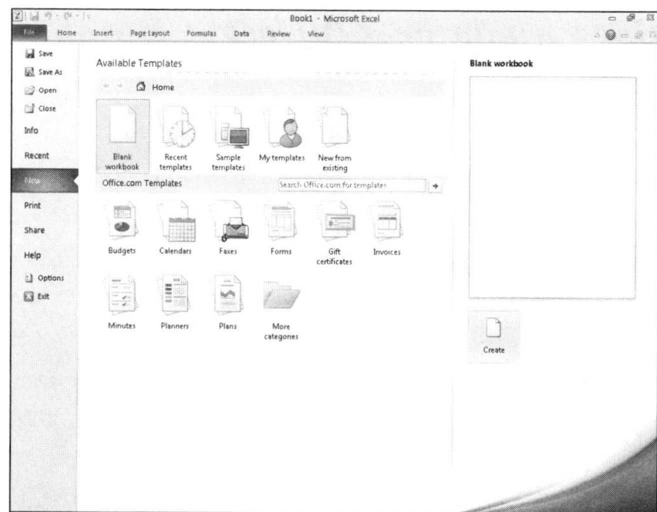

Figure 7-3

Save an Excel Workbook

1. Click the File tab. From Backstage view that appears, choose Save. The Save As dialog box appears, as seen in Figure 7-4.

Optionally, to save a workbook, click the Save button on the Quick Access Toolbar or press Ctrl + S.

2. By default, Excel saves your files in the Libraries⇨Documents folder. If you want to save your file in a different folder, use the icons on the left to navigate to the folder you want .
3. In the File Name text box, type a descriptive name for the file.
4. Click Save. Excel saves the workbook in the location with the name you specified.

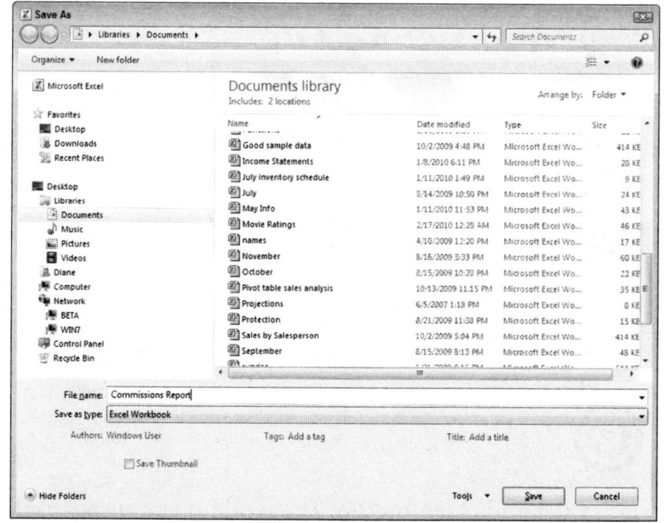

Figure 7-4

Save a File in a Different Format

1. Click the File tab. From Backstage view that appears, choose Save As.
2. In the File Name text box of the Save As dialog box that appears, type a descriptive name for the file.
3. Open the Save as Type drop-down menu.
4. In the list of file formats that appears, choose one of the 27 different file formats (see Figure 7-5).

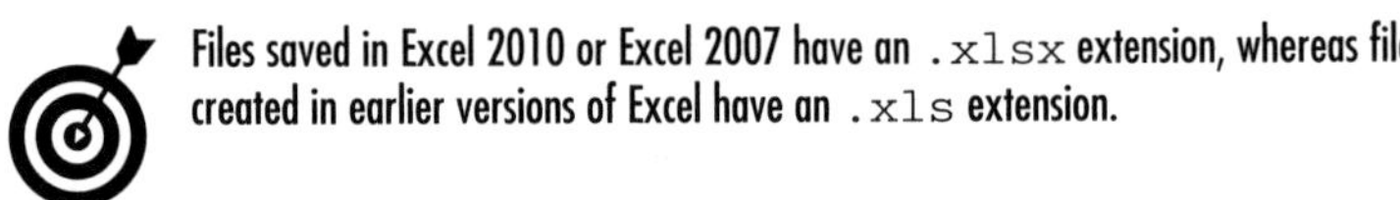

Files saved in Excel 2010 or Excel 2007 have an `.xlsx` extension, whereas files created in earlier versions of Excel have an `.xls` extension.

5. Click Save. Depending on the format you choose, Excel may prompt you for additional information.

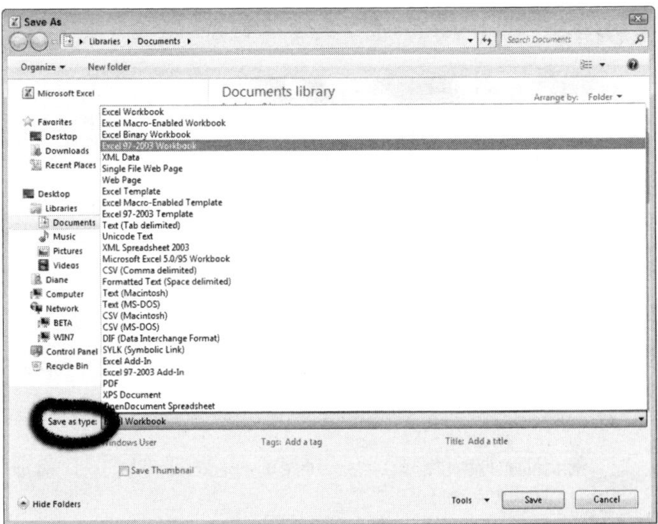

Figure 7-5

Open an Existing File

1. Click the File tab. From Backstage view that appears, choose Open. The Open dialog box appears, as shown in Figure 7-6.

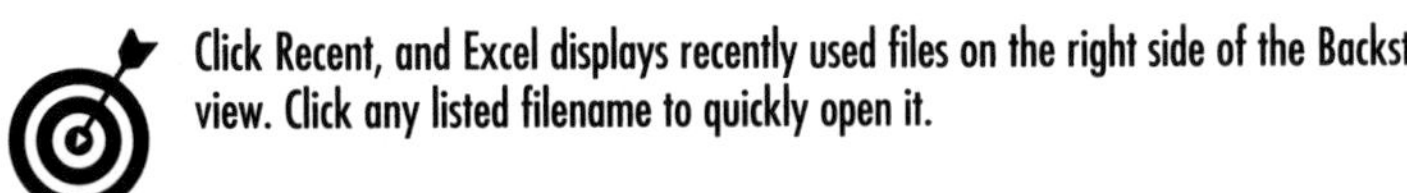

Click Recent, and Excel displays recently used files on the right side of the Backstage view. Click any listed filename to quickly open it.

2. If necessary, navigate to the appropriate folder and select the file you want to open.

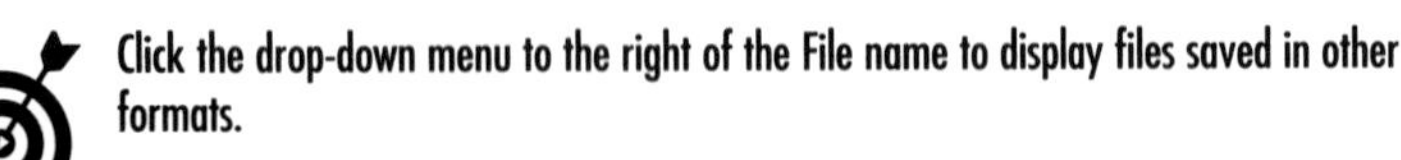

Click the drop-down menu to the right of the File name to display files saved in other formats.

3. Click the Open button. The workbook appears in the Excel workspace, ready for you to edit.

Figure 7-6

Convert a Prior-Version File to Excel 2010

1. Open a workbook created in an earlier version of Excel; the title bar indicates that Excel opened the document in Compatibility Mode.
2. Click the File tab; from Backstage view, choose Convert. Excel displays a message indicating you are about to convert the current workbook (see Figure 7-7).
3. Click OK, and another conversion message appears.
4. Click Yes, and Excel saves the file in the new format. Excel replaces the older version of the workbook, using the same name you used for the older version of the document. If the older version was an Excel 97–2003 or earlier document, Excel 2010 changes the extension to `.xlsx`.

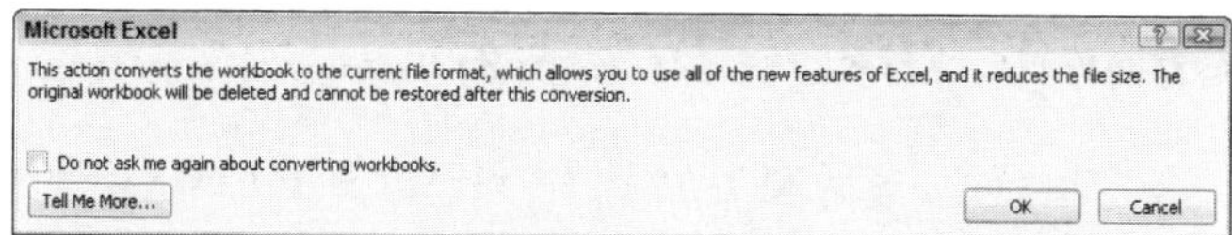

Figure 7-7

Delete a File

1. Open Excel, but do not open the file you want to delete. Click the File tab and choose Open or Save As. Depending on your choice, the Open or the Save As dialog box appears.
2. If necessary, navigate to the folder containing the file you want to delete.
3. Right-click the unwanted file.
4. Choose Delete from the shortcut menu that appears (see Figure 7-8). A confirmation message appears.
5. Click Yes. Excel deletes the file.
6. Click the Cancel button to close the Open or the Save As dialog box.

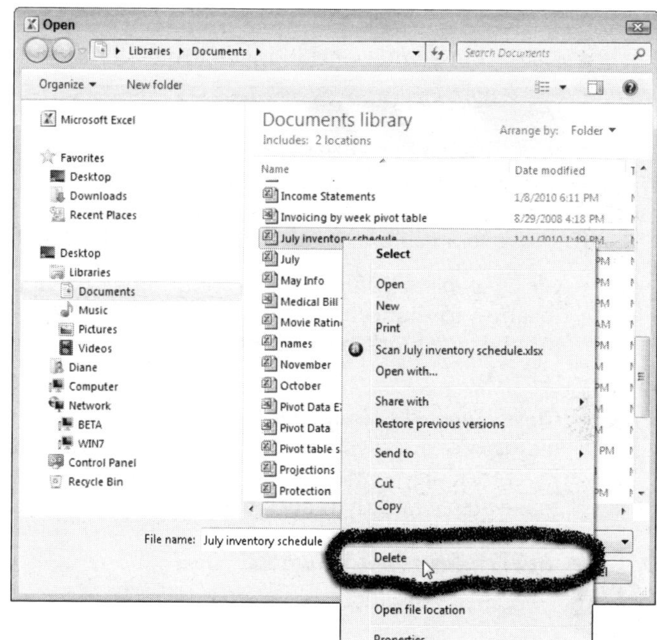

Figure 7-8

Change the Active Cell

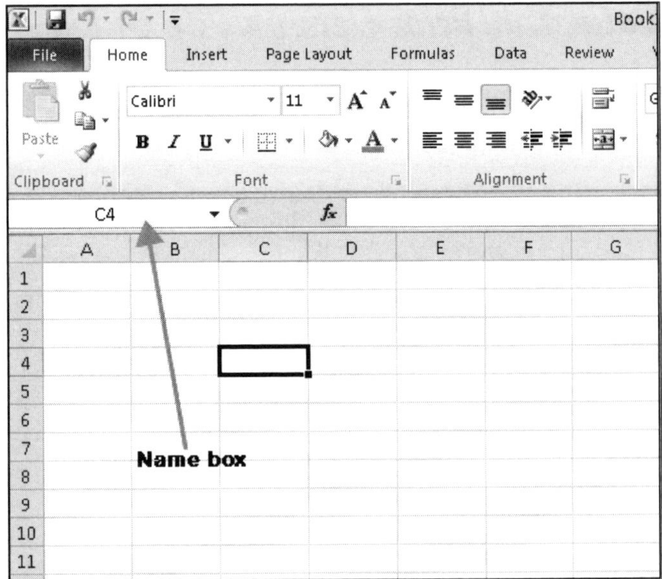

Figure 7-9

1. Display a spreadsheet in Excel. The name box displays the active cell location.
2. Move the focus to an adjacent cell with one the following techniques:
   - *Down:* Press Enter or the down-arrow (↓) key.
   - *Up:* Press the up-arrow (↑) key.
   - *Right:* Press the right-arrow (→) key.
   - *Left:* Press the left-arrow (←) key.
3. To move to a cell farther away, use one of these techniques:
   - *Click the mouse pointer on any cell* to move the active cell location to that cell. You can use the scroll bars to see more of the worksheet. In Figure 7-9, the cell focus is in cell C4.
   - *Choose Home➪Editing➪Find & Select➪Go To.* The Go To dialog box displays, as shown in Figure 7-10. In the Reference field, enter the address of the cell you want to make active and then click OK.

Press F5 to display the Go To dialog box.

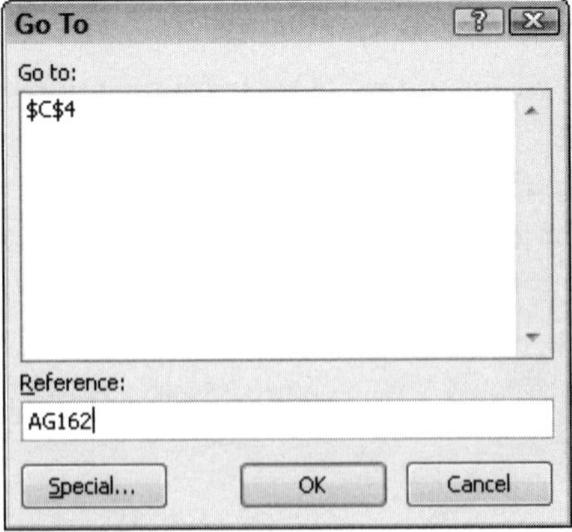

Figure 7-10

   - *Press Ctrl+Home.* Excel jumps to cell A1.
   - *Press Ctrl+End.* Excel jumps to the lower-right cell of the worksheet data.
   - *Press Ctrl+Page Down.* Excel moves to the next worksheet in the workbook.
   - *Press Ctrl+Page Up.* Excel moves to the previous worksheet in the workbook.

Enter Cell Data

1. Type the label or value in the desired cell.
2. Press Enter. The data is entered into the current cell, and Excel makes the next cell down active (see Figure 7-11). How Excel aligns the data depends on what it is:

To enter a value as a label, type an apostrophe before the value.

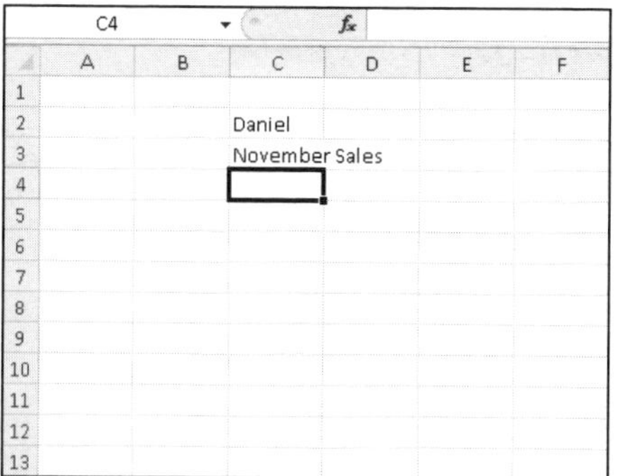

Figure 7-11

- *Label:* Excel aligns the data to the left side of the cell. If the descriptive information is too wide to fit, Excel extends that data past the cell width if the next cell is blank. If the next cell isn't blank, Excel displays only enough text to fit the display width. Widening the column displays additional text.
- *Whole value:* If the data is a whole value, such as 59 or 3215, Excel aligns the data to the right side of the cell.
- *Value with a decimal:* If the data is a decimal value, Excel aligns the data to the right side of the cell, including the decimal point, with the exception of a trailing 0. For example, in Figure 7-12, if you enter **392.57,** then **392.57** displays; if you enter **392.50**, however, **392.5** displays.

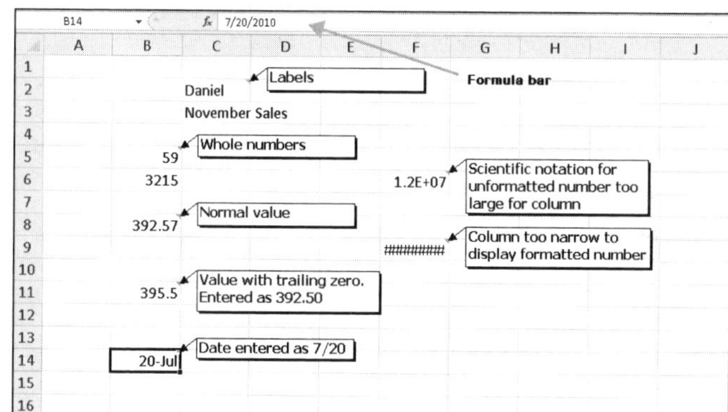

Figure 7-12

If a value displays as scientific notation or number signs, such as the ones you see in Figure 7-12, it means the value is too long to fit into the cell. You need to widen the column width. (See Chapter 9.)

- *Date:* If you enter a date, such 7/20, Jul 20, or 20 July, Excel automatically returns 20-Jul in the cell. However, the formula bar displays 07/20/2009 (or whatever the current year). Figure 7-12 also illustrates an example of date entry.

Undo Data Entry

1. Enter data into a spreadsheet.
2. To undo any actions or correct any mistakes you make when entering data, perform one of the following:
   - *Choose Undo from the Quick Access Toolbar.*
   - *Press Ctrl+Z.*
3. Keep repeating your favorite Undo method until the cells reflect the data you want.
4. To undo several steps at once, click the Undo arrow and select the step from which you want to begin the Undo action (see Figure 7-13).

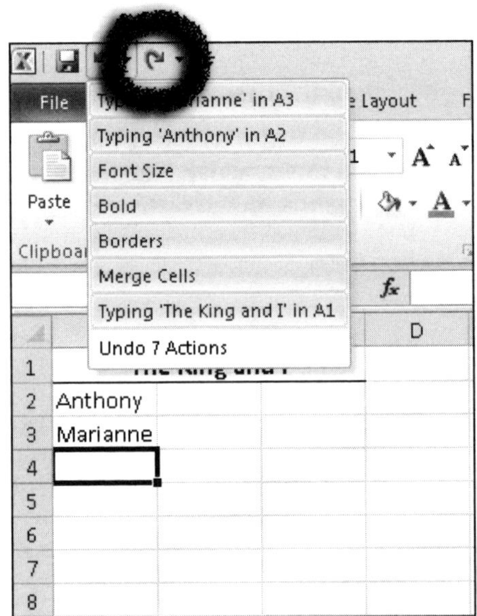

Figure 7-13

Edit Cell Data

1. To delete the entire contents of a cell, use one of the following methods:
   - *Choose Home⇨Editing⇨Clear and choose the option you want.*
   - *Press Delete.*

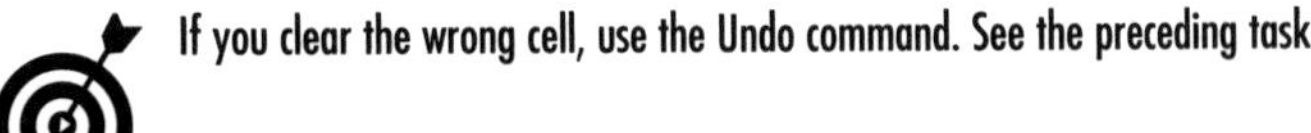

If you clear the wrong cell, use the Undo command. See the preceding task.

2. To edit the cell contents, use one of these methods:
   - *Delete the contents and retype new cell information.*
   - *Click in the formula bar and edit the cell contents.*
   - *Double-click the cell contents and edit the cell contents from the cell* (see Figure 7-14).

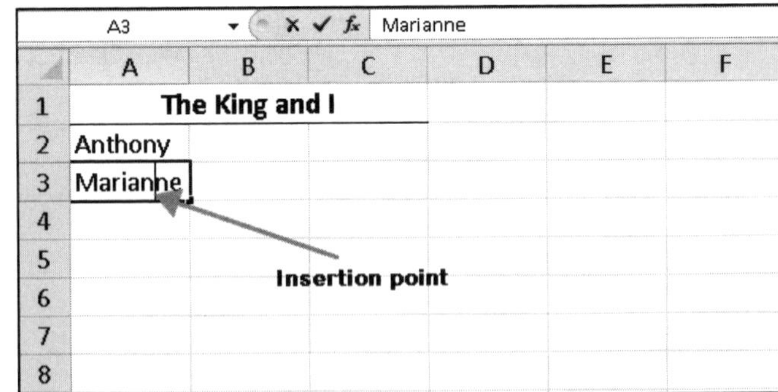

Figure 7-14

Select Multiple Cells

1. Click the first cell in the group you want to select.
2. Depending on the cells you want to select, perform one of the following actions.
   - *To select contiguous cells,* hold down Shift and select the last cell you want. Excel highlights all cells in the selected area, with the exception of the first cell. (Don't worry; it's selected, too.) Figure 7-15 shows a sequential area selected from cell B5 to cell B16. Notice the black border surrounding the selected area.
   - *To select noncontiguous cells,* hold down Ctrl and click each additional cell you want to select. Figure 7-16 shows the noncontiguous cells A4, A18, and B5 through B18 selected.
   - *To select a single entire column,* click a column heading.
   - *To select multiple columns,* drag across multiple column headings.
   - *To select a single entire row,* click the row number.
   - *To select multiple rows,* drag across multiple row numbers.
   - *To select the entire worksheet,* click the small gray box (called the Select All button) located to the left of column A and above row 1. Optionally, you can select all cells in a worksheet by pressing Ctrl+A.

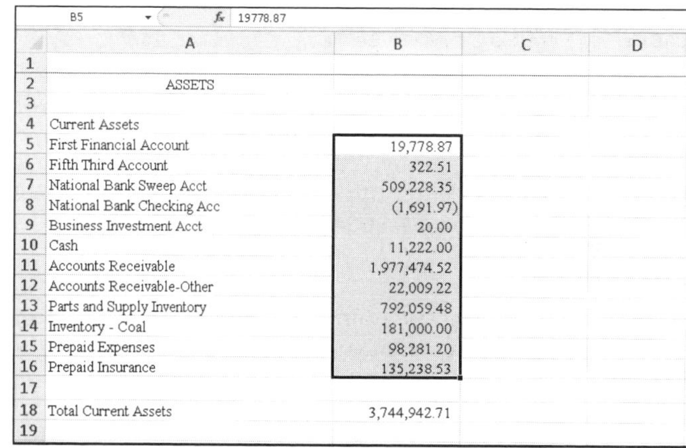

B5 | fx 19778.87

	A	B	C	D
1				
2	ASSETS			
3				
4	Current Assets			
5	First Financial Account	19,778.87		
6	Fifth Third Account	322.51		
7	National Bank Sweep Acct	509,228.35		
8	National Bank Checking Acc	(1,691.97)		
9	Business Investment Acct	20.00		
10	Cash	11,222.00		
11	Accounts Receivable	1,977,474.52		
12	Accounts Receivable-Other	22,009.22		
13	Parts and Supply Inventory	792,059.48		
14	Inventory - Coal	181,000.00		
15	Prepaid Expenses	98,281.20		
16	Prepaid Insurance	135,238.53		
17				
18	Total Current Assets	3,744,942.71		
19				

Figure 7-15

B5 | fx 19778.87

	A	B	C
1			
2	ASSETS		
3			
4	Current Assets		
5	First Financial Account	19,778.87	
6	Fifth Third Account	322.51	
7	National Bank Sweep Acct	509,228.35	
8	National Bank Checking Acc	(1,691.97)	
9	Business Investment Acct	20.00	
10	Cash	11,222.00	
11	Accounts Receivable	1,977,474.52	
12	Accounts Receivable-Other	22,009.22	
13	Parts and Supply Inventory	792,059.48	
14	Inventory - Coal	181,000.00	
15	Prepaid Expenses	98,281.20	
16	Prepaid Insurance	135,238.53	
17			
18	Total Current Assets	3,744,942.71	
19			
20	Property and Equipment		
21	Settlement Purchase	3,965,000.00	

Figure 7-16

Extend a Series with AutoFill

1. Type the first cell of data with a day or month, such as Wednesday or September. AutoFill works with days of the week, months of the year, or yearly quarters (such as 2nd Qtr). You can enter the entire word, or you can enter the abbreviated form (Wed or Sep).

2. Press Enter.

3. Position the mouse pointer on the fill handle (the small black box at the lower-right corner of the data cell). Your mouse pointer turns into a small black cross (see Figure 7-17).

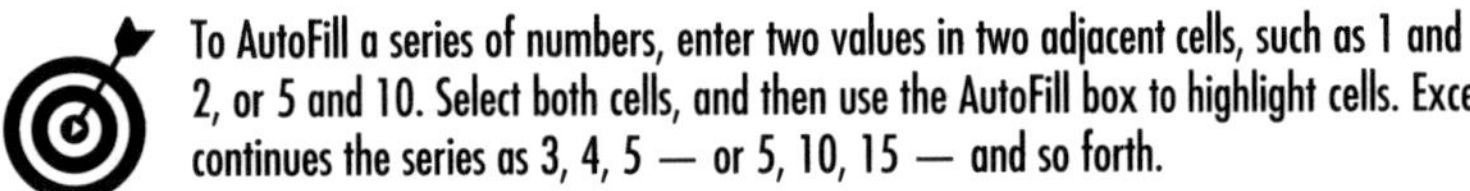

To AutoFill a series of numbers, enter two values in two adjacent cells, such as 1 and 2, or 5 and 10. Select both cells, and then use the AutoFill box to highlight cells. Excel continues the series as 3, 4, 5 — or 5, 10, 15 — and so forth.

4. Drag the small black box across the cells you want to fill. You can drag the fill handle across cells up, down, left, or right.

5. Release the mouse. Excel fills in the selected cells with a continuation of your data. Figure 7-18 shows how Excel fills in the cells with the rest of the days of the week. This figure also shows the different formats for the days of the weeks, months, and some numbers.

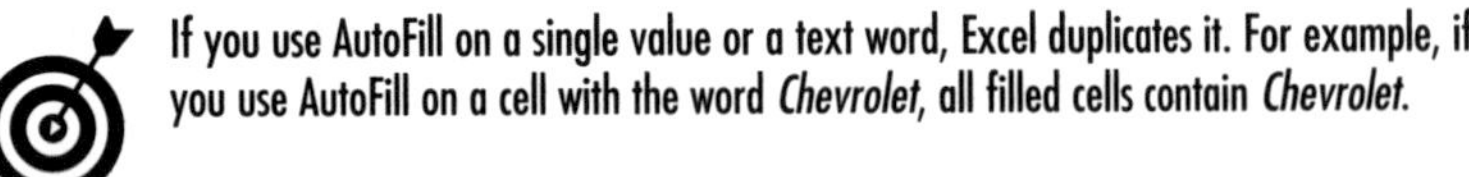

If you use AutoFill on a single value or a text word, Excel duplicates it. For example, if you use AutoFill on a cell with the word *Chevrolet,* all filled cells contain *Chevrolet.*

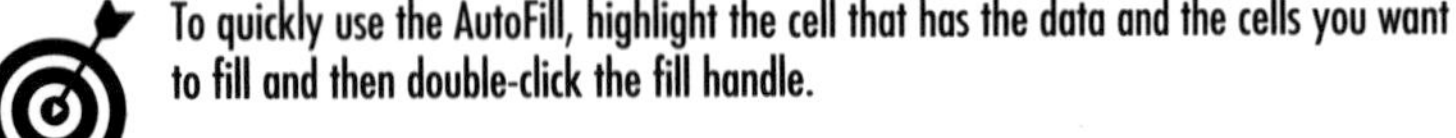

To quickly use the AutoFill, highlight the cell that has the data and the cells you want to fill and then double-click the fill handle.

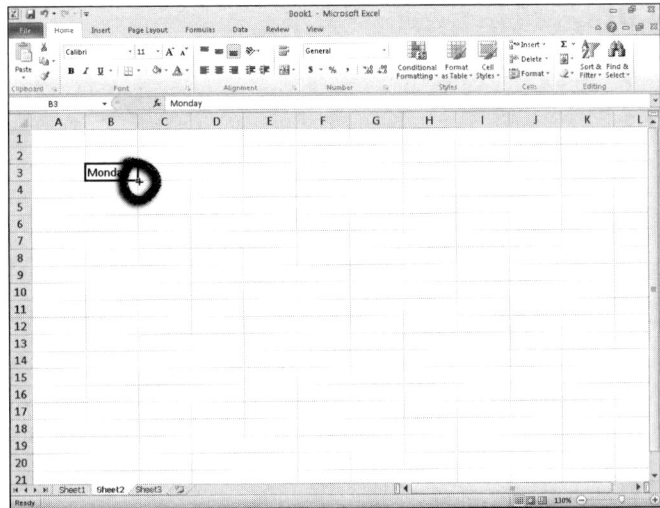

Figure 7-17

	B	C	D	E	F	G	H	I	J	K	L	M
1												
2												
3	Monday		Jan		Mon	Tue	Wed	Thu	Fri	Sat	Sun	
4	Tuesday		Feb									
5	Wednesday		Mar		January	February	March	April	May	June	July	
6	Thursday		Apr									
7	Friday		May		1	2	3	4	5	6	7	
8	Saturday		Jun									
9	Sunday		Jul		2	4	6	8	10	12	14	
10	Monday		Aug									
11	Tuesday		Sep		5	10	15	20	25	30	35	
12	Wednesday		Oct									
13	Thursday		Nov									
14	Friday		Dec									
15	Saturday		Jan									
16												
17												
18												
19												
20												
21												

Figure 7-18

Copy and Paste Cell Data

1. Select the area of data you want to copy.
2. Choose Home⇨Clipboard⇨Copy. A *marquee* (which looks like marching ants) surrounds the cells (see Figure 7-19). Excel copies the selected information to the Windows Clipboard.
3. Click the cell to which you want to copy the selected area.
4. Choose Home⇨Clipboard⇨Paste. The selected cells are pasted into the new location. The formatting is the same as in the original cells.
5. Paste the cells into another location or press Esc(ape) to cancel the marquee.

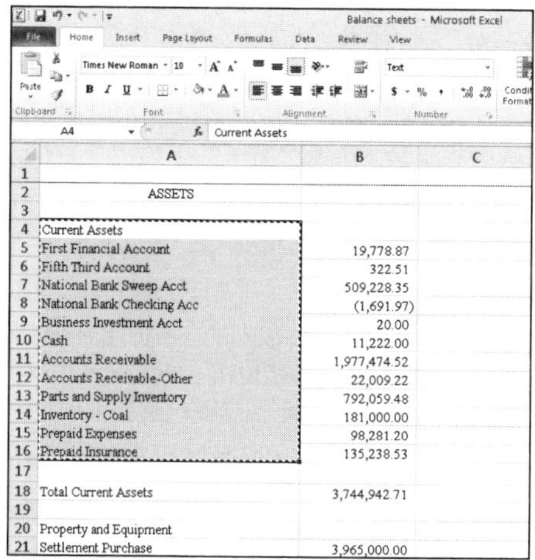

Figure 7-19

Move Data

1. Select the group of cells you want to move.
2. Choose Home⇨Clipboard⇨Cut. The marquee surrounds the cells.
3. Click the beginning cell where you want to place the area you want moved.
4. Choose Home⇨Clipboard⇨Paste. The selected cells are pasted into the new location.
5. Paste the cells into another location or press Esc(ape) to cancel the marquee. In Figure 7-20, you can see that the data originally located in cells A4 through A16 now placed in cells D2 through D14. The formatting is the same as in the original cells.

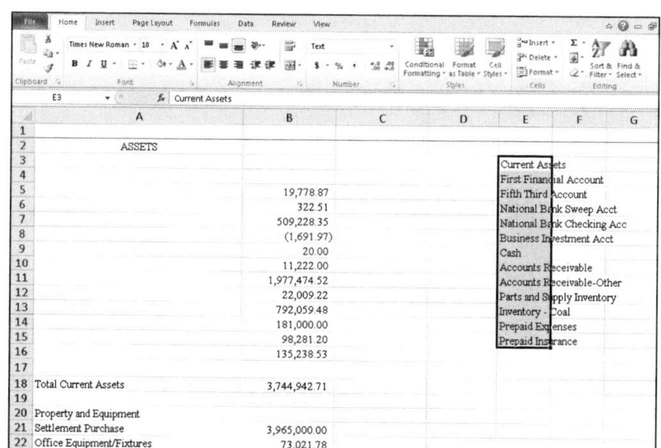

Figure 7-20

Drag and Drop Data

1. Select the data you want to move. Excel highlights the selected area.
2. Position the mouse pointer over the border surrounding the selected cells. The mouse pointer turns into a four-headed arrow.
3. Drag the data to the new worksheet location. As you move around the worksheet, Excel displays a gray border indicating the destination cell location (see Figure 7-21).
4. Release the mouse button. Excel moves the data to the new area.

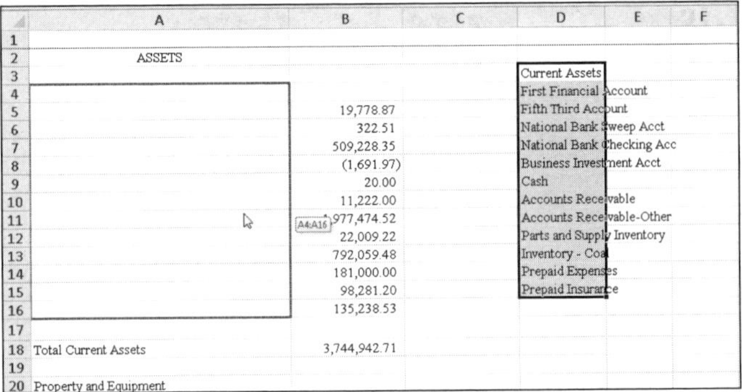

Figure 7-21

Transpose Data

1. Select the cells you want to transpose.
2. Choose Home➪Clipboard➪Copy or press Ctrl+C.
3. Click the beginning cell where you want the transposed cells. The new area must be outside the selected area.
4. On the Home tab of the Ribbon, in the Clipboard group, click the Paste down-arrow (not the Paste icon). A menu of options appears. Pause your mouse over the icons to identify the Transpose icon. It's the seventh icon.
5. Choose Transpose. As you see in Figure 7-22, Excel copies the selected cells into the new area, transposing rows into columns or columns into rows.

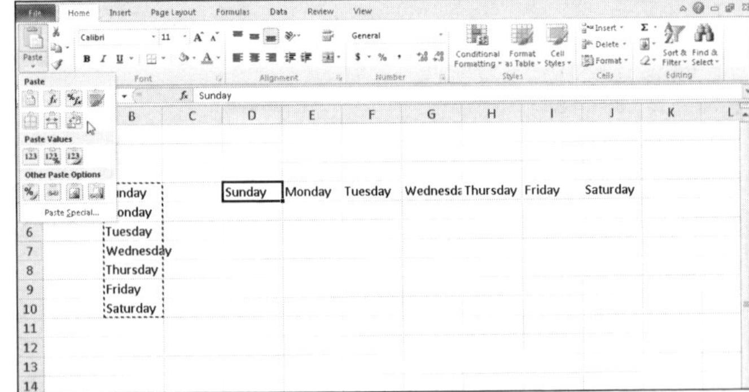

Figure 7-22

Insert Rows and Columns

1. Select the row numbers or column letters where you want the new rows or columns. Excel highlights the entire rows or columns, as seen in Figure 7-23.
2. Choose Home⇨Cells⇨Insert. Excel inserts the same number of rows or columns that you selected in Step 1. Data in the selected columns and columns to the right moves to the right. Data in the selected rows and lower moves down.

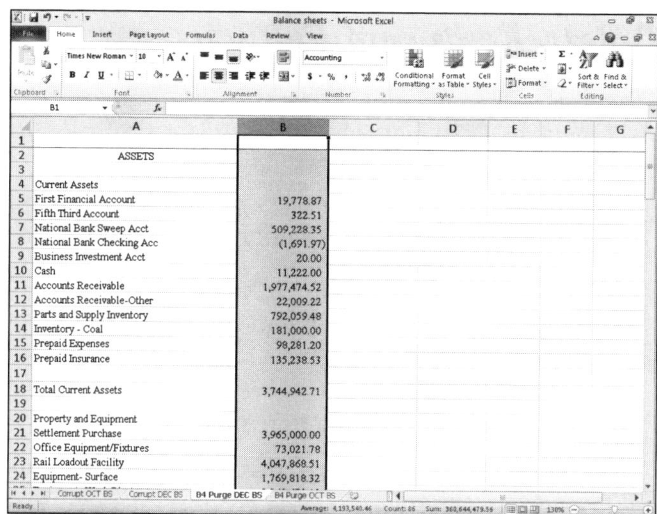

Figure 7-23

Insert Cells

1. Select the cell area where you want to insert blank cells. Be sure to select the same number of cells as you want to insert. Excel highlights the selected area.
2. Choose Home⇨Cells and then click the Insert arrow.
3. From the menu of options that appears, choose Insert Cells. The Insert dialog box seen in Figure 7-24 appears.
4. Make a selection and then click OK:
   - *Shift Cells Right:* Select this option if you want data in the cells in the same row moved to the right. Excel doesn't move the data in the cells to the left of the selection.
   - *Shift Cells Down:* Select this option if you want data in the lower cells in the same column moved down. Excel doesn't move data in the cells above the selection.
   - *Entire Row:* Select this option if you want to add a new row and move data lower.
   - *Entire Column:* Select this option if you want to add a new column and move data to the right.

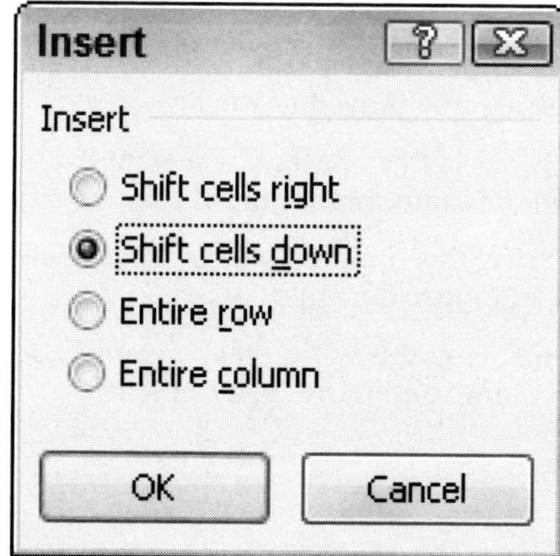

Figure 7-24

Delete Rows and Columns

1. Select the row numbers or column letters you want to remove. Excel highlights the entire rows or columns (see Figure 7-25).
2. Choose Home⇨Cells⇨Delete. Excel removes any data in the rows or columns and moves existing data up or right. This fills the void from the deleted rows or columns.

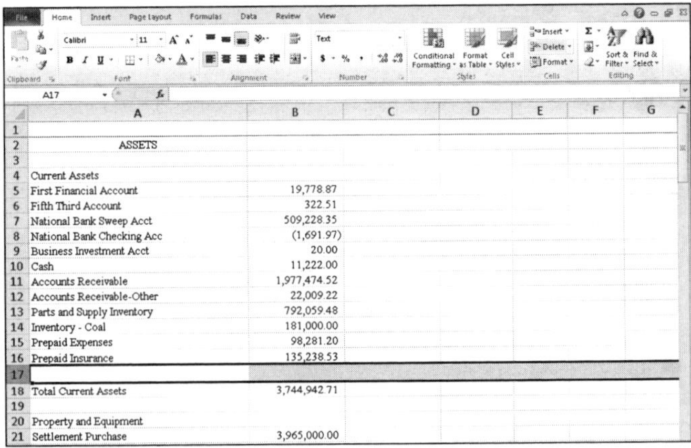

Figure 7-25

Delete Cells

1. Select the cells you want to remove.
2. Choose Home⇨Cells and then click the Delete arrow.
3. From the menu of options that appears, choose Delete Cells. The Delete dialog box appears, as seen in Figure 7-26.
4. Select a deletion option and then click OK:
   - *Shift Cells Left:* Select this option if you want data in the cells in the same row moved to the left.
   - *Shift Cells Up:* Select this option if you want data in the lower cells in the same column moved up.
   - *Entire Row:* Select this option if you want to delete the current row and move data up.
   - *Entire Column:* Select this option if you want to delete the current column and move data to the left.

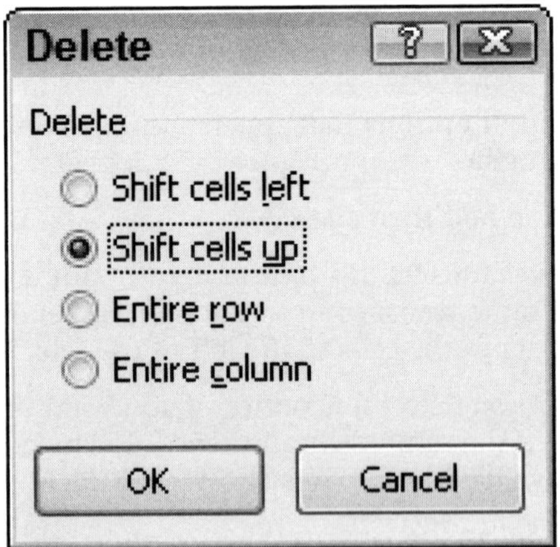

Figure 7-26

Working with Excel Formulas

This chapter is mostly about the math. With Excel, you can create formulas to perform calculations. The calculations can be simple, (such as adding 2 + 3), or they can be extremely complex (such as those used to calculate depreciation). Don't despair, though, because Excel does most of the work. Excel includes almost 400 built-in calculations — *functions* — in 11 categories. Functions contain *arguments,* which appear in parentheses following the function name. The arguments are the details that you provide to Excel to indicate which numbers to calculate in the function. Some functions require several arguments to function correctly, but again I say, don't worry; Excel contains a Function Wizard to walk you through the entire process.

The primary tasks in this chapter include

- Creating simple and complex formulas by typing them into a cell
- Analyzing data with Excel's time-saving functions
- Creating cell ranges separated by colons for a sequential cell selection or by commas to list specific cell locations
- Validating data entry for proper values

Chapter 8

Get ready to . . .

Create Simple Formulas with Operators

1. Enter values in two different cells. Remember, however, formulas do not need to reference cell addresses: They can contain actual numbers.

2. In the cell where you want to perform the calculation for the two values, type an equal sign (=).

All Excel formulas begin with an equal sign.

3. Click or type the first cell address or type the first value you want to include in the formula. In the example in Figure 8-1, I'm adding two cell references (B5 and B6).

	A	B	C	D	E
1					
2					
3					
4					
5		19778.87			
6		135238.53			
7		=B5+B6			
8					
9					
10					
11					

Figure 8-1

Excel displays a color border that surrounds the cell reference you enter.

4. Type an operator. Operators can include
   - +: Addition
   - –: Subtraction
   - *: Multiplication
   - /: Division
   - %: Percent
   - ^: Exponentiation

5. Type the second cell address or the second value you want to include in the formula.

6. Press Enter, and Excel displays the results of the calculation in the selected cell (see Figure 8-2).

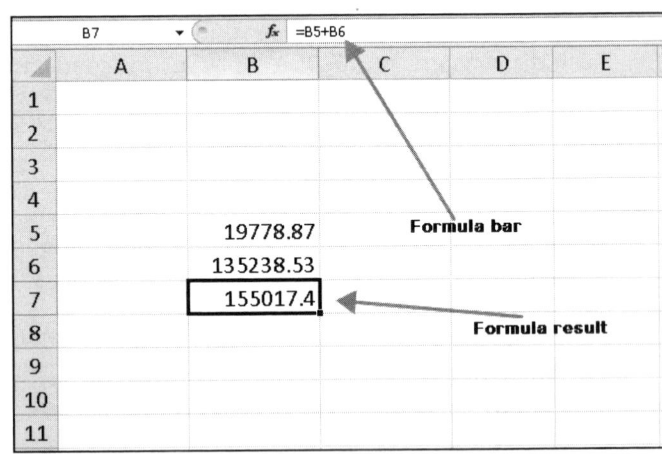

Figure 8-2

Create Compound Formulas

1. Type values in three or more different cells.
2. Select the cell where you want the formula.
3. Type the equal sign and then the first cell reference.
4. Type the first operator and then the second cell reference.
5. Type the second operator and then the third cell reference, as seen in Figure 8-3.

Compound formulas are not limited to three references, and you can use cell references multiple times in a compound formula.

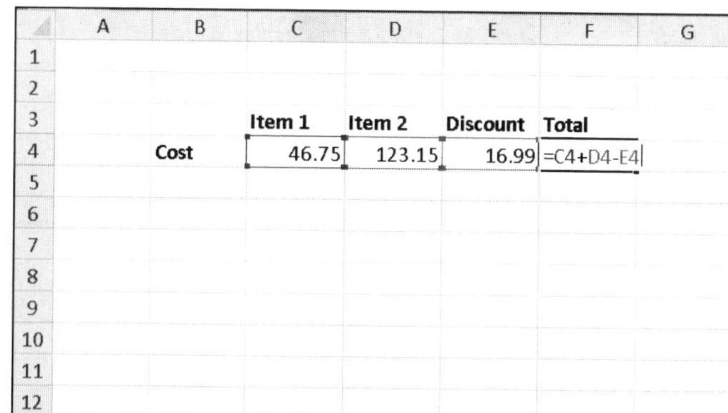

Figure 8-3

6. Press Enter. Excel displays the results of the calculation in the selected cell. The actual formula appears in the formula bar (see Figure 8-4).

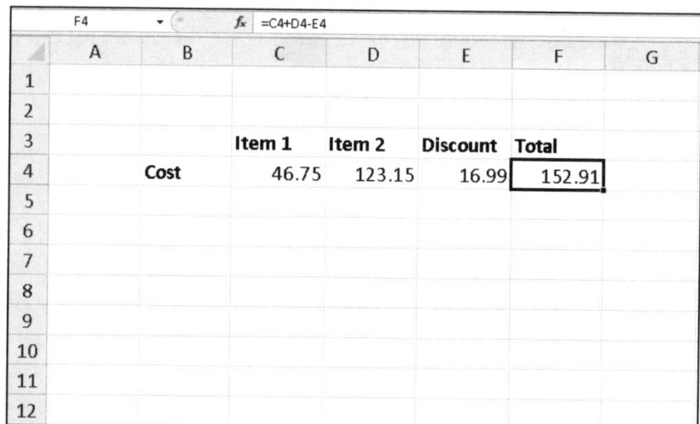

Figure 8-4

If you were paying attention in your high school algebra class, you might remember the Rule of Priorities (also known as order of precedence). In a compound formula, Excel calculates multiplication and division before it calculates addition and subtraction. This means that you must include parentheses for any portion of a formula you want calculated first. As an example, `3+5*2` gives a result of `13`, but `(3+5)*2` gives a result of `16`.

Compound formulas can have multiple combinations in parentheses and can contain any combination of operators and references. A formula might read `((B5+C5)/2)*SalesTax`. This formula adds `B5` and `C5`, divides that result by `2`, and then multiplies that result times the value in the cell named `SalesTax`. (See Name Cell Ranges, later in this chapter.)

A great tool to review formulas is the capability to display the actual formula in the worksheet rather than the formula result. Choose Formulas⇨Formula Auditing⇨Show Formulas. Click the Show Formulas button again to return to the formula result.

Add Numbers with AutoSum

1. Click the cell beneath a contiguous list of values.

2. Choose Formulas➪Function Library➪AutoSum. Excel places a marquee (marching ants) around the cells directly above the current cell (see Figure 8-5).

   If the cells directly above the current cell have no values, Excel selects the cells directly to the left of the current cell. If you want to add a group of different cells, highlight them.

3. Press Enter to display the sum total of the selected cells.

   The formula bar displays the formula beginning with the equal sign and the word SUM. The selected cells appear in parentheses, the first and last cells separated by a colon.

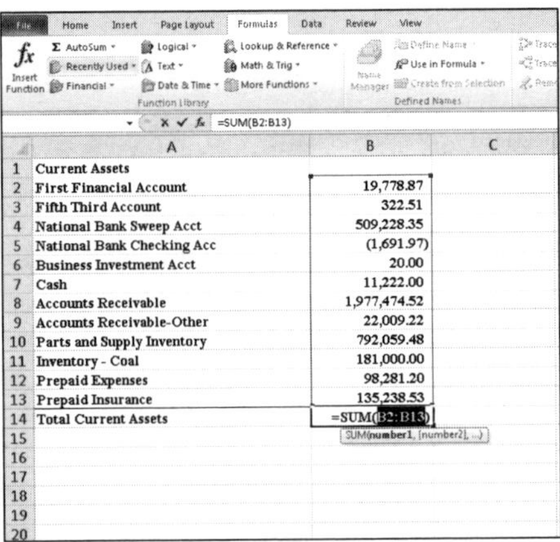

Figure 8-5

Find an Average Value

1. After selecting the cell beneath a sequential list of values, click Formulas➪Function Library and click the AutoSum arrow. Excel displays a list of calculation options, including the following (see Figure 8-6).

   - *Average:* Calculated by adding a group of numbers and then dividing by the count of those numbers
   - *Count Numbers:* Counts the number of cells in a specified range that contain numbers
   - *Max:* Determines the highest value in a specified range
   - *Min:* Determines the lowest value in a specified range

3. Choose Average. A marquee appears around the group of cells. Highlight a different group of cells if necessary.

4. Press Enter. The selected cell displays the average value of the cell group.

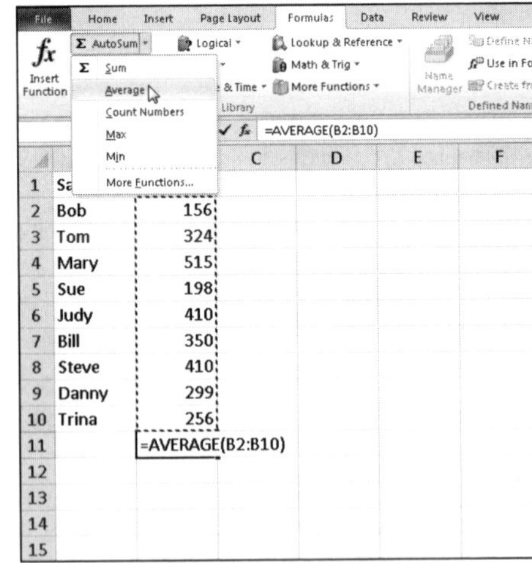

Figure 8-6

Copy Formulas with AutoFill

1. Position the mouse on the AutoFill box in the lower-right corner of a cell with a formula. Make sure that the mouse pointer turns into a black cross.
2. Drag the AutoFill box to include the cells to which you want to copy the formula (see Figure 8-7). The AutoFill method of copying formulas is helpful if you're copying a formula to surrounding cells.

Copied formulas are slightly different than the originals because of the relative change in position. For example, if the formula in cell E16 is `C16+D16` and you copy the formula to the next cell down (to cell E17), Excel automatically changes the formula to `C17+D17`. If you do not want the copied formula to change, you must make the originating formula an *absolute reference formula;* see the upcoming task "Define an Absolute Reference."

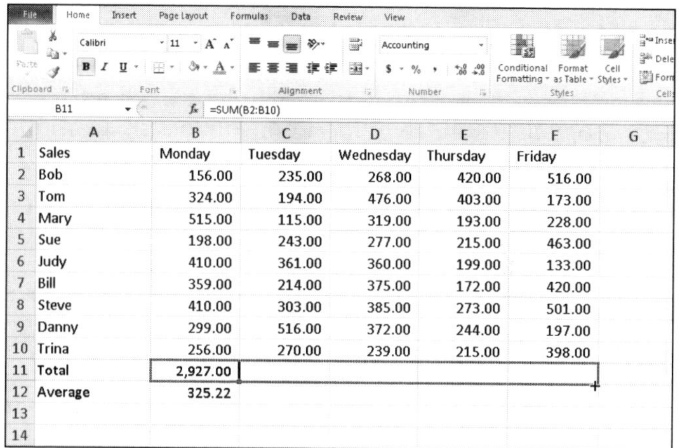

B11 =SUM(B2:B10)

	A	B	C	D	E	F	G
1	Sales	Monday	Tuesday	Wednesday	Thursday	Friday	
2	Bob	156.00	235.00	268.00	420.00	516.00	
3	Tom	324.00	194.00	476.00	403.00	173.00	
4	Mary	515.00	115.00	319.00	193.00	228.00	
5	Sue	198.00	243.00	277.00	215.00	463.00	
6	Judy	410.00	361.00	360.00	199.00	133.00	
7	Bill	359.00	214.00	375.00	172.00	420.00	
8	Steve	410.00	303.00	385.00	273.00	501.00	
9	Danny	299.00	516.00	372.00	244.00	197.00	
10	Trina	256.00	270.00	239.00	215.00	398.00	
11	Total	2,927.00					
12	Average	325.22					
13							
14							

Figure 8-7

Edit a Formula

1. Double-click the cell containing the formula you want to edit. The formula appears instead of the result (see Figure 8-8).

Optionally, press F2 to expand the formula so that you can edit it.

2. Use the arrow keys to navigate to the character you want to change.
3. Using the Backspace key, delete any unwanted characters and type any additional characters.
4. Press Enter.

Press Delete to delete the entire formula and start over.

=AVERAGE(B2:B10)

	A	B	C	D	E	F	G
1	Sales	Monday	Tuesday	Wednesday	Thursday	Friday	
2	Bob	156.00	235.00	268.00	420.00	516.00	
3	Tom	324.00	194.00	476.00	403.00	173.00	
4	Mary	515.00	115.00	319.00	193.00	228.00	
5	Sue	198.00	243.00	277.00	215.00	463.00	
6	Judy	410.00	361.00	360.00	199.00	133.00	
7	Bill	359.00	214.00	375.00	172.00	420.00	
8	Steve	410.00	303.00	385.00	273.00	501.00	
9	Danny	299.00	516.00	372.00	244.00	197.00	
10	Trina	256.00	270.00	239.00	215.00	398.00	
11	Total	2,927.00	2,451.00	3,071.00	2,334.00	3,029.00	
12	Average	=AVERAGE(B2:B10)					
13		AVERAGE(number1, [number2], ...)					
14							

Figure 8-8

Define an Absolute Reference

1. To prevent a formula from changing a cell reference as you copy it to a different location, you lock in an absolute cell reference by using one of these methods:
   - *Lock in a cell location.* Type a dollar sign in front of both the column reference and the row reference (as in $A$2). If the original formula in cell E5 is `=$A$2*D5` and you copy the formula to cell E6, the copied formula remains the same instead of changing to `=$A$2*D6`, which is how it would read were it not absolute (see Figure 8-9).
   - *Lock in the row or column location only.* Type a dollar sign in front of the column reference (**$D3**) or in front of the row reference (**D$3**).
2. Copy the formula, as needed, to other locations.

	A	B	C	D	E	F	G
1	Sales Tax Rate						
2	7%						
3							
4	Invoice #	Quantity	Cost	Subtotal	Sales Tax	Total	
5	101	15	3.57	53.55	3.75		
6	102	13	9.48	123.24	=$A$2*D6		
7	103	5	17.51	87.55			
8	104	1	127.95	127.95			
9							
10							
11							
12							
13							

Figure 8-9

Copy Values by Using Paste Special

1. Select a cell (or group of cells) containing a formula and then choose Home➪Clipboard➪Copy. A marquee appears around the selected cell.
2. Select the cell where you want the copied values; then choose Home➪Clipboard and click the Paste arrow. A menu of options appears.
3. Choose Paste Special. The Paste Special dialog box appears, as shown in Figure 8-10.
4. Select the Values option.
5. Click OK. Excel pastes the result of the formula, not the actual formula. If the original formula changes, this value doesn't change.

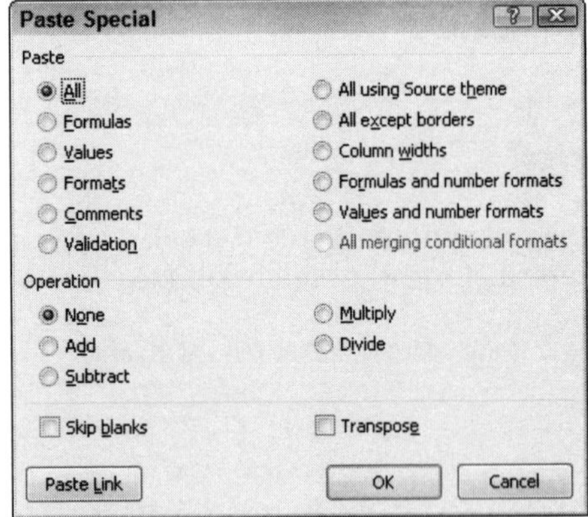

Figure 8-10

Build a Formula with the Function Wizard

1. Select the cell where you want to enter a function.
2. Click Formulas⇨Function Library⇨Insert Function.
3. From the Insert Function dialog box that appears, select a function category from the Or Select a Category drop-down list (see Figure 8-11).

To make the functions easier to locate, Excel separates them into categories including Financial, Date & Time, Math & Trig, Statistical, Lookup & Reference, Database, Text, Logical, Information, Engineering and Cube categories. For example, the Sum function is in the Math category; Average, Count, Max, and Min are Statistical functions. Functions that calculate a payment value are considered Financial functions.

4. Select a function name from the Select a Function list. A brief description of the function and its arguments appears under the list of function names.
5. Click OK. The Function Arguments dialog box displays. The contents of this dialog box depend upon the function that you selected. Figure 8-12 shows the PMT function that calculates a loan payment based on constant payments and interest.
6. Type the first argument amount or cell reference or click the cell in the worksheet. If you click the cell, Excel places a marquee around the selected cell.
7. Press Tab to move to the next argument.
8. Type or select the second argument.
9. Repeat Steps 7 and 8 for each necessary argument.
10. Click OK. Excel calculates the result.

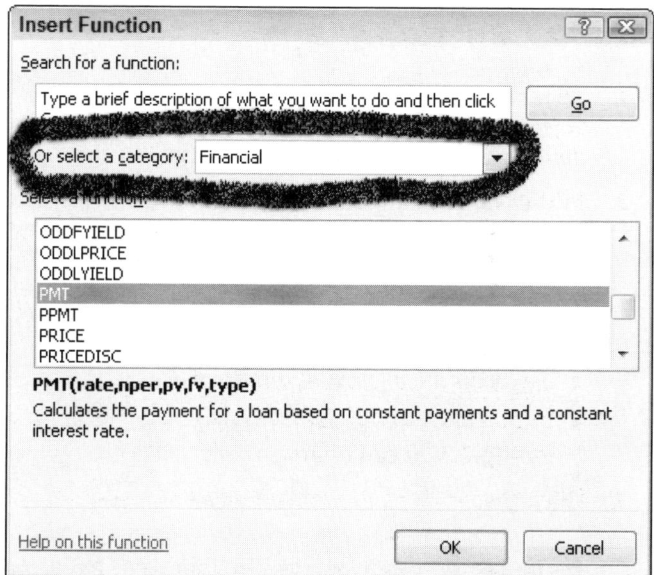

Figure 8-11

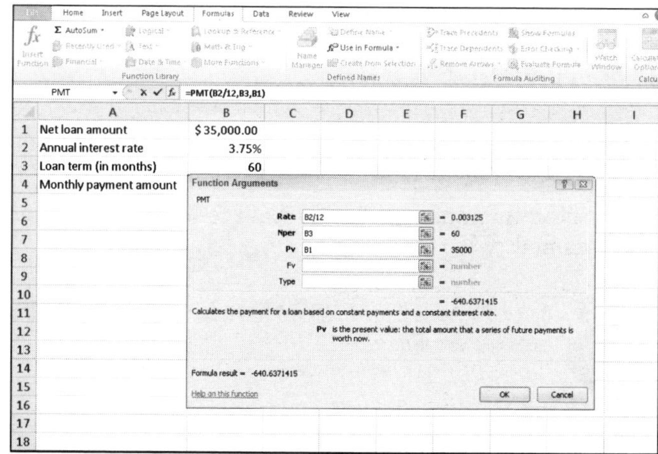

Figure 8-12

Name Cell Ranges

1. After selecting the cells you want to name, click Formulas⇨Defined Names⇨Define Name. The New Name dialog box appears (see Figure 8-13).

2. In the Name field, type a name (up to 255 characters) for the range. Range names are not case-sensitive; however, range names must follow these conventions:

   - *The first character must be a letter, an underscore, or a backslash.*
   - *No spaces are allowed in a range name.*
   - *Do not use a name that is the same as a cell address.* For example, you can't name a range CD57.

3. Click OK.

You can include range names in formulas, such as =F6*PayRate, where a specific cell is named PayRate.

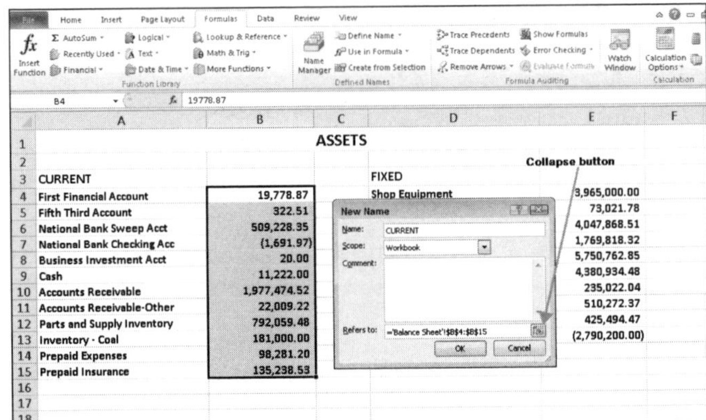

Figure 8-13

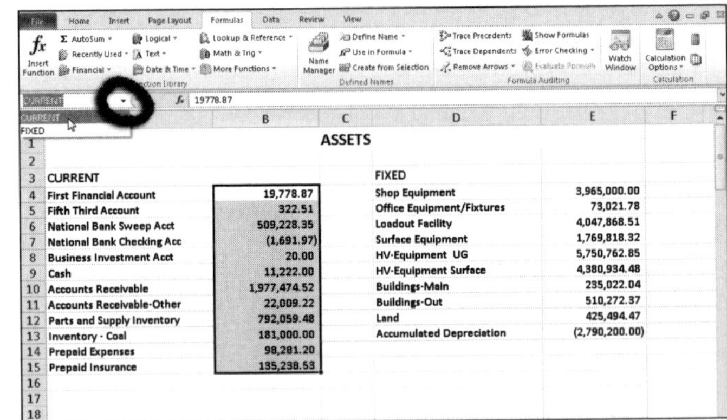

Figure 8-14

Use Named Ranges

1. Click the down arrow in the Name field. A list of named ranges appears (see Figure 8-14).

2. Select the range name you want to access. Excel highlights the named cells.

Optionally, choose Home⇨Editing⇨Find & Select⇨Go To. Double-click the range name you want to access.

Manage Range Names

1. Choose Formulas➪Defined Names➪Name Manager. The Name Manager dialog box, shown in Figure 8-15, appears.

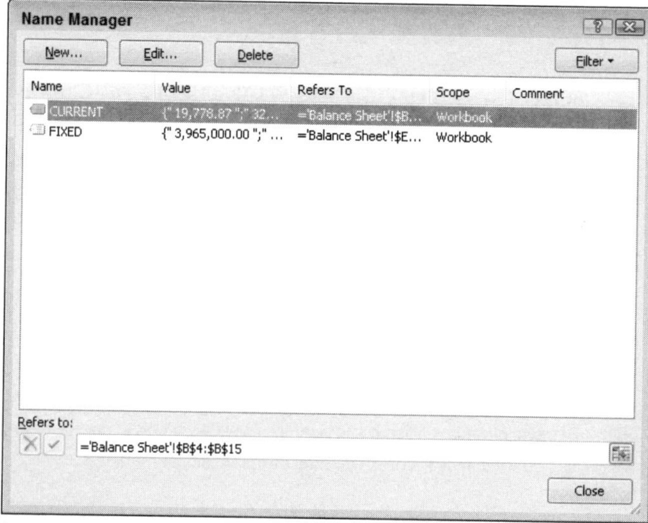

Figure 8-15

2. Select one of the following options.

   - *Click the New button,* which displays the New Name dialog box (refer to Figure 8-13), where you can enter a range name and enter the cell location to which it refers.

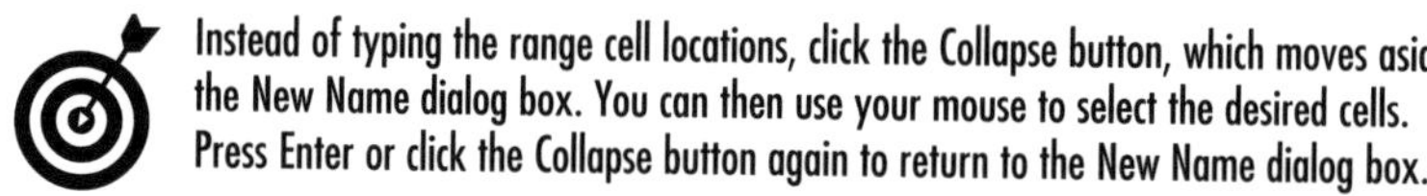

Instead of typing the range cell locations, click the Collapse button, which moves aside the New Name dialog box. You can then use your mouse to select the desired cells. Press Enter or click the Collapse button again to return to the New Name dialog box.

   - *Click an existing range name and then click the Edit button* to display the Edit Name dialog box shown in Figure 8-16. Use this dialog box to change the range name or the range cell location reference.

   - *Click an existing range name and then click the Delete button.* A confirmation message appears making sure that you want to delete the range name.

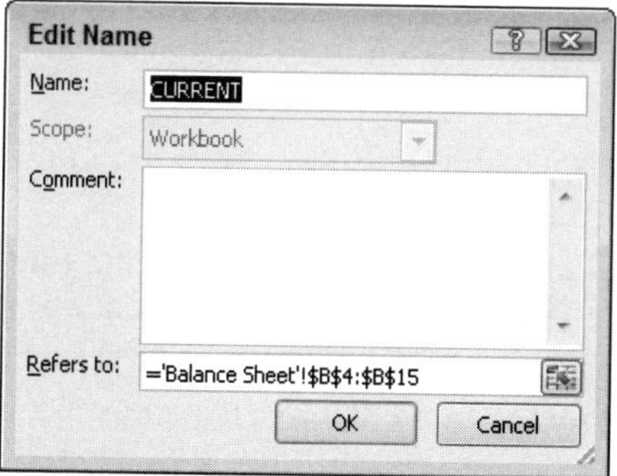

Figure 8-16

If you have a lot of range names, you can click the Filter button and elect to display only the items meeting selected criteria.

3. Click the Close button to close the Name Manager dialog box.

Validate Data Entry

1. Select the cell or cells you want Excel to validate. Next, choose Data➪Data Tools➪Data Validation. The Data Validation dialog box displays.
2. From the Settings tab, open the Allow drop-down list and choose the type of validation, such as
   - *Values,* such as Whole Number or Decimal, where you specify the upper and lower limits of allowable data values.
   - *List,* such as a list you define, a range of cells in the existing worksheet, or a named range (see Figure 8-17).

When creating a list, if you want the available choices to appear when the cell is selected, make sure to select the In-Cell Dropdown check box.

   - *Dates or Times,* where you specify ranges or limitations such as greater than or less than or even a specific date.
   - *Text Length,* where the number of characters in the data must be within the limits that you specify.
3. If necessary, display the Data drop-down list and select criteria such as Between, Greater Than, and so on.
4. Select optional criteria (such as maximum and minimum values) or specify a data location. Enter values or cell addresses. Precede a value with an equal sign (=) to specify a range name.
5. (Optional) From the Input Message tab, enter a comment to display whenever someone clicks the validated cell.
6. On the Error Alert tab, choose from the Style drop-down list whether Excel warns you or completely stops you from entering an invalid entry. (See an example of an alert in Figure 8-18.)
7. Click OK.

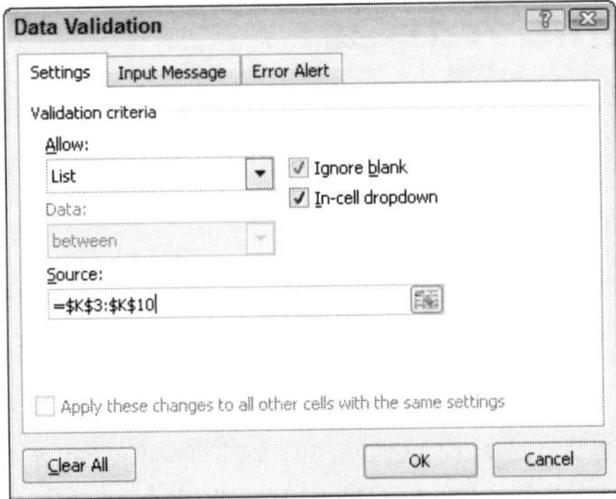

Figure 8-17

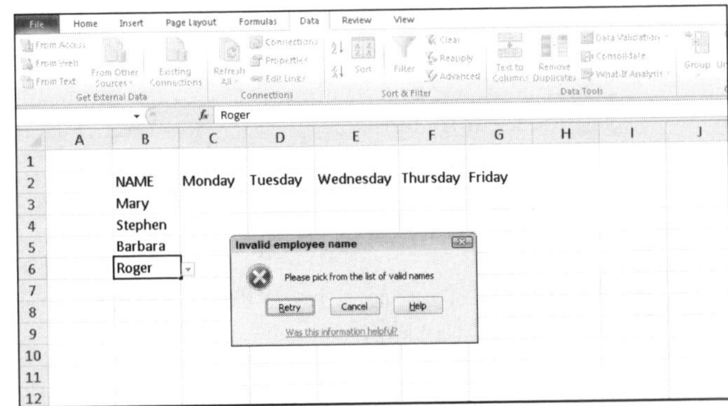

Figure 8-18

Formatting Worksheets

Chapter 9

Whoever said, "Looks aren't everything" wasn't staring at an unformatted Excel spreadsheet. Columns often aren't wide enough; fonts are too small to read; dates display in an unusual manner; and when columns of data are stacked next to each other, information sometimes overlaps.

Fortunately, Excel includes a plethora of features to make your data more presentable and easier to read. After you master the Excel formatting features in this chapter, you can

- Change the font type, size, and style of text, values, or dates.
- Add cell borders and backgrounds.
- Change the alignment of data in a cell from the standard left-aligned for text and right-aligned for values or dates.
- Turn values into currency or percentages.
- Create titles, using the Excel Merge and Center button.
- Change column width and row height.
- Save time by copying formatting from cell to cell.

Get ready to . . .

Format Values

1. Select the cells you want to format. You can select a few cells, entire rows, entire columns, or the entire worksheet. (See Chapter 7 for information on selecting multiple cells.)

2. Choose Home➪Number➪Number Format. A list of options appears. Figure 9-1 shows values formatted in various Excel styles. Notice the different dollar sign placement in the Accounting and Currency types.

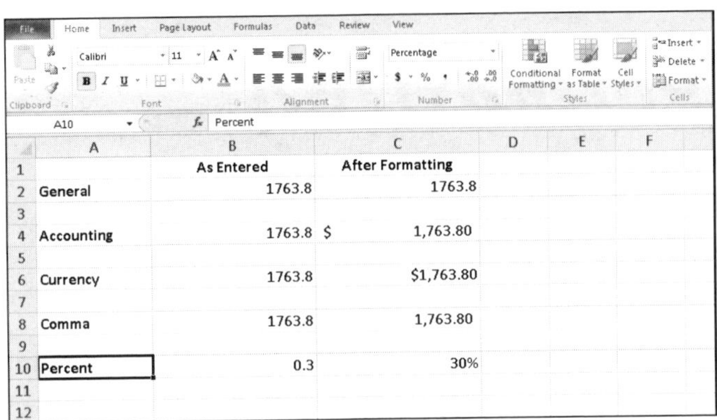

Figure 9-1

The Number group on the Ribbon also displays three icons you can use to quickly format as Accounting Number Format, Percent Style, or Comma. The Accounting Number Format option has a drop-down list from which you can select different international currency symbols. The Comma Style option adds two decimal places and a comma between the thousands. It does not include a dollar sign. Percent Style adds a percent sign and no decimal points.

Another method to select number formatting is using the Number dialog box launcher, which displays the Format Cells dialog box. Number format selections are on the Number tab.

Add or Remove Decimal Points

1. Select the cells you want to format. You can select a few cells, entire rows, entire columns, or the entire worksheet.

2. To remove digits to the right of the decimal point, choose Home➪Number➪Decrease Decimal. To add decimal digits, click the Increase Decimal button. Each click adds or removes a number to the far right of the decimal point and rounds the value in the cell (see Figure 9-2).

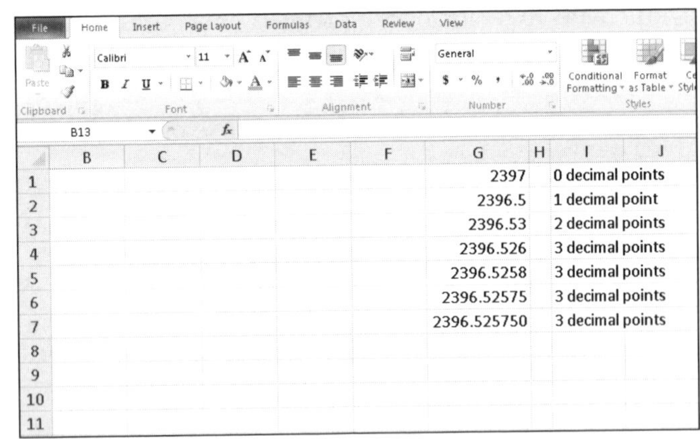

Figure 9-2

Excel numbers can display up to 30 decimal places.

If you see a cell with values displaying #####, you need to widen the column width. See the upcoming task, "Adjust Column Width."

Adjust Column Width

1. To adjust the width of columns headings, highlight the ones to be widened. If you want to adjust a single column, click any cell in that column.

If your worksheet contains many numbers, you can widen the columns to make the worksheet less cluttered. Columns that especially need widening are those containing cells with truncated text entries or numbers that Excel shows as ######.

2. Choose a method to adjust column width:

   - *Manually change column width.* Position the mouse pointer on the right boundary of the column heading until it turns into a double-ended arrow. Drag until the column is the width that you want. As you move the pointer, a balloon message displays the new width. In Figure 9-3, I'm expanding column A.

Excel displays cell width in characters and pixels instead of in inches. The minimum column width is 0 characters, and the maximum is 255 characters.

   - *Set column width to a specific setting.* Choose Home➪Cells➪Format➪ Column Width. The Column Width dialog box, shown in Figure 9-4, appears. Type the exact width you want; then click OK.
   - *Automatically change the column width so it fits the widest entry:* Double-click the boundary on the right side of the column heading, or choose Home➪Cells➪Format➪AutoFit Column Width. Excel sets the width slightly larger than the longest entry in the column.

The default column width is 8.43 based on the default 11-point Calibri font. If you change the default font type or size, Excel may also change the standard column width. You can manually set a default column width by choosing Home➪Cells➪Format➪Standard Width.

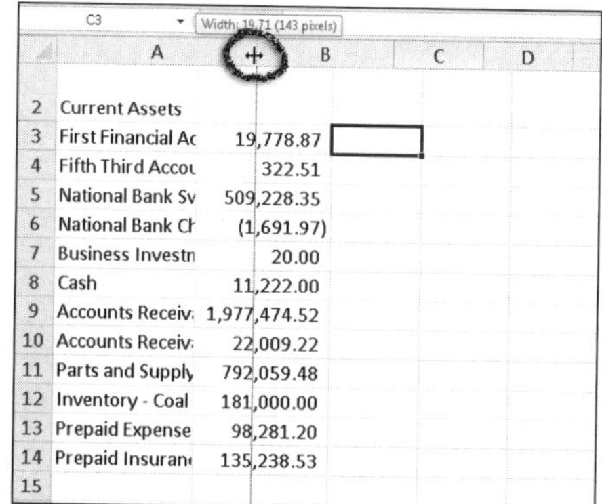

Figure 9-3

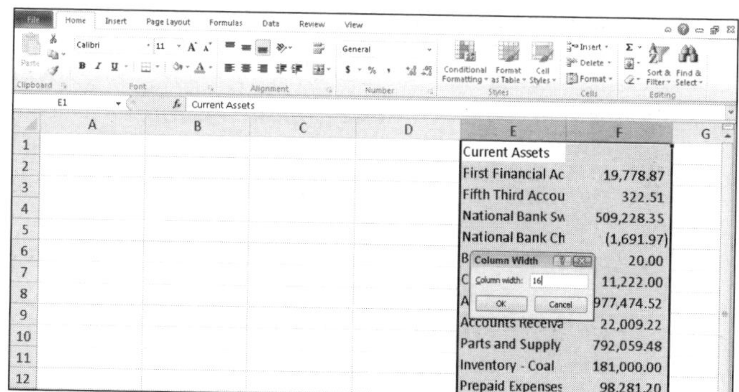

Figure 9-4

Change Row Height

1. Highlight the row headings whose height you want to adjust. If you want to adjust a single row, click any cell in that row.

2. Choose a method to adjust row height:

   - *Manually change row height.* Position the mouse pointer on the bottom boundary of the row heading until it turns into a double-ended arrow. Drag until the row is the height that you want. As you move the pointer, a balloon message displays the new height. In Figure 9-5, I'm increasing the height of rows 1 and 2.

Excel displays row height in characters and pixels instead of inches.

   - *Set row height to a specific setting.* Choose Home➪Cells➪Format➪Row Height. The Row Height dialog box appears, as shown in Figure 9-6. Type the exact width you want; then click OK.

   - *Automatically change the height of the row so it fits the tallest entry in the row.* Double-click the boundary on the bottom of the row heading, or choose Home➪Cells➪Format➪AutoFit Row Height. Excel examines the rows contents and sets the height slightly larger than the tallest entry.

The default row height is 15, based on the default 11-point Calibri font. If you change the default font type or size, Excel may also change the standard row height. You cannot manually set a default row height.

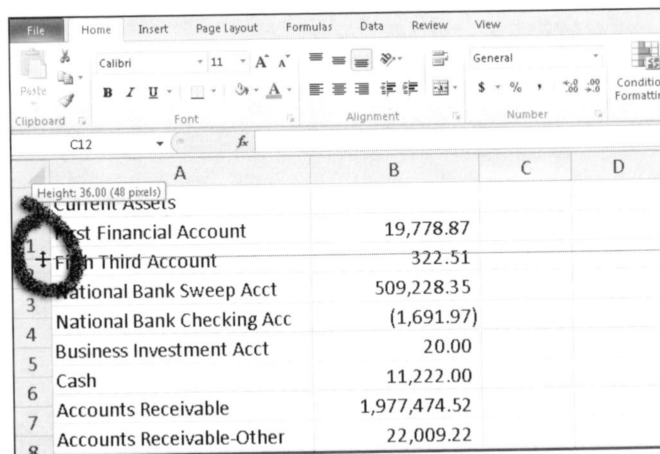

Figure 9-5

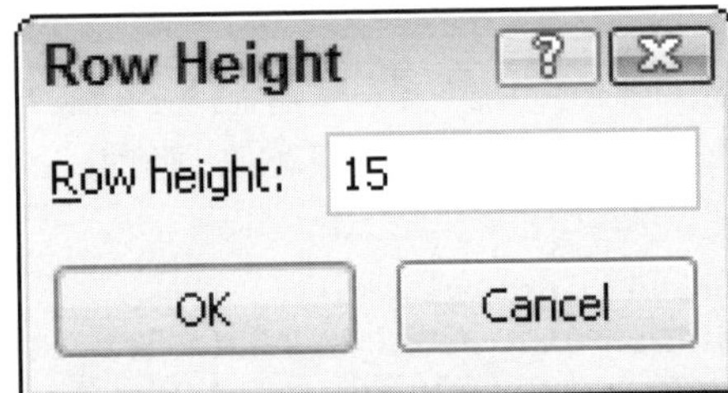

Figure 9-6

Align Data

1. Select the cells you want to align.
2. Choose Home➪Alignment; then, select one of these alignment buttons:
   - *Align Text Left:* Horizontally aligns the data along the left edge of the cell.
   - *Center:* Centers the data horizontally in the middle of the cell. If you modify the column width, the data remains centered to the new column width. Cells D3 through I3 are center-aligned in Figure 9-7.
   - *Align Text Right:* Horizontally aligns the data along the right edge of the cell.

Values formatted as Accounting can display only as right-aligned. You can change alignment on all other formatting styles.

   - *Top Align:* Aligns the data vertically along the top edge of the cell.
   - *Middle Align:* Centers the data vertically in the cell.
   - *Bottom Align:* Default; aligns the data along the bottom edge of the cell. Notice the heading in Figure 9-8. Cell C1 shows a top vertical alignment, whereas cell C2 shows the default bottom alignment.

Optionally, you can view additional alignment options and align both the horizontal and vertical alignment at the same time using the Format Cells dialog box. From the Home tab, click the Alignment group dialog box launcher. If necessary, click the Alignment tab and then set any desired alignment options; then click OK.

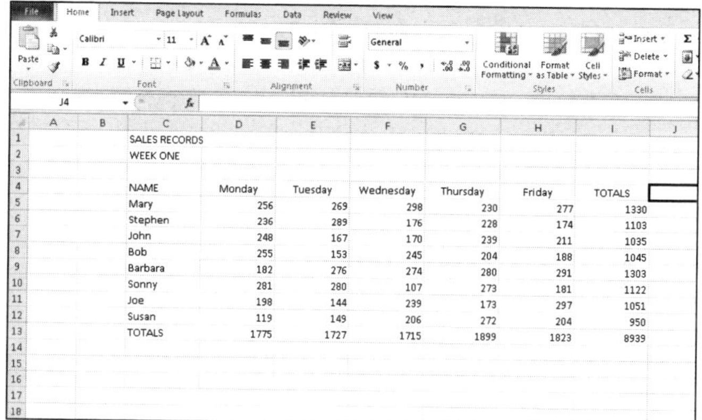

SALES RECORDS
WEEK ONE

NAME	Monday	Tuesday	Wednesday	Thursday	Friday	TOTALS
Mary	256	269	298	230	277	1330
Stephen	236	289	176	228	174	1103
John	248	167	170	239	211	1035
Bob	255	153	245	204	188	1045
Barbara	182	276	274	280	291	1303
Sonny	281	280	107	273	181	1122
Joe	198	144	239	173	297	1051
Susan	119	149	206	272	204	950
TOTALS	1775	1727	1715	1899	1823	8939

Figure 9-7

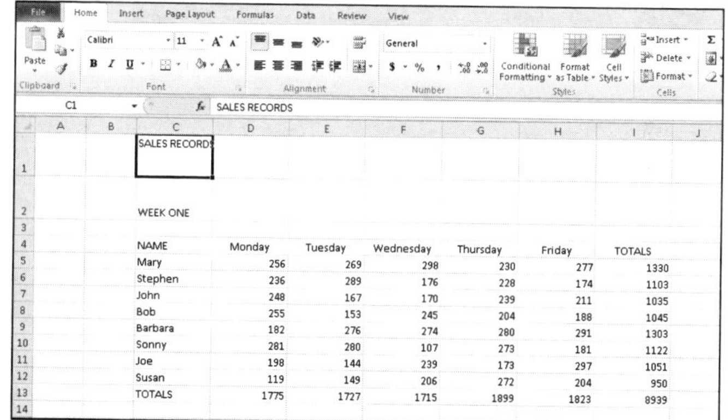

SALES RECORDS
WEEK ONE

NAME	Monday	Tuesday	Wednesday	Thursday	Friday	TOTALS
Mary	256	269	298	230	277	1330
Stephen	236	289	176	228	174	1103
John	248	167	170	239	211	1035
Bob	255	153	245	204	188	1045
Barbara	182	276	274	280	291	1303
Sonny	281	280	107	273	181	1122
Joe	198	144	239	173	297	1051
Susan	119	149	206	272	204	950
TOTALS	1775	1727	1715	1899	1823	8939

Figure 9-8

Create a Title by Merging Cells

1. Select the cell containing the data you want to merge and the cells you want to include in the merge. The data cell must be in the left cell of the selection and the other cells cannot contain data (see Figure 9-9).
2. Choose Home⇨Alignment⇨Merge & Center. All the selected cells merge into one larger cell, and the data is horizontally centered.

If you select cells vertically and choose the Merge & Center command, Excel merges the cells and vertically bottom-aligns the data.

After clicking Merge & Center, you can change the alignment. Click the Merge & Center button again to unmerge the cells from each other.

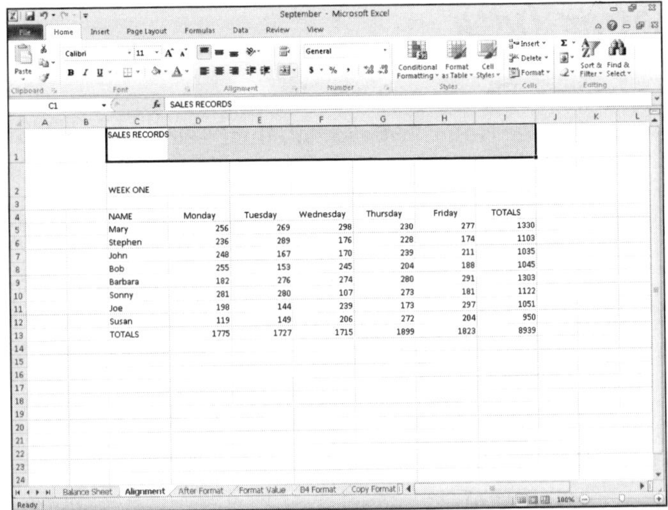

Figure 9-9

Change Font Color

1. Select the cells you want to format.
2. Choose Home⇨Font and then click the Font Color arrow to select a color (see Figure 9-10). The Live Preview feature shows you the selected cells in the new font colors.

Click More Colors to display the Colors dialog box from which you can select additional colors as well as create your own custom color.

Another method to select font color is through the Font dialog box launcher, which displays the Format Cells dialog box. Font color selection is found on the Font tab.

If you choose a light font color, add background shading to make the font color show up.

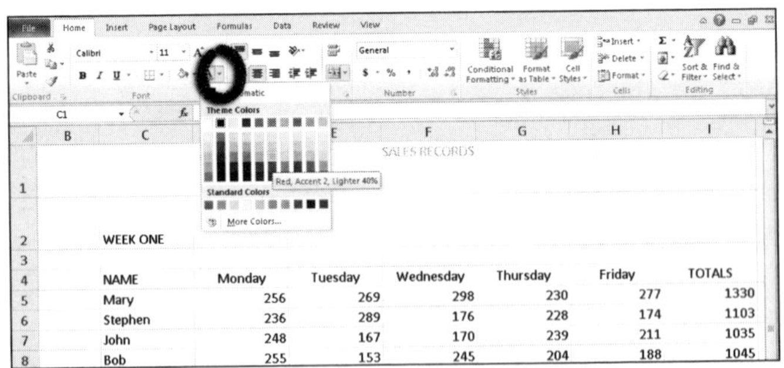

Figure 9-10

Select Font Attributes

1. Select the cells you want to format.
2. Click Home⇨Font⇨Font (arrow), and select a font. As you hover your mouse over a type face, Excel displays the selected cells in the different fonts.
3. Choose Home⇨Font⇨Font Size (arrow) and then select a font size.

Optionally, click the Increase Font Size or the Decrease Font Size buttons to increment or decrease the font size 1 point at a time.

4. Click Home⇨Font and click an attribute, such as Bold, Italic, or Underline (see Figure 9-11). Shortcut keys for Bold, Italic, and Underline are Ctrl+B, Ctrl+I, and Ctrl+U, respectively.

The Bold, Italic, and Underline buttons are *toggle switches* — clicking one turns it on, and then clicking it again turns it off.

The default underline style is a single underline. Click the Underline arrow to select Double Underline. Or, choose additional underline options through the Font dialog box launcher, which displays the Format Cells dialog box. Underline options appear on the Font tab.

Apply Cell Background Colors

1. Select the cells to which you want to add background color.
2. From the Font group, click the Fill Color arrow. A gallery of colors appears (see Figure 9-12).
3. Select the cell background color you want.

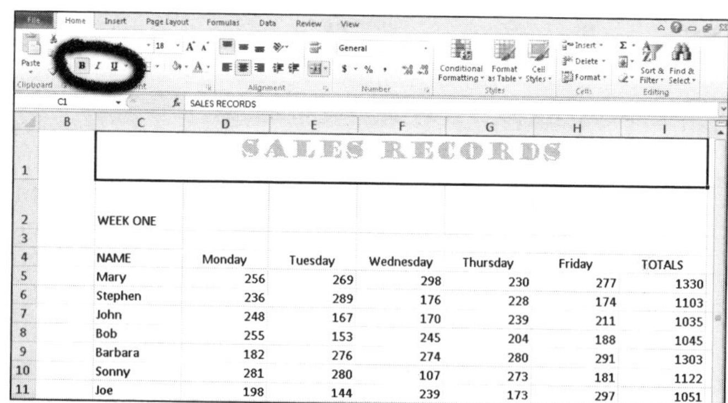

Figure 9-11

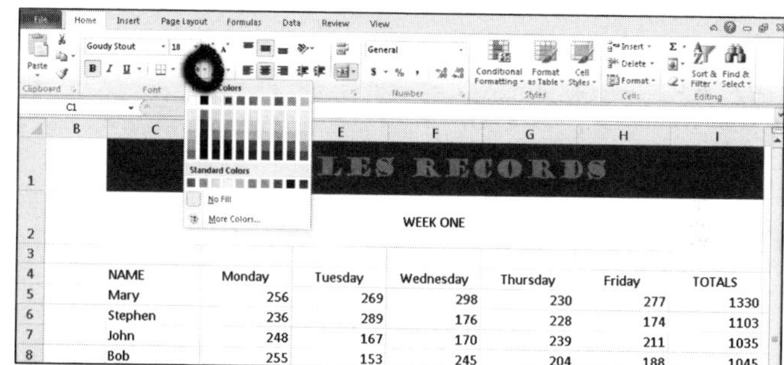

Figure 9-12

Select No Fill to remove any cell background shading, or choose More Colors to create your own shading color.

A good combination to use with a black-and-white printer is a black background and a white font color.

Wrap Text in a Cell

1. Select the cells you want to format.
2. Choose Home⇨Alignment⇨Wrap Text. As in Figure 9-13, if the selected text cells contain more text than will fit the width of the cell, Excel displays it on multiple lines. Excel automatically increases row height to accommodate the additional text lines.

Selecting the Shrink to Fit option from the Alignment tab of the Format Cells dialog box (instead of choosing the Wrap Text option) allows Excel to automatically change the font size in the selected cell. This forces the data to fit within the cell's current width. Use caution with this option; the text may become unreadable.

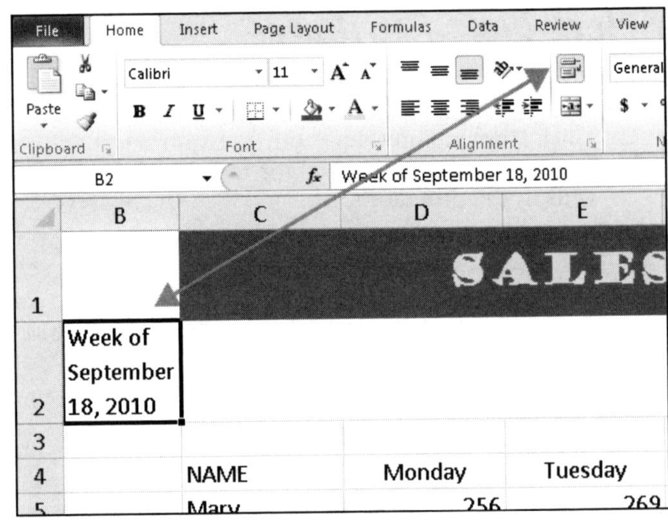

Figure 9-13

Place Borders around Cells

1. To add a border, select the appropriate cells.
2. Choose Home⇨Font and then click the Borders drop-down list arrow. A variety of border options appears, as shown in Figure 9-14.

The Borders tooltip button might display Bottom Border, Top Border, or whatever border was last used.

3. Select the border you want. Excel applies the border to the selected cells.

For more border styles, colors, and options, select More Borders to open the Format Cells dialog box.

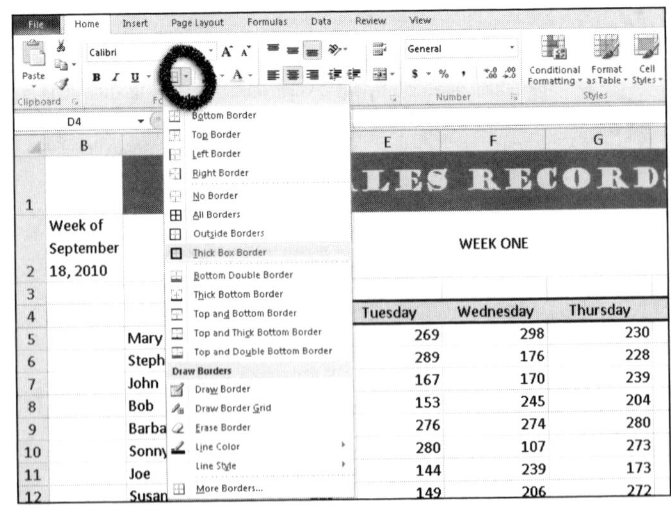

Figure 9-14

Work with Date Formats

1. Enter a date into a cell. Depending on what you type, Excel probably displays the date in a different format. Figure 9-15 illustrates some date examples.

Dates are actually numeric values, and you can use them in Excel calculations. See the next task.

2. From the Home tab, click the Number dialog box launcher to display the Format Cells dialog box.
3. Click the Date category. The right side of the screen displays a variety of different date formats.
4. Select a format for the selected cells.
5. Click OK.

Optionally, choose Short Date or Long Date from the Number Format drop-down list of the Number group on the Home tab.

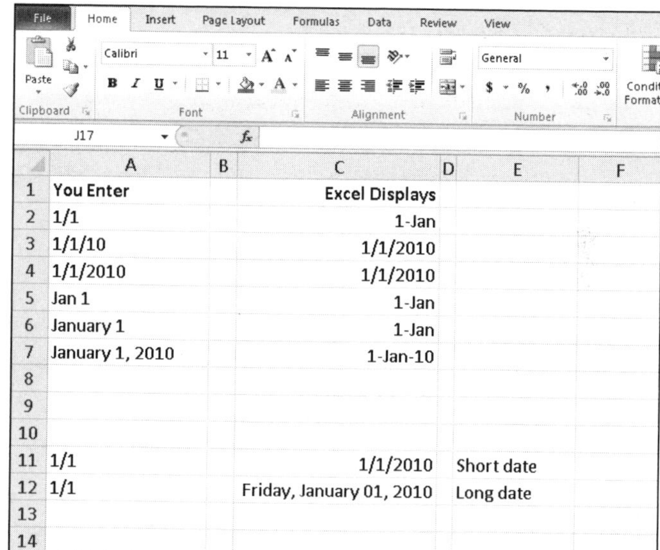

Figure 9-15

Copy Formatting

1. Click a cell containing formatting you want to copy.
2. Choose Home➪Clipboard➪Format Painter. The mouse pointer is a white plus sign along with a paint brush like the one you see in Figure 9-16.
3. Click or drag across the cells you want to format. Excel immediately applies formats such as font, size, colors, borders, and alignment.

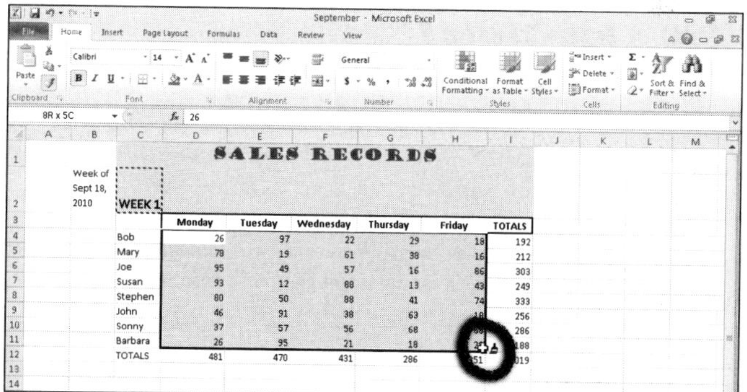

Figure 9-16

Double-click the Format Painter tool to lock it in so you can paint additional cells without having to reselect the tool. Click the Format Painter tool again to unlock it.

Indent Data in Cells

1. Select the cells you want to indent.
2. Choose Home⇨Alignment⇨Increase Indent. Each Increase Indent click adds a small amount of space between the cell border and the data itself (see Figure 9-17). How Excel indents depends on how you format the cell:
   - *If the data is left aligned:* Excel indents from the left.
   - *If the data is right aligned:* Excel indents from the right.
   - *If the data is centered:* With the first click, Excel indents to the right, but subsequent clicks cause Excel to move the data to the left.

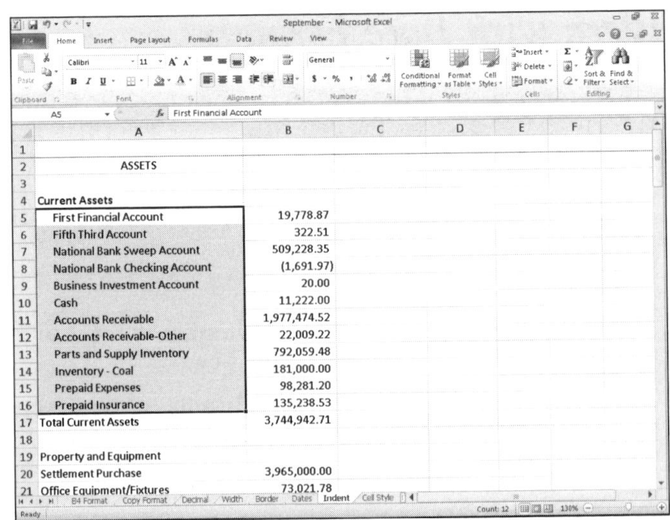

Figure 9-17

Click the Decrease Indent button to remove indentation.

Use Cell Styles

1. Select the cells you want to format.
2. Choose Home⇨Style⇨Cell Styles. As shown in Figure 9-18, Excel displays a gallery of predefined styles.

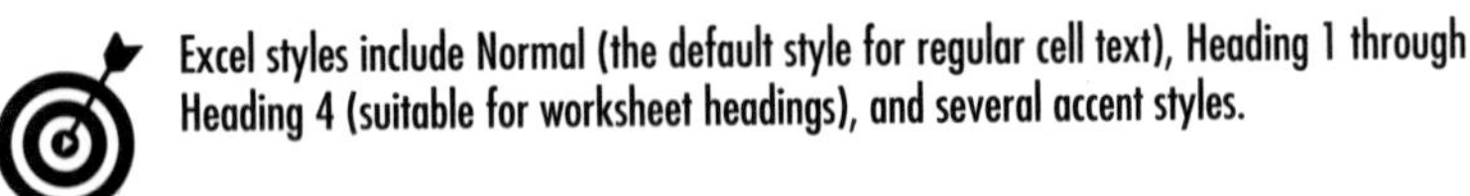

Excel styles include Normal (the default style for regular cell text), Heading 1 through Heading 4 (suitable for worksheet headings), and several accent styles.

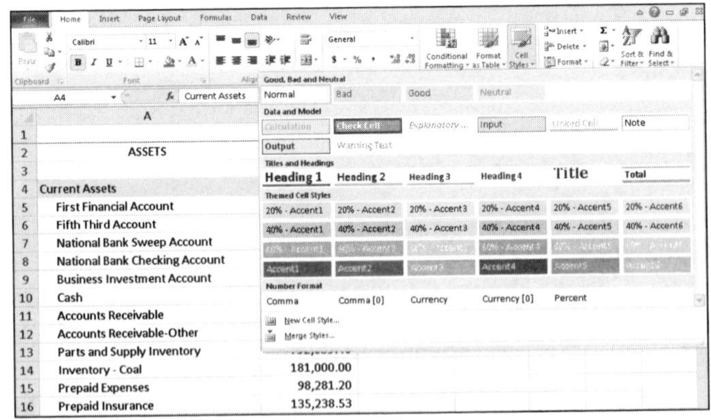

Figure 9-18

3. Select the style you want to use. The cells take the new appearance.

Cell styles originate from the Office themes and are coordinated based on the current theme. Select a different theme by choosing Page Layout⇨Themes⇨Themes.

Managing Workbooks

I want to begin this chapter by clearing up a couple of terms. First of all, a *worksheet* — sometimes called a *spreadsheet* — is a collection of cells that can have more than one million rows down and more than 16,000 rows across. Each cell of each sheet can contain more than 32,000 characters.

Secondly, a *workbook* is a collection of worksheets. By default, each time you create a new Excel workbook, it contains three worksheets. Each workbook, however, can have an almost unlimited number of worksheets, limited only by your computer memory. The resulting possible number of cells in a single workbook is too huge to even dream about, but the fact remains that you *could* create a single huge workbook. Realistically, however, you'll probably have a number of different workbooks, each with a number of worksheets.

Excel makes it easy to work with multiple worksheets. You can maneuver between the sheets by clicking a sheet tab. And you can use navigation buttons for situations when you have a lot of tabs. This chapter is primarily about working with multiple sheets. You discover how to insert, delete, move, and copy worksheets, rename the tabs that reference them, and create formulas that reference other worksheets or workbooks.

Finally, you discover several ways to change your worksheet view.

Chapter

10

Get ready to . . .

Insert Additional Worksheets

1. Choose Home➪Cells➪Insert➪Insert Sheet. Excel automatically inserts a new blank worksheet on top of the selected sheet (see Figure 10-1). Excel automatically assigns the next number — such as Sheet4.

Optionally, just click the Insert Sheet tab located after the last named worksheet tab.

2. Click a different worksheet tab. That worksheet becomes the current sheet.

Optionally, press Ctrl+Page Up to move to the previous worksheet or press Ctrl+Page Down to move to the next worksheet.

Another way to insert a worksheet is to right-click a worksheet tab and then choose Insert from the resulting shortcut menu. The Insert dialog box opens. Choose Worksheet and then click OK.

3. If your workbook has more worksheets than you can see at the bottom, click the First, Previous, Next, or Last navigation buttons in the bottom-left corner of the workbook.

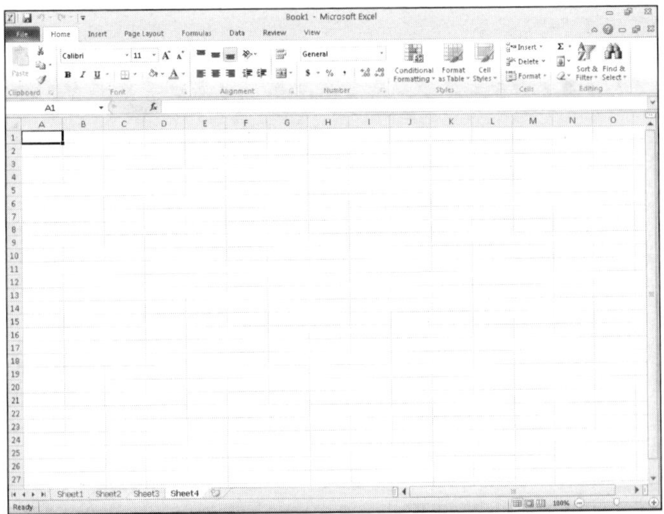

Figure 10-1

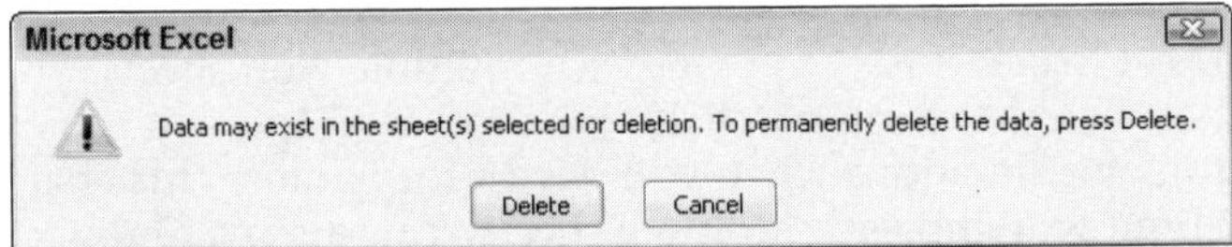

Figure 10-2

Another way to delete a worksheet is to right-click the worksheet tab and select Delete from the resulting shortcut menu.

Delete Worksheets

1. Choose Home➪Cells➪Delete➪Delete Sheet. If any cells in the selected sheet have data in them, a warning message appears, as shown in Figure 10-2.
2. Click the Delete button.

Use caution when deleting worksheets. The Undo feature does not work with the Delete Sheet function.

Rename Worksheets

1. Click anywhere on the sheet you want to rename.
2. Choose Home⇨Cells⇨Format⇨Rename Sheet. The worksheet tab becomes highlighted. Leave it highlighted so that you can replace it with a new name.

Optionally, right-click the worksheet tab and choose Rename from the shortcut menu that appears.

3. Type a unique name for the worksheet, as shown in Figure 10-3. Press Enter to accept the change.

Two worksheets in a single workbook cannot have the exact same name.

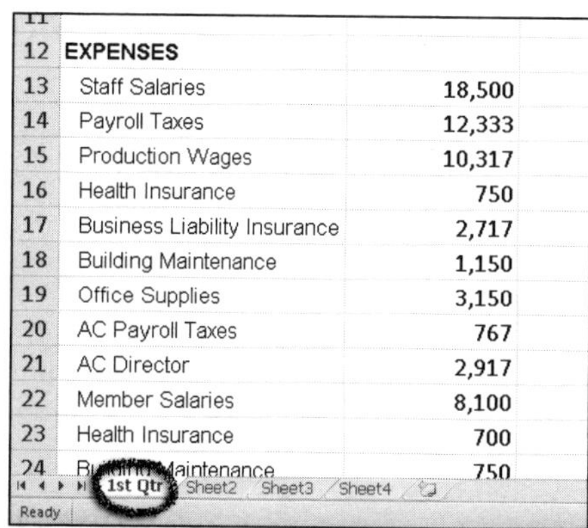

12	EXPENSES	
13	Staff Salaries	18,500
14	Payroll Taxes	12,333
15	Production Wages	10,317
16	Health Insurance	750
17	Business Liability Insurance	2,717
18	Building Maintenance	1,150
19	Office Supplies	3,150
20	AC Payroll Taxes	767
21	AC Director	2,917
22	Member Salaries	8,100
23	Health Insurance	700
24	B[illegible]aintenance	750

Figure 10-3

Copy Worksheets

1. Click anywhere on the worksheet that you want to duplicate.
2. Choose Home⇨Cells⇨Format⇨Move or Copy Sheet. The Move or Copy dialog box appears.

Optionally, right-click the worksheet tab and select Move or Copy Sheet.

3. Select the Create a Copy check box (see Figure 10-4).
4. Select where in the order of the worksheets you want the duplicate sheet placed.
5. Click OK. Excel duplicates the sheet and gives it the same name as the copied sheet, plus Excel numbers it sequentially.

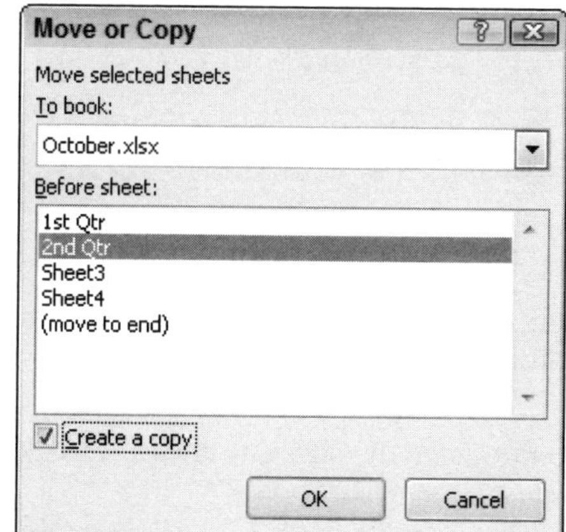

Figure 10-4

Move or Copy Worksheets to a Different Workbook

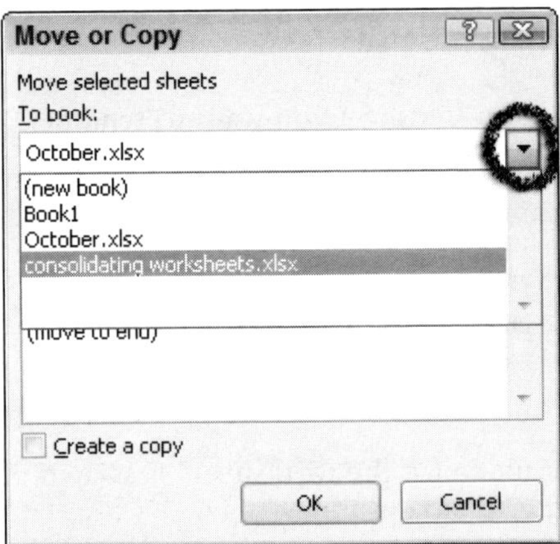

Figure 10-5

1. Open the workbook to which you will move the worksheet.
2. Open the workbook that contains the worksheets you want to move.
3. Click anywhere on the worksheet that you want to move. If you don't see the sheet you want, click the tab navigation buttons until you see it.

If you want to move or copy multiple worksheets, hold down Ctrl and click additional tabs. If you want to move or copy all the existing worksheets to another workbook, right-click a sheet tab and choose Select All Sheets from the menu that appears.

4. Choose Home➪Cells➪Format➪Move or Copy Sheet. The Move or Copy dialog box opens.

Optionally, right-click a selected tab and choose Move or Copy Sheet.

5. From the To Book drop-down list (as shown in Figure 10-5), select the workbook to which you want to move or copy the sheets.
6. If you want to duplicate the sheets to the other workbook, select the Create a Copy check box.
7. Select where in the order of the existing worksheets you want the moved sheet placed.
8. Click OK. Excel moves or copies the worksheets to the other workbook. In Figure 10-6, the sheet named 1st Qtr. was copied from the Book1 workbook to the Consolidating Worksheets workbook.

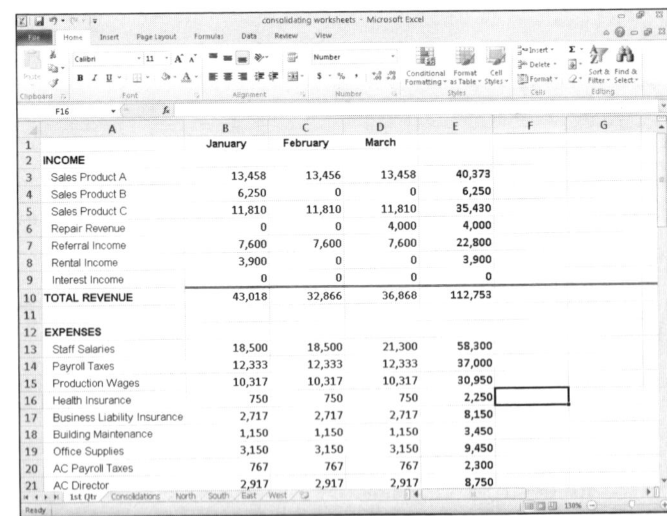

	A	B	C	D	E
1		January	February	March	
2	INCOME				
3	Sales Product A	13,458	13,456	13,458	40,373
4	Sales Product B	6,250	0	0	6,250
5	Sales Product C	11,810	11,810	11,810	35,430
6	Repair Revenue	0	0	4,000	4,000
7	Referral Income	7,600	7,600	7,600	22,800
8	Rental Income	3,900	0	0	3,900
9	Interest Income	0	0	0	0
10	TOTAL REVENUE	43,018	32,866	36,868	112,753
11					
12	EXPENSES				
13	Staff Salaries	18,500	18,500	21,300	58,300
14	Payroll Taxes	12,333	12,333	12,333	37,000
15	Production Wages	10,317	10,317	10,317	30,950
16	Health Insurance	750	750	750	2,250
17	Business Liability Insurance	2,717	2,717	2,717	8,150
18	Building Maintenance	1,150	1,150	1,150	3,450
19	Office Supplies	3,150	3,150	3,150	9,450
20	AC Payroll Taxes	767	767	767	2,300
21	AC Director	2,917	2,917	2,917	8,750

Figure 10-6

Hide and Unhide Worksheets

1. Click anywhere on the worksheet that you want to hide.
2. Choose Home➪Cells➪Format➪Hide & Unhide➪Hide Sheet. Excel hides the worksheet from view. All formula references to a hidden worksheet are still valid even when a worksheet is hidden.

Optionally, right-click a worksheet tab and choose Hide (or Unhide).

3. To unhide the worksheet, choose Home➪Cells➪Format➪Hide & Unhide➪Unhide Sheet. A dialog box appears, like the one in Figure 10-7, listing all hidden worksheets in the active workbook.
4. Select the worksheet you want to unhide and then click OK.

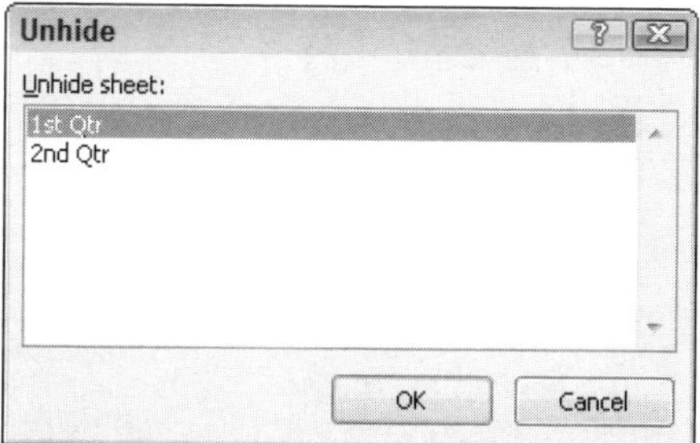

Figure 10-7

Change Worksheet Tab Colors

1. To recolor the tab of a worksheet, click anywhere in that worksheet.
2. Choose Home➪Cells➪Format➪Tab Color. The Tab Color gallery appears, as shown in Figure 10-8.

Optionally, right-click a worksheet tab and choose Tab Color.

3. Select a color.

Select No Color to remove a tab color.

When a worksheet with a colored tab is the current worksheet, Excel does not display the tab color in full. It displays only a colored line under the tab name. The tab becomes full color when the worksheet is not the active one.

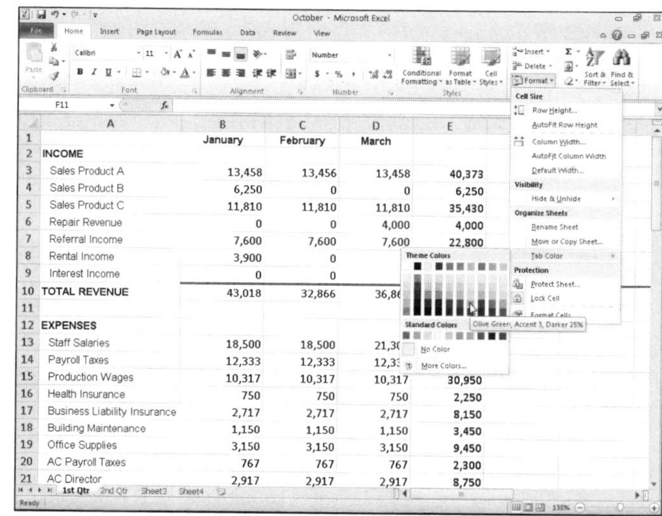

Figure 10-8

Generate References to Other Worksheets

1. Select the cell into which you want to enter a reference.
2. Perform one of the following actions:
   - *To display a value located in another cell on the same worksheet:* Type the equal sign and then the cell address. For example, type **=C23**. If the value in C23 changes, the cell with the reference to C23 also changes.
   - *To display a value located in a cell on a different worksheet but in the same workbook:* Type the equal sign. Next, click the worksheet tab containing the cell you want to reference and then click the actual cell you want to reference. Press **Enter**. Excel displays the equal sign, the worksheet name, an exclamation point, and the cell reference (see Figure 10-9).
   - *To include a cell located on a different worksheet, but in the same workbook, in a formula:* Begin to type the formula. In the place where you want to position the distant cell reference, click the worksheet containing the cell and then click the actual cell. Follow this with the remainder of the formula. Figure 10-10 illustrates an example of a formula using a reference to a different worksheet.

Optionally, you can manually type the referenced sheet and cell address, but you must be sure to include the exclamation point.

Formulas referencing other worksheets or other workbooks can also be compound formulas or used in a function.

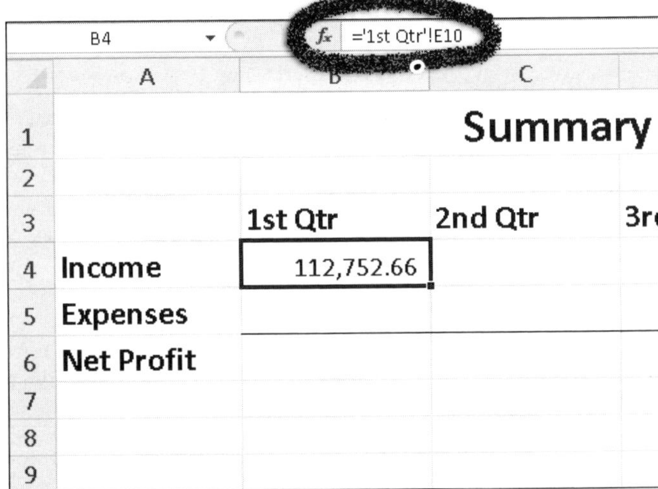

Figure 10-9

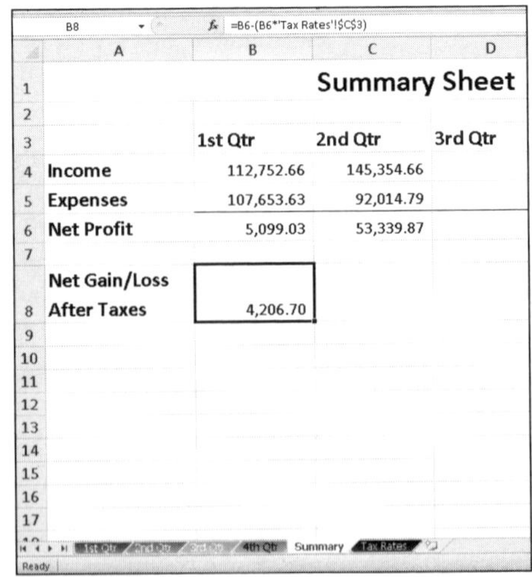

Figure 10-10

Cross-Reference Other Workbooks

1. Open the workbook to which you will refer. For simplicity's sake, call this Workbook2.

2. Click the desired cell in the workbook where you want to create a reference. Call this Workbook1.

3. In Workbook1, begin the formula or reference with an equal sign.

4. If using a function or formula, enter any portion that you want to precede the cross-reference.

5. Click the cell that you want to reference from Workbook2.

6. Finish the remainder of the formula or press Enter. Excel displays the equal sign, an apostrophe, and then the Workbook2 path and filename in brackets followed by the worksheet name, a closing apostrophe, an exclamation point, and then the absolute cell reference. For example, `[Check Register.xlsx]2010'!$B$40` refers to the value in cell B40 of the sheet named 2010 in the Excel file named Check Register. See Figure 10-11 for an example of a cross reference.

Excel uses absolute references (with dollar signs) when referring to other workbooks.

7. When you open a workbook containing a cross reference, Excel displays a Security Warning message such as the one shown in Figure 10-12, prompting you with a security alert so it can determine whether to update the cross referenced cell. Click the Enable Content button if you want Excel to check the originating workbook for changes to the referenced cell.

8. You might see another confirmation message. If so, click Continue.

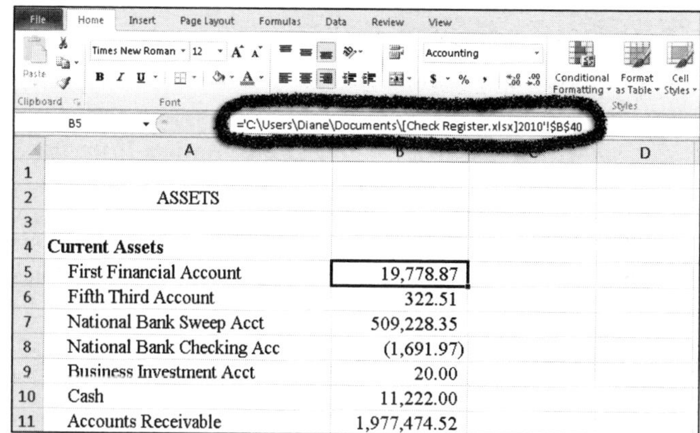

Figure 10-11

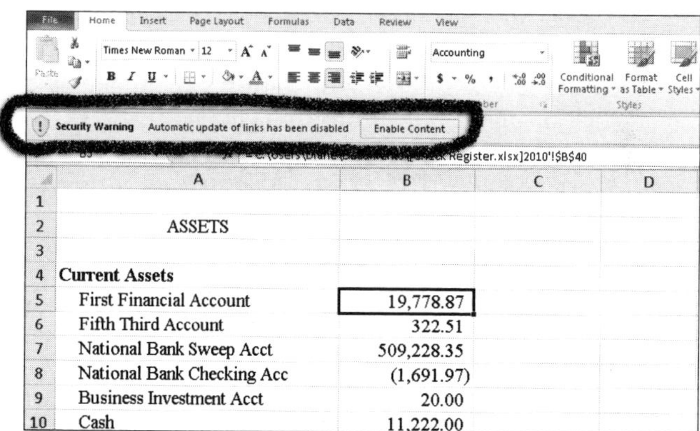

Figure 10-12

Zoom In or Out

1. Choose View⇨Zoom⇨Zoom.
2. Select a magnification percentage option from the Zoom dialog box that appears; see Figure 10-13. A higher zoom setting makes the text appear larger (you see less on screen); a lower setting shows more cells on screen (data appears smaller). Zooming does not affect the printed data size. Click OK.

If you select the Custom option, you can enter your own setting from 10% to 400%.

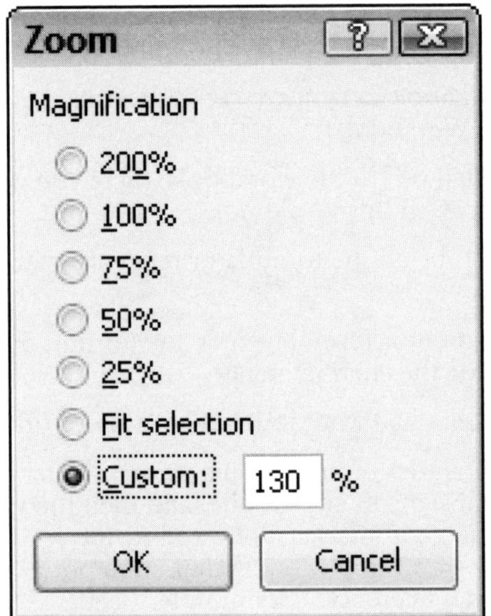

Figure 10-13

Use the Zoom Controls

1. Click the Zoom In (+) button on the Zoom control slider. Excel increases the magnification percentage by 10% for each click of the Zoom In button (see Figure 10-14).

The Zoom percentage displays on the status bar.

2. Click the Zoom Out (–) button on the Zoom control. Excel decreases the magnification percentage by 10% for each click of the Zoom Out button.
3. Drag the Zoom slider bar to the right. Excel increases magnification.
4. Drag the Zoom slider bar to the left. Excel decreases magnification.

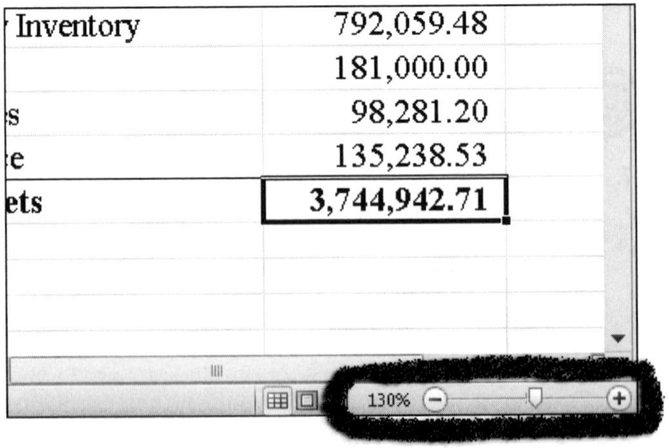

Figure 10-14

Change Worksheet Views

1. Choose View➪Workbook Views➪Page Layout. As shown in Figure 10-15, Page Layout view displays your worksheets on individual pages that correspond to printed pages. A ruler appears on the top and in the header and footer area. See Chapter 14 for more on headers and footers.

Use the Zoom controls to increase or decrease magnification.

2. Choose View➪Workbook Views➪Normal. Excel returns to the default Normal view, which shows one continuous page of columns and rows.

3. Choose View➪Workbook Views➪Page Break Preview. The Welcome to Page Break Preview dialog box appears.

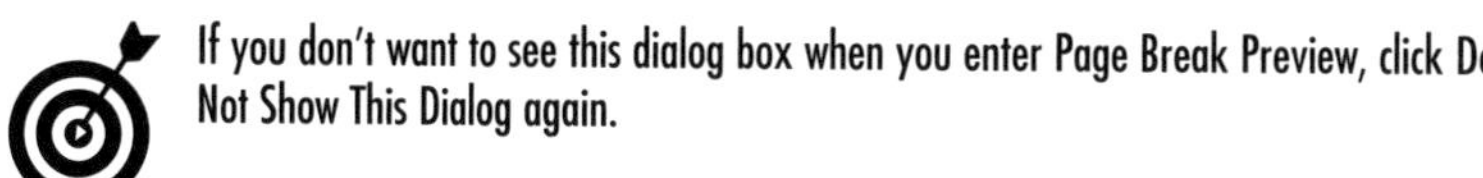

If you don't want to see this dialog box when you enter Page Break Preview, click Do Not Show This Dialog again.

4. Click OK. The Excel mode changes to Page Break Preview, where Excel indicates page breaks with lines (see Figure 10-16). You can drag these lines to modify where pages break. See Chapter 13 for more on using page breaks.

To return to Normal view, choose View➪Worksheet Views➪Normal.

5. Choose View➪Worksheet Views➪Full Screen. You see only the worksheet itself with its row and column headings, worksheet tabs, and the title bar. The Ribbon, Quick Access Toolbar, and status bar are hidden.

6. Press the Esc(ape) key. Excel returns to the view you last used.

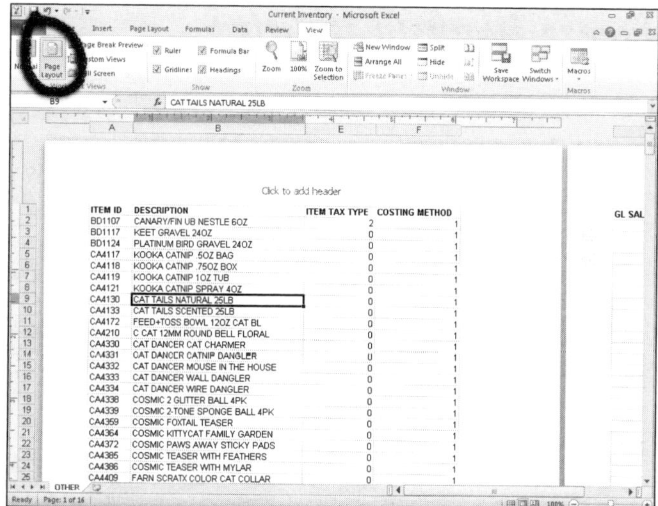

Figure 10-15

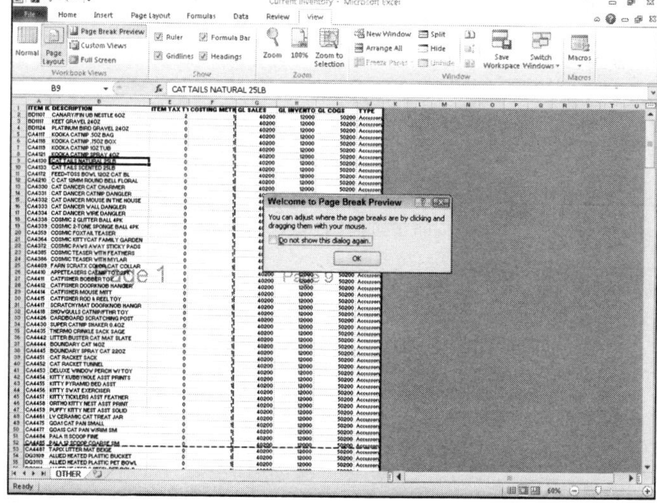

Figure 10-16

Freeze Worksheet Titles

1. Choose what you want to freeze:

   - *Columns:* Select the column to the right of the columns you want to freeze. For example, click cell B1 to freeze only column A.
   - *Rows:* Select the row below the rows you want to freeze. For example, click cell A4 to freeze rows 1, 2, and 3.
   - *Columns and rows:* Click the cell below the rows and to the right of the columns you want to freeze. For example, click cell B2 to freeze both column A and row 1 (as shown in Figure 10-17).

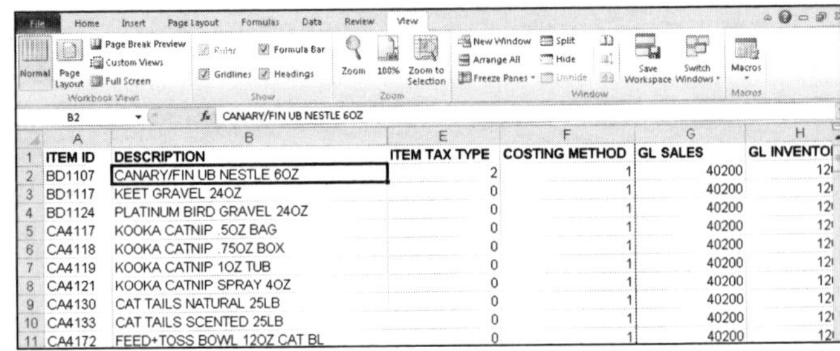

Figure 10-17

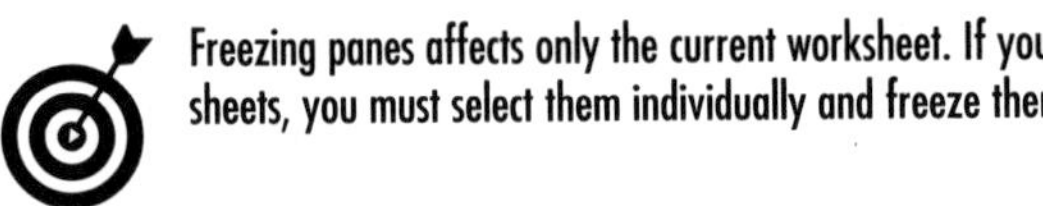

Freezing panes affects only the current worksheet. If you want to freeze other worksheets, you must select them individually and freeze them.

2. Choose View⇨Window⇨Freeze Panes⇨Freeze Panes. A thin, black line appears to separate the sections. As you see in Figure 10-18, as you scroll down and to the left, row 1 and column A remain visible even though you see rows 41–63 in the bottom section and columns E–K on the right.

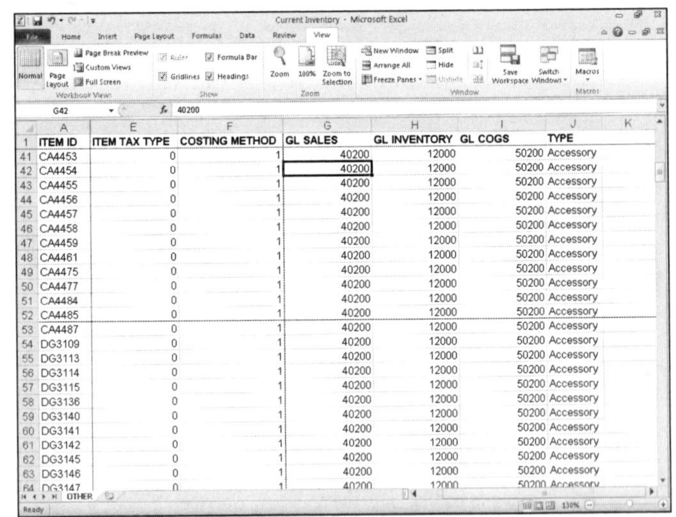

Figure 10-18

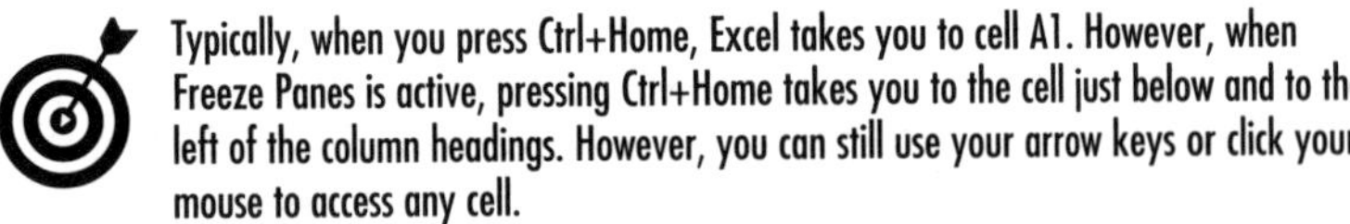

Typically, when you press Ctrl+Home, Excel takes you to cell A1. However, when Freeze Panes is active, pressing Ctrl+Home takes you to the cell just below and to the left of the column headings. However, you can still use your arrow keys or click your mouse to access any cell.

3. Choose View⇨Window⇨Freeze Panes⇨Unfreeze Panes to remove the freeze from row and column headings.

Using Excel Tools

Tools are designed to help make your work easier. Imagine life many years ago when our ancestors had to build their houses with hand tools instead of the wonderful collection of power tools now so readily available.

Excel has many tools, also. And just like power tools, they make your work in Excel easier.

In this chapter, you work with Excel tools to help you sort, find, and analyze your data. You'll discover what I call Assistance Tags which are the funny-looking little icons that appear when you perform certain Excel functions, such as paste data, or enter a formula that may contain an error. Assistance Tags offer you options right at the tip of your mouse pointer.

You'll also find tools that help you break larger data into smaller data and combine smaller data into larger data. All these tools help you create better and more informative Excel worksheets.

Chapter

11

Get ready to . . .

Use the Ribbon to Sort

1. For the easiest sorting, create a list in contiguous order and with headings specifying the contents of each column. Figure 11-1 illustrates an ideal data array.
2. In the column you want to sort by, click any cell containing data.

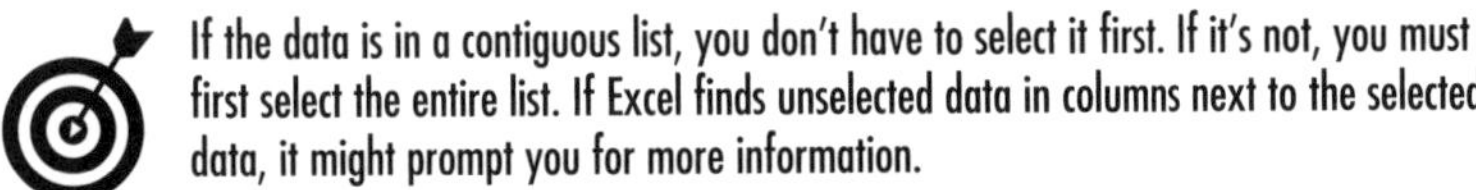

If the data is in a contiguous list, you don't have to select it first. If it's not, you must first select the entire list. If Excel finds unselected data in columns next to the selected data, it might prompt you for more information.

3. Choose Data➪Sort & Filter➪Sort A to Z. (If the current cell contains a value, the button reads Sort Smallest to Largest.) Excel sorts the entire list in ascending order.

Sorting text data in ascending order sorts text A–Z, sorting numeric information in ascending order sorts low to high (1–10), and sorting dates in ascending order places the earliest date first.

Excel sorts in the following pattern: numbers; spaces; special characters, which are ! " # $ % & ( ) * , . / : ; ? @ [\ ] ^ _ ` { | } ~ + < = >; and, finally, alphabetic letters.

4. Choose Data➪Sort & Filter➪Sort Z to A (or Largest to Smallest). Excel sorts the entire list by descending order. Figure 11-2 shows the Totals column sorted in descending order (from highest to lowest).

If Excel incorrectly sorts a cell that contains a value, make sure that the cell is formatted as a number and not as text.

Sorting text data in descending order sorts text Z–A, sorting numeric information in descending order sorts high to low (10–1); and sorting dates in descending order places the latest date first.

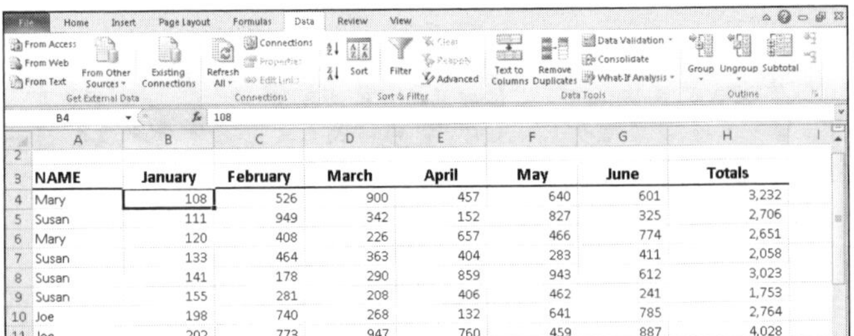

NAME	January	February	March	April	May	June	Totals
Mary	108	526	900	457	640	601	3,232
Susan	111	949	342	152	827	325	2,706
Mary	120	408	226	657	466	774	2,651
Susan	133	464	363	404	283	411	2,058
Susan	141	178	290	859	943	612	3,023
Susan	155	281	208	406	462	241	1,753
Joe	198	740	268	132	641	785	2,764
Joe	202	773	947	760	459	887	4,028

Figure 11-1

NAME	January	February	March	April	May	June	Totals
Susan	626	901	726	955	794	698	4,700
Stephen	998	802	967	902	366	614	4,649
Stephen	814	618	704	548	949	628	4,261
Sonny	819	960	624	672	779	339	4,193
Barbara	796	710	725	763	958	188	4,140
Susan	823	815	540	240	849	857	4,124
Susan	791	936	924	443	116	909	4,119
Barbara	836	324	756	905	278	966	4,065
Joe	202	773	947	760	459	887	4,028
Barbara	813	488	845	951	645	259	4,001
Bob	488	781	449	951	363	948	3,980
Joe	743	180	421	922	760	911	3,937
Susan	389	950	839	644	109	978	3,909
Stephen	961	598	892	559	666	209	3,885
John	208	480	649	977	642	925	3,881
Joe	675	242	897	884	230	925	3,853
Susan	624	895	792	806	239	420	3,776
Susan	364	721	700	579	860	476	3,700
Susan	710	610	940	342	171	884	3,657
Joe	710	668	129	324	822	989	3,642
Joe	519	280	881	910	285	759	3,634

Figure 11-2

Work with the Sort Command

1. Select or click in the list of data that you want to sort.

Select only a single column of data if you want to sort that column independently of the rest of the data.

2. Choose Data➪Sort & Filter➪Sort. The Sort dialog box opens.
3. If your data includes column headings, make sure the My Data Has Headers check box is selected. If the data doesn't include column headings, deselect the option.

Excel doesn't include header rows in the sort process.

4. From the Sort By drop-down list, select the column by which you want to sort (see Figure 11-3).
5. From the Sort On drop-down list, choose Values. (I discuss the other options later in this chapter.)
6. From the Order drop-down list, select how you want to sort the data:
   - *By text values:* Choose A to Z or Z to A.
   - *By numeric data:* Choose Smallest to Largest or Largest to Smallest.
   - *By dates:* Choose Oldest to Newest or Newest to Oldest.

Click the Options button if you want to make the sorting case-sensitive (noncapitalized words before capitals).

7. Click OK. Excel sorts data in the following order: numbers, special characters, alphabetic characters, and then blanks. Figure 11-4 illustrates the data sorted by name.

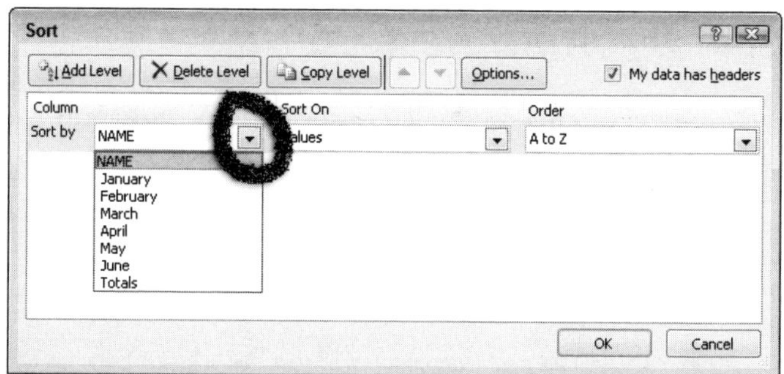

Figure 11-3

	A	B	C	D	E	F	G	H
2								
3	NAME	January	February	March	April	May	June	Totals
4	Barbara	796	710	725	763	958	188	4,140
5	Barbara	836	324	756	905	278	966	4,065
6	Barbara	813	488	845	951	645	259	4,001
7	Barbara	434	623	330	616	860	375	3,238
8	Barbara	318	248	545	706	614	724	3,155
9	Barbara	285	276	805	330	887	406	2,989
10	Barbara	492	263	358	741	968	163	2,985
11	Barbara	377	588	299	196	327	342	2,129
12	Bob	488	781	449	951	363	948	3,980
13	Bob	672	169	501	711	913	589	3,555
14	Bob	671	619	708	962	386	155	3,501
15	Bob	233	882	602	477	241	817	3,252
16	Bob	606	161	641	487	176	880	2,951
17	Bob	853	256	628	325	356	412	2,830
18	Bob	575	240	948	145	485	195	2,588
19	Bob	439	577	660	200	108	450	2,434
20	Joe	202	773	947	760	459	887	4,028
21	Joe	743	180	421	922	760	911	3,937
22	Joe	675	242	897	884	230	925	3,853
23	Joe	710	668	129	324	822	989	3,642
24	Joe	519	280	881	910	285	759	3,634

Figure 11-4

Sort by Multiple Criteria

1. Select or click in the list of data you want to sort.
2. Choose Data⇨Sort & Filter⇨Sort. The Sort dialog box opens.
3. If your data includes column headings, make sure that the My Data Has Headers check box is selected. If the data doesn't include column headings, deselect the option.

Although the most common sort is by rows (top to bottom), you can also sort by columns (left to right). In the Sort dialog box, click the Options button; then, under the Orientation section, choose Sort Left to Right. Finally, click OK.

4. Set up the primary sort criteria as in the previous section.

Excel sorts dates formatted with slashes, such as 11/22/68, as numeric data. Dates with the day or month spelled out must be sorted differently.

5. Click the Add Level button.
6. In the Then By section, select the secondary column you want to sort by if two or more items are identical in the first Sort By option (see Figure 11-5).
7. Select how you want to sort the second data criteria. Repeat as needed.

To delete an entry, select the sort entry and choose Delete Level. You must keep at least one sort entry in the list.

8. Click OK. Excel performs the sort process. Figure 11-6 illustrates data rows sorted first by Name and then by Totals.

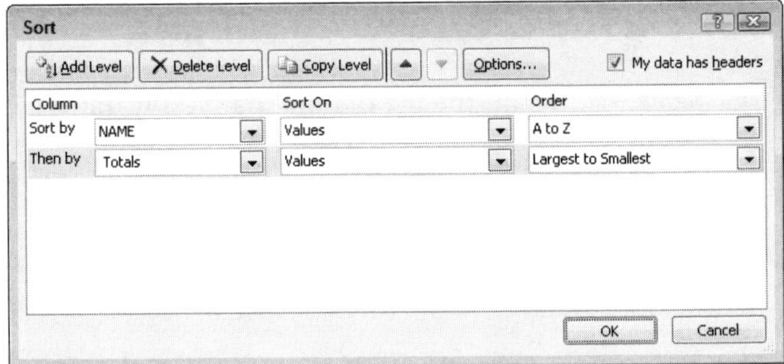

Figure 11-5

	A	B	C	D	E	F	G	H
2								
3	NAME	January	February	March	April	May	June	Totals
4	Barbara	796	710	725	763	958	188	4,140
5	Barbara	836	324	756	905	278	966	4,065
6	Barbara	813	488	845	951	645	259	4,001
7	Barbara	434	623	330	616	860	375	3,238
8	Barbara	318	248	545	706	614	724	3,155
9	Barbara	285	276	805	330	887	406	2,989
10	Barbara	492	263	358	741	968	163	2,985
11	Barbara	377	588	299	196	327	342	2,129
12	Bob	488	781	449	951	363	948	3,980
13	Bob	672	169	501	711	913	589	3,555
14	Bob	671	619	708	962	386	155	3,501
15	Bob	233	882	602	477	241	817	3,252
16	Bob	606	161	641	487	176	880	2,951
17	Bob	853	256	628	325	356	412	2,830
18	Bob	575	240	948	145	485	195	2,588
19	Bob	439	577	660	200	108	450	2,434
20	Joe	202	773	947	760	459	887	4,028
21	Joe	743	180	421	922	760	911	3,937
22	Joe	675	242	897	884	230	925	3,853
23	Joe	710	668	129	324	822	989	3,642
24	Joe	519	280	881	910	285	759	3,634

Figure 11-6

During an Excel sort, apostrophes (') and hyphens (-) are ignored unless two text strings are the same except for a hyphen. In that situation, the text with the hyphen is sorted as the latter.

Sort by Cell Format

1. Select or click in the list of data you want to sort.

Sorting by cell format is helpful when you have specified conditional formatting conditions. It can sort all items meeting your conditions to the top or bottom of the data table.

2. Choose Data⇨Sort & Filter⇨Sort. The Sort dialog box opens.
3. If your data includes column headings, make sure that the My Data Has Headers check box is selected. If the data doesn't include column headings, deselect the option.
4. Select your first sort criteria field.
5. From the Sort On drop-down list, select one of the following:
   - *Cell Color:* Choosing this option sorts the cells based on the cell background formatting (see Figure 11-7).
   - *Font Color:* Choosing this option sorts the cells based on the font color of the cell contents regardless of background formatting.
6. Open the Order drop-down list. Several options appear, including Automatic and each color you used in your selected field.
7. Select the cell fill color or font color that you want to sort by.
8. Choose whether you want the formatted cells to appear at the top of the data range or at the bottom of the data range.
9. Add any additional sort criteria.
10. Click OK. In Figure 11-8, you see the data sorted with the green-filled cells at the top.

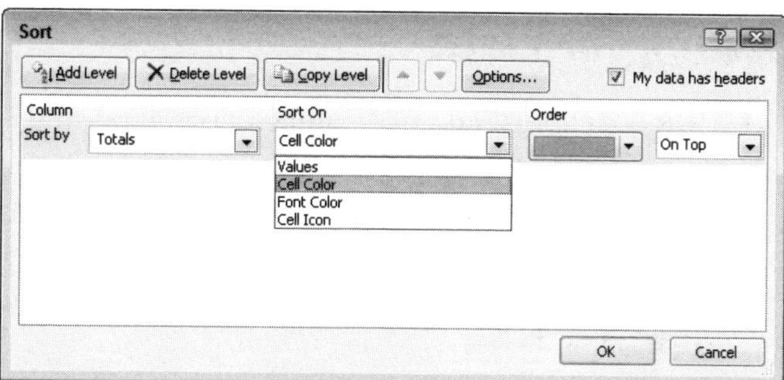

Figure 11-7

	A	B	C	D	E	F	G	H
1	CUSTOMER EVALUATIONS							
2								
3	NAME	January	February	March	April	May	June	[illegible]
4	Barbara	796	710	725	763	958	[illegible]	4,140
5	Bob	488	781	449	951	363	[illegible]	3,980
6	Joe	202	773	947	760	459	[illegible]	4,028
7	John	208	480	649	977	642	[illegible]	3,881
8	Mary	467	176	783	962	718	[illegible]	3,294
9	Sonny	819	960	624	672	779	[illegible]	4,193
10	Stephen	998	802	967	902	366	[illegible]	4,649
11	Susan	626	901	726	955	794	[illegible]	4,700
12	Barbara	836	324	756	905	278	966	[illegible]
13	Barbara	813	488	845	951	645	259	4,001
14	Barbara	434	623	330	616	860	375	3,238
15	Barbara	318	248	545	706	614	724	3,155
16	Barbara	285	276	805	330	887	406	2,989
17	Barbara	492	263	358	741	968	163	2,985
18	Barbara	377	588	299	196	327	342	2,129
19	Bob	672	169	501	711	913	589	3,555
20	Bob	671	619	708	962	386	155	3,501
21	Bob	233	882	602	477	241	817	3,252
22	Bob	606	161	641	487	176	880	2,951

Figure 11-8

Search for Data

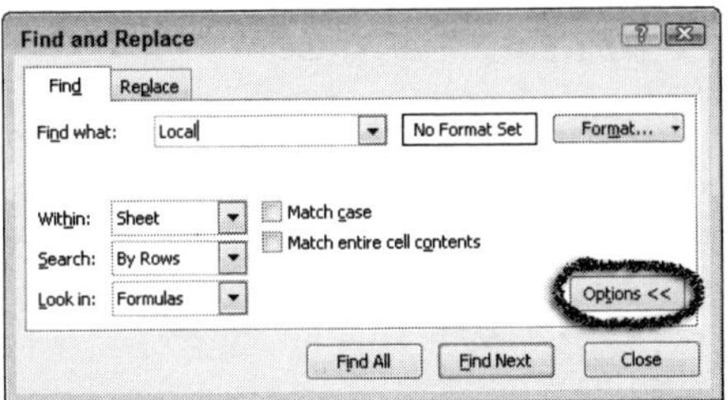

Figure 11-9

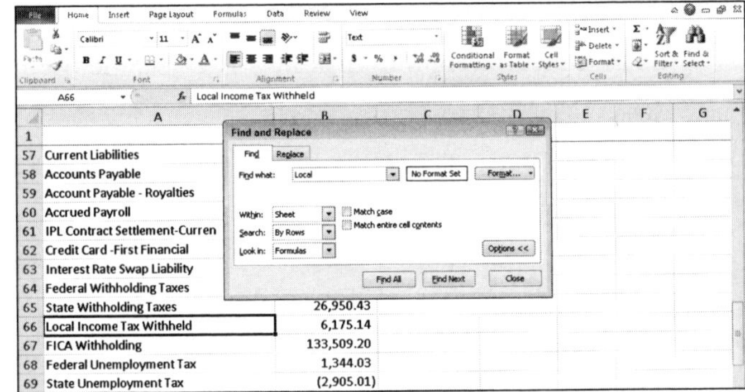

Figure 11-10

1. Choose Home➪Editing➪Find & Select➪Find. The Find and Replace dialog box appears.
2. In the Find What field, enter the value or word you want to locate.
3. Click the Options button and specify any desired options (see Figure 11-9):
   - *Within:* Search just the current worksheet or the entire workbook.
   - *Search:* Select whether to search first across the rows or down the columns.
   - *Look In:* Select whether you want to search through the values or formula results, through the actual formulas, or in the comments.

Select Formulas when you're looking for a formula that references a specific cell address.

   - *Match Case:* Select this check box if you want your search to be case-specific (for example, BOBCAT instead of BobCat or Bobcat).
   - *Match Entire Cell Contents:* Select this check box if you want your search results to list only the items that exactly match your search criteria.
4. Click Find Next. Excel jumps to the first occurrence of the match (see Figure 11-10). If this isn't the entry you're looking for, click Find Next again. Excel advises you if it doesn't locate the data that you're searching for.
5. Click Close when you locate the entry you want.

Find All Data Occurrences

1. Choose Home➪Editing➪Find & Select➪Find. The Find and Replace dialog box appears.
2. In the Find What field, enter the value or word you want to locate.
3. Click Options and specify any desired options.
4. Click the Find All button. The Find and Replace dialog box expands showing a list of each cell entry that contains your data (see Figure 11-11).
5. Click any entry. The specified cell is selected. When finished, click Close.

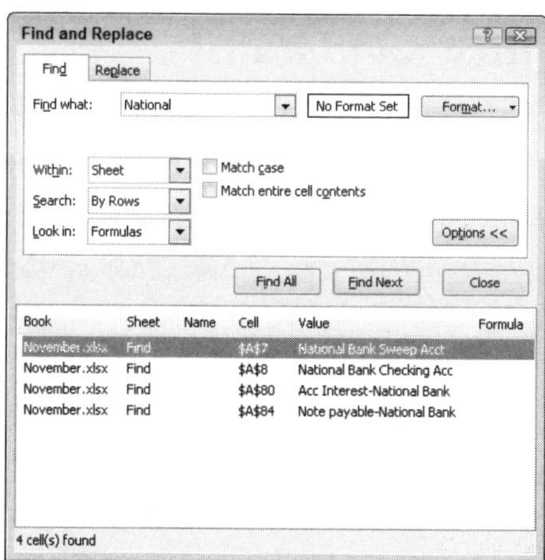

Figure 11-11

Locate Cells by Format

1. Choose Home➪Editing➪Find & Select➪Find. The Find and Replace dialog box appears.
2. Click the Format button. The Find Format dialog box appears.

To select formatting from an existing cell, from the Find and Replace dialog box, click the Format drop-down list arrow and click the Choose Format from Cell button. Click the desired cell; then continue with the Find and Replace options.

3. From the various tabs, select the formatting options that you're searching for. In Figure 11-12, I'm looking for any cell formatted in Times New Roman font.
4. Click OK. The Find Format dialog box closes, and the Find and Replace dialog box displays a sample of the format that you selected.
5. Click the Find Next or the Find All button. Excel finds the formatting occurrence.

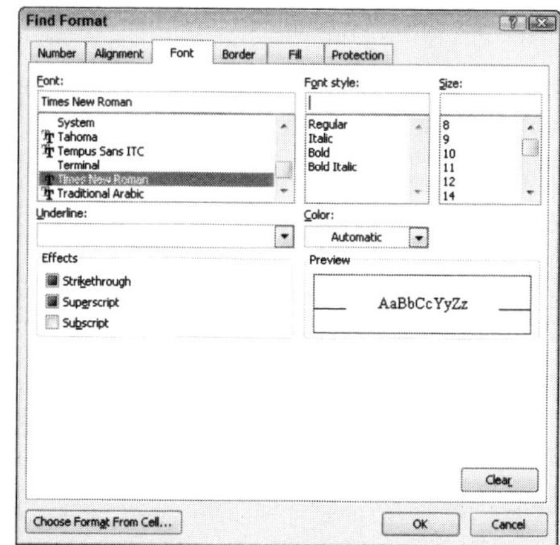

Figure 11-12

Use the Replace Command

1. Choose Home⇨Editing⇨Find & Select⇨Replace. The Find and Replace dialog box appears with the Replace tab active (see Figure 11-13).

If you want to replace data in only certain cells, rows, or columns, select the desired area before you open the Find and Replace dialog box.

2. In the Find What field, enter the data you want to locate.

Click the Options button to display and select additional search preferences, including formatting.

3. In the Replace With field, enter the data with which you want to replace the found data.
4. Click Find Next to locate the first found occasion; or, click Find All to display a list of all occurrences.
5. If you want to use the replacement data on a single occurrence, click Replace. Excel performs the replacement and locates the next occurrence.
6. If you want to replace all occurrences at the same time, click Replace All. Excel displays an information box, like the one in Figure 11-14, indicating the number of replacements made.
7. Click OK.

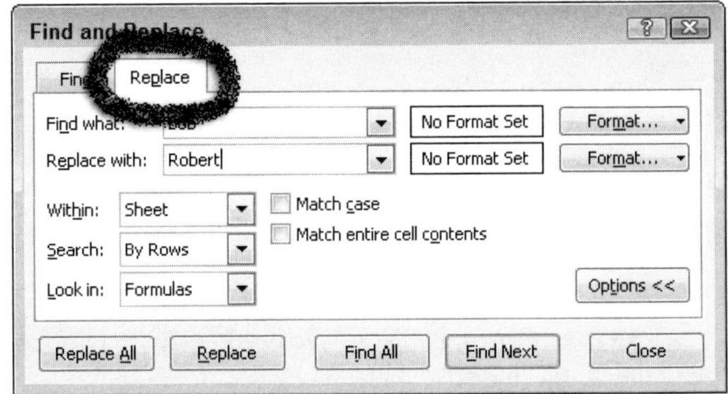

Figure 11-13

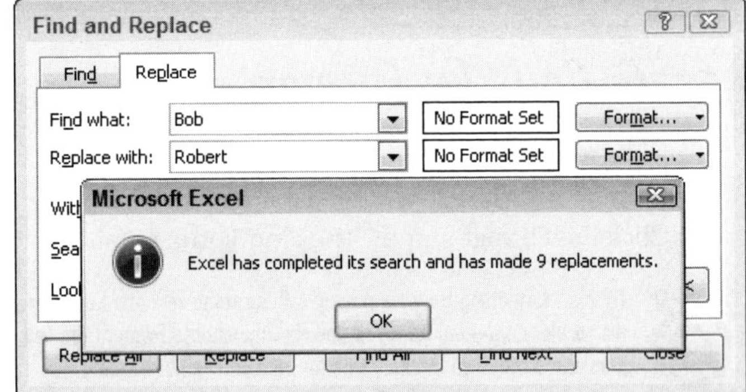

Figure 11-14

Create an AutoFilter

1. After clicking anywhere in your data, choose Data➪Sort & Filter➪Filter. Excel displays a filter arrow in each database column.

Optionally, choose Home➪Sort & Filter➪Filter.

2. Click the arrow in the column heading from which you want to find a common value. Excel displays a drop-down list, which includes one of each unique entry (up to 10,000 entries) in the selected column, as you see in Figure 11-15.

3. Remove the check mark from Select All. All items become unselected.

4. Click the entry you want to filter and then click OK. Excel displays only the records that match your choice. In Figure 11-16, you see the records only for the name Mary.

The filter arrows on filtered columns take on a different appearance to indicate that a filter is in use.

To sort any column, click the column filter arrow and choose a sort option.

To make the AutoFilter menu wider or longer, drag the grip handle at the bottom.

5. To clear the filter, click the filter arrow and choose Clear Filter from *"field name"* where "field name" represents the field you are currently filtering.

6. When you finish filtering your data, choose Data➪Sort & Filter➪Filter to turn off the AutoFilter. You can turn the AutoFilter on and off as often as you need to.

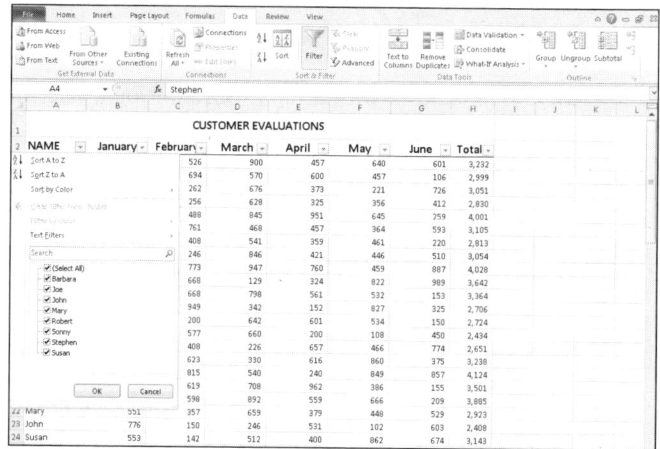

Figure 11-15

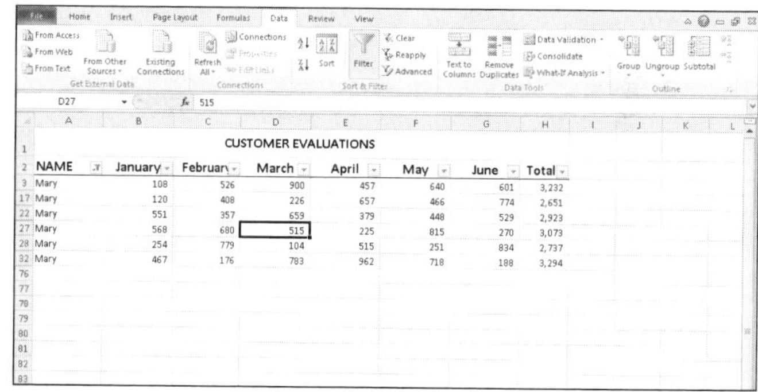

Figure 11-16

Generate a Subtotal

1. Sort the field to use for generating subtotals. The subtotal data must have no blank rows or columns, and each column in the database must have a label in the first row.
2. Choose Data⇨Outline⇨Subtotals. The Subtotal dialog box appears.
3. Select the field you want to subtotal from the At Each Change In drop-down list.
4. Select a function from the Use Function drop-down list. Choices include Sum (totals the values in a field), Count (returns the quantity of items in a field), Average (determines the average value of a field), Max and Min (display the highest and lowest value in a field), and Product (returns the value of all the numbers in a field multiplied together). The options also include four statistical functions: StdDev, StdDevp, Var, or Varp.
5. Select the fields holding the data you want to subtotal from the Add Subtotal To list (see Figure 11-17). You can select more than one field to subtotal; however, if you're using the Sum function, Excel totals only the fields containing values.
6. Select the Replace Current Subtotals check box if you already have subtotal calculations. Excel replaces the previous subtotals with the new ones.
7. Select the Page Break between Groups check box if you want Excel to begin each subtotaled group on a new page.
8. Clear the Summary below Data check box if you want Excel to place the subtotals at the top of each group instead of under each group.
9. Click OK. Excel performs the subtotal. Figure 11-18 shows the Totals field data subtotaled by Name.

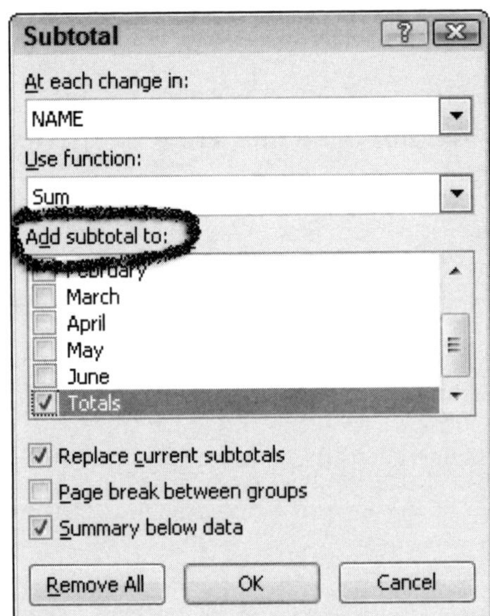

Figure 11-17

CUSTOMER EVALUATIONS

NAME	January	February	March	April	May	June	Totals
Barbara	813	488	845	951	645	259	4,001
Barbara	434	623	330	616	860	375	3,238
Barbara	492	263	358	741	968	163	2,985
Barbara	796	710	725	763	958	188	4,140
Barbara	836	324	756	905	278	966	4,065
Barbara	318	248	545	706	614	724	3,155
Barbara	377	588	299	196	327	342	2,129
Barbara	285	276	805	330	887	406	2,989
Barbara Total							26,702
Joe	824	408	541	359	461	220	2,813
Joe	202	773	947	760	459	887	4,028
Joe	710	668	129	324	822	989	3,642
Joe	519	280	881	910	285	759	3,634
Joe	198	740	268	132	641	785	2,764
Joe	675	242	897	884	230	925	3,853
Joe	743	180	421	922	760	911	3,937
Joe	785	623	324	791	174	765	3,462
Joe Total							28,133
John	793	262	676	373	221	726	3,051
John	776	150	246	531	102	603	2,408
John	966	809	587	200	258	745	3,565
John	208	480	649	977	642	925	3,881
John	810	412	196	586	613	654	3,271
John Total							16,176

Figure 11-18

Control Individual Subtotals

1. Create subtotals for your data. (See the "Generate a Subtotal" section, earlier in this chapter.)
2. Hide and show data using the following methods:
   - *See only the grand total.* Click the 1 on the subtotal headings.
   - *See the subtotal categories and amounts (the detail is hidden).* Click the 2 on the subtotal headings (the column on the left side of the worksheet). As shown in Figure 11-19, you see the total for each name, but not the detail. The detail data is not lost, only hidden.

Excel uses its `SUBTOTAL` function to create the subtotals.

   - *Show all the detail and subtotals.* Click the 3 on the subtotal headings. Excel displays the individual worksheet rows.
3. Click the Hide Detail button (minus sign) next to any subtotal row. The selected subtotal detail collapses.
4. Click the Show Detail button (plus sign) next to any subtotal row. The detail data for the selected row appears.

Optionally, choose Data⇨Outline and click the Show Detail or the Hide Detail button.

Remove Subtotals

1. Choose Data⇨Outline⇨Subtotal. The Subtotal dialog box appears (see Figure 11-20).
2. Click the Remove All button. Excel removes all subtotal information from the database, including the Expand and Collapse icons from the left side of the worksheet. Your data remains in the order you last sorted it.

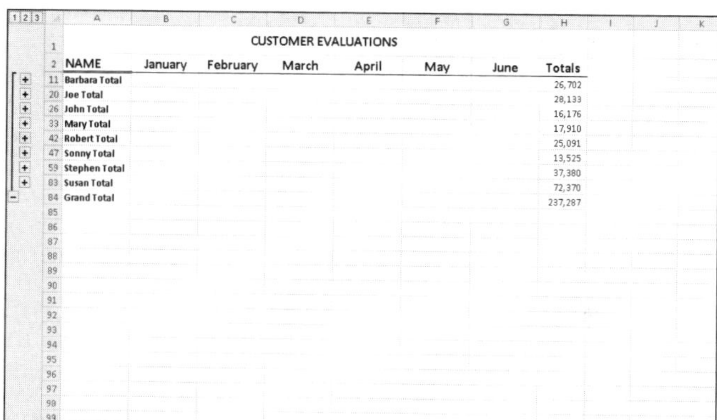

Figure 11-19

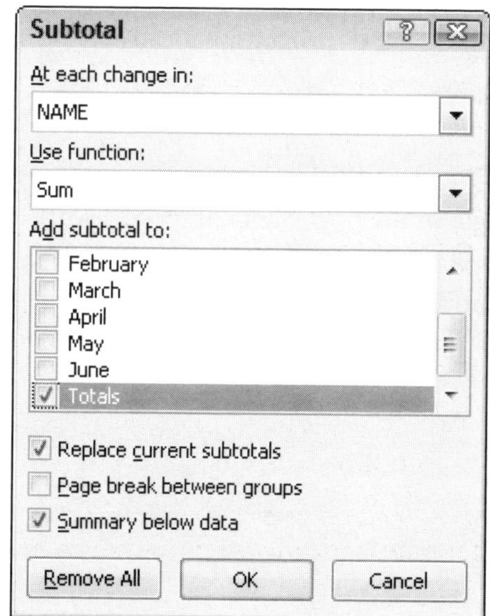

Figure 11-20

Work with Assistance Tags

1. From the worksheet, click a Assistance Tag icon. Each Assistance Tag type appears with a different icon appearance including:
   - *Paste:* This icon appears over pasted data (as shown in Figure 11-21), offering choices for pasting such as whether to include formatting, values, or both.
   - *AutoFill:* This icon appears after you enter data in a worksheet, offering tips on how to fill in the text or data.
   - *Insert:* This icon appears next to inserted cells, rows, or columns, offering a list of formatting options.
   - *Hyperlinks:* This icon appears next to a "perceived" hyperlink and allows you to not automatically create a hyperlink.
   - *Error Checking:* This icon appears over potential formula errors in the same way as the Error-Checking feature. Error-Checking Assistance Tags are indicated by a small, green triangle in the upper-left corner of a worksheet cell (see Figure 11-22).
2. Choose the option you want.

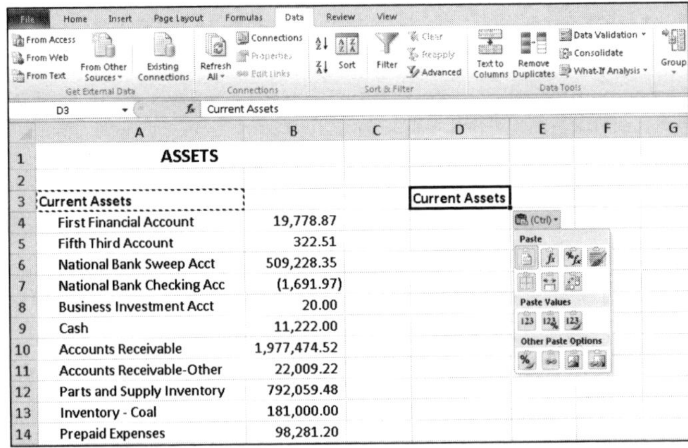

Figure 11-21

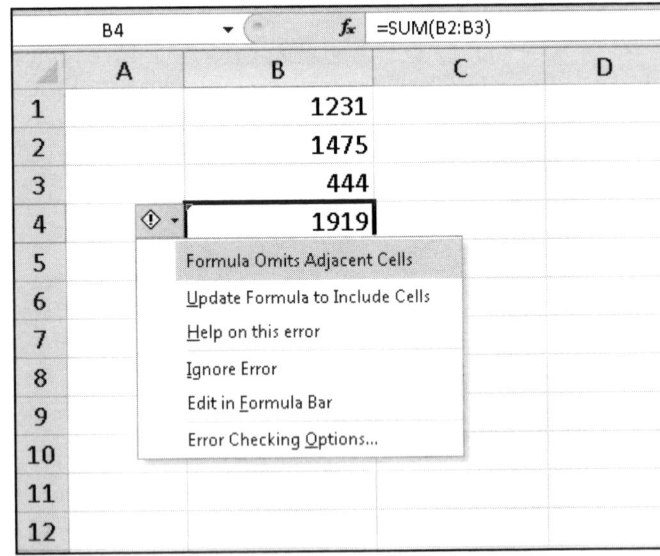

Figure 11-22

Split Data into Multiple Columns

1. If necessary, insert blank columns to the left of the cells you want to convert into multiple columns. If you want your data in three columns, you must have two blank columns.
2. Select the cells you want to convert.

You can't split empty cells, and you can't split merged cells. You must first unmerge the cells.

3. Choose Data➪Data Tools➪Text to Columns. The Convert Text to Columns Wizard appears.
4. Select the Original Data type that best suits your existing date. For example, if you're separating text that is variable in length (such as a first name and last name), select Delimited. The Delimited data type works best if your data has a similar format. If all cells contain a specific number of characters, choose Fixed Width.

If your data type is delimited, be sure that each section is separated by a common character, such as a comma, a period, an apostrophe, or a tab.

5. Click Next. The option you see next depends upon which data type you selected in Step 4.
6. If you selected Fixed Width, click the ruler bar where you want the data to split. If you selected Delimited, enter the character you use to separate your text. In Figure 11-23, the text is separated by a comma.
7. Click Finish. Excel separates the selected cells into multiple columns. See Figure 11-24.
8. Click OK.

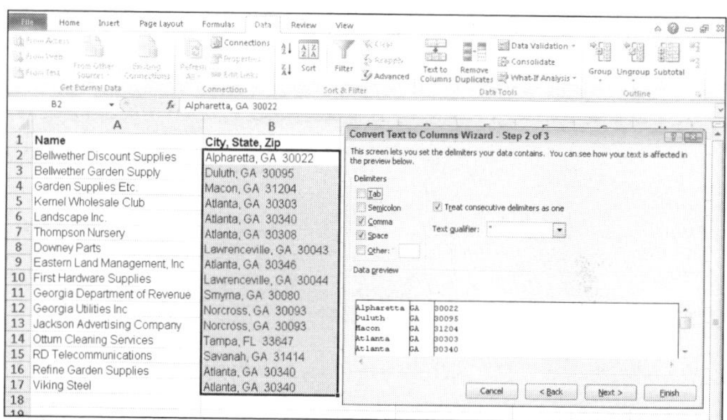

Figure 11-23

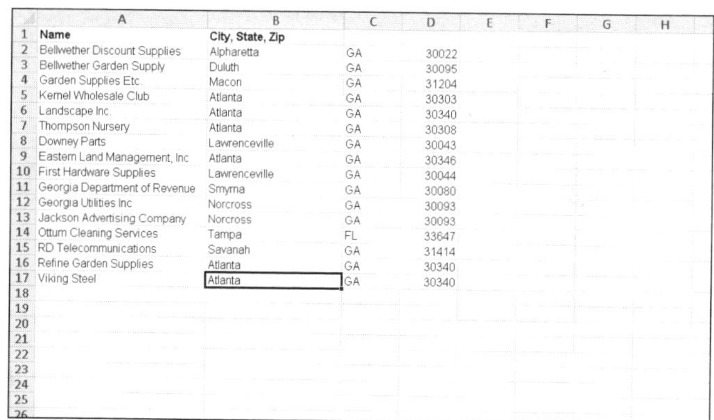

	A	B	C	D
1	Name	City, State, Zip		
2	Bellwether Discount Supplies	Alpharetta	GA	30022
3	Bellwether Garden Supply	Duluth	GA	30095
4	Garden Supplies Etc.	Macon	GA	31204
5	Kernel Wholesale Club	Atlanta	GA	30303
6	Landscape Inc.	Atlanta	GA	30340
7	Thompson Nursery	Atlanta	GA	30308
8	Downey Parts	Lawrenceville	GA	30043
9	Eastern Land Management, Inc	Atlanta	GA	30346
10	First Hardware Supplies	Lawrenceville	GA	30044
11	Georgia Department of Revenue	Smyrna	GA	30080
12	Georgia Utilities Inc	Norcross	GA	30093
13	Jackson Advertising Company	Norcross	GA	30093
14	Ottum Cleaning Services	Tampa	FL	33647
15	RD Telecommunications	Savanah	GA	31414
16	Refine Garden Supplies	Atlanta	GA	30340
17	Viking Steel	Atlanta	GA	30340

Figure 11-24

Merge Columns

1. Click in the cell where you want to put the merged data.
2. Choose Formulas⇨Function Library⇨Insert Function.
3. From the Or Select a Category drop-down list, choose Text.
4. Select Concatenate.
5. Click OK. The Function Arguments dialog box appears.
6. Type the first cell address or click the cell you want to add to the combination. Excel enters the cell address in the Text1 field.

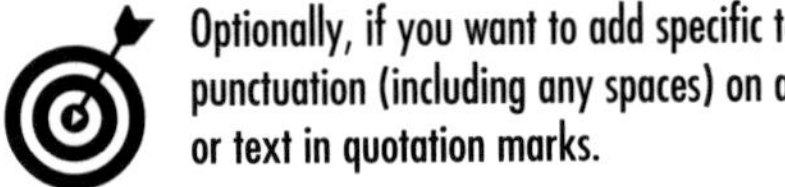

Optionally, if you want to add specific text that's not in a cell address, type the text or punctuation (including any spaces) on any line. Excel places any spaces, punctuation, or text in quotation marks.

7. In the Text2 field, click the cell or type the text that you want next. Each element must go on its own line. Figure 11-25 shows an example with a space (Text2) inserted between the first name (Text1) and the last name (Text3).
8. Click OK. Figure 11-26 shows the list of first and last names each combined into a single cell.

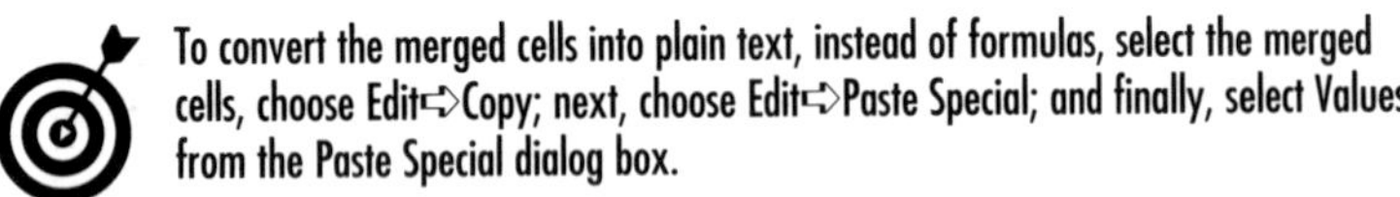

To convert the merged cells into plain text, instead of formulas, select the merged cells, choose Edit⇨Copy; next, choose Edit⇨Paste Special; and finally, select Values from the Paste Special dialog box.

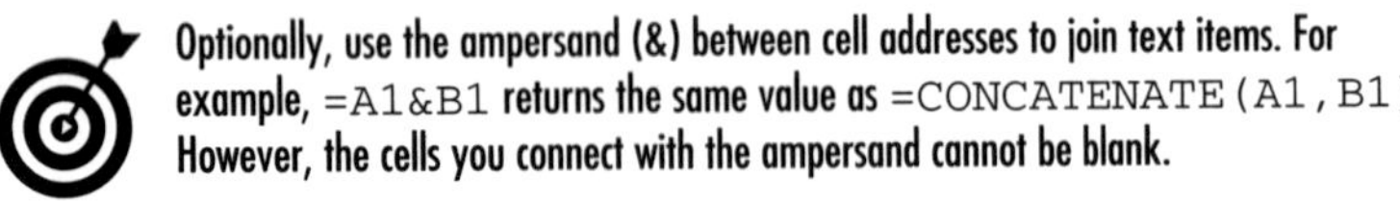

Optionally, use the ampersand (&) between cell addresses to join text items. For example, `=A1&B1` returns the same value as `=CONCATENATE(A1,B1)`. However, the cells you connect with the ampersand cannot be blank.

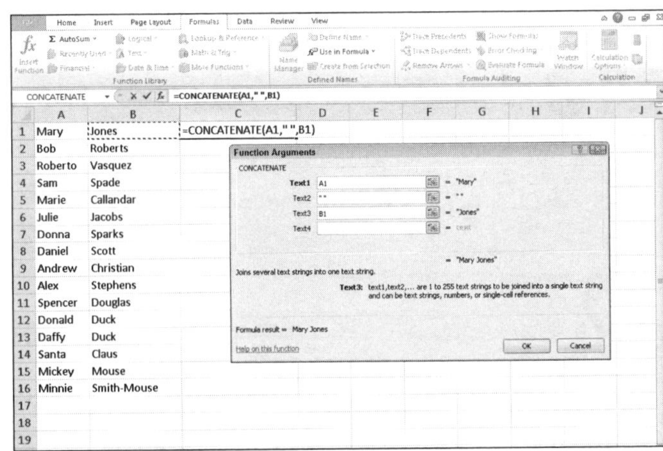

Figure 11-25

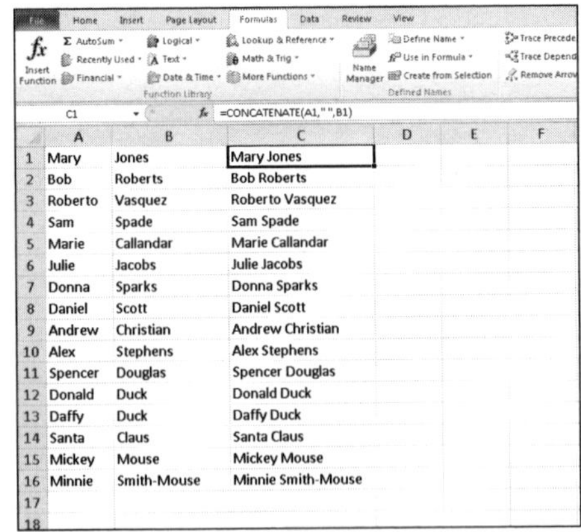

Figure 11-26

Creating Charts in Excel

Get ready to . . .

Whoever said that a picture is worth a thousand words is most certainly referring to a chart. Face it: We *like* looking at pictures more than we like looking at sheets of data. Charts, sometimes referred to as *graphs*, provide an effective way to illustrate your worksheet data by making the relationships between numbers easier to see. A chart turns numbers into shapes and enables you to compare the shapes to each other. Charts let you get your thoughts across with simplicity and strength, and because different charts may cause you to draw varied conclusions, they also prod you to ask questions about what you're seeing. Whatever the idea you're trying to convey, charts make it easier.

If you've ever spent hours drawing a chart on graph paper, you'll really appreciate the ease with which you can create dozens of different chart styles using your Excel data. With just a few decisions on your part and a few clicks of the mouse, you have a 2-D or 3-D illustration of your data.

New to Excel 2010 are *Sparklines*, which are miniature charts that you can add to individual worksheet cells. Sparklines, like regular charts, help bring meaning and context to the data that you're reporting, but they're embedded into the cells they're describing. Therefore, you get both elements in the space of one!

In this chapter, discover how to

- ➡ Add Sparklines to a worksheet.
- ➡ Quickly and easily create a chart.
- ➡ Modify a chart's appearance or content.

Add Sparklines

1. Select the cell where you want the Sparkline. Typically, this is next to the data.
2. Choose Insert➪Sparklines and choose a Sparkline type: Line, Column, or Win/Loss. The Create Sparklines dialog box appears, as shown in Figure 12-1.
3. In the Data Range field, enter (or drag across the cells with your mouse) the cells containing the data you want to plot.
4. Change, if necessary, in the Location Range field, the cell in which you want the Sparkline.
5. Click OK. Excel creates a Sparkline chart in the selected cell.

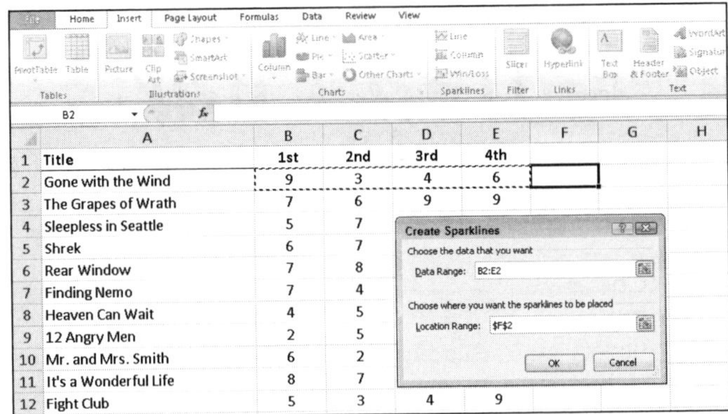

Figure 12-1

To delete a Sparkline, click the Sparkline cell and choose Sparkline Tools Design➪Group➪Clear.

To save time when creating multiple Sparklines in a data array (such as in the Figure 12-1 example), use the AutoFill handle to copy the Sparkline settings. This creates a Sparkline *group*, and changes that you make to one Sparkline affect all the Sparklines in the group.

Add Sparkline Markers

1. Select the Sparkline cells on which you want to add markers.
2. Choose Sparkline Tools Design➪Show/Hide and check the markers you want displayed. In Figure 12-2, you see only the high point markers.

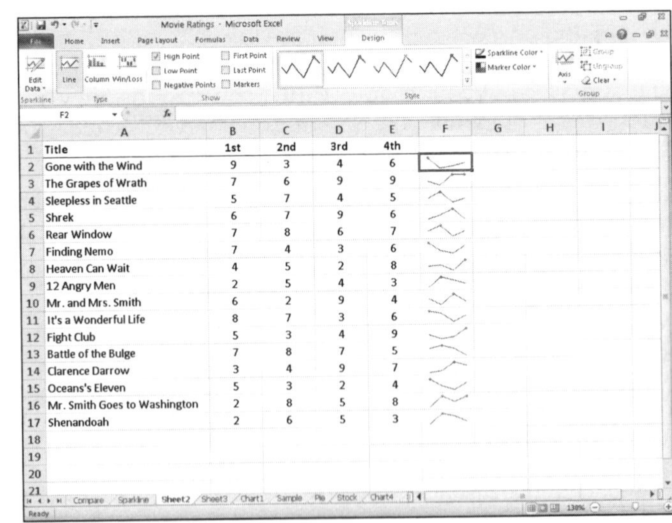

Figure 12-2

To change the Sparkline type, with the Sparkline cells selected, choose Sparkline Tools Design➪Type and choose a different type.

Change Sparkline Styles

1. Select the Sparkline cells on which you want to change the style.

If the Sparklines are in a group and you want to change only one of the Sparklines, choose Sparkline Tools Design➪Group➪Ungroup.

2. Choose Sparkline Tools Design➪Style and click the More button. A gallery of Sparkline styles appears, as shown in Figure 12-3.

3. Select the Sparkline style you want. All selected Sparklines change to the selected style.

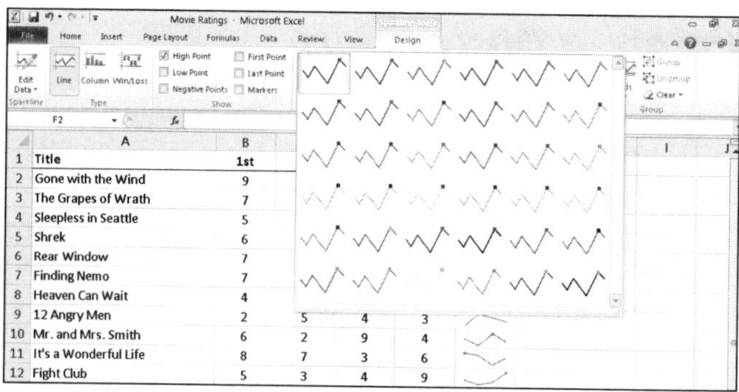

Figure 12-3

Edit Sparkline Data

1. Select the Sparkline cells on which you want to change the data.

2. Choose Sparkline Tools Design➪Sparkline and click the arrow on the Edit Data button.

3. From the menu that appears, choose from

- *Edit Group Location and Data* if you're working with a group of Sparklines.
- *Edit Single Sparklines Data* if you want to change only one Sparkline's data location. The Edit Sparklines dialog box shown in Figure 12-4 appears.

4. In the Data Range field, enter the new data area you want to include in the Sparklines.

5. In the Location Range field, enter or select a new Sparkline location.

6. Click OK.

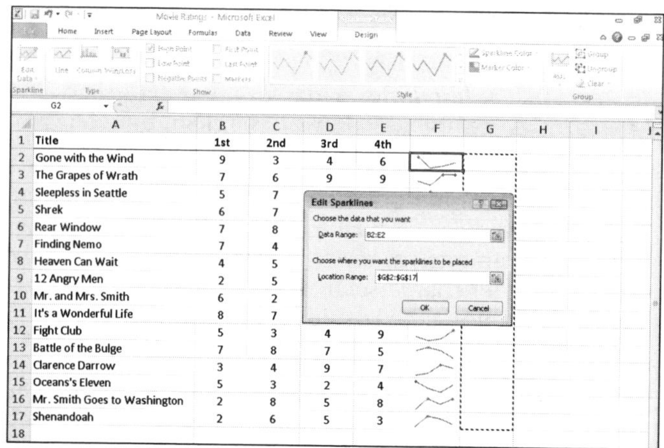

Figure 12-4

Create a Basic Chart

1. Select the data (contiguous or non contiguous) that you want to plot in the chart. See Figure 12-5 for an example of contiguous data selected for a chart.

2. Press **F11**. Excel immediately adds a new sheet (Chart1) to your workbook with the data plotted into a column chart. Each subsequent chart page is numbered sequentially (Chart2, Chart3, and so forth). Figure 12-6 shows you the various elements that can make up a chart:

	A	B	C	D	F	G	H
1		January	February	March	TOTALS		
2	Mary	256	269	298	1,646		
3	Stephen	236	289	176	1,402		
4	John	248	167	170	1,170		
5	Bob	255	153	245	1,306		
6	Susan	119	149	206	948		
8	TOTALS	2,228	2,054	2,190	6,472		
9							
10							
11							
12							

Figure 12-5

Some newer keyboards use a different function for the F11 key. If pressing F11 does not produce a chart, use the Insert tab as explained in the next section.

- *Title:* A descriptive name for the overall chart. By default, titles are not added in a basic chart, but you can add them later manually or by using the Chart Wizard.
- *X, or category axis:* Column or row headings from your selected data, which Excel uses for category axis names. In a column chart, the categories display along the bottom. In other charts (such as a bar chart), the category axis displays along the left side.
- *X axis title:* A descriptive name for the category axis. By default, a category label isn't added in a basic chart, but you can add one later manually or with the Chart Wizard.

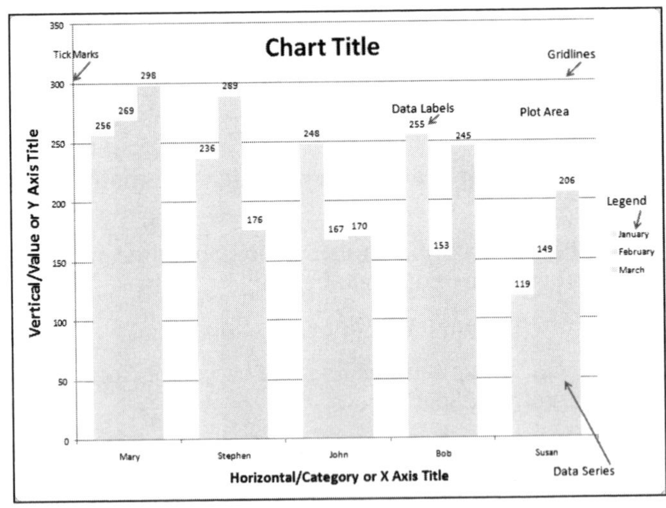

Figure 12-6

- *Y, or value axis:* A scale representing the zero or the lowest and highest numbers in the plotted data. The Value axis is usually located on the left side on a column chart or on the bottom on a bar chart.
- *Y axis title:* A descriptive name for the values. By default, a value label isn't added in a basic chart, but you can add one later manually or by using the Chart Wizard.
- *Legend:* The box, usually located on the right, that identifies the patterns or colors assigned to the chart data series. In Figure 12-7, the legend shows the colors used to represent January, February, and March.
- *Tick marks:* The small extensions of lines that appear outside the gray area and represent divisions of the value or category axis.
- *Gridlines:* These lines extend from the tick marks across the chart area to allow you to easily view and evaluate data.
- *Series:* Excel uses the worksheet cell values to generate the series. Each element, called a *data marker,* represents a single worksheet cell value. Related data markers make up a data series and have the same pattern or color. In Figure 12-8, you can see the comparison of the data values to the Y axis and the series values.
- *Plot area:* The background that represents the entire plotted chart area.

To delete a chart, right-click the Chart tab and choose Delete. When Excel asks for a confirmation, click Delete.

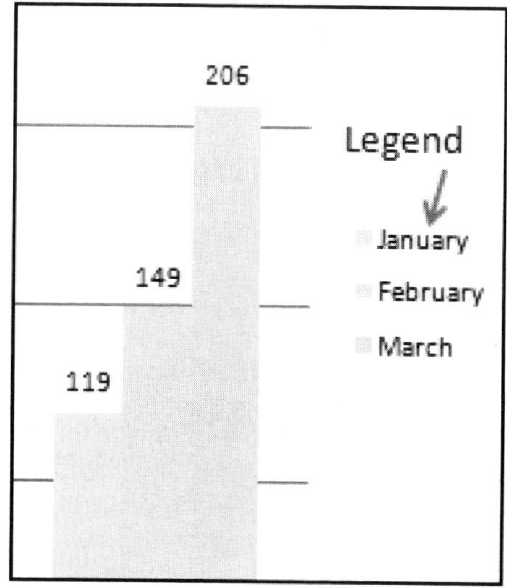

Figure 12-7

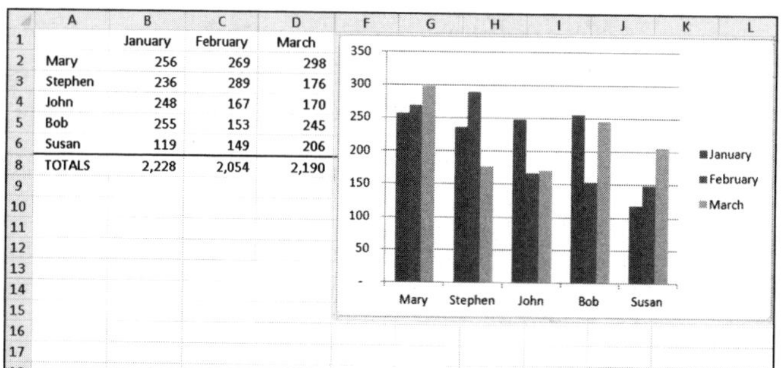

	A	B	C	D
1		January	February	March
2	Mary	256	269	298
3	Stephen	236	289	176
4	John	248	167	170
5	Bob	255	153	245
6	Susan	119	149	206
8	TOTALS	2,228	2,054	2,190

Figure 12-8

Insert a Chart

1. Select the data you want to plot in the chart.

Typically, if you are selecting values such as monthly figures, you don't want to include totals in your chart.

2. Choose Insert⇨Charts, and then click the down-arrow for the chart style you want. Excel can create many different chart types; each compares data in a different manner (see Figure 12-9). Some of the most commonly used chart types include the following:

Click a chart type to see a sample and an explanation of the chart.

- *Column:* Compares values to categories, using a series of vertical columns to illustrate the series.
- *Bar:* Like column charts, compares values to categories but uses a series of horizontal bars to illustrate the series.
- *Line:* Similar to bar charts but uses dots to represent the data points and lines to connect the data points.
- *Pie:* Compares parts to a whole. Usually, a pie chart has only one data series. Figure 12-10 illustrates data appropriate for a pie chart.
- *Area:* Displays the trend of each value, usually over a specified period of time.
- *X-Y Scatter:* Includes two value axes: one showing a set of numerical data along the X axis and the other showing data along the Y axis.

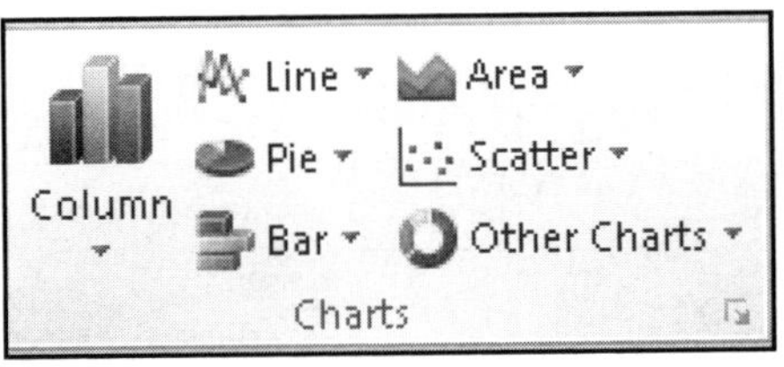

Figure 12-9

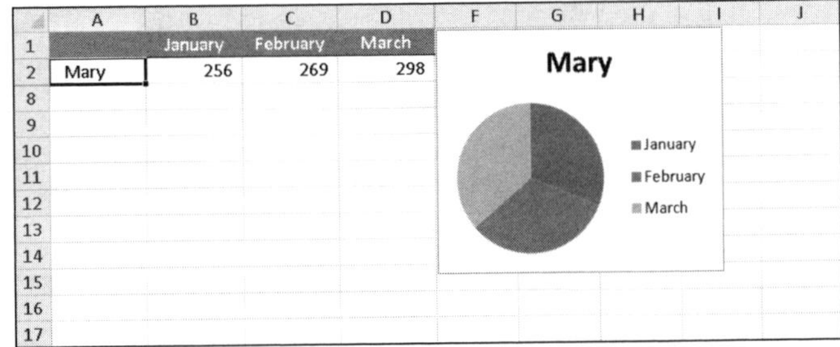

Figure 12-10

- *Surface:* Shows trends in values in a continuous curve.
- *Doughnut:* Displays data similarly to a pie chart; compares parts to a whole, but contains multiple series.
- *Stock:* Typically (but not exclusively) used to illustrate the fluctuation of stock prices. In a stock chart, data order is very important, and the row headings are typically High, Low, and Close; or Open, High, Low, and Close. See Figure 12-11 for an example of a stock chart and related data.
- *Radar:* Displays changes in values relative to a center point by comparing the cumulative values of multiple data series.
- *Bubble:* Similar to scatter charts, but compares three sets of values by displaying a series of circles.
- *Cylinder, Cone, and Pyramid:* The three chart types to create a column or bar chart by using 3-D cylindrical, conical, or pyramid shapes.

3. Choose a chart subtype. Depending on the chart type, some chart subtypes show the data series next to each other; others show the data elements stacked on top of each other. Some charts are 2-D, and others are 3-D. As you see in Figure 12-12, Excel creates the chart on the worksheet where your data resides.

You'll soon discover how you can change the chart location to its own sheet. But just in case you don't like your changes, make sure to save your worksheet, which also saves your chart, before modifying chart attributes.

The chart is a graphic object. You can resize or delete it like you would any graphic object.

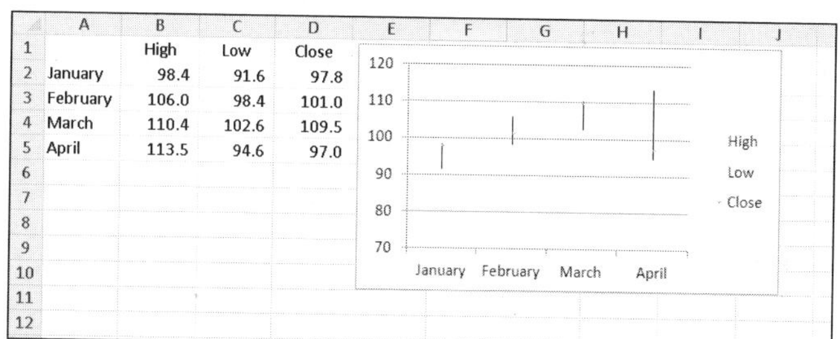

Figure 12-11

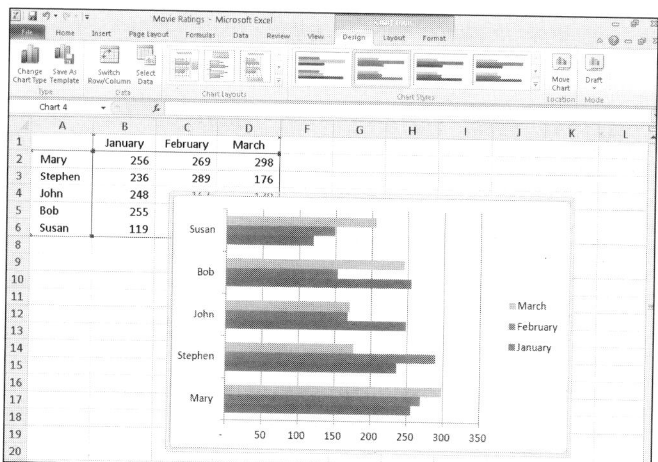

Figure 12-12

Change the Chart Type

1. Click the chart to select it whether it appears on its own sheet or on a data worksheet. The Chart Tools tab, with three subtabs, appears.
2. Choose Chart Tools Design➪Type➪Change Chart Type.
3. From the Change Chart Type dialog box that appears, select the different chart type and subtype you want (see Figure 12-13).
4. Click OK. Excel modifies the existing chart.

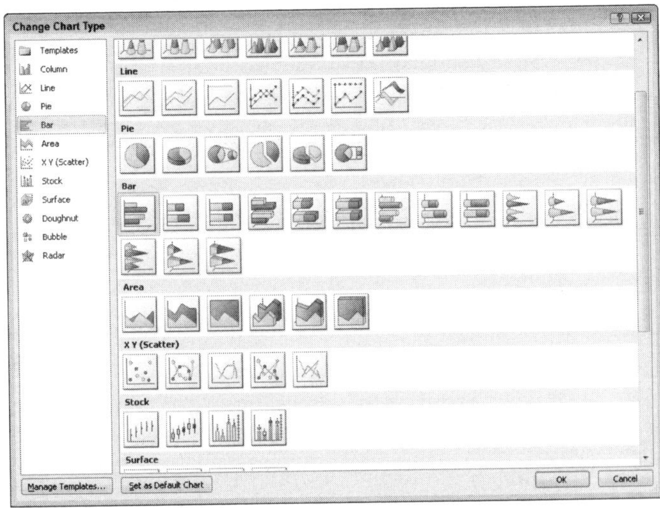

Figure 12-13

Adjust the Chart Location

1. Click anywhere on the chart that you want to move.

If you don't select the chart first, the Chart Tools tab doesn't appear.

2. On the Chart Tools Design tab, choose Location➪Move Chart. The Move Chart dialog box appears (see Figure 12-14).
3. Select a location:
   - *New Sheet:* Creates a new worksheet and places the chart on the sheet.
   - *Object In:* Moves the chart to an existing sheet in the workbook. Click the drop-down arrow to select the worksheet to which you want to move the chart.
4. Click OK. Your chart is moved to the location you specify.

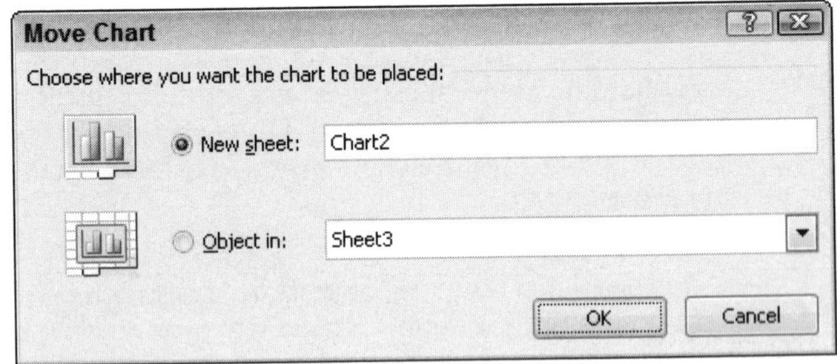

Figure 12-14

To move the chart to a different location on the current worksheet, position the mouse over the edge of the chart and drag it to a new location.

Display a Chart Title

1. Click anywhere on the chart you want to modify.
2. Choose Chart Tools Layout➪Labels➪Chart Title. A list of options appears:
   - *None:* The default choice; you don't want to display a title. Also use this option to remove a chart title.
   - *Centered Overlay Title:* Centers the title over the chart but retains the existing size of the chart.
   - *Above Chart:* Centers the title over the chart but adds room at the top so the title doesn't interfere with the chart itself.
3. Make a selection. A text box with the words `Chart Title` (as you can see in Figure 12-15) appears on the chart.
4. Click the `Chart Title` placeholder text and begin typing the desired title.
5. Press Enter. The text you type replaces `Chart Title`.
6. Click anywhere outside of the chart title to deselect it.
7. (Optional) Choose Chart Tools Layout➪Labels➪Chart Title, More Title Options. The Format Chart Title dialog box in Figure 12-16 appears.
8. Select Fill and then choose any desired background options for the chart title. Live Preview allows you to view various options without first selecting them.
9. Select Border Color, Border Style, and other title options, including color, shadows, 3-D formatting, and much more.

You can't apply 3-D formatting or select a shadow if your title doesn't have a border.

10. Click Close.

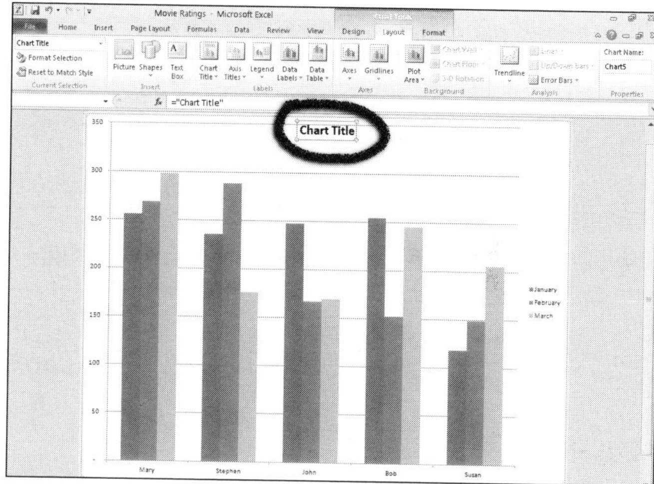

Figure 12-15

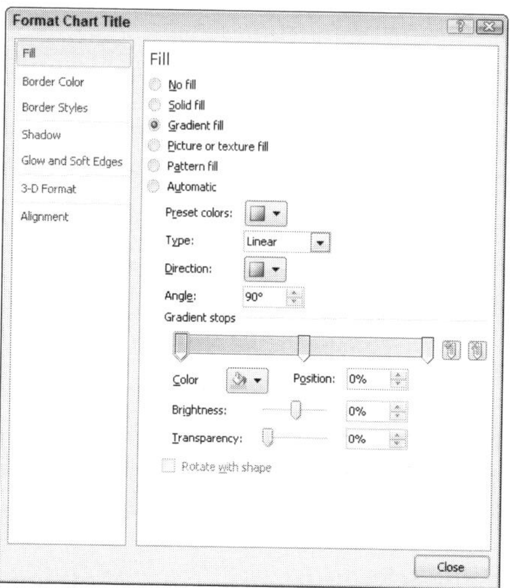

Figure 12-16

Customize the Chart Legend

1. Click anywhere on the chart that you want to modify.
2. Choose Chart Tools Layout➪Labels➪Legend.
3. Select a placement for the legend or click None to turn off the chart legend (see Figure 12-17).
4. Choose Chart Tools Layout➪Labels➪Legend➪More Legend Options.
5. The More Legend Options box offers the same type of formatting options as the Chart Title. Choose any desired options.
6. Click Close.

Figure 12-17

Add a Data Table

1. Click anywhere on the chart that you want to modify.

Data tables can be added to charts on a regular worksheet, but it isn't a common practice because the worksheet itself already displays the data.

2. Choose Chart Tools Layout➪Labels➪Data Table. Options include a choice not to show a data table, show a data table but not show a chart legend, or to show a data table and include the chart legend.

Data tables display the chart values in a grid beneath the chart. They are very helpful if a reader needs to see exact values along with a graphical display, such as when using a 3-D chart.

3. Make a Data Table selection.
4. Click OK. A data table, as seen in Figure 12-18, displays at the bottom of the chart showing the actual values.

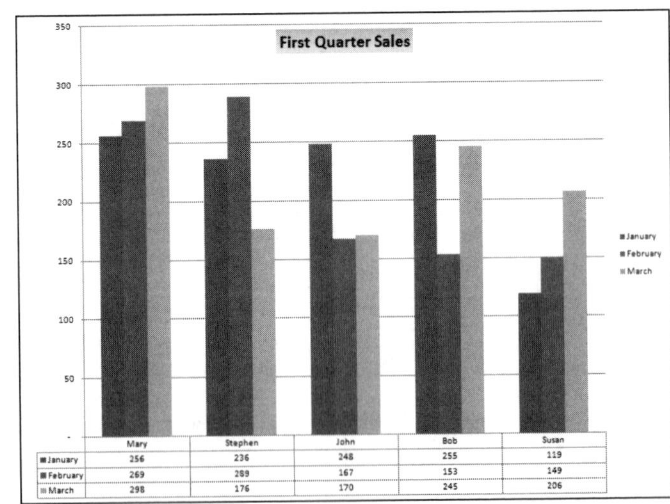

Figure 12-18

Show Data Labels

1. Click anywhere on the chart that you want to modify.
2. Choose Chart Tools Layout➪Data Labels. A menu of data label placement options appears.

You can use Data Labels to help identify the data series values, which are sometimes difficult to read on the Y axis scale.

3. Select a placement option. Figure 12-19 shows the data labels with a placement of Outside End.
4. Choose Chart Tools Layout➪Data Labels➪More Data Label Options. The Format Data Labels dialog box appears.
5. If you don't want the data label to be the series value, choose a different option from the Label Options area (such as the series or category names).
6. In the Number option, select a number style for the data labels.
7. Select any additional options and then click Close.

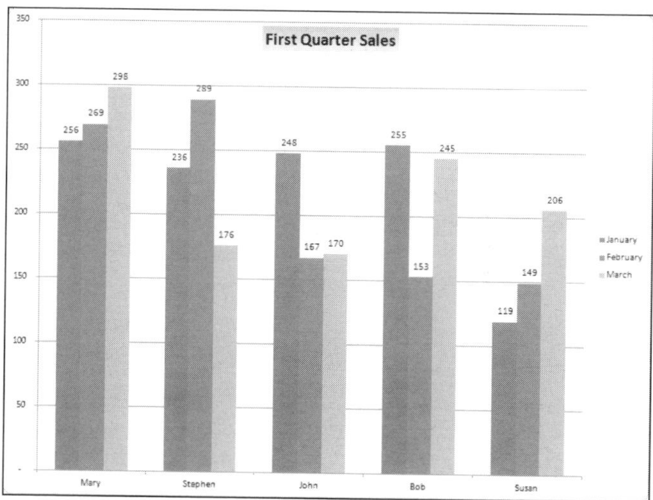

Figure 12-19

Select a Chart Color Style

1. Click anywhere on the chart that you want to modify.
2. Choose Chart Tools Design➪Chart Styles and click the More button, which displays the Chart Styles Gallery, as shown in Figure 12-20.
3. Select a chart theme. Scroll down . . . there's more at the bottom.

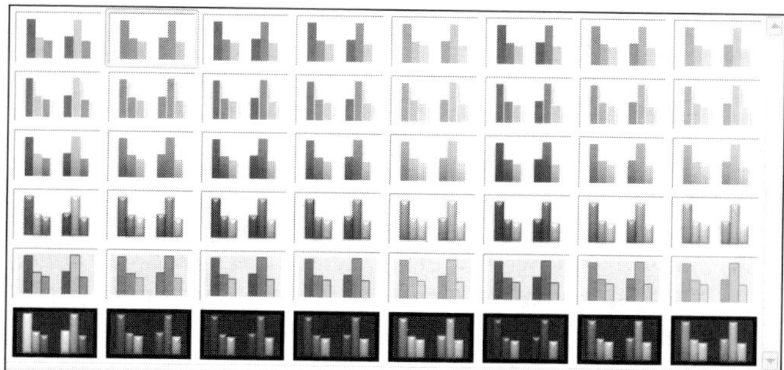

Figure 12-20

Place a Picture in a Data Series

1. Right-click the series or data point that you want to modify.
2. From the shortcut menu that appears, choose Format Data Series. The Format Data Series dialog box appears.
3. Click the Fill option; from the Fill options that appear on the right, select Picture or Texture Fill and then click File. The Insert Picture dialog box appears.
4. Locate and select the picture you want to use. Click Insert. The Format Data Series dialog box reappears.
5. Click Close. Figure 12-21 illustrates a pie chart where the one series was replaced with a photograph of spring flowering trees. As an extra example, you see the other series replaced with texture, patterns and gradients.

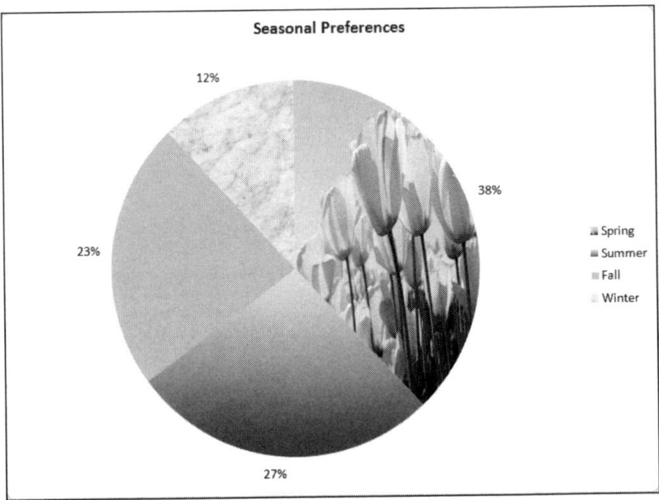

Figure 12-21

Adjust Chart Data

1. Click anywhere on the chart that you want to modify and choose Chart Tools Design➪Data➪Select Data. The Select Data Source dialog box opens with the current chart data selected in the worksheet (see Figure 12-22).
2. Drag in the worksheet to select the new data range. The Select Data Source dialog box collapses so you can easily see your data.
3. Release the mouse button. The Select Data Source box reappears, and the new data range appears in the Chart Data Range box.
4. Click OK. The Select Data Source dialog box closes.

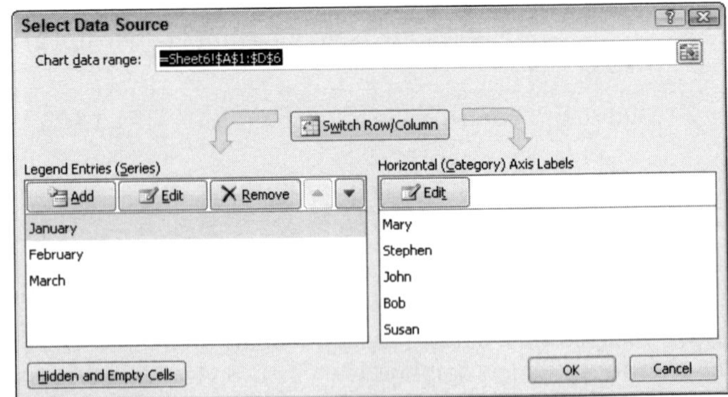

Figure 12-22

Printing in Excel

When you finish compiling your worksheet, you'll probably want to print a copy or e-mail a copy to someone else. This chapter shows you a number of Excel tools that you can use to improve your document layout, including headers, footers, page orientation, and margins.

When you're printing, Excel assumes that you want to print the entire worksheet area unless you specify otherwise. You discover in this chapter how to tell Excel exactly what you want to print. This chapter also includes these topics:

- Working with page breaks
- Adjusting the paper size
- Making a worksheet fit when you must get a few last rows or columns on a single page
- Printing gridlines or row and column headings on the page, as well as other options for printing your worksheet or chart
- Sharing a workbook with others via e-mail

Chapter 13

Get ready to . . .

Preview Before Printing

1. Click the File tab. From Backstage view that appears, choose Print. A print settings section appears on the left, and a preview of the worksheet appears on the right.
2. From the preview area (shown in Figure 13-1), select from the following options:
   - If you have multiple pages, click the Page buttons (in the bottom center) to view additional pages.
   - Click the Zoom icon in the lower right corner to enlarge the view. Click it again to reduce the view.
   - Select the *Show Margins* icon to display the page margins; then drag any margin line to manually set margin size. Click the Show Margins icon again to turn off the margin lines.

See "Set Page Margins" later in this chapter to choose from predefined margins settings.

See the upcoming task "Print Worksheets and Charts" to review the Print Settings options.

3. Click the File tab to return to Normal view.

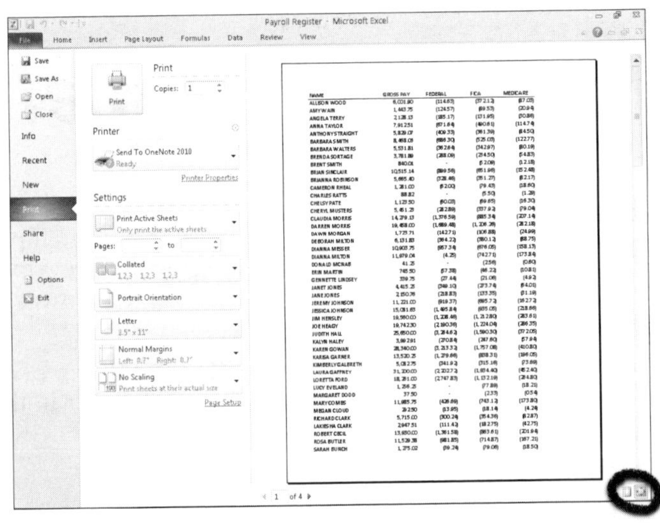

Figure 13-1

Add a Manual Page Break

1. Click a cell in the row where you want the new page to begin.
2. Choose Page Layout➪Page Setup➪Breaks➪Insert Page Break. Dotted page break lines appear, similar to the ones shown in Figure 13-2.

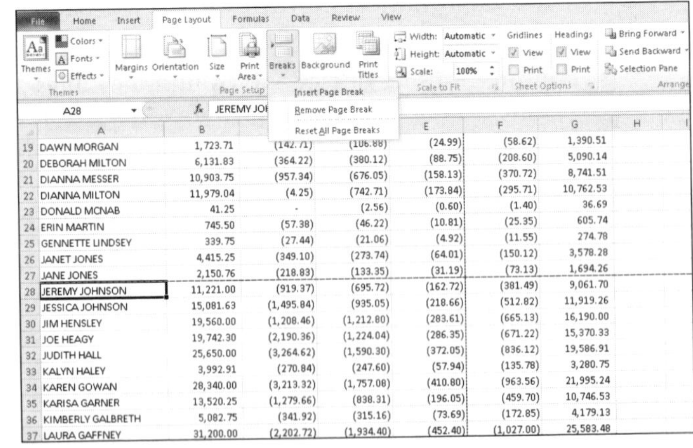

	A	B	C	D	E	F	G
19	DAWN MORGAN	1,723.71	(142.71)	(106.88)	(24.99)	(58.62)	1,390.51
20	DEBORAH MILTON	6,131.83	(364.22)	(380.12)	(88.75)	(208.60)	5,090.14
21	DIANNA MESSER	10,903.75	(957.34)	(676.05)	(158.13)	(370.72)	8,741.51
22	DIANNA MILTON	11,979.04	(4.25)	(742.71)	(173.84)	(295.71)	10,762.53
23	DONALD MCNAB	41.25	-	(2.56)	(0.60)	(1.40)	36.69
24	ERIN MARTIN	745.50	(57.38)	(46.22)	(10.81)	(25.35)	605.74
25	GENNETTE LINDSEY	339.75	(27.44)	(21.06)	(4.92)	(11.55)	274.78
26	JANET JONES	4,415.25	(349.10)	(273.74)	(64.01)	(150.12)	3,578.28
27	JANE JONES	2,150.76	(218.83)	(133.35)	(31.19)	(73.13)	1,694.26
28	JEREMY JOHNSON	11,221.00	(919.37)	(695.72)	(162.72)	(381.49)	9,061.70
29	JESSICA JOHNSON	15,081.63	(1,495.84)	(935.05)	(218.66)	(512.82)	11,919.26
30	JIM HENSLEY	19,560.00	(1,208.46)	(1,212.80)	(283.61)	(665.13)	16,190.00
31	JOE HEAGY	19,742.30	(2,190.36)	(1,224.04)	(286.35)	(671.22)	15,370.33
32	JUDITH HALL	25,650.00	(3,264.62)	(1,590.30)	(372.05)	(836.12)	19,586.91
33	KALYN HALEY	3,992.91	(270.84)	(247.60)	(57.94)	(135.78)	3,280.75
34	KAREN GOWAN	28,340.00	(3,213.32)	(1,757.08)	(410.80)	(963.56)	21,995.24
35	KARISA GARNER	13,520.25	(1,279.66)	(838.31)	(196.05)	(459.70)	10,746.53
36	KIMBERLY GALBRETH	5,082.75	(341.92)	(315.16)	(73.69)	(172.85)	4,179.13
37	LAURA GAFFNEY	31,200.00	(2,202.72)	(1,934.40)	(452.40)	(1,027.00)	25,583.48

Figure 13-2

Specify a Print Area

1. Highlight the area you want to print. See Figure 13-3.

Unless you specify a specific print area when you print, Excel prints the entire worksheet.

2. Choose Page Layout➪Page Setup➪Print Area➪Set Print Area. Dotted lines appear around the print area. When you print the worksheet, only the area contained within the dotted lines prints. See "Print Worksheets and Charts," later in this chapter.

To reset Excel to print the entire worksheet, choose Page Layout➪Page Setup➪Print Area➪Clear Print Area.

Optionally, highlight the area you want to print. Then, after clicking the File tab, click the Print option. From the Print What settings of the Print Settings panel, choose Selection.

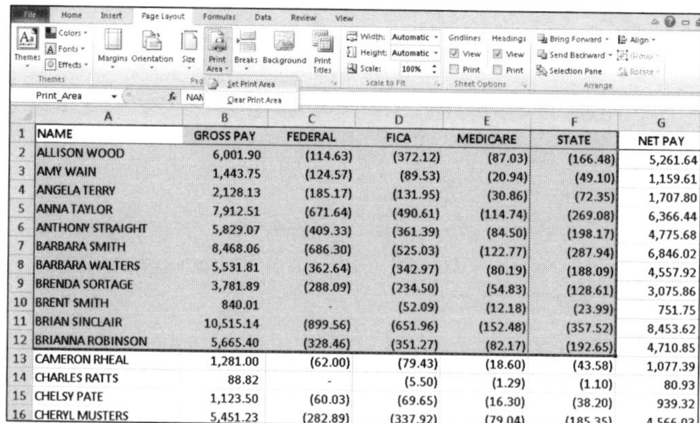

Figure 13-3

Adjust Paper Orientation and Size

1. Choose Page Layout➪Page Setup➪Orientation.
2. Select whether you want Portrait or Landscape orientation.

Portrait orientation prints the top of the document along the short edge of the paper, and *Landscape* prints it along the long edge of the paper.

3. Choose Page Layout➪Page Setup➪Size. A drop-down list of paper sizes appears.
4. Select a paper size. Your choices depend upon the printer you use. The two most common choices in the United States are Letter (8.5" x 11") and Legal (8.5" x 14"). See Figure 13-4.

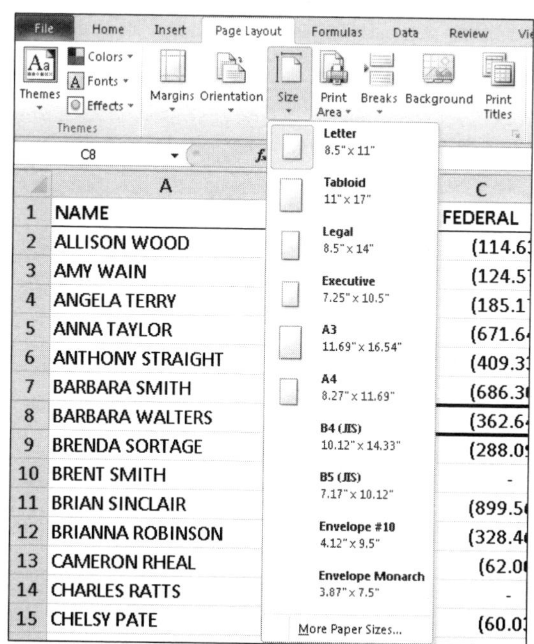

Figure 13-4

Make Worksheets Fit Better on a Page

1. Choose Page Layout⇨Scale to Fit.
2. Click the Scale to Fit dialog box launcher. The Page Setup dialog box opens.
3. From the Scaling area, choose how many pages wide you want the document. Make a selection from the options seen in Figure 13-5:
   - *Adjust To:* Enlarge or shrink the printed font size by setting a percentage option between 10 and 400.
   - *Fit To:* Force Excel to a specified number of pages wide and high.

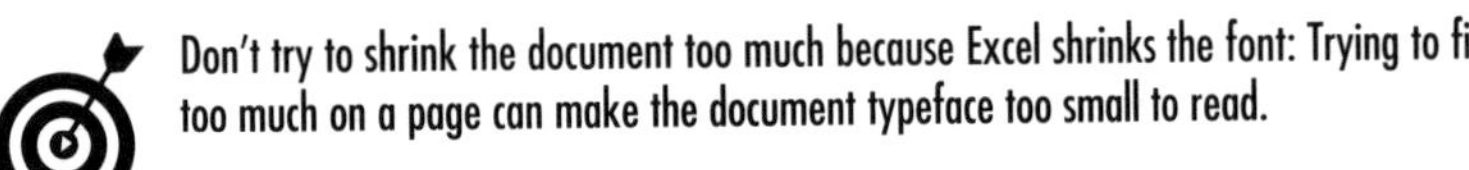
Don't try to shrink the document too much because Excel shrinks the font: Trying to fit too much on a page can make the document typeface too small to read.

4. Click OK.

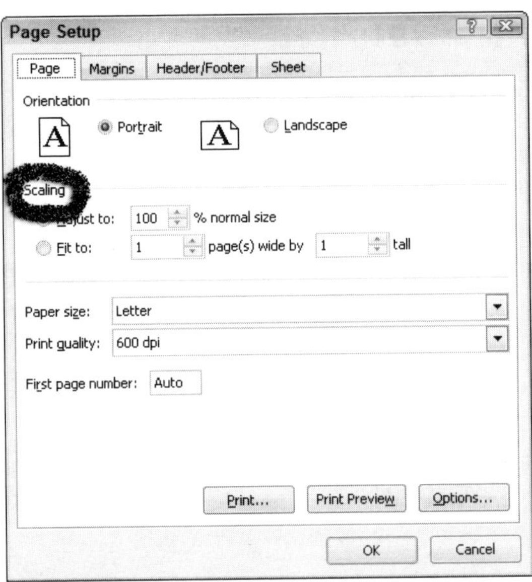

Figure 13-5

Optionally, instead of opening the Page Setup dialog box, select width, height, and scaling options from the Scale to Fit group.

Set Page Margins

1. Choose Page Layout⇨Page Setup⇨Margins. Figure 13-6 shows a list of margin options.
2. Select from the margins options shown, or choose Custom Margins to open the Page Setup dialog box, where you can set your own margin options.

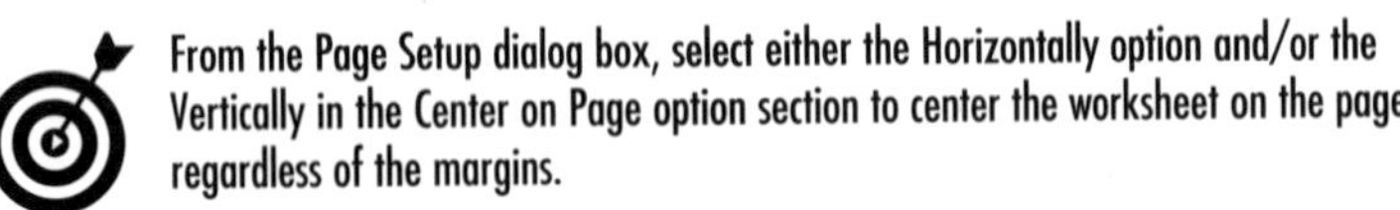
From the Page Setup dialog box, select either the Horizontally option and/or the Vertically in the Center on Page option section to center the worksheet on the page, regardless of the margins.

3. Click OK.

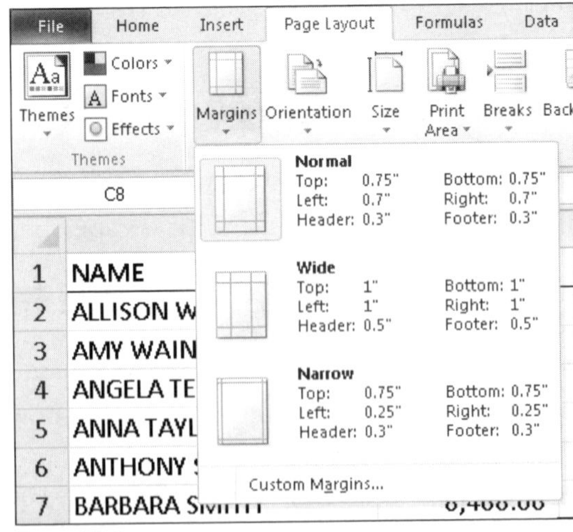

Figure 13-6

Specify Repeating Rows and Columns

1. Choose Page Layout⇨Page Setup⇨Print Titles. The Page Setup dialog box opens.
2. On the Sheet tab, in the Rows to Repeat at Top field, type a dollar sign ($) followed by the row numbers or column letters that you want to print as titles. Entering **$1:$1**, as you see in Figure 13-7, repeats row 1 at the beginning of each page.

Click the worksheet icon on the right to collapse the Page Setup dialog box so that you can select the rows or columns you want to include. Click the button again to return to the Page Setup dialog box.

3. Click OK.

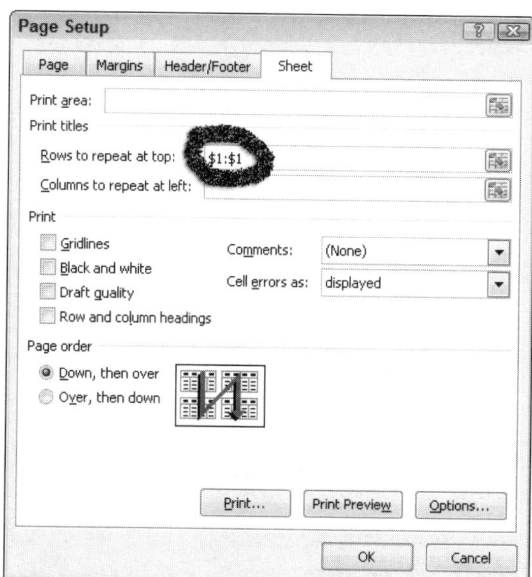

Figure 13-7

Print Gridlines and Row and Column Headings

1. Choose Page Layout⇨Sheet Options and choose from the following options:
   - *Gridlines⇨Print:* Select this option to print the gridlines surrounding each cell in the worksheet.

By default, the Gridlines View option is selected. If you don't want to see the gridlines while you're working on the worksheet, clear this option.

   - *Headings⇨Print:* Select this option to print the row numbers or column letters around the worksheet. Figure 13-8 illustrates a worksheet printed with gridlines and row and column headings.

By default, gridlines are a lighter shade of blue. You can change the gridline color by clicking the File tab and choosing Options, Then selecting a different gridline color from the Advanced section.

	A	B	C	D	E
1	NAME	GROSS PAY	FEDERAL	FICA	MEDICARE
2	ALLISON WOOD	6,001.90	(114.63)	(372.12)	(87.03)
3	AMY WAIN	1,443.75	(124.57)	(89.53)	(20.94)
4	ANGELA TERRY	2,128.13	(185.17)	(131.95)	(30.86)
5	ANNA TAYLOR	7,912.51	(671.64)	(490.61)	(114.74)
6	ANTHONY STRAIGHT	5,829.07	(409.33)	(361.39)	(84.50)
7	BARBARA SMITH	8,468.06	(686.30)	(525.03)	(122.77)
8	BARBARA WALTERS	5,531.81	(362.64)	(342.97)	(80.19)
9	BRENDA SORTAGE	3,781.89	(288.09)	(234.50)	(54.83)
10	BRENT SMITH	840.01	-	(52.09)	(12.18)
11	BRIAN SINCLAIR	10,515.14	(899.56)	(651.96)	(152.48)
12	BRIANNA ROBINSON	5,665.40	(328.46)	(351.27)	(82.17)
13	CAMERON RHEAL	1,281.00	(62.00)	(79.43)	(18.60)
14	CHARLES RATTS	88.82	-	(5.50)	(1.29)
15	CHELSY PATE	1,123.50	(60.03)	(69.65)	(16.30)
16	CHERYL MUSTERS	5,451.23	(282.89)	(337.92)	(79.04)
17	CLAUDIA MORRIS	14,279.13	(1,376.59)	(885.34)	(207.14)
18	DARREN MORRIS	19,458.00	(1,689.48)	(1,206.26)	(282.18)
19	DAWN MORGAN	1,723.71	(142.71)	(106.88)	(24.99)
20	DEBORAH MILTON	6,131.83	(364.22)	(380.12)	(88.75)
21	DIANNA MESSER	10,903.75	(957.34)	(676.05)	(158.13)
22	DIANNA MILTON	11,979.04	(4.25)	(742.71)	(173.84)
23	DONALD MCNAB	41.25	-	(2.56)	(0.60)
24	ERIN MARTIN	745.50	(57.38)	(46.22)	(10.81)
25	GENNETTE LINDSEY	339.75	(27.44)	(21.06)	(4.92)
26	JANET JONES	4,415.25	(349.10)	(273.74)	(64.01)

Figure 13-8

Add a Standard Header or Footer

1. Choose View➪Workbook Views➪Page Layout. You see the header area of your worksheet. Headers and Footers are divided into three sections: Left, Center, and Right. *Headers* appear at the top of each printed page, and *footers* appear at the bottom of each printed page.
2. Click anywhere in the header or footer area. A blinking insertion point appears in the area, and the Header & Footer Tools Design tab appears above the Ribbon.
3. Choose Header & Footer Tools Design ➪Header & Footer➪ Header (or Footer). A list of predefined headers or footers appears, as shown in Figure 13-9.
4. Select the header or footer you want to use.

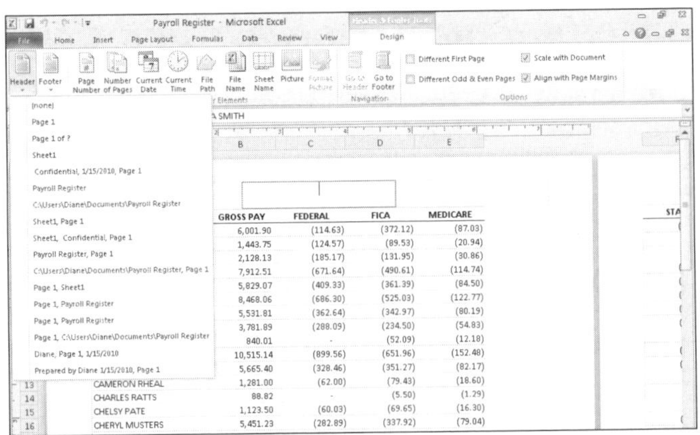

Figure 13-9

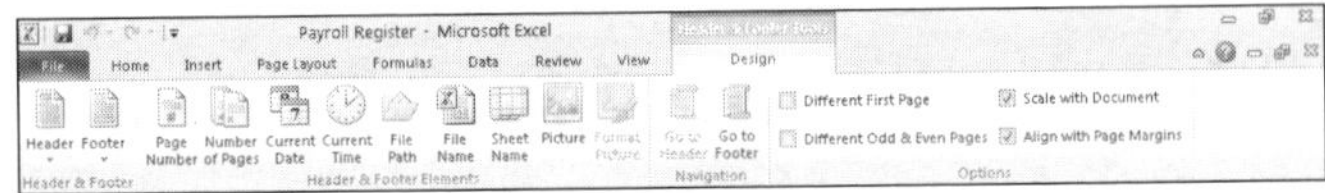

Figure 13-10

View Other Header and Footer Options

1. From Page Layout view (Views➪Workbook Views), click in the header or footer area.
2. Choose Header & Footer Tools Design. From the Options group, select any of the options shown in Figure 13-10:
   - *Different First Page:* Excel won't print the header or footer on the first page.
   - *Different Odd & Even Pages:* You want a header or footer for the odd-numbered pages of the document.
   - *Scale with Document:* Use the same font size and scaling as the worksheet. If you want the header and footer font size and scaling independent of the worksheet scaling, clear this check box.
   - *Align with Page Margins:* Align the header and footer with the left and right margins of the worksheet.

Create a Custom Header or Footer

1. Choose View➪Workbook Views➪Page Layout view.

Click Go to Footer to jump to the footer area.

2. From Page Layout view, in any desired header or footer section, type the text you want for the header (or footer). As you see in Figure 13-11, you can format the header and footer text just like you would any cell data.

3. Choose Header & Footer Tools➪Design and click any options from the Header & Footer Elements group:

   - *Page Number:* Insert a code that indicates the page number.
   - *Number of Pages:* Insert a code that indicates the total number of pages.

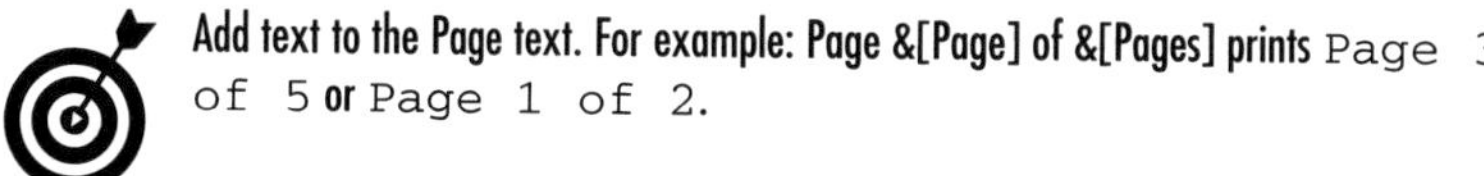

Add text to the Page text. For example: Page &[Page] of &[Pages] prints `Page 3 of 5` or `Page 1 of 2`.

   - *Current Date* or *Current Time:* Insert the print date or time of day, respectively. See Figure 13-12.
   - *File Path, File Name,* or *Sheet Name:* Include file information.
   - *Picture:* Insert a graphic image, such as a company logo.
   - *Format Picture:* Resize, rotate, or crop a header or footer graphic image.

4. Click anywhere outside the header or footer area to return to Page Layout view.

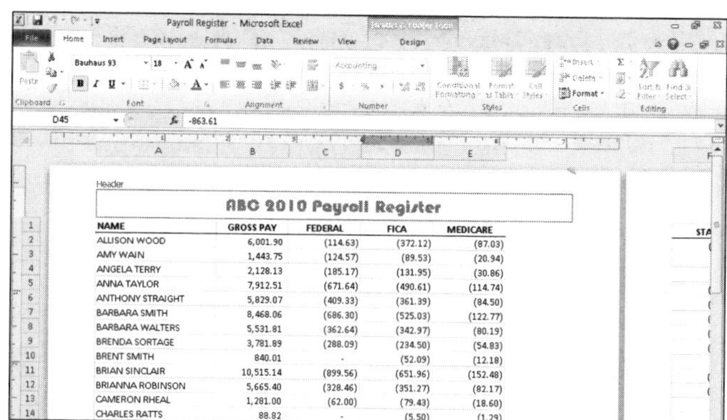

Figure 13-11

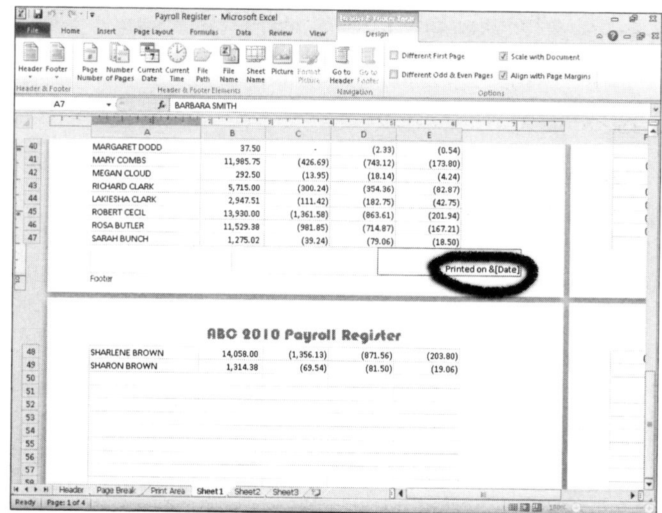

Figure 13-12

Print Worksheets and Charts

1. Click the File tab. From Backstage view, choose Print. A Print Settings section appears on the left, and a preview of the worksheet appears on the right.
2. From the Print Settings area shown in Figure 13-13, choose from the following options:
   - *Copies:* Select the number of copies you want to print.
   - *Printer:* Select the printer to which you want to print.
   - *Settings:* Choose whether to print the current worksheet, a preselected area, or the entire workbook. You can also specify to print only certain pages. Other settings, such as whether to print double-sided (if your printer has the capability), print collation order, orientation, paper size, and margins are also available.
3. Click the Print button.

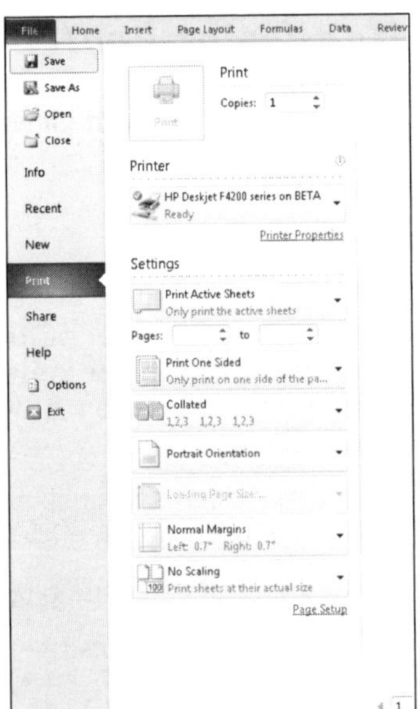

Figure 13-13

E-Mail a Workbook

1. Click the File tab. choose Share➪Send Using E-Mail and then click Send as Attachment. As you see in Figure 13-14, your e-mail program launches with the workbook as an attachment.

Recipients must have Excel installed on their computer to open the workbook file.

2. Enter the recipient e-mail information and any additional text in the body of the message.

Optionally, instead of sending as an Excel attachment (an editable file), you can send the workbook as a PDF or XPS attachment (not editable).

3. Click Send.

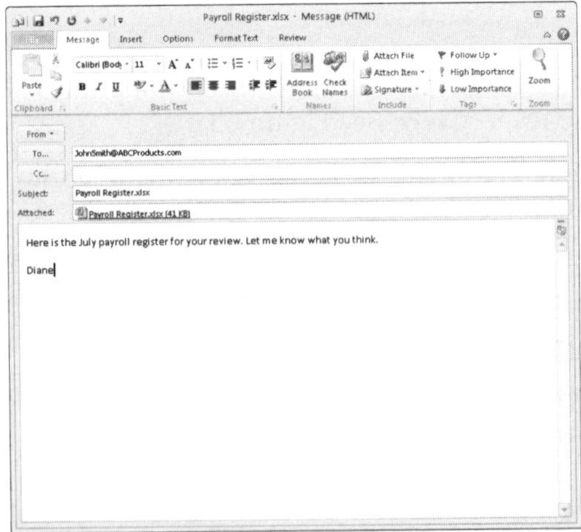

Figure 13-14

Part III
PowerPoint

Chapter 14: Creating a Presentation 149

Chapter 15: Editing a Presentation 157

Chapter 16: Working with Objects 167

Chapter 17: Adding Tables, Charts, and Diagrams ...177

Chapter 18: Finishing the Presentation 189

Chapter 19: Presenting the Presentation 199

Creating a Presentation

Chapter 14

The first step of any journey through PowerPoint is to open the program and create a new presentation or open an existing presentation. (Obviously, you can't do anything in PowerPoint until you launch the program.)

In this chapter, I talk about how to launch PowerPoint and begin to create a new presentation. I also show you how to save a presentation and then safely exit the program.

Note: I assume you have the Microsoft Office 2010 suite or Microsoft Office PowerPoint 2010 installed. If you need to perform an installation, refer to the user documentation accompanying your installer CD for installation instructions.

Get ready to . . .

Start PowerPoint

1. Start your computer and log on to Windows.
2. Choose Start➪All Programs➪Microsoft Office➪Microsoft PowerPoint 2010. Microsoft PowerPoint opens, and a blank presentation appears as shown in Figure 14-1. PowerPoint calls this opening view *Normal view*.

To create a convenient program shortcut on your desktop, locate Microsoft PowerPoint 2010 on your Start menu and then right-click the PowerPoint application icon to open a contextual menu. Choose Send To➪Desktop (Create Shortcut). Just double-click the shortcut icon that now appears on your desktop to launch PowerPoint.

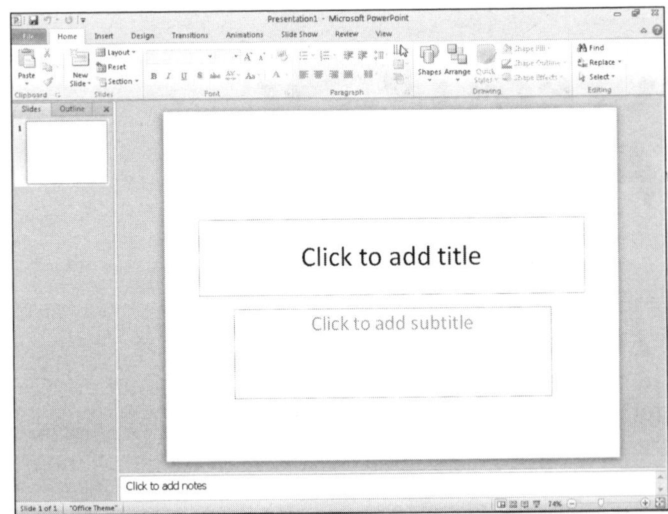

Figure 14-1

Open a Saved Presentation

1. Open PowerPoint.
2. Click the File tab. From Backstage view that appears, click Open. The Open dialog box appears (see Figure 14-2). Alternatively, press Ctrl+O to open the Open dialog box.
3. From the Folders or the Favorite Links sections, navigate your hard drive and locate the folder where you have a saved presentation.
4. Click a presentation to select it.

If you want to open multiple presentations, press the Ctrl key and click each presentation you want to open in the Open dialog box. Click Open, and PowerPoint opens all the selected presentations.

5. Click Open, and the presentation opens in PowerPoint.

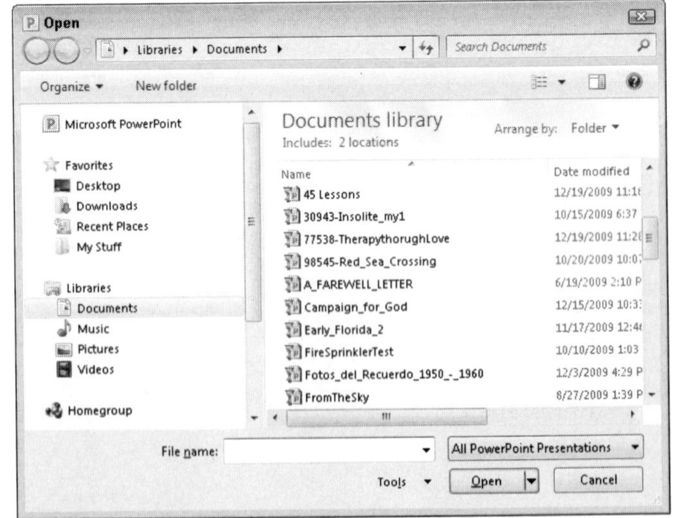

Figure 14-2

Create a New Presentation

1. In PowerPoint, click the File tab. From Backstage view that appears, choose New.
2. In the Available Templates and Themes pane (see Figure 14-3), select one of the following options to create a presentation:
   - *Home:* Click an option from here to display the templates installed with PowerPoint that reside locally on your computer.
   - *Office.com Templates:* Click any category here to display a selection of templates that you can download from Microsoft.
3. Click the Create button.

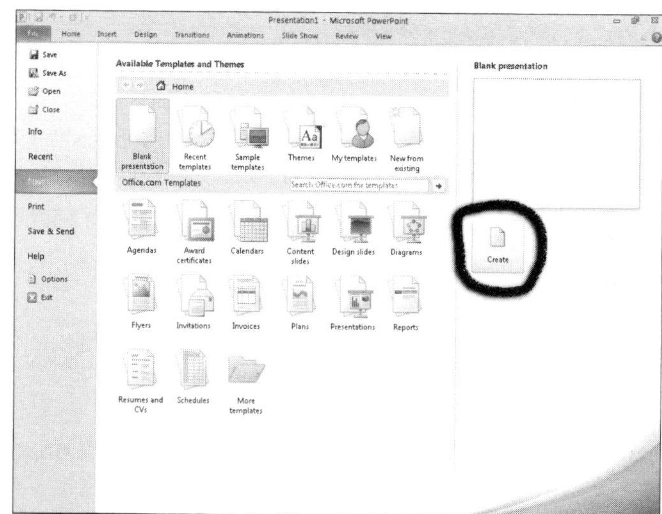

Figure 14-3

Use Slides from Another File

1. Open or create a presentation in PowerPoint, choose Home⇨Slides, and click the New Slide arrow.
2. Click Reuse Slides. The Reuse Slides pane opens on the right side of the screen.
3. Click the Browse button and then choose Browse File. Locate and click the presentation from which you want to reuse slides.
4. Click Open. All the slides in the selected presentation appear in the Reuse Slides pane, as shown in Figure 14-4.
5. Click the slides you want to reuse. PowerPoint automatically inserts the slide into your current presentation.
6. Click the Close (X) button to close the Reuse Slides pane.

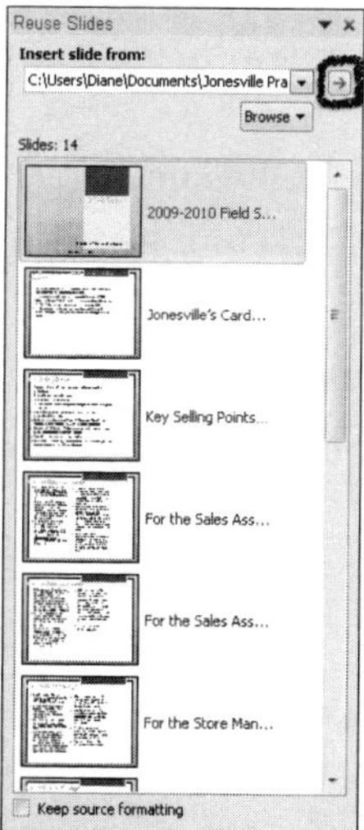

Figure 14-4

Save a Presentation

1. Open or create a presentation in PowerPoint.
2. Click the File tab. From Backstage view that appears, choose Save As. The Save As dialog box appears (see Figure 14-5).
3. Type a name for your presentation in the File Name text box.
4. From the Folders or the Favorite Links sections, navigate your hard drive and locate the folder where you want to save your presentation.
5. Click Save to save the file.

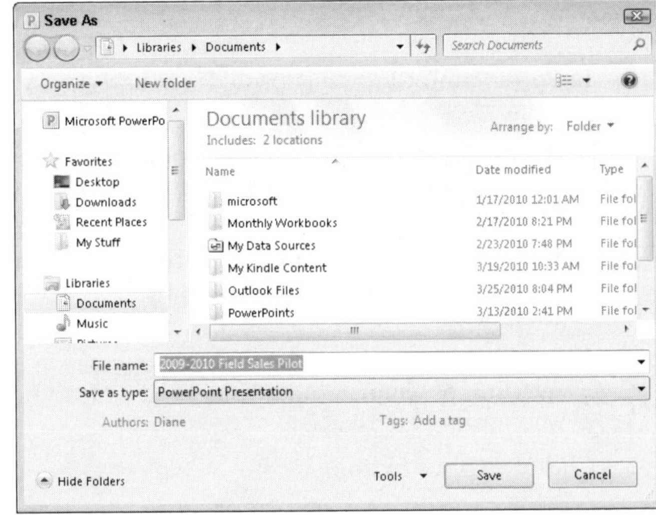

Figure 14-5

Save a Presentation in a Different Format

1. Start PowerPoint and create or open a presentation.
2. Click the File tab. From Backstage view that appears, choose Save As. The Save As dialog box appears.
3. Name your file by typing a name in the File Name text box.
4. Click the drop-down list arrow for Save as Type. A list of file types appears, as shown in Figure 14-6.
5. Choose the file type that you want.
6. From the Folders or the Favorite Links sections, navigate your hard drive and locate the folder where you want to save your presentation.
7. Click Save to save the file.

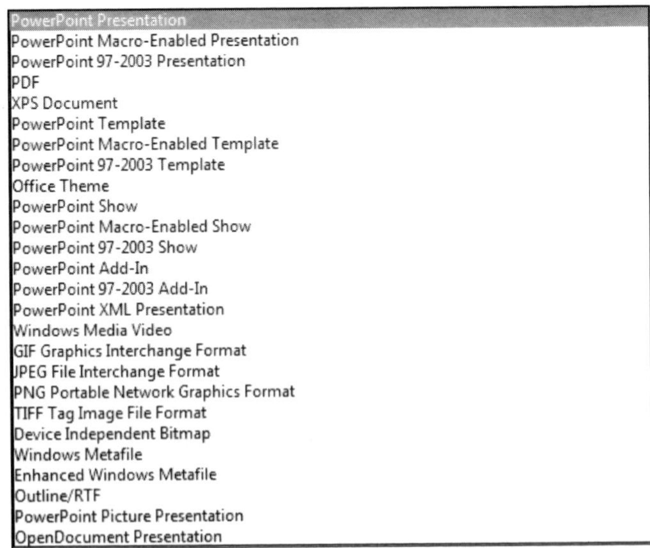

Figure 14-6

Close a Presentation

1. Open or create a PowerPoint presentation.
2. Click the File tab. From Backstage view that appears, choose Close.
3. If you haven't saved the file since your last edit, PowerPoint prompts you with a dialog box to save your changes before the file closes (see Figure 14-7). After closing a file, PowerPoint remains open and ready for you to create a new presentation or open another presentation.

Alternatively, you can click the X in the top-right corner of the PowerPoint document window or press Ctrl+F4.

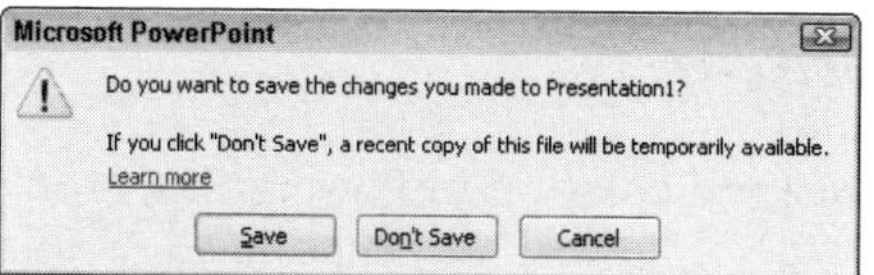

Figure 14-7

Exit PowerPoint

1. Open or create a presentation in PowerPoint.
2. Click the File tab. From Backstage view that appears, choose Exit (see Figure 14-8).
3. If you haven't saved the file since your last edit, PowerPoint prompts you to save your changes before the file closes.
4. Click Yes to save your last edits and exit, or click No to exit PowerPoint without saving your changes.

You can also press Alt+F4 to exit PowerPoint.

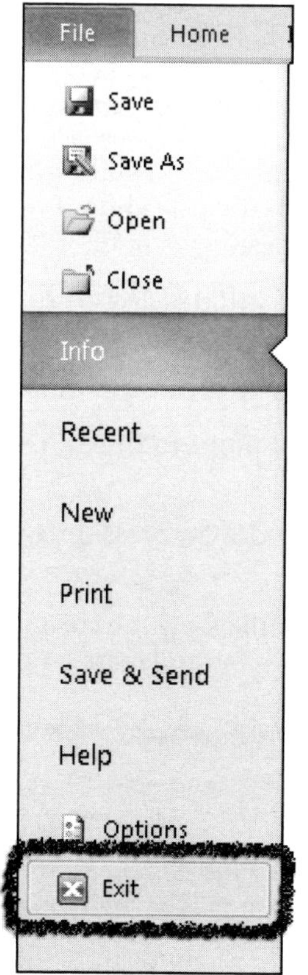

Figure 14-8

Create an Outline

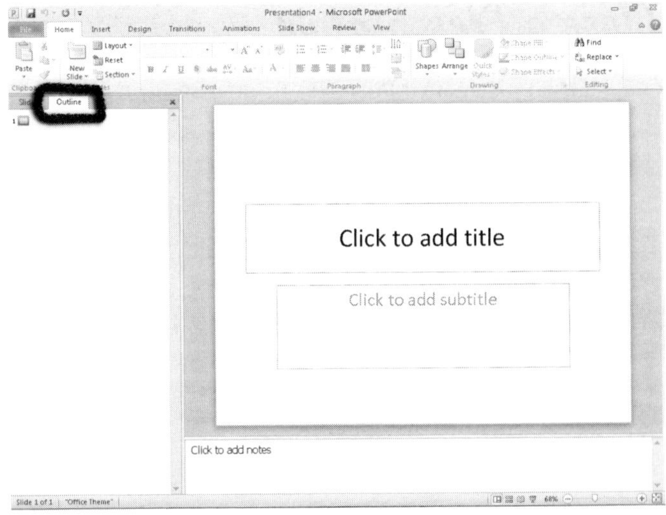

Figure 14-9

1. Open or create a presentation in PowerPoint. From the slide thumbnail panel, click the Outline tab to show the Outline pane (see Figure 14-9).
2. Click to the right of the small slide icon and type the main title in the title slide and then do one of the following:
   - *Title only:* If you want just a title to appear, press Enter. PowerPoint creates a second slide.
   - *Add a subtitle:* Press Tab on the second slide, and the insertion point moves up beneath the title slide. Type a subtitle and then press Enter to create a new slide.
3. Press Shift+Tab to move the insertion point to the left, which creates a new slide.
4. Type a slide title on slide 2 and then press Enter.
5. Press Tab to move the insertion point to the right one level, which is a bullet point.
6. Type text for the bullet point and then press Enter to add additional bullet points.
7. When you're finished adding bullets on the current slide, press Enter and then press Shift+Tab to create a new slide.

Press Tab to move the outline level to the right; press Shift+Tab to move the outline level to the left.

8. Press Enter to create a new slide, and repeat Steps 4–7 to continue adding titles and bullet points (see Figure 14-10).

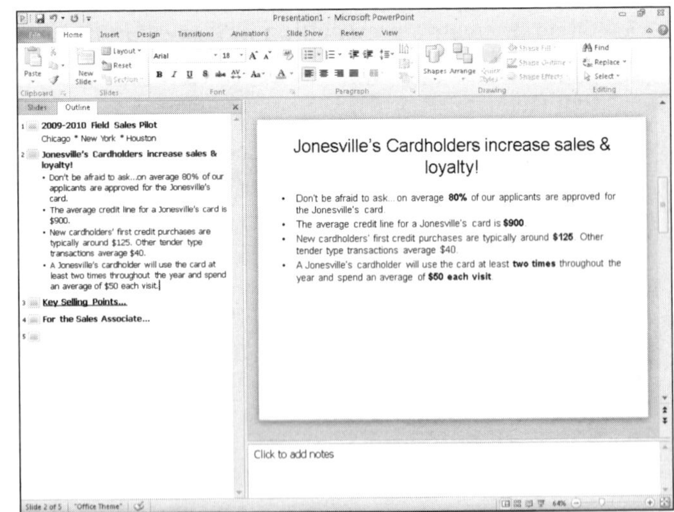

Figure 14-10

Import a Microsoft Word Outline

1. Open or create a presentation in PowerPoint and then click the Home tab.
2. From the Slides group, click the New Slide arrow. A list of options appears.
3. Choose Slides from Outline. The Insert Outline dialog box opens (see Figure 14-11).
4. From the Folders or the Favorite Links sections, navigate your hard drive and locate the folder where you saved your Microsoft Word outline.
5. Click the Word outline you want to import. The document name is highlighted.
6. Click Insert.

Files you import as outlines from Word files should be formatted with Level 1 and Level 2 styles in Microsoft Word. If you import a file and the Level 2 heads don't import as subcategories in PowerPoint, return to the Word file and check the formatting.

7. Click the Outline tab in PowerPoint to view the outline (see Figure 14-12).

Add a New Slide

1. Open or create a presentation in PowerPoint.
2. Click the Slides tab, which displays the slides as thumbnails.

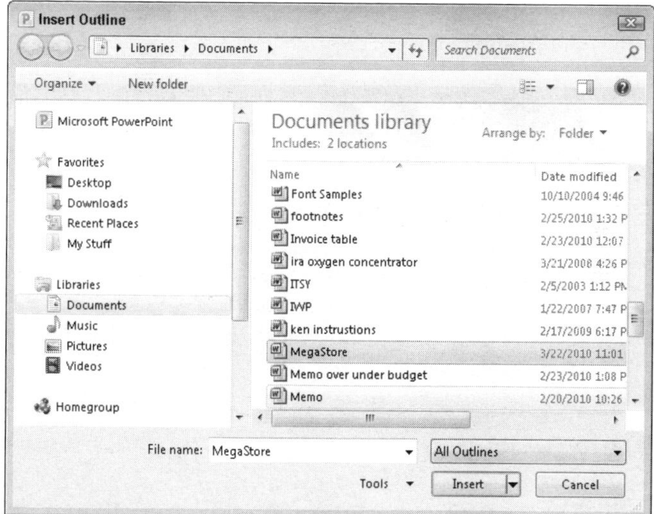

Figure 14-11

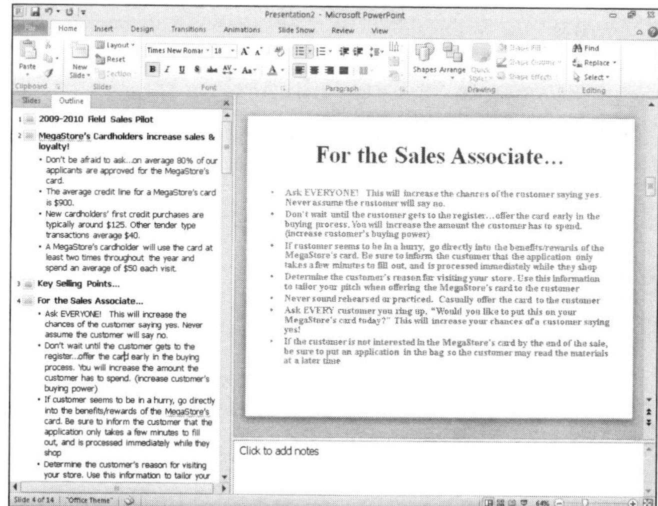

Figure 14-12

3. Click the slide preceding the slide you want to add in your presentation.

When you add new slides to a presentation, the new slide is added after the selected slide.

4. Choose Home➪Slides➪New Slide or press Ctrl+M (see Figure 14-13).
5. Choose the slide layout you want for the new slide.
6. Type text in either Slide mode or Outline mode for the title and bullet points.

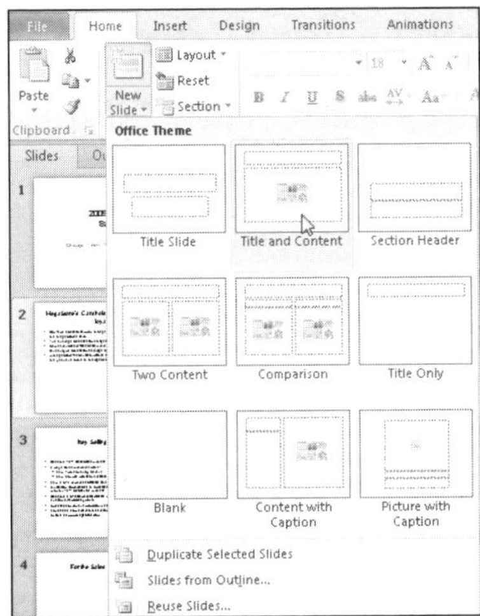

Figure 14-13

Delete a Slide

1. Open or create a presentation in PowerPoint.
2. From the slide thumbnail pane, click the Slides tab and select the slides you want to delete. Thick borders appear around the selected slides.

Alternatively, you can select a slide in the Slide Sorter view and press the Delete (Del) key. See Chapter 15 for information on the Slide Sorter view.

3. Perform one of the following actions:
   - Press the Delete key.
   - Right-click the unwanted slide and choose Delete Slide from the menu that appears (see Figure 14-14).

If you accidently delete the wrong slides, immediately press Ctrl+Z or click the Undo button on the Quick Access toolbar.

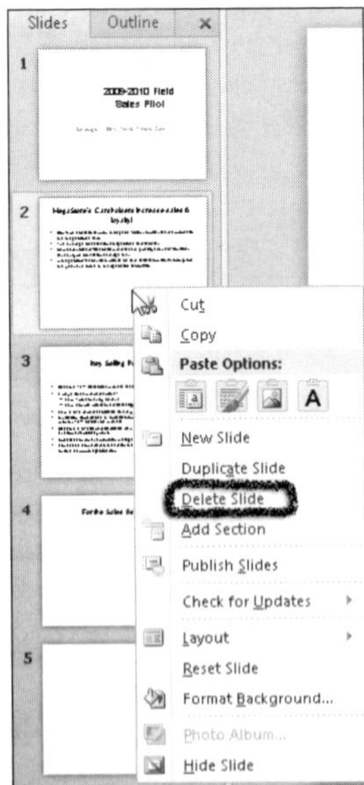

Figure 14-14

Editing a Presentation

After putting together the pieces of your PowerPoint presentation, you will most likely need to make some changes. Fortunately, PowerPoint provides a number of editing features that you can use to modify your presentation.

This chapter is about editing. Whether you want to edit the actual text on a slide, the text font, or even the slide layout, this chapter shows you how to accomplish those tasks. Discover how to give your slides additional pizzazz by adding clip art, pictures, sound files, and video files.

You'll also discover how to work in Slide Sorter view, where you can get a good overall look at your presentation by providing a thumbnail size view of each slide. In Slide Sorter view, you'll realize how easy it is to rearrange or delete slides.

Chapter 15

Get ready to . . .

Change a Slide Type

1. Open the PowerPoint presentation. From the slide thumbnail pane, click the Slides tab and select the slides that you want to modify.
2. Choose Home⇨Slides⇨Layout. The gallery of available slide layouts appears, as shown in Figure 15-1.
3. Choose the layout you want. The selected slides change, and objects are rearranged according to the new layout.

Depending on the layout you choose as well as the current view, you may see some new placeholders.

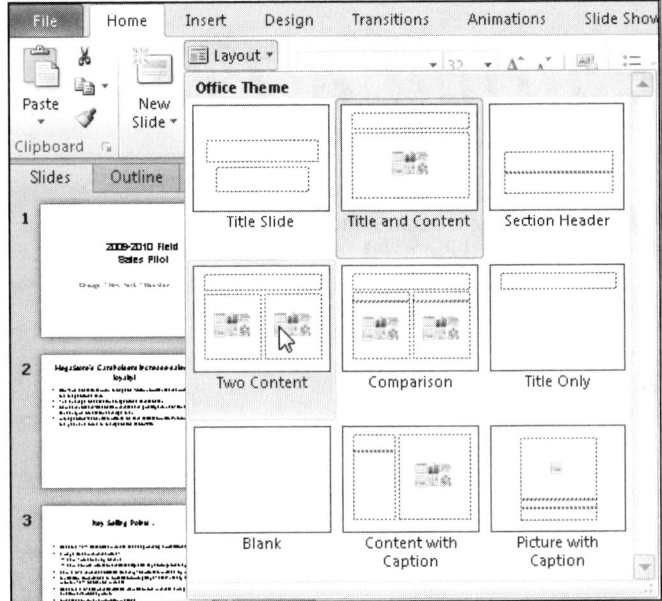

Figure 15-1

Copy Slides

1. Open a PowerPoint presentation.
2. From the slide thumbnail pane, click the Slides tab and select the slides you want to copy.
3. Choose Home⇨Clipboard⇨Copy or right-click the selected slide and choose Copy from the contextual menu that appears.
4. Either in the same presentation or a different presentation, from the slide thumbnail pane, click the Slides tab and select the slide preceding the position where you want the new slide.
5. Choose Home⇨Clipboard⇨Paste, or right-click the selected slide and choose Paste from the contextual menu that appears. PowerPoint copies the selected slides into the new location, as shown in Figure 15-2.

If you accidentally paste the slide into the wrong position, drag the slide to the correct position in the slide thumbnail pane or in Slide Sorter view.

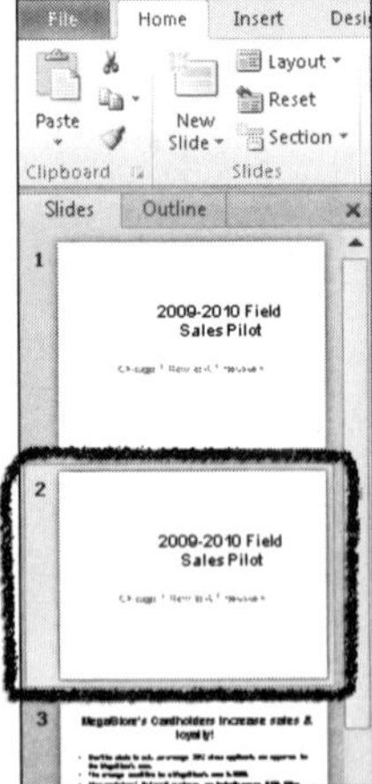

Figure 15-2

Add Text to a Slide

1. On a PowerPoint presentation slide, click in a text box placeholder. A box indicating the object boundary appears, along with a blinking insertion point.
2. Type the desired text. As shown in Figure 15-3, text appears as you type.
3. Click outside the text box.
4. If you're using a Title and Content layout, you can click the box under the title and begin typing text. PowerPoint places bullet points next to the text. If you're using a Title Slide layout, clicking the next box adds a subtitle to the slide.

To create a second level of bullet points, press Tab to indent the text. Press Shift+Tab to return to the previous level.

Format the text font, size, or color by selecting the text, choosing Home⇨Font, and choosing new text options.

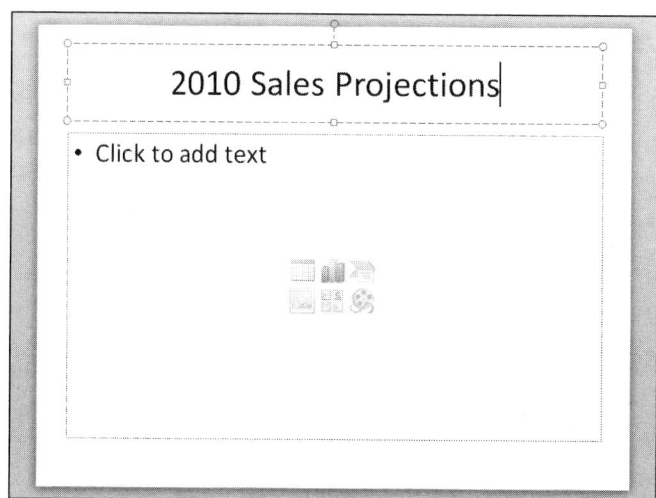

Figure 15-3

Edit Slide Text

1. From the slide thumbnail pane in an open PowerPoint presentation, click the Slides tab and select the slide you want to modify. The slide appears in the slide pane.
2. Click the cursor inside the text placeholder. A blinking cursor appears.
3. Drag the mouse across the text you want to edit. The selected text becomes highlighted. (See Figure 15-4.)
4. Type new text to replace the selected text.

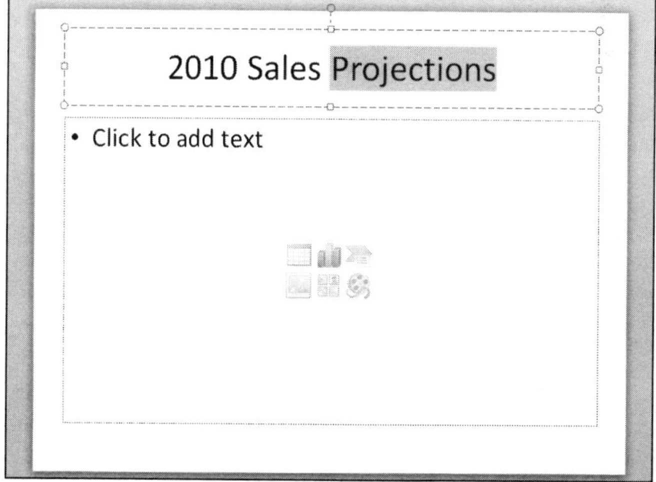

Figure 15-4

Move a Text Placeholder

1. From the slide thumbnail pane in an open PowerPoint presentation, click the Slides tab and select the slide you want to modify. The slide appears in the slide pane.
2. Click the slide placeholder containing the text you want to move. The placeholder has a border and eight handles around it.
3. Move the cursor to the placeholder border so that it changes from an I-beam to a black, four-headed arrow (see Figure 15-5). Do not place the cursor over one of the eight handles.
4. Drag the placeholder to a new position.

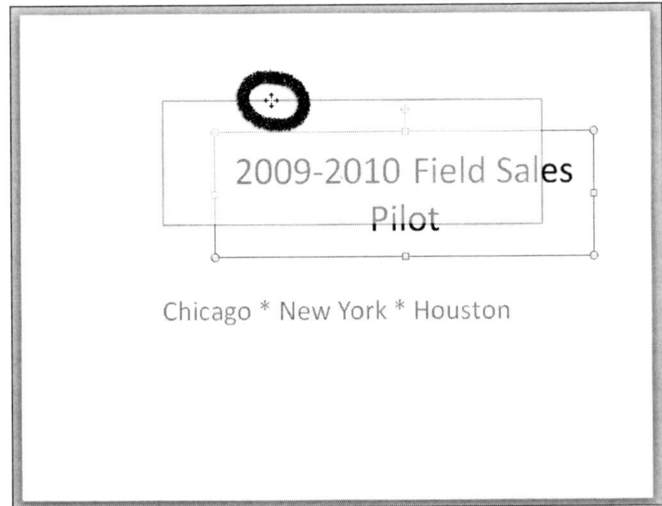

Figure 15-5

Resize a Text Placeholder

1. From the slide thumbnail pane in an open PowerPoint presentation, click the Slides tab and select the slide you want to modify. The slide appears in the Slide pane.
2. Click the slide placeholder containing the text you want to move. The placeholder has a border and eight handles around it.
3. Move the cursor over one of the placeholder handles. The mouse pointer changes from an I-beam to a white, double-headed arrow (see Figure 15-6).
4. Drag any one of the small circles on the corners or the four squares at the midpoint of each border in or out to make the placeholder box smaller or larger, respectively.
5. Release the mouse button when you finish resizing the text box.

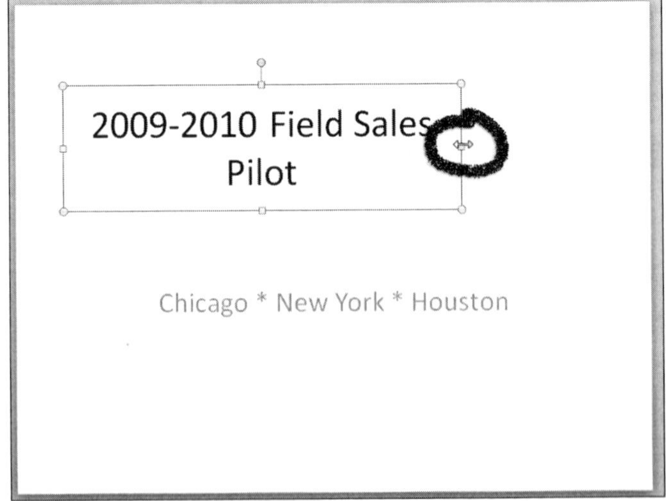

Figure 15-6

Format Text

1. From the slide thumbnail pane in an open PowerPoint presentation, click the Slides tab and select the slide you want to modify. The slide appears in the slide pane.

2. If you want to format only a portion of the text, drag across the text you want to modify to highlight the text. If you want to format the entire text box, click the border around the text box.

3. From the Font group on the Home tab, choose from the following:

   - *Font:* Click the down-arrow next to the font name to choose from a menu of fonts (see Figure 15-7).
   - *Font Size:* Click the down-arrow next to the font size to choose from a menu of font sizes.
   - *Increase or Decrease Font:* Click the larger A to increase the font size; click the smaller A to decrease the font size.
   - *Font Attributes:* Click the **B** for bold, ***I*** for Italics, **U** for Underline, **S** for Shadowing, or **abc** for Strikethrough.
   - *Character Spacing:* Click this button to change the spacing between characters.
   - *Change Case:* Click this button to display a menu where you can change the selected text to Sentence case, lower case, UPPER CASE, Capitalize Each Word, and tOGGLE cASE.
   - *Font Color:* Click this option to select a color for the selected text (see Figure 15-8).

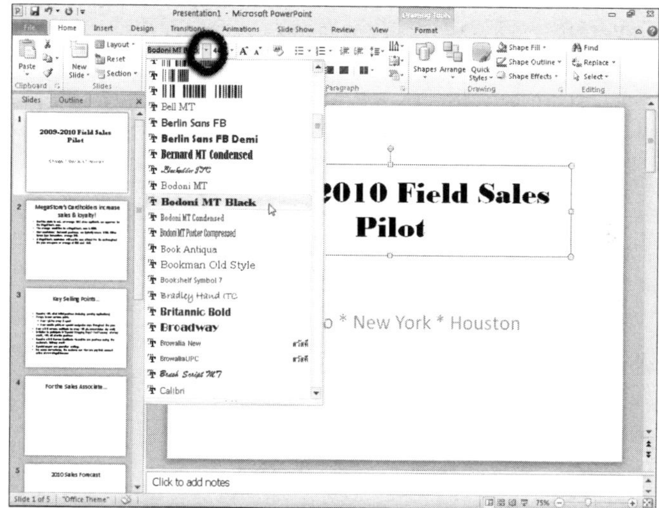

Figure 15-7

Figure 15-8

Organize Slides in the Slide Sorter

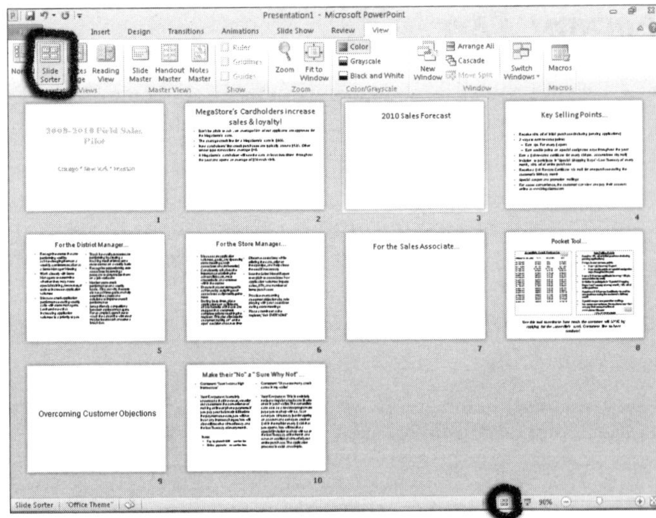

Figure 15-9

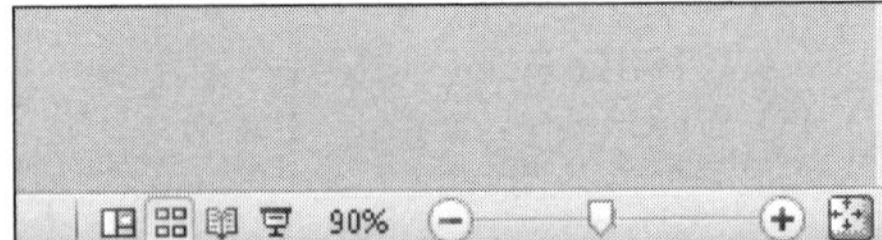

Figure 15-10

1. From an open PowerPoint presentation, choose View➪Presentation Views➪Slide Sorter, or click the Slide Sorter view button (located with the View icons on the status bar). PowerPoint changes the view to Slide Sorter view, where you can see thumbnail representations of all slides in the presentation. Figure 15-9 illustrates a presentation in Slide Sorter view.

2. Click the zoom controls at the bottom of the window (see Figure 15-10). Use the plus (+) icon to make the slides larger in the window, or use the minus (–) icon to make the slides smaller in the window.

If your mouse has a scroll wheel, hold down the Ctrl key and roll the scroll wheel forward to enlarge the view, or roll the scroll wheel backward to shrink the view.

3. Drag a slide either between two slides or to the far left or right of a slide in a row. A vertical line appears. When you release the mouse button, the selected slide drops between the slides on either side of the vertical line.

You can't edit individual slides while in Slide Sorter view.

4. From Slide Sorter view, double-click a slide, click the Normal view icon in the zoom control area, or choose View➪Presentation Views➪Normal. PowerPoint displays the slide in Normal view, where you can edit the slide contents.

Insert Clip Art

1. From the slide thumbnail pane in an open PowerPoint presentation, click the Slides tab and select the slide you want to modify. The slide appears in the slide pane.

2. In a slide content placeholder, click the Clip Art icon (see Figure 15-11). (Hover your mouse over the icons to see the tooltip for the Clip Art icon.) The Clip Art task pane appears on the right.

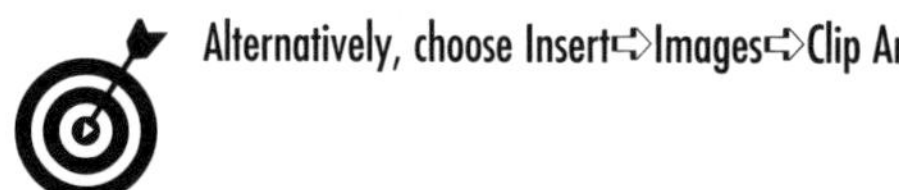

Alternatively, choose Insert➪Images➪Clip Art.

3. In the Search For box, enter a keyword that describes the art you're looking for.

In the Search For box, if you type two words — such as *yellow leaves* — PowerPoint searches for clips using the keywords *yellow* and *leaves.* If you type two words enclosed by quotation marks — "yellow leaves" — the program searches for clips that contain the phrase *yellow leaves.* If you type two words separated by a comma — yellow, leaves — PowerPoint searches for art with the keywords *yellow* or *leaves.*

4. In the Results Should Be box, click the down-arrow and select your desired media type. Choose from Illustrations (clip art drawings), Photographs, Audio, and Video.

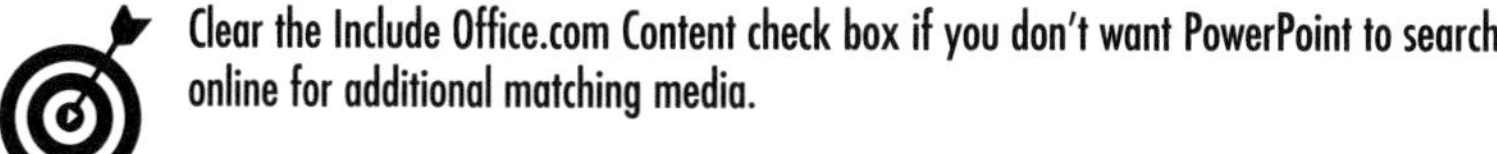

Clear the Include Office.com Content check box if you don't want PowerPoint to search online for additional matching media.

5. Click the Go button. The Clip Art pane displays media that matches your search criteria.

6. In the results panel, click the thumbnail you want. PowerPoint inserts it into your slide, as shown in Figure 15-12.

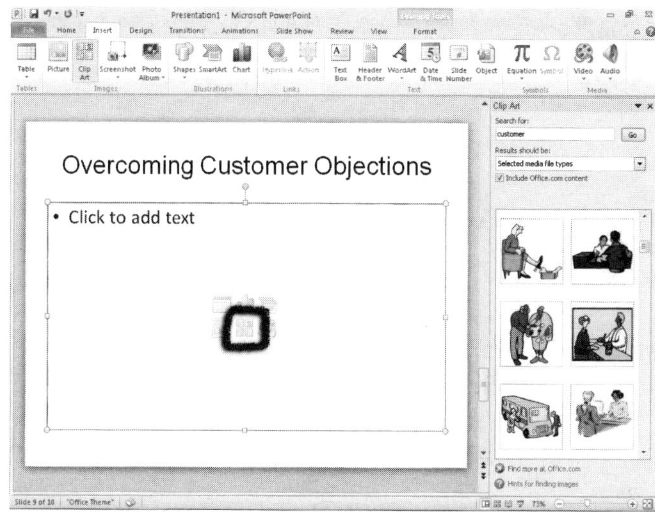

Figure 15-11

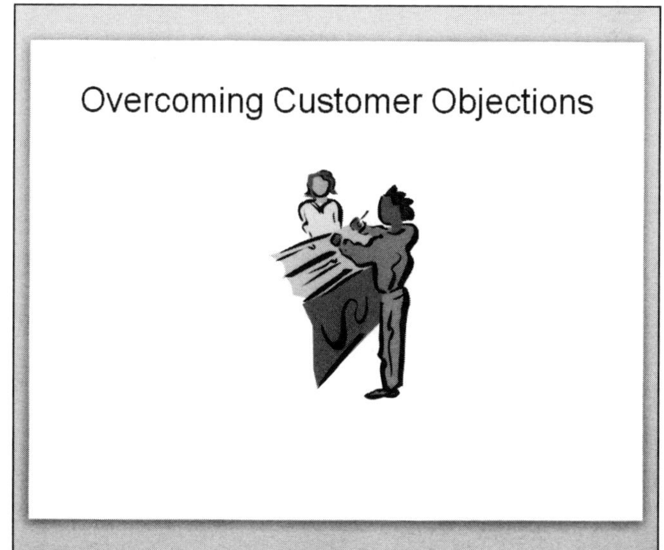

Figure 15-12

To delete the clip art from the slide, click the image and press Delete.

7. Click the Clip Art task pane Close button (X).

Insert a Saved Picture

1. From the slide thumbnail pane in an open PowerPoint presentation, click the Slides tab, and select the slide you want to modify. The slide appears in the slide pane.
2. In a slide content placeholder, click the Insert Picture from File icon. Hover your mouse over the icons to determine which icon is the Insert Picture from File icon. The Insert Picture dialog box seen in Figure 15-13 opens.

Alternatively, choose Insert⇨Images⇨Picture. Using this option may make the image fill the entire slide.

3. From the Folders or the Favorite Links sections, navigate your hard drive and locate the folder where you have a saved picture. Pictures can include digital photographs or other graphic images, such as a company logo.
4. Click the picture you want. To add multiple pictures at the same time, hold down Ctrl while you click the images.
5. Click the Open button. PowerPoint inserts the image onto the slide, as shown in Figure 15-14.

See Chapter 16 for information on cropping, resizing, rotating, and flipping pictures and other artwork.

To delete the picture, click the image and press Delete.

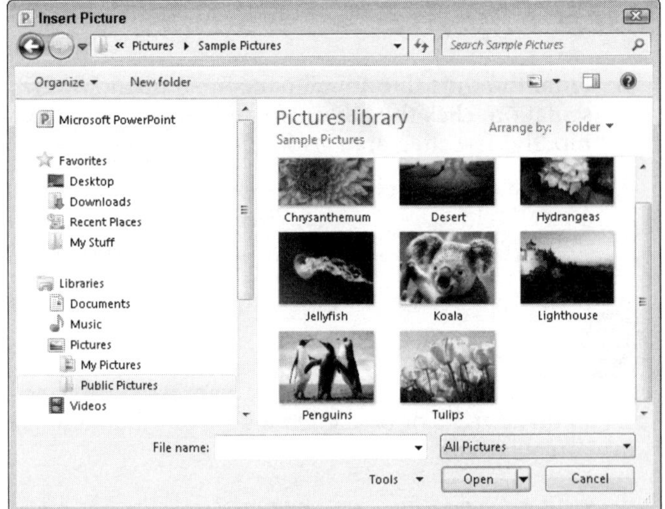

Figure 15-13

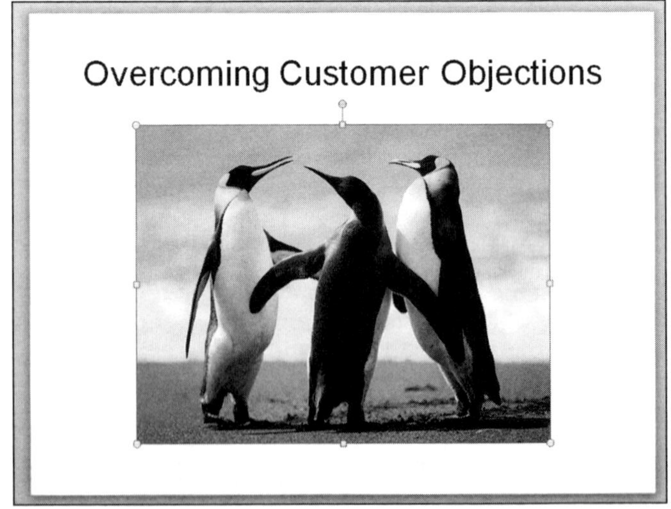

Figure 15-14

Insert a Sound

1. From the slide thumbnail pane in an open PowerPoint presentation, click the Slides tab and select the slide you want to modify. The slide appears in the slide pane.
2. Choose Insert⇨Media and click the arrow on the Audio button.
3. Choose Audio from File. The Insert Audio dialog box opens.

If you want a sound file from Clip Art, see the earlier task on inserting clip art which also offers video and sound files.

4. From the Folders or the Favorite Links sections, navigate your hard drive and locate the folder where you have a saved audio file.
5. Select the sound file you want and then click the Insert button. A sound icon appears on the slide, as shown in Figure 15-15. Also notice the two new Audio Tools tabs that appear on the Ribbon.

To delete the sound file from the slide, click the sound icon and press Delete.

6. With the sound icon selected, click the Audio Tools Playback tab. A series of sound playback options appears (see Figure 15-16).
7. Select the options you want for the sound file, including volume, whether to loop (repeat) the sound file, when to play the sound file, and other editing options.
8. Choose Audio Tools⇨Playback⇨Preview⇨Play to listen to the sound file.

You can also play or pause the sound file from the toolbar that appears under the sound icon.

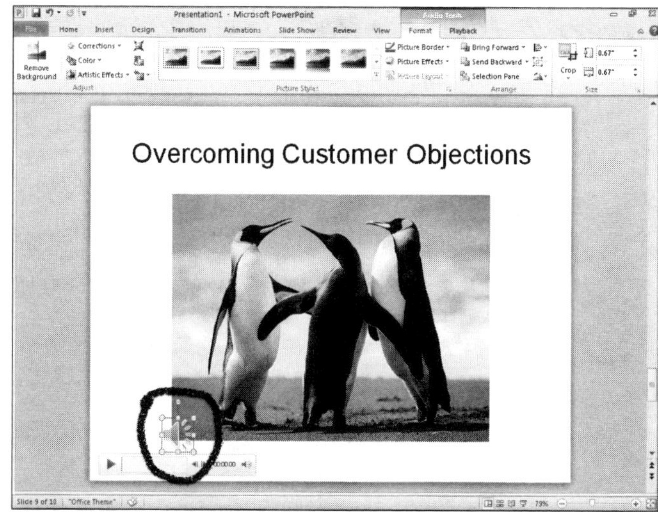

Figure 15-15

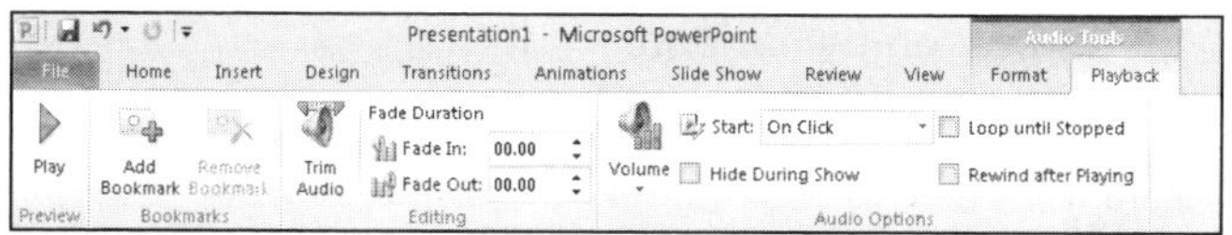

Figure 15-16

Insert a Video File

1. From the slide thumbnail pane in an open PowerPoint presentation, click the Slides tab, and select the slide you want to modify. The slide appears in the slide pane.
2. In a slide content placeholder, click the Insert Media Clip icon (see Figure 15-17). The Insert Video window appears.

You can also choose Insert➪Media, click the arrow on the Video button, and choose Video from File.

3. From the Folders or the Favorite Links sections, navigate your hard drive and locate the folder where you have a saved video file.
4. Select the video file you want and then click Insert. The first frame of the movie (which is probably blank) appears on your slide, along with the two new Video Tools tabs that appear on the Ribbon.

To delete the video file from the slide, click the video icon and press Delete.

5. With the video icon selected, click the Video Tools Playback tab. A series of video playback options appears (see Figure 15-18).
6. Select the options you want for the video file, including volume, whether to play the movie in a full screen or a frame, whether to loop (repeat) the movie, when to play the movie, and other editing options.
7. Choose Video Tools➪Playback➪Preview➪Play to play the video.

You can also play or pause the video file from the toolbar that appears under the video icon.

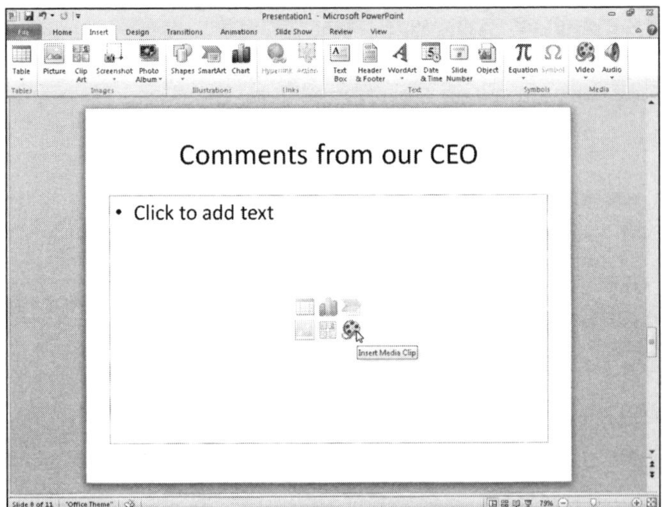

Figure 15-17

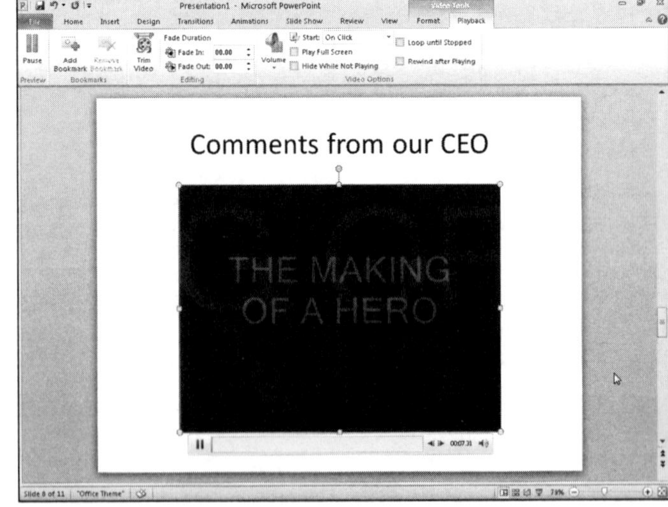

Figure 15-18

Working with Objects

Chapter 16

Everything you see and touch has a shape. In the PowerPoint world, shapes are 2-D or 3-D and are the result of a geometric design. PowerPoint calls them *objects*. You can add shapes to a slide to provide more information and better illustrate the slide topic. In Chapter 15, you discover how to insert pictures in a slide, and in Chapter 17, you discover how to insert charts. Charts and picture are also objects.

However, after you create one or more shapes, you'll probably want to manipulate them more by changing their appearance, size, or position on the slide. That's what this chapter is about: creating and manipulating shapes and other objects.

Here, you'll discover how to

- Crop, resize, rotate, and flip pictures.
- Adjust picture clarity.
- Draw shapes and lines.
- Change object color, object style, and line styles.
- Manipulate multiple objects.

Get ready to . . .

Crop a Picture

1. Open the PowerPoint presentation. From the slide thumbnail pane, click the Slides tab and select the slide containing the picture that you want to modify.
2. Select the picture you want to crop. The picture has handles around it, and the Picture Tools Format tab appears on the Ribbon.

Cropping is one of the easiest things you can do to improve the composition of your picture and hone in on the focal point.

3. Choose Picture Tools⇨Format⇨Size⇨Crop. Cropping handles appear around the image corners and middle edges.
4. Drag one of the cropping handles inward to indicate the portion of the image you want removed. To crop equally on two sizes simultaneously, press the Ctrl key while you drag a side, top, or bottom center crop handle. To crop equally on all four sides simultaneously, press the Ctrl key while you drag a corner handle. A shaded area represents the area being cropped (see Figure 16-1).
5. Click the Crop tool again or click anywhere outside of the picture to finalize the crop. The picture appears cropped in its new size (see Figure 16-2).

If you crop too much off the image, you can restore a cropped area by dragging the crop handle outward from your picture.

To restore a picture to its original size, click the picture and choose Picture Tools⇨Format⇨Adjust⇨Reset Picture. (It's the last icon in the group.)

Figure 16-1

Figure 16-2

Resize a Picture

1. Open the PowerPoint presentation. From the slide thumbnail pane, click the Slides tab and select the slide containing the picture that you want to modify.
2. Select the picture you want to resize. The picture has handles around it.
3. Position your mouse pointer over one of the handles. The mouse pointer turns into a white, double-headed arrow.
4. Drag a corner handle to resize both the width and height of the image; drag a top or bottom middle handle to resize the height of the image only, or drag the left or right middle handle to resize the width of the image only. To keep the center of the object in the same place, press the Ctrl key while you drag. As you drag, you see both the original image size and the new image size (see Figure 16-3).
5. Release the mouse button when the image is the desired size.

To precisely resize the image, choose Picture Tools⇨Format⇨Size and enter the desired image height and width.

Figure 16-3

Rotate a Picture

1. Open the PowerPoint presentation. From the slide thumbnail pane, click the Slides tab and select the slide containing the picture that you want to modify.
2. Select the picture you want to rotate. The picture has handles around it. You also see a green rotation handle at the top of the image.
3. Drag the green rotation handle until the image is the angle you want it, and then release the mouse button (see Figure 16-4).

Figure 16-4

Flip a Picture

1. Open the PowerPoint presentation. From the slide thumbnail pane, click the Slides tab. Select the slide and then the picture that you want to modify.
2. Choose Picture Tools⇨Format⇨Arrange⇨Rotate. A menu appears.
3. Choose Flip Vertical or Flip Horizontal, depending on how you want your image. In Figure 16-5, the koala was originally facing left, but after flipping horizontally, is now facing right.

If you're flipping an object other than a picture — say, a shape or a Clip Art object — choose Drawing Tools⇨Format⇨Rotate.

Figure 16-5

Adjust Picture Brightness and Contrast

1. Open the PowerPoint presentation. From the slide thumbnail pane, click the Slides tab. Select the slide and then the picture that you want to modify.
2. Choose Picture Tools⇨Format⇨Adjust⇨Corrections. A gallery of options appears, as shown in Figure 16-6.
3. As you hover your mouse over a gallery choice, the Live Preview feature allows you to see the picture with the brightness and contrast changes. Select the option you want.

To adjust the picture's color tone and saturation, choose Picture Tools⇨Format⇨Adjust⇨Color and choose from the options displayed.

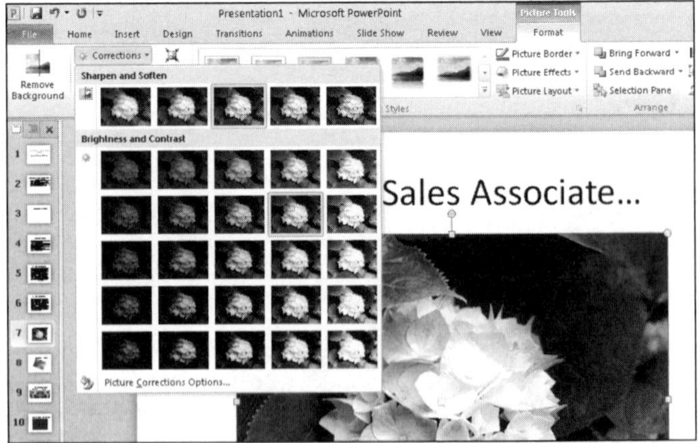

Figure 16-6

Add Transparency to an Object

1. Open the PowerPoint presentation. From the slide thumbnail pane, click the Slides tab. Select the slide and then the object that you want to modify.
2. Choose Drawing Tools (or Picture Tools)⇨Format⇨Adjust⇨Color⇨Set Transparent Color. The mouse pointer becomes a white arrow with another arrow on the tip of it.
3. On the object, click the color that you want to make transparent. That area becomes transparent, as shown in the before-and-after image in Figure 16-7.

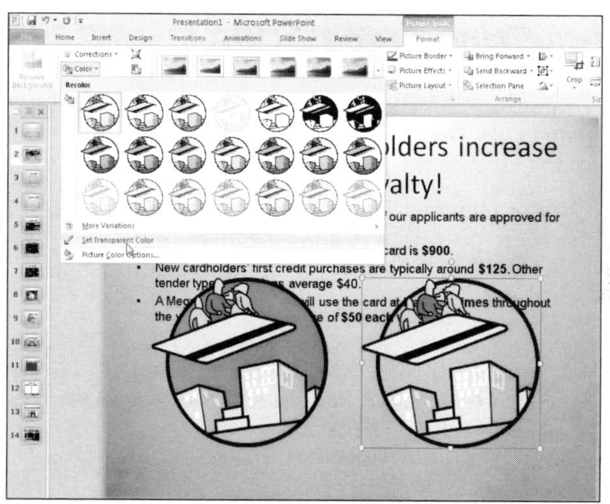

Figure 16-7

Draw Shapes

1. Open the PowerPoint presentation. From the slide thumbnail pane, click the Slides tab. Select the slide on which you want to draw a shape.
2. Choose Insert⇨Illustrations⇨Shapes. A gallery of shapes appears, as shown in Figure 16-8. Hover your mouse over any shape to see a tooltip describing the shape.
3. Click the shape you want to draw. The mouse pointer becomes a black cross.

When drawing a box or circle, hold down the Shift key while drawing the shape to constrain the shape into a perfect square or perfect circle. When drawing lines, holding the Shift key draws a perfectly straight line.

4. Drag on the slide to create the shape. When you release the mouse button, the shape appears on the slide.

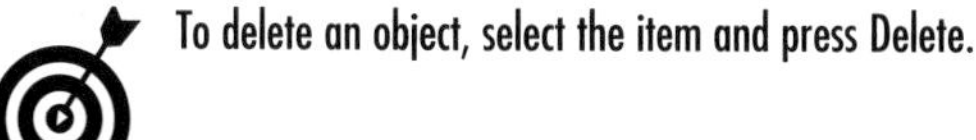

To delete an object, select the item and press Delete.

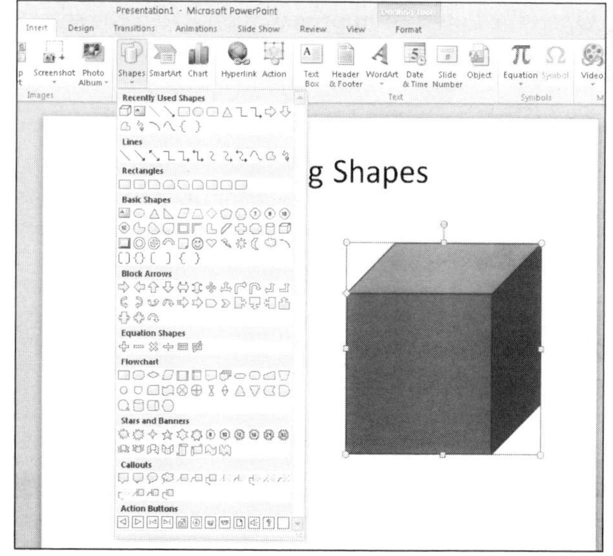

Figure 16-8

Change the Shape Style

1. Open the PowerPoint presentation. From the slide thumbnail pane, click the Slides tab. Select the slide and then click the shape you want to modify.
2. Choose Drawing Tools➪Format➪Shape Styles and then click the More button to display a gallery of styles, as shown in Figure 16-9.
3. Choose the style you want.

You can also change the shape fill by choosing Drawing Tools➪Format➪Shape Styles➪Shape Fill. From the resulting menu, you can also choose Pictures, Gradients, or Textures for the shape.

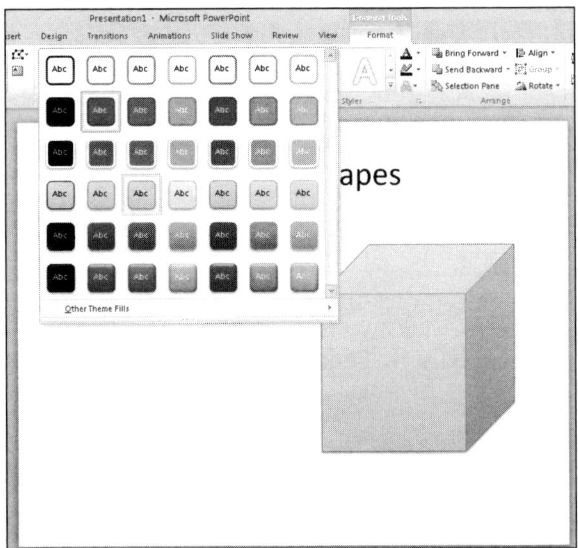

Figure 16-9

Change Line Color

1. Open the PowerPoint presentation. From the slide thumbnail pane, click the Slides tab. Select the slide and then click the shape or line you want to modify.
2. Choose Drawing Tools➪Format➪Shape Styles➪Shape Outline. A color palette appears (see Figure 16-10).
3. Select the color you want for your line or as the outline of your shape object.

To remove an outline from a shape, choose Drawing Tools➪Format➪Shape Styles➪Shape Outline➪No Outline.

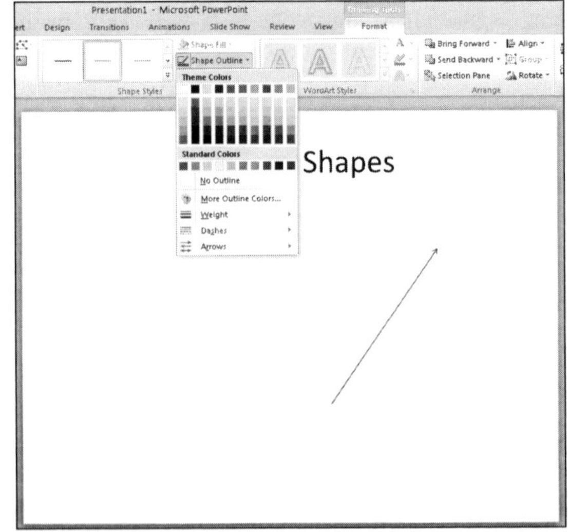

Figure 16-10

Change Line Style

1. Open the PowerPoint presentation. From the slide thumbnail pane, click the Slides tab. Select the slide and then click the shape or line you want to modify.
2. Choose Drawing Tools➪Format➪Shape Styles➪Shape Outline➪Weight. From the fly-out menu that appears, choose a line thickness.
3. Choose Drawing Tools➪Format➪Shape Styles➪Shape Outline➪Dashes. From the fly-out menu that appears, choose a line style (see Figure 16-11).
4. Choose Drawing Tools➪Format➪Shape Styles➪Shape Outline➪Arrows. From the fly-out menu that appears, choose an arrow head style.

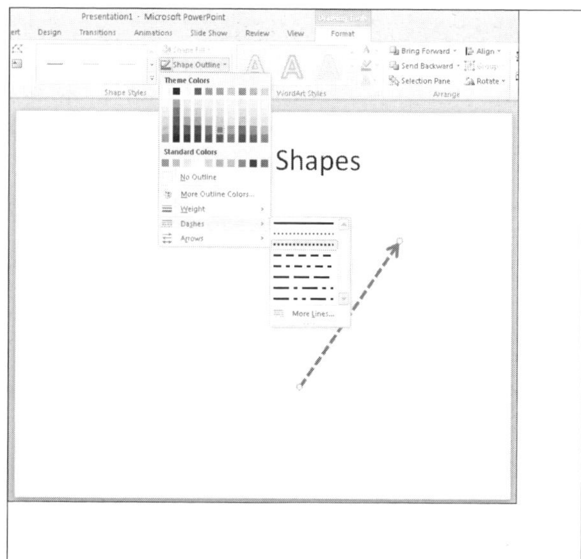

Figure 16-11

Move Objects

1. Open the PowerPoint presentation. From the slide thumbnail pane, click the Slides tab. Select the slide and then click the shape or line you want to move. The object has a border and eight handles around it; however, if the object is a line, it will have only two handles around it and no border.
2. Move the cursor over any place except over a handle, on the line or shape. The cursor becomes a four-headed black arrow; then click and drag the object to a new location (see Figure 16-12).
3. To nudge a line or shape horizontally or vertically, press an arrow key to move the object in the direction of the arrow key.

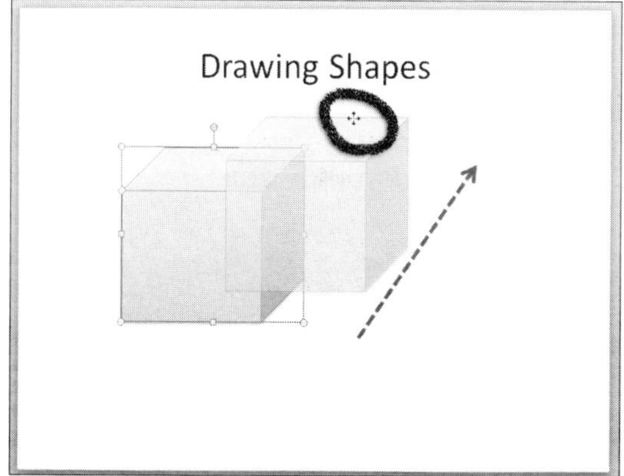

Figure 16-12

Stack Objects

1. Open the PowerPoint presentation. From the slide thumbnail pane, click the Slides tab. Select the slide and then select one of the overlapping objects that you want to reorder.
2. Choose Drawing (or Picture) Tools➪Format➪Drawing➪Arrange and choose one of the two options:
   - Click the Bring Forward arrow. Choose *Bring to Front* to place the selected object in front of all objects, or choose *Bring Forward* to place the selected object up one object level. In Figure 16-13, on the left, you see the arrow — originally in the middle of the object stack — and on the right as it is moved to the top of the stack.
   - Click the Send Backward arrow. Choose *Send to Back* to place the selected object behind all objects, or choose *Send Backward* to place the selected object down one object level

Align Objects

1. Open the PowerPoint presentation. From the slide thumbnail pane, click the Slides tab. Select the slide and then select at least two objects that you want to align.

Hold down the Ctrl key to select multiple objects.

2. Choose Drawing Tools (or Picture Tools)➪Format➪Arrange➪Align. A menu of options appears.
3. Select the desired alignment option. If you select Align Top, the objects align at the position of the highest object in the selection. If you select Align Left, the objects align at the position of the leftmost object in the selection. If you want two object aligned directly centered with each other, align them twice: once with Align Center and then again with Align Middle (see Figure 16-14).

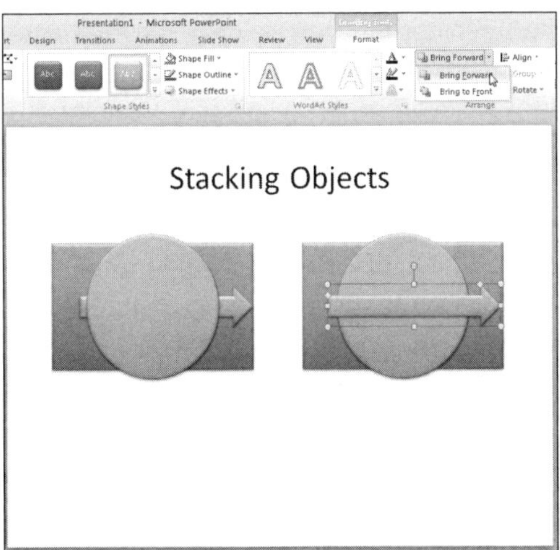

Figure 16-13

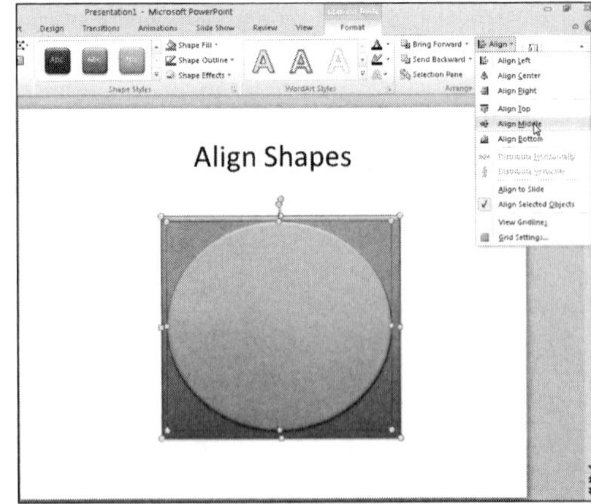

Figure 16-14

Distribute Objects

1. Open the PowerPoint presentation. From the slide thumbnail pane, click the Slides tab. Select the slide and then select at least three objects that you want to distribute the space between.
2. Choose Drawing Tools (or Picture Tools)➪Format➪Arrange➪Align. A menu of options appears.
3. Select the desired distribution option. If you choose Distribute Horizontally, PowerPoint moves the objects so that the horizontal space is equal between the selected objects. If you choose Distribute Vertically, PowerPoint moves the objects so that the vertical space is equal between the selected objects (see Figure 16-15).

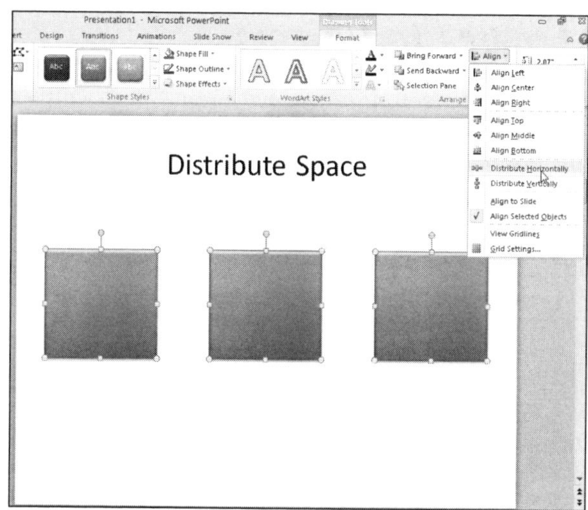

Figure 16-15

Group Objects

1. Open the PowerPoint presentation. From the slide thumbnail pane, click the Slides tab. Select the slide and then select at least two objects that you want to group. The objects can be pictures, shapes, clip art, or WordArt.
2. Choose Drawing Tools (or Picture Tools)➪Format➪Arrange➪Group. The selected objects are now grouped as a single object. Any changes you make to the object — such as resizing, moving, changing color, and so forth — apply to all elements in the group. In Figure 16-16, on the left, you see a rectangle, a circle, and an arrow as separate objects; on the right, you see the same objects grouped into a single item.

To separate the objects, choose Drawing Tools (or Picture Tools)➪Format➪Arrange➪Ungroup.

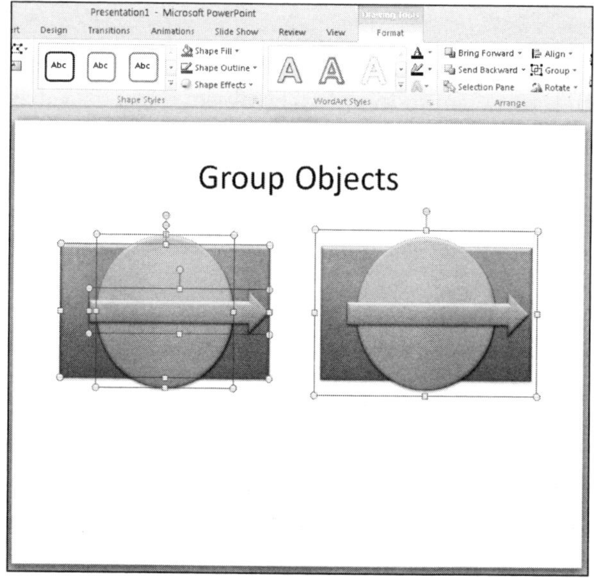

Figure 16-16

Add Frames to Objects

1. Open the PowerPoint presentation. From the slide thumbnail pane, click the Slides tab. Select the slide and then the object that you want to modify. The object could be a shape, text, clip art, picture, or WordArt object.
2. Choose Picture Tools (or Drawing Tools)➪Format➪Picture Styles.
3. Click the More button (the small button below the Picture Styles scroll bar). A gallery of styles appears, as shown in Figure 16-17.
4. As you hover your mouse over a gallery choice, the Live Preview feature allows you to see the object with a frame around it. Select the frame style you want.

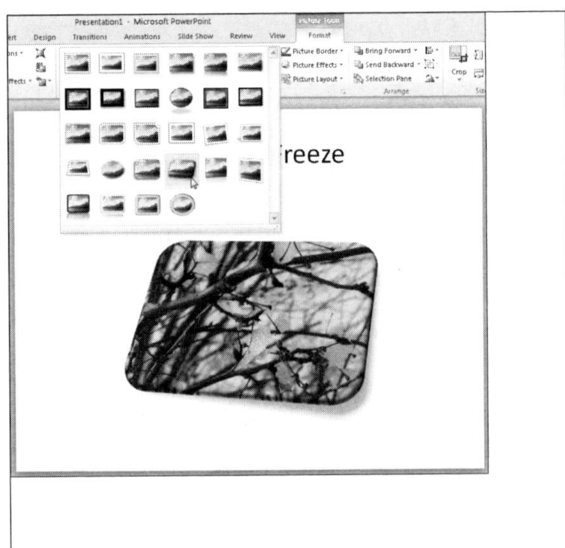

Figure 16-17

Add Effects to Objects

1. Open the PowerPoint presentation. From the slide thumbnail pane, click the Slides tab. Select the slide and then the object that you want to modify. The object could be a shape, text, clip art, picture, or WordArt object.
2. Choose Picture Tools (or Drawing Tools)➪Format➪Picture Styles➪Picture Effects. A menu of effects appears. The choices that appear depend on the object type that you're working with.
3. Choose the effect you want. A fly-out gallery appears, as shown in Figure 16-18.
4. As you hover your mouse over a gallery choice, the Live Preview feature allows you to see the object with the effect. Select the effect you want.

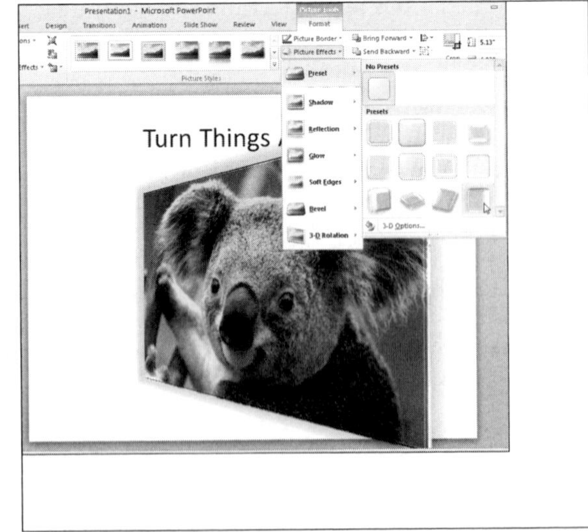

Figure 16-18

Adding Tables, Charts, and Diagrams

Data is often grasped more quickly and with more understanding and impact when presented in a simple, organized, and visual way. In PowerPoint, tables and charts are two ways to effectively present data — especially quantitative, complex, or tedious data. This chapter describes the powerful options within PowerPoint to work with charts and tables. You can create tables and charts from scratch within PowerPoint or import them from Microsoft Word or Excel.

Then, after you create your table or chart, use PowerPoint to change virtually all the elements, from modifying a table's font, columns and rows, borders, and shading to adding effects. And in addition to many types of charts to choose from, you can also use PowerPoint to alter almost all charts objects. For example, modify a chart's type, font, axis, grid, borders, shading, labels, legend, and effects.

Similarly, you can use SmartArt diagrams, which also offer a visual solution to presenting complicated data, especially data such as processes, workflow, relationships, and causes and effects.

Like tables and graphs, organization charts and diagrams provide important but complex and sometimes tedious information visually, making it easier and quicker for the viewer to comprehend. And with Microsoft Office 2010's SmartArt feature, creating these charts and diagrams has never been easier. This chapter covers everything you need to know to create both effective and attractive org charts and diagrams.

Chapter 17

Get ready to . . .

Insert a Table

1. Open the PowerPoint presentation. From the slide thumbnail pane, click the Slides tab and select the slide on which you want to create a table.
2. Do one of the following to create a table:
   - In the slide content placeholder, click the Insert Table icon. From the Insert Table dialog box that appears, enter the number of columns and rows you want and then click OK.
   - Choose Insert➪Tables➪Table. From the drop-down palette that appears, move your mouse cursor to select your desired number of columns and rows for the table, as shown in Figure 17-1.
   - Choose Insert➪Tables➪Table➪ Insert Table. From the Insert Table dialog box that appears, enter the number of columns and rows you desire, and then click OK.

When you create a table, PowerPoint displays two additional Table Tools tabs. Use the Design tab options to change the appearance of the table, and use the Layout tab options when you want to change the table structure.

3. Click within a table cell and type your desired text, as shown in Figure 17-2. If you type to the end of the cell, the text automatically wraps to the next line. Press Enter to insert another line within a cell.

Press the up-arrow or down-arrow key to move up or down in a column. Press the left and right arrows to move side to side within the table. Press Tab to advance to the next cell to the right. If you're at the end of the row, you advance to the first cell in the next row.

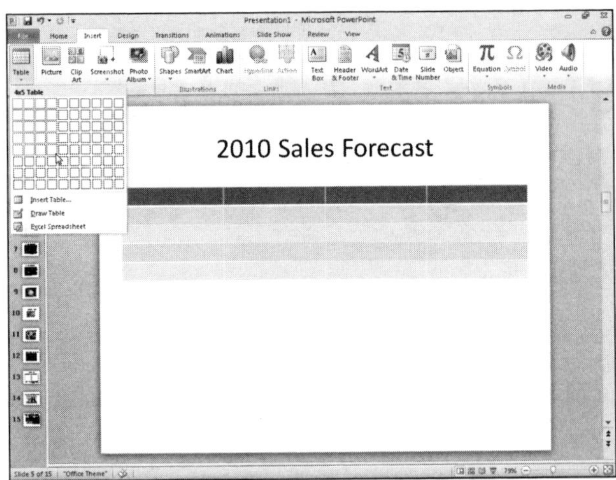

Figure 17-1

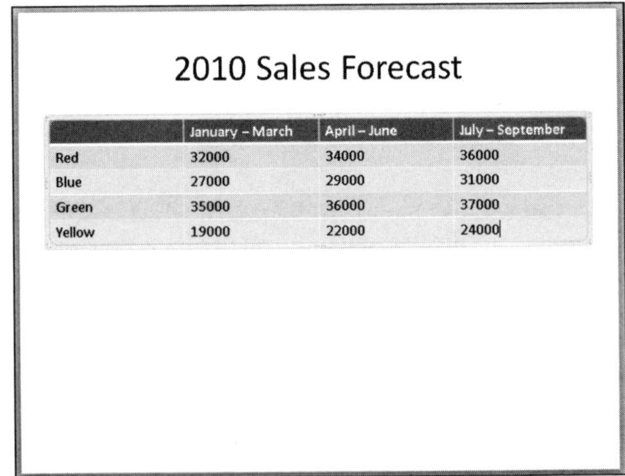

Figure 17-2

Copy a Table from Word or Excel

1. Open Word and select the desired table; in Excel, click the upper-left cell of the table and drag diagonally to select the cells you want. See Figure 17-3, which shows selected Excel data.
2. In Word or Excel, choose Home⇨Clipboard⇨Copy.

Alternatively, press Ctrl+C to copy the table.

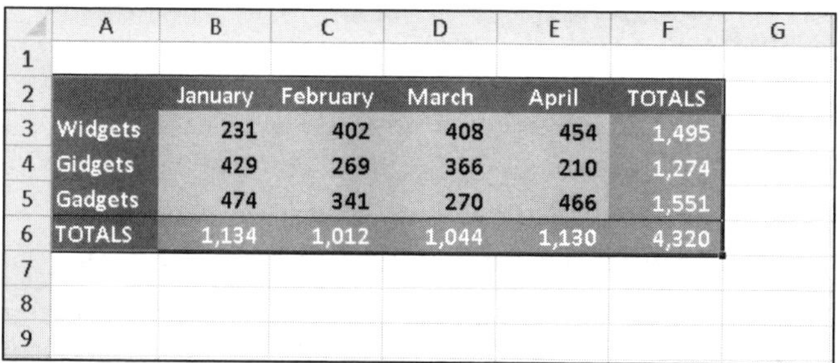

	A	B	C	D	E	F	G
1							
2		January	February	March	April	TOTALS	
3	Widgets	231	402	408	454	1,495	
4	Gidgets	429	269	366	210	1,274	
5	Gadgets	474	341	270	466	1,551	
6	TOTALS	1,134	1,012	1,044	1,130	4,320	
7							
8							
9							

Figure 17-3

3. Open the PowerPoint presentation. From the slide thumbnail pane, click the Slides tab and then select the slide on which you want to create a table.
4. Choose Home⇨Clipboard⇨Paste. The table appears on the slide, as shown in Figure 17-4.

Alternatively, press Ctrl+V to paste the table.

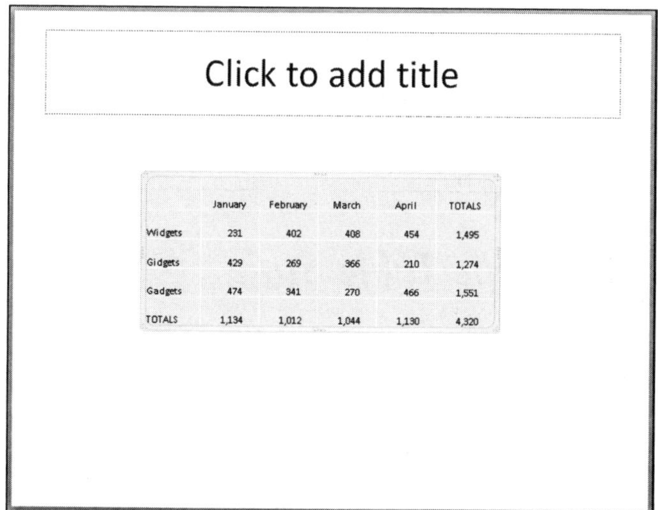

	January	February	March	April	TOTALS
Widgets	231	402	408	454	1,495
Gidgets	429	269	366	210	1,274
Gadgets	474	341	270	466	1,551
TOTALS	1,134	1,012	1,044	1,130	4,320

Figure 17-4

5. Resize the table by dragging a corner sizing handle; click and drag the table to reposition it.

Format Table Text

1. Open the PowerPoint presentation. From the slide thumbnail pane, click the Slides tab and then select the slide that contains your table.
2. Highlight your text within the cell, row, or column.
3. Click the Home tab. From the Font group, choose any desired font attributes, such as font name, font size, or special formatting, as shown in Figure 17-5.
4. To format text alignment within the table cells, click the Home tab. From the Paragraph group, click the left, right, or center alignment buttons.

You can also change alignment options by choosing Table Tools⇨Layout⇨Alignment and choosing an alignment option. From here, you can also align text to the top, bottom, or center of the cells.

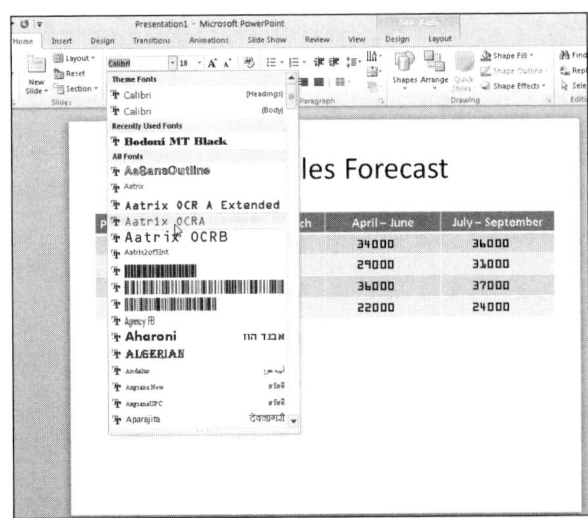

Figure 17-5

Format the Table Style

1. Open the PowerPoint presentation. From the slide thumbnail pane, click the Slides tab and then select the slide that contains your table.
2. Click the edge of the table to select the entire table. Note that if you click inside a cell, only the cell borders will be formatted.
3. Choose Table Tools⇨Design⇨Table Styles. Click the More button to display a gallery of table styles, as shown in Figure 17-6. Choose the table style you want.
4. (Optional) Choose Table Tools⇨Design⇨Table Style Options and select additional options for formatting, such as Banded Rows, a Header Row, and First Column.

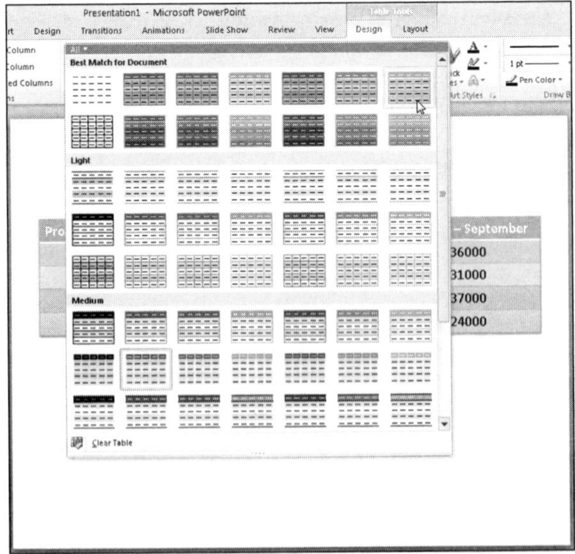

Figure 17-6

Modify Table Size

1. Open the PowerPoint presentation. From the slide thumbnail pane, click the Slides tab and then select the slide that contains your table.
2. To add a row, click in the row above or below where the new row is to be inserted. Choose Table Tools⇨Layout⇨Rows & Columns and then choose Insert Above or Insert Below.
3. To add a column, click in the column to the right or left where the new column is to be inserted. Choose Table Tools Layout⇨Rows & Columns and then choose Insert Left or Insert Right. See a newly inserted column in Figure 17-7.

You can also click the row or column next to where you want to insert a new one. Then right-click and choose Insert Rows Above, Insert Rows Below, Insert Columns to the Right, or Insert Columns to the Left from the contextual menu.

4. To change the height of any row, position the pointer on the lower border of the row you want modified. Your cursor changes to a double-headed arrow, as shown in Figure 17-8.
5. Click and drag the border up or down to increase or decrease the row height, respectively.
6. To change the width of any column, position the pointer on the right border of the column you want modified.
7. Click and drag the border to the left or right to increase or decrease the width, respectively.

To change the height of all rows evenly or the width of all columns evenly, click anywhere on the table to select it. Choose Table Tools⇨Layout⇨Cell Size and then click the Distribute Rows button or the Distribute Columns button. PowerPoint sets the table rows or columns to the same height, and the table content adjusts to fit.

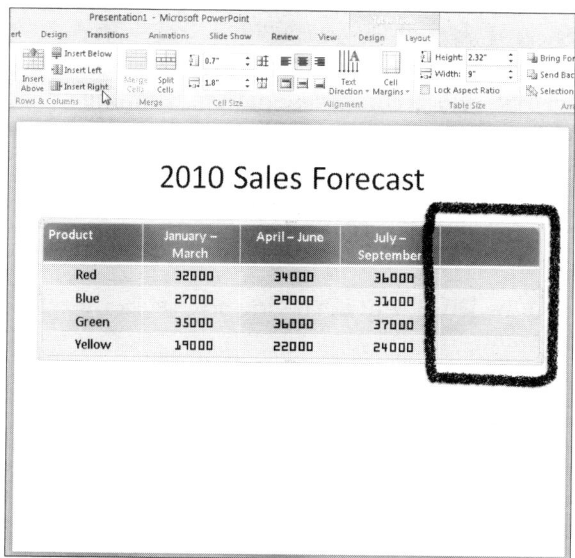

Figure 17-7

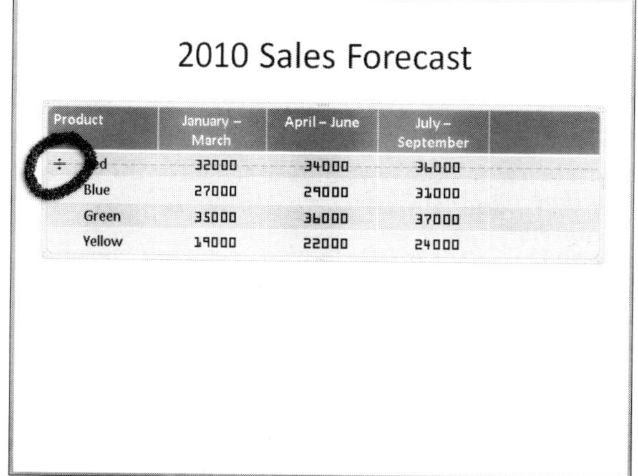

Figure 17-8

Insert a Chart

1. Open the PowerPoint presentation. From the slide thumbnail pane, click the Slides tab and then select the slide on which you want to create a chart.
2. In a slide content placeholder, click the Insert Chart icon or choose Insert➪Illustrations➪Chart. The Insert Chart dialog box appears.
3. From the left side of the dialog box, select the type of chart you want.
4. From the right side of the dialog box, select a chart subtype and then click OK.
5. Excel 2010 opens along the side of PowerPoint and displays a worksheet with sample data. Click in the Excel cells and enter your own data and labels, as shown in Figure 17-9. Your chart and data appear in the PowerPoint slide.
6. In Excel, click the File tab and choose Exit. Excel closes, and the PowerPoint window enlarges.

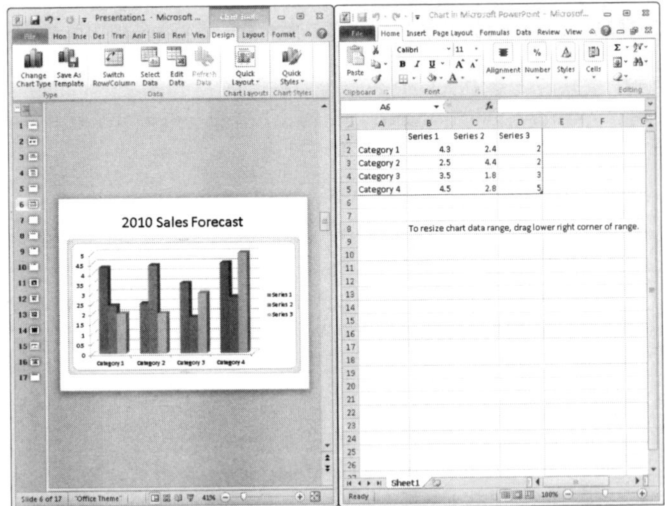

Figure 17-9

Change a Chart Type

1. Open the PowerPoint presentation. From the slide thumbnail pane, click the Slides tab and then select the slide and the chart you want to modify.
2. Choose Chart Tools➪Design➪Type➪Change Chart Type. The Change Chart Type dialog box appears (see Figure 17-10).
3. Select a chart type and a chart subtype and then click OK. Your modified chart appears.

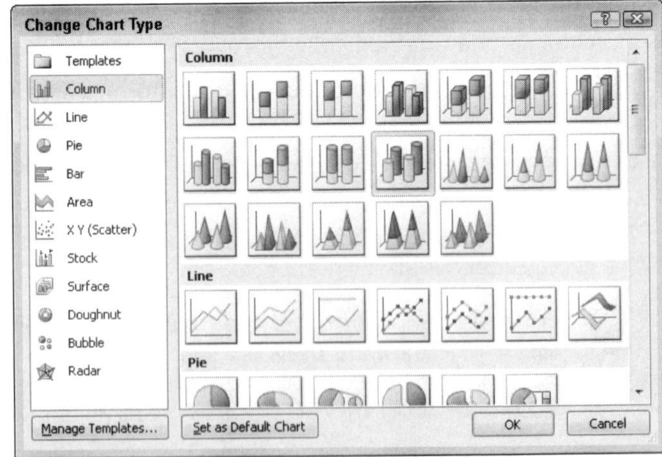

Figure 17-10

Edit Chart Data

1. Open the PowerPoint presentation. From the slide thumbnail pane, click the Slides tab. Select the slide and then the chart that you want to modify.
2. Choose Chart Tools➪Design➪Design➪Edit Data. The Excel spreadsheet reappears.
3. Modify the Excel data as desired. The PowerPoint chart immediately reflects the changes (see Figure 17-11).
4. In Excel, click the File tab and choose Exit. Excel closes, and the PowerPoint window enlarges.

Embed an Excel Chart

1. Open the PowerPoint presentation. From the slide thumbnail pane, click the Slides tab and select the slide where you want the chart.
2. Choose Insert➪Text➪Object. The Insert Object dialog box appears.
3. Select Create from File and then click the Browse button.
4. Locate the Excel file containing the chart and click OK. The Insert Object dialog box reappears (see Figure 17-12).
5. Select the Link option if you want the changes made to the Excel file to be reflected on the chart on the PowerPoint slide.
6. Click OK. The chart appears on the PowerPoint slide.

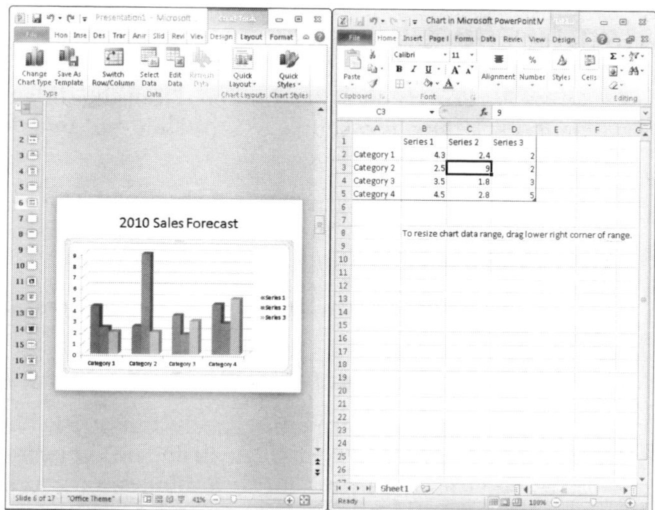

Figure 17-11

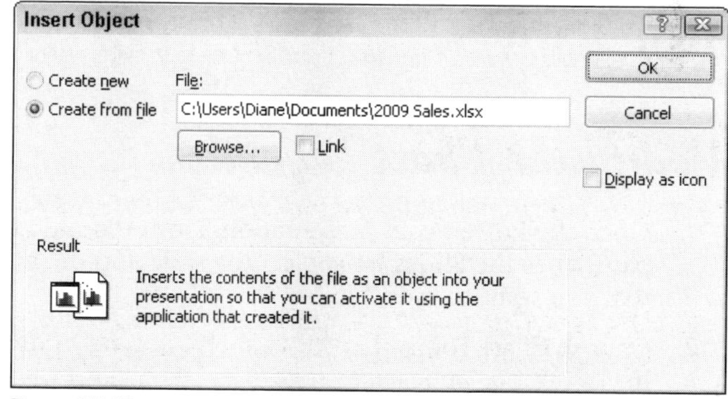

Figure 17-12

Modify the Chart Title

1. Open the PowerPoint presentation. From the slide thumbnail pane, click the Slides tab. Select the slide and then the chart that you want to modify.
2. Choose Chart Tools⇨Layout⇨Labels⇨Chart Title. A drop-down list of options appears. The thumbnails give you a visual representation of the legend's placement.
3. Select a chart title location. A placeholder title box appears on the chart.
4. Type the chart title text (see Figure 17-13).
5. Choose Chart Tools⇨Layout⇨Labels⇨Chart Title⇨More Title Options. The Format Chart Title dialog box appears. From here, you can modify other title attributes, such as Fill, Border Color, Border Styles, Shadow, and so on.

To add a title for a chart axis, choose Chart Tools⇨Layout⇨Labels⇨Axis Titles. Choose either Primary Horizontal Axis Title or Primary Vertical Axis Title. Then, from the submenu, choose your desired position of the horizontal or vertical axis title.

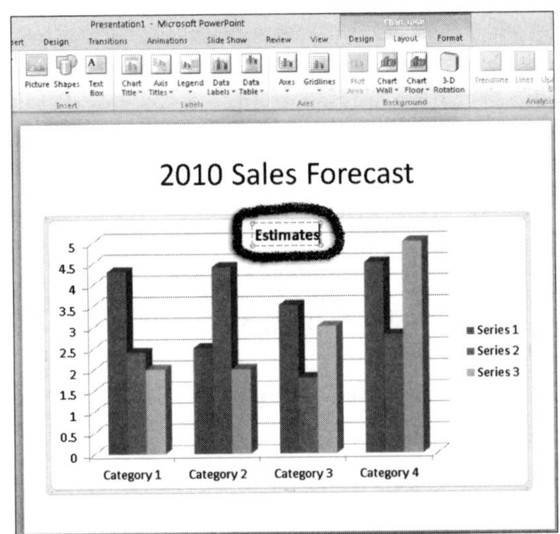

Figure 17-13

Modify the Chart Legend

1. Open the PowerPoint presentation. From the slide thumbnail pane, click the Slides tab. Select the slide and then the chart that you want to modify.
2. Choose Chart Tools⇨Layout⇨Labels⇨Legend. A drop-down list of options appears, as shown in Figure 17-14.
3. Choose the legend placement option you want.

To modify the legend appearance, choose Chart Tools⇨Layout⇨Labels⇨Legend⇨More Legend Options.

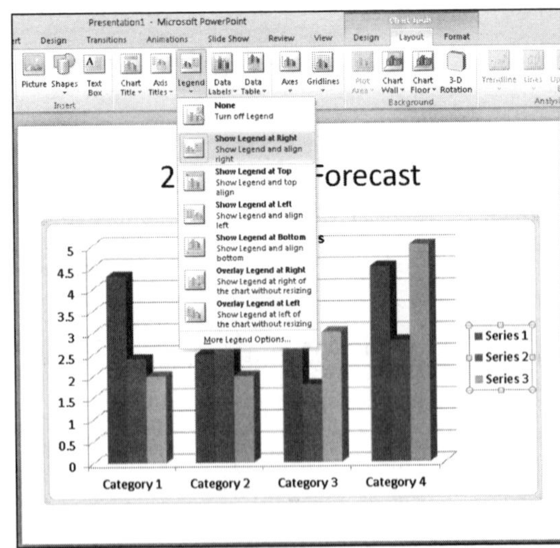

Figure 17-14

Create a SmartArt Diagram

1. Open the PowerPoint presentation. From the slide thumbnail pane, click the Slides tab and select the slide where you want the SmartArt.
2. From the content placeholder, click the Insert SmartArt graphic or choose Insert➪Illustrations➪SmartArt. The Choose a SmartArt Graphic dialog box appear, as shown in Figure 17-15.
3. Select the type of graphic you want from the list at the left; for example, if you want an organization chart, choose Hierarchy.
4. Choose your desired layout for that graphic type and then click OK. The graphic appears on the slide.
5. To add text to the graphic, click inside the text placeholder and type. If there is no text placeholder, simply click in the shape and type. You can also enter your text in the Text pane. If you don't see the Text pane, choose SmartArt Tools➪Design➪Create Graphic➪Text Pane.

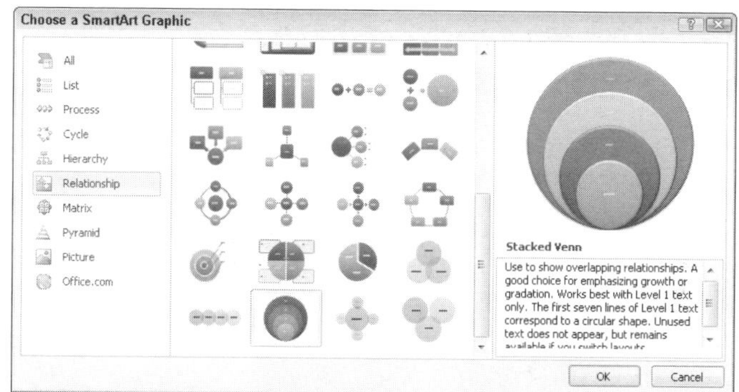

Figure 17-15

Modify a Diagram Style

1. Open the PowerPoint presentation. From the slide thumbnail pane, click the Slides tab. Select the slide and then the SmartArt graphic you want to modify.
2. Choose SmartArt Tools➪Design➪SmartArt Styles➪More button. You see a gallery of styles like the one in Figure 17-16.
3. Choose the style you want.

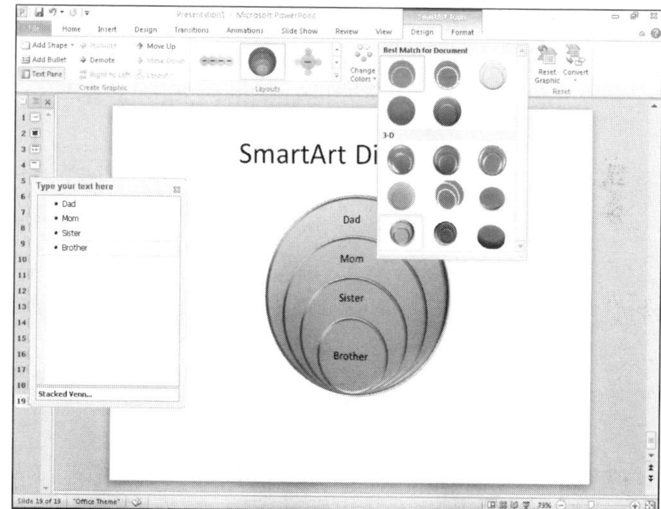

Figure 17-16

Format and Edit Diagrams

1. Open the PowerPoint presentation. From the slide thumbnail pane, click the Slides tab. Select the slide and then the SmartArt graphic you want to modify.
2. Select one or more individual shapes in the graphic, choose SmartArt Tools⇨Format, and do any or all of the following:
   - *Change a shape.* Choose Shapes⇨Change Shape and select a different shape from the drop-down palette shown in Figure 17-17.
   - *Resize a shape.* Choose Shapes⇨Larger (or Smaller) to size a shape. You can also place your mouse cursor over a selected shape corner and drag to a desired size.
   - *Change a shape's outline style.* Click the Shape Styles More button to display different shape outline styles. Select the style you want.
   - *Change a shape's color.* Choose Shapes Styles⇨Shape Fill and choose a different color for a shape. You can also choose a gradient or even a photo for a shape.
   - *Change a shape's line style.* Choose Shapes Styles⇨Shape Outline and choose a different color, line weight, or line style (for example, dashed) for a shape.
   - *Add a shape effect.* Choose Shapes Styles⇨Shape Effects and choose a different effect, such as a shadow, glow, or reflection for a shape (see Figure 17-18).
3. Click the Home tab. From the Font group, change the shape font size, font style, or text color.

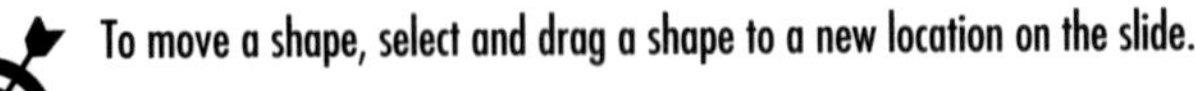
To move a shape, select and drag a shape to a new location on the slide.

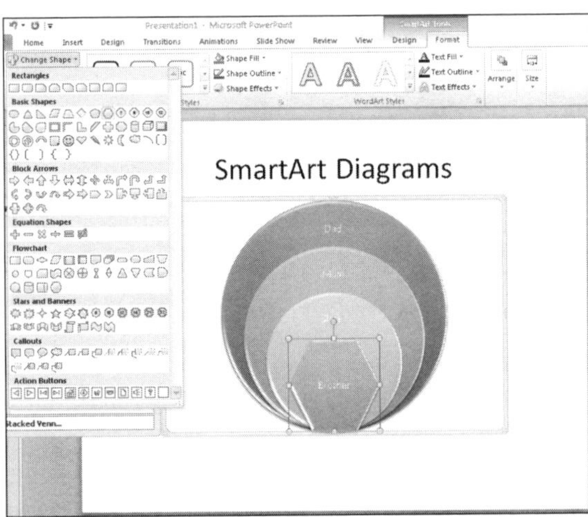

Figure 17-17

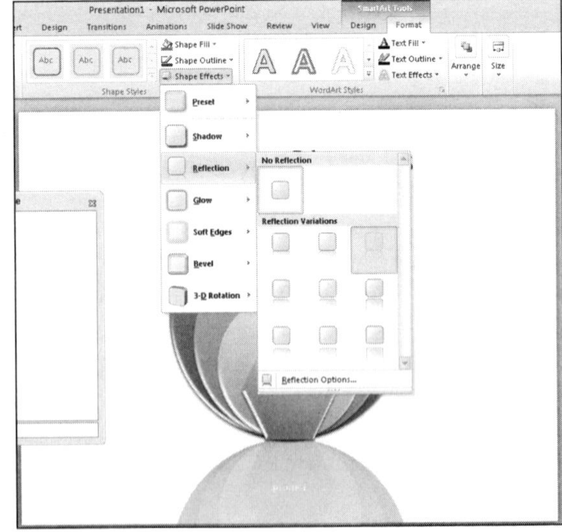

Figure 17-18

Add Shapes to a Diagram

1. Open the PowerPoint presentation. From the slide thumbnail pane, click the Slides tab. Select the slide and then the SmartArt graphic you want to modify.

2. Choose SmartArt Tools⇨Design⇨Create Graphic and open the Add Shape drop-down list. A menu of options appears. The options available depend on the type of SmartArt graphic you have.

3. Choose one of the following from the submenu (see Figure 17-19):

   - *Add Shape After:* Adds a shape at the same level after the existing shape.
   - *Add Shape Before:* Adds a shape at the same level before the existing shape.
   - *Add Shape Above:* Adds a shape one level above the existing shape.
   - *Add Shape Below:* Adds a shape one level below the existing shape.
   - *Add Assistant:* Adds a shape between the existing shape and any shapes below the existing shape. This option is available only with certain hierarchy graphics.

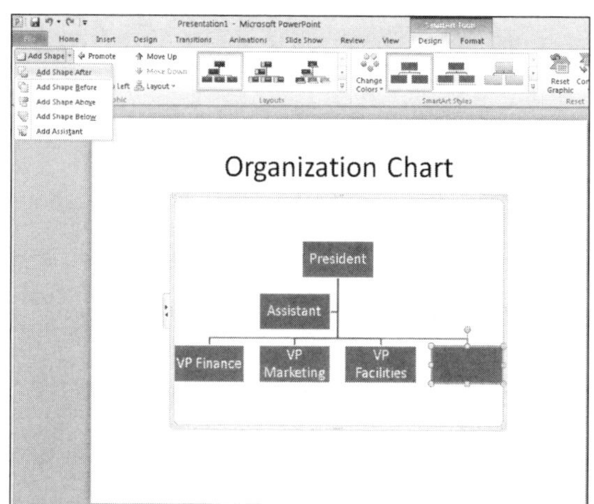

Figure 17-19

Delete Shapes from a Diagram

1. Open the PowerPoint presentation. From the slide thumbnail pane, click the Slides tab. Select the slide and then the SmartArt graphic you want to modify.

2. Select one or more shapes you want to remove and then press Delete (see Figure 17-20).

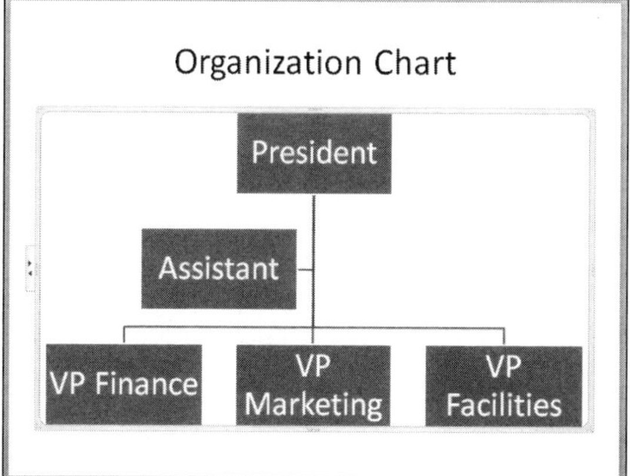

Figure 17-20

Change the Diagram Color Scheme

1. Open the PowerPoint presentation. From the slide thumbnail pane, click the Slides tab. Select the slide and then the SmartArt graphic you want to modify.
2. Choose SmartArt Tools⇨Design⇨SmartArt Styles⇨Change Colors. A gallery of colors appears, as shown in Figure 17-21.
3. Select the color option you want.

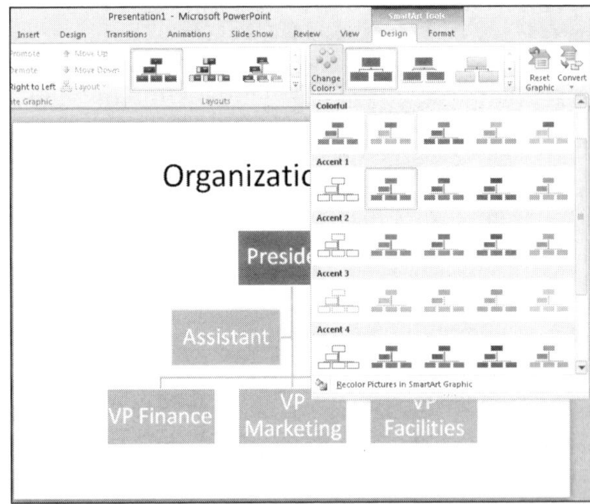

Figure 17-21

Change the Diagram Type

1. Open the PowerPoint presentation. From the slide thumbnail pane, click the Slides tab. Select the slide and then the SmartArt graphic you want to modify.
2. Choose SmartArt Tools⇨Design⇨Layouts and then click the More button. A gallery of SmartArt sub-layouts for your current SmartArt type appears (see Figure 17-22).
3. Select the new layout from the SmartArt gallery. Or, if you want a completely different SmartArt diagram type, click More Layouts. The Choose a SmartArt Graphic dialog box appears.
4. Select a different diagram type and subtype, and then click OK. After converting to another type, you might have to rearrange the elements in your diagram, as well as modify your text attributes.

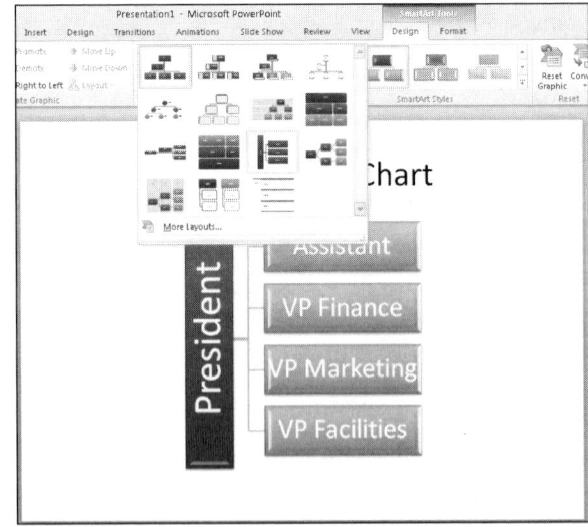

Figure 17-22

Finishing the Presentation

*T*hese days, you hear lots of talk about brand identification. Manufacturers want you to quickly identify a product as theirs with a glimpse of their packaging, which usually consists of a common color theme, logo, and general appearance. That same uniformity is important in a presentation. Maintaining appearance helps your audience stay focused and on topic.

PowerPoint provides a series of *masters* to help you keep uniformity throughout your presentation. By placing your logo on a slide master, your brand name stays in view through every slide. PowerPoint masters also determine the size, position, and appearance of a title and other elements, such as bullet points. You also save time when you modify a master because you don't have to create the same modification on each slide.

In this chapter, you work with

- Themes and backgrounds provided by PowerPoint, which provide uniform color, background, and fonts
- Masters where you can place your logo and modify other generalized appearances
- Speaker notes where you create reminders for the presenter to use with the presentation
- Printing slides and audience handouts that you can give to your audience to help them follow along with your presentation

Chapter 18

Get ready to . . .

Apply a Theme

1. Open or create a PowerPoint presentation.
2. Choose Design➪Themes. Choose your desired theme. Hover your mouse over any theme to get a preview. Note that themes affect the formatting of colors, fonts, and effects of all elements on your slide.
3. Click the More button to see more themes (see Figure 18-1). To see additional themes online, click the More button and then choose More Themes on Microsoft Office Online to download additional themes online.

The same themes are available in Word 2010 and Excel 2010, enabling you to keep all your documents and presentations consistent in look and feel.

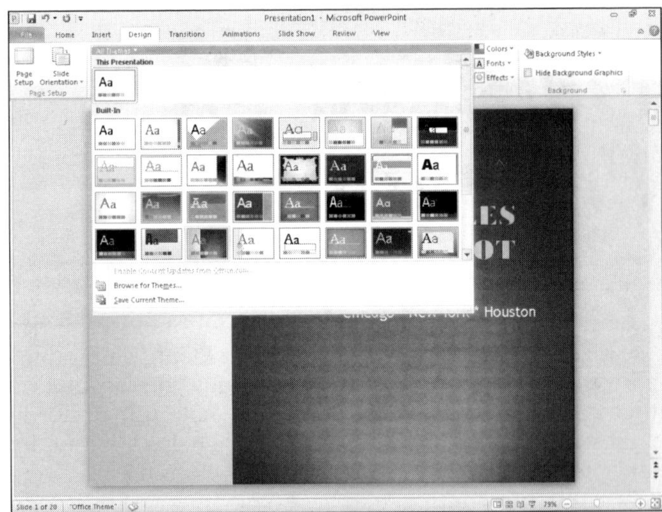

Figure 18-1

Change Theme Colors

1. Open or create a presentation in PowerPoint.
2. On the Ribbon, click the Design tab. In the Themes group, click Theme Colors (or the Theme Colors button).
3. Choose your desired predefined color palette from the drop-down palette (see Figure 18-2).
4. To further customize your colors, choose Create New Theme Colors from the drop-down palette. In the Create New Theme Colors dialog box, select your desired colors for each of the 12 color "slots" provided.
5. Name your customized color palette and click Save for later use. Your saved theme now appears in the Themes gallery.

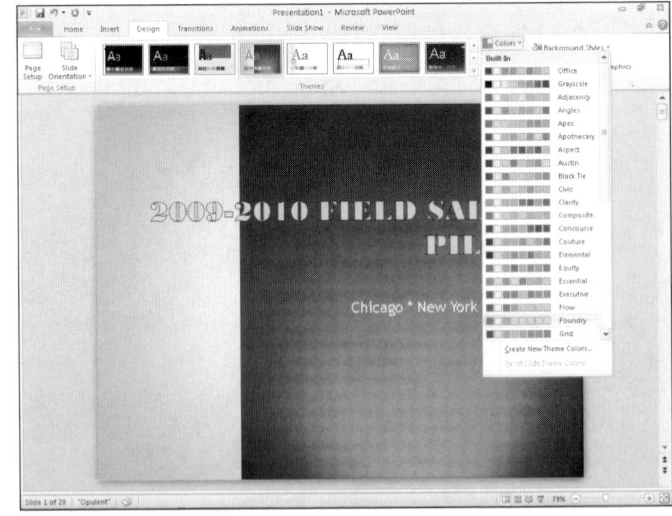

Figure 18-2

Change Theme Fonts

1. Open or create a presentation in PowerPoint.
2. Choose Design⇨Themes⇨Fonts and click the Font down arrow. A list of fonts appears (see Figure 18-3).
3. Choose your desired font set.
4. To further customize your fonts, choose Create New Theme Fonts from the drop-down list. In the Create New Theme Fonts dialog box, choose your desired Heading and Body fonts from the drop-down lists.
5. Name your new font set and click Save for later use. Your saved theme now appears in the Themes gallery.

Always make sure that both optimum readability and legibility are your prime considerations when choosing fonts for your presentation. The Georgia, Verdana, and Times New Roman fonts were designed for best onscreen display.

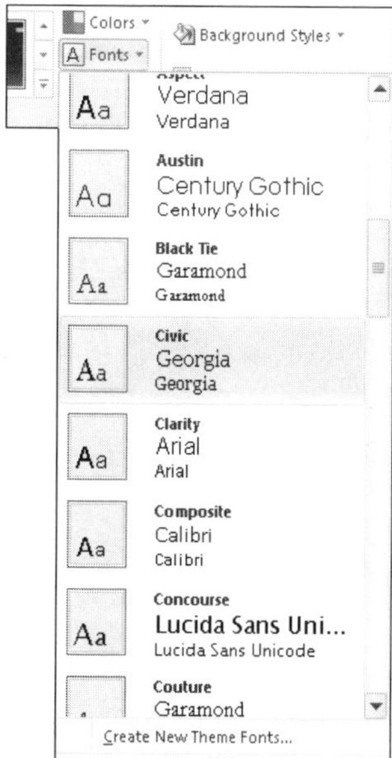

Figure 18-3

Choose Theme Effects

1. Open or create a presentation in PowerPoint.
2. Choose Design⇨Themes⇨Effects.
3. Choose your desired effect from the drop-down list (see Figure 18-4). Note that unlike colors and fonts, you can't create your own theme effects.

You can apply effects to SmartArt graphics, shapes, pictures, WordArt, text, and tables.

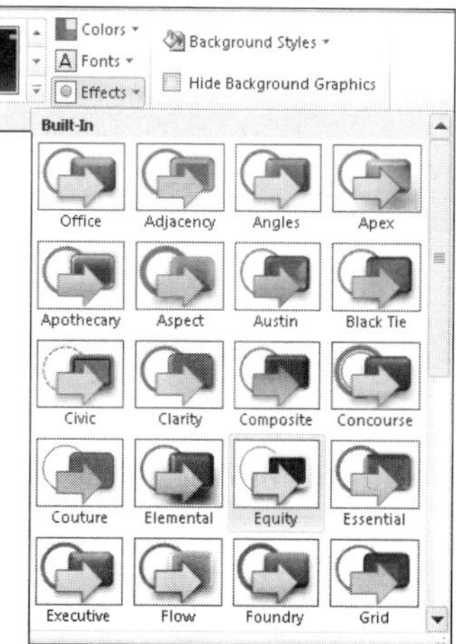

Figure 18-4

Work with Slide Masters

1. Open or create a presentation in PowerPoint and choose View➪Master Views➪Slide Master. PowerPoint switches to Master view, and a Slide Master tab appears. In the slide thumbnail pane, you see a Slide Master and each layout master.

The top slide in the slide thumbnail pane is the Slide Master. The slides under the Slide Master are the masters for each slide layout.

2. Click the Slide Master. The Slide Master appears in the slide pane (see Figure 18-5).
3. Make any desired changes, such as placing any text, a picture, or a logo.
4. When you finish editing the master, choose Slide Master➪Close➪Close Master View.

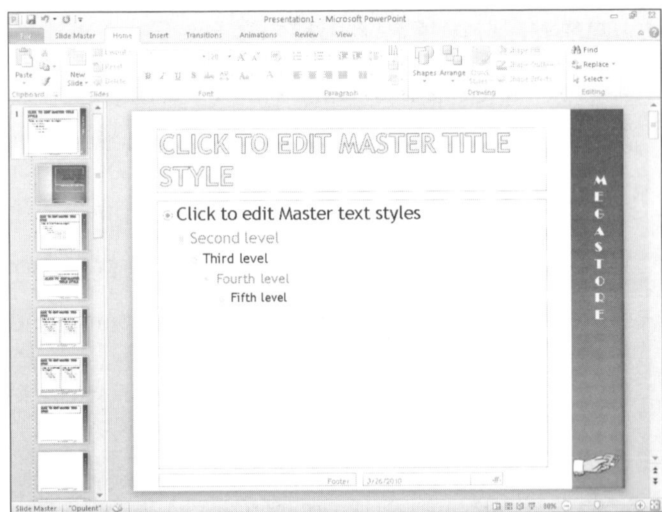

Figure 18-5

Change a Slide Master Background

1. Open or create a presentation in PowerPoint and choose View➪Master Views➪Slide Master.
2. Choose Design➪Background➪Background Styles. A gallery of styles appears; see Figure 18-6.
3. Hover your mouse over any background choice. Live Preview shows you how your current slide looks with the new background.
4. Select the background option you want. The background applies to all slides in the presentation.

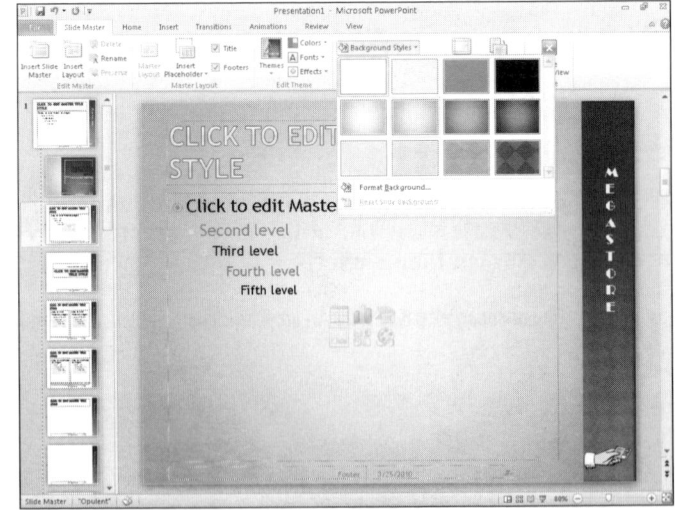

Figure 18-6

Create Your Own Background

1. Open or create a presentation in PowerPoint and choose Design➪Background➪Background Styles. A gallery of styles appears.
2. Click the Format Background option. The Format Background dialog box appears, as shown in Figure 18-7.
3. Select the Fill option (on the left) and then choose one of the following options. Additional settings appear, depending upon which option you choose:
   - *Solid Fill:* Click the Preset colors button to choose a color. This option provides a single uniform color.
   - *Gradient Fill:* Select the two colors that you want to blend, along with the direction, the type, and stops in which the colors blend. This option provides a gradual blending of two colors.
   - *Picture or Texture Fill:* This option allows you to select a photograph, clip art, or a texture for the background. Use pictures sparingly on a slide background because they can detract from the slide content.
4. Click the Apply to All button and then click Close to apply the setting to all slides, or click Close to apply the setting to the current slide only. In Figure 18-8, the background is applied to all slides.

For a really cool background effect, choose a texture fill background. From the Format Background dialog box, select Artistic Effects section and then the Artistic Effect button. You'll see a list of interesting effects you can try on your textured background, such as Pencil Grayscale or Film Grain.

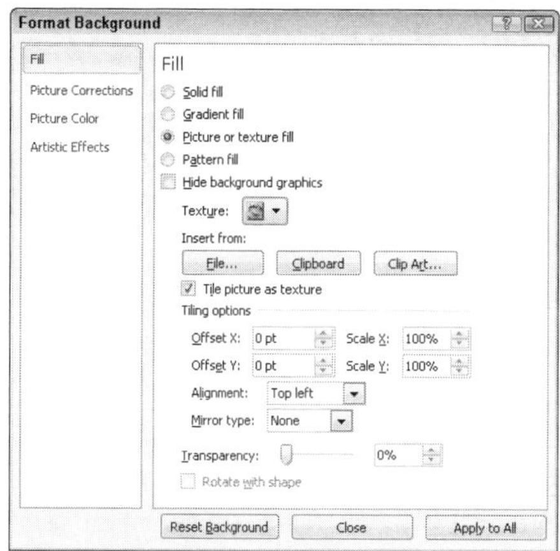

Figure 18-7

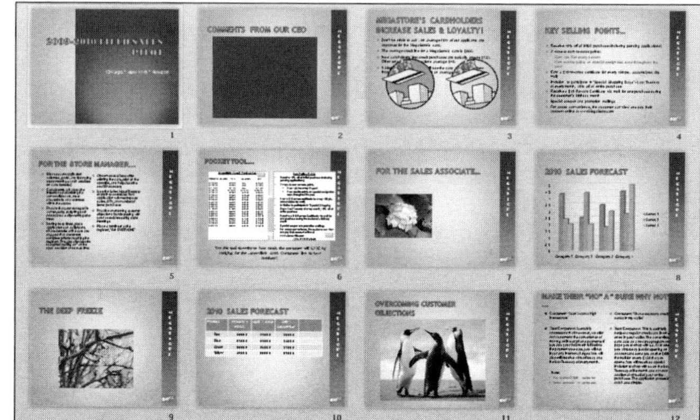

Figure 18-8

Create Speaker Notes

1. Open or create a presentation in PowerPoint. From the slide thumbnail pane, click the Slides tab and then select the slide on which you want to create speaker notes. The slide appears in the slide pane.
2. Choose View➪Presentation Views➪Notes Page. You see a full-screen view with half the page displaying the slide and the other half displaying a notes placeholder. Optionally, you can enter notes in the Notes pane located directly under each slide in Normal view, but the working area is small, so you might want to enlarge it by dragging the separator bar between the slide and the Notes pane (see Figure 18-9).
3. Click in the Notes placeholder and type your speaker note text, like that shown in Figure 18-10.
4. Press the Page Down key (on the keyboard) to display the next slide and note placeholder. Enter any desired notes. Press the Page Up key to display the previous slide.
5. When you finish entering speaker notes, choose View➪Presentation Views➪Normal.

You can format speaker note text the same as you would slide text. Highlight the text, click the Home tab, and then make any desired choices from the Font group.

Figure 18-9

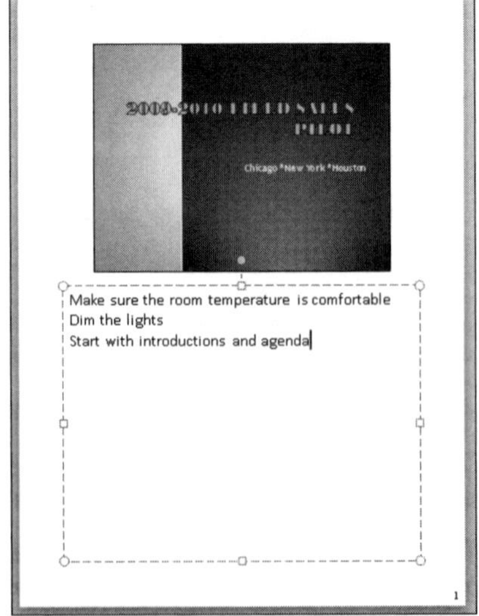

Figure 18-10

Edit the Notes Master

1. Open or create a presentation in PowerPoint.
2. Choose View⇨Master Views⇨Notes Master.
3. To add a background fill to the Notes Master, choose Notes Master⇨Background⇨Background Styles and choose a style (see Figure 18-11).
4. To change the default Portrait Notes page orientation to Landscape, choose Notes Master⇨Page Setup⇨Notes Page Orientation and select Landscape.
5. To resize the slide size as it appears on the Speaker Note, choose Notes Master and then click the slide placeholder. Drag any of the handles to resize the slide placeholder.

To move the slide placeholder, click the placeholder to select it and drag the placeholder border to a new location.

6. To hide the slide image on the Notes Master, choose Notes Master⇨Placeholders and remove the check mark from Slide Image. I do not recommend turning off this option because having the slide on the Notes page helps the speaker remember which slide he's referencing.
7. To add a graphic image to the Notes pages, from the Notes Master view, choose Insert⇨Images ⇨Picture or Insert Images⇨ClipArt. Navigate to the image you want and then insert it. When the object is inserted on the Notes Master page, move the object below the slide. Objects placed on the slide area in the Notes Master won't be visible on the notes pages (see Figure 18-12).
8. Click Notes Master⇨Close Master View to return to Normal view.

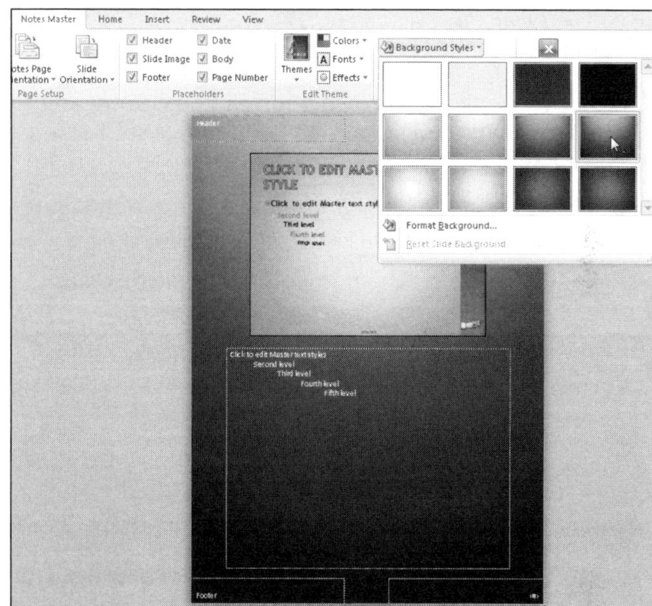

Figure 18-11

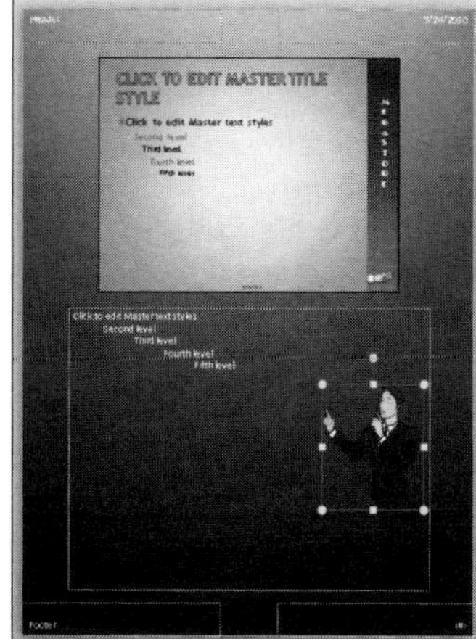

Figure 18-12

Establish Print Options

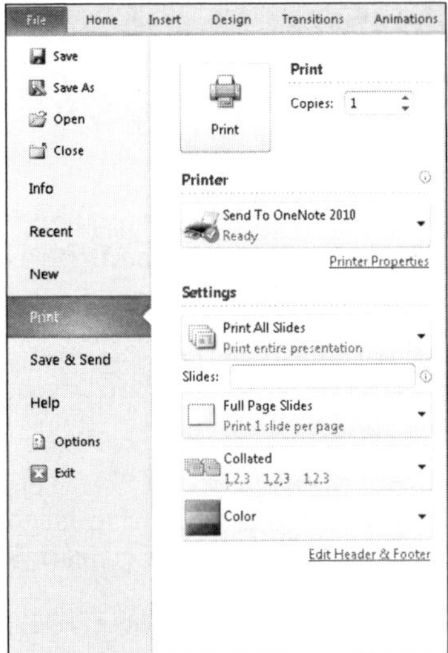

Figure 18-13

1. Open or create a presentation in PowerPoint and then choose Print from the File tab. A print settings section appears on the left, and a preview of the first slide appears on the right.
2. From the print settings section, as shown in Figure 18-13, choose from the following options:
   - *Copies:* Select the number of copies you want to print.
   - *Printer:* Select the printer to which you want to print.
   - *Settings:* Specify other settings, such as whether to print all slides, a preselected group of slides, or the current slide. Optionally, you can specify whether to print double-sided (if your printer has the capability); print-collation order; whether you want to print the slides, the outline, the Notes pages, or the handouts; and whether to print in color, grayscale, or pure black and white. If you select color and you're printing to a non-color printer, PowerPoint prints in grayscale.

Optionally, from the third Settings option list, select the Frame Slides option if you want to print a small thin border around your slides.

3. From the Preview section (see Figure 18-14), click the Next Page or the Previous Page button to view the other slides. You can also use the Zoom slider to enlarge the preview view.
4. Click the Print button after making your selections. PowerPoint prints your presentation.

Figure 18-14

Print Audience Handouts

1. Open or create a presentation in PowerPoint and then choose Print from the File tab.
2. From the Settings section, click the second drop-down option to display a list of items you could print. See Figure 18-15.
3. Select your desired handout layout. Choose 1, 2, 3, 4, 6, or 9 slides per page. Note that if you choose the 3-slide layout, blank lines will be added next to each slide to allow for audience members to take notes during the presentation.

See the previous "Establish Print Options" task for information on additional printing choices.

4. Click the Print button.

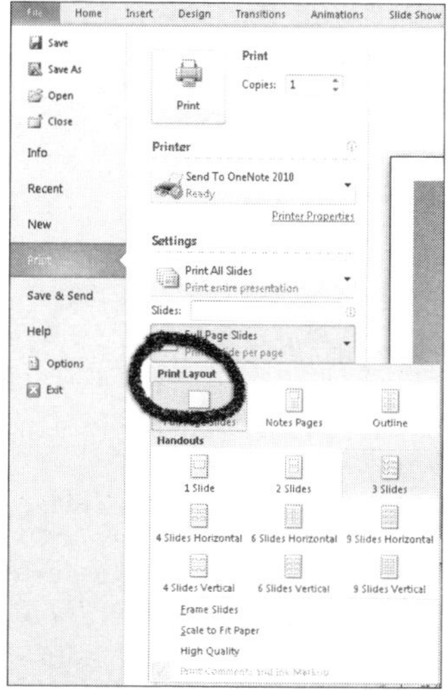

Figure 18-15

Print Speaker Notes

1. Open or create a presentation in PowerPoint and then choose Print from the File tab.
2. From the Settings section, click the second drop-down option to display a list of items you could print (see Figure 18-16).
3. From the Print Layout category, select Notes Pages.

See the "Establish Print Options" task, earlier in this chapter, for information on additional printing choices.

4. Click the Print button.

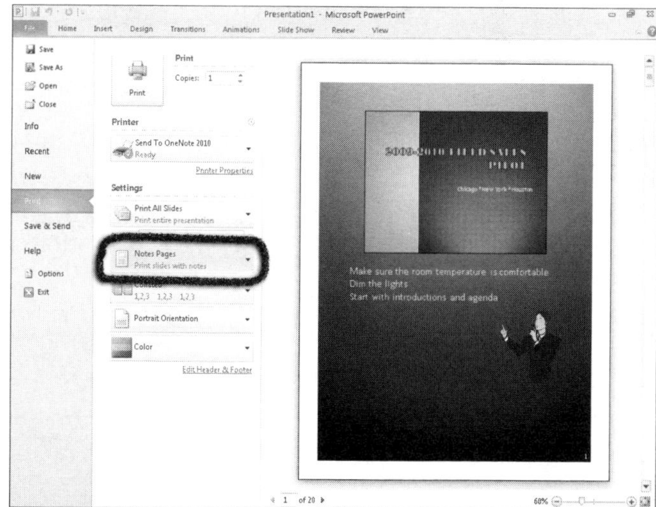

Figure 18-16

Print the Outline

1. Open or create a presentation in PowerPoint.
2. Click the File tab and choose Print.
3. From the Settings section, click the second drop-down option to display a list of items you could print (see Figure 18-17).
4. From the Print Layout category, select Outline.

See the "Establish Print Options" task, earlier in this chapter, for information on additional printing choices.

5. Click the Print button.

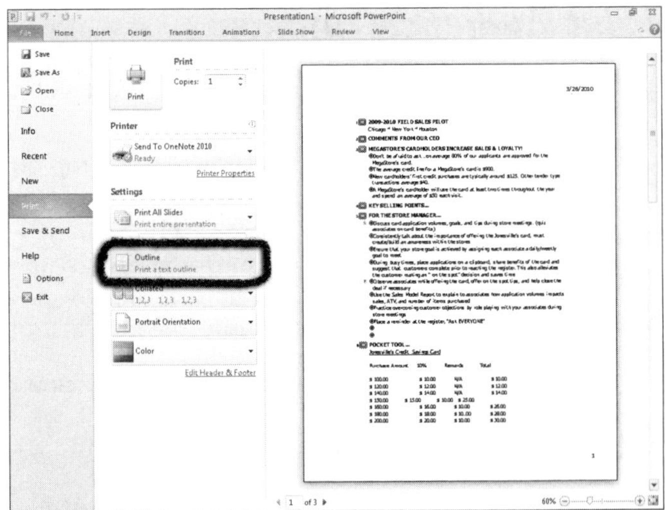

Figure 18-17

E-Mail the Presentation

1. Open or create a presentation in PowerPoint.
2. From the File tab, choose Save & Send.
3. Choose Send Using E-mail.
4. Click Send as Attachment (see Figure 18-18). Your e-mail program launches with the presentation as an attachment.
5. Enter or select a recipient. Optionally, change the subject line. By default, PowerPoint uses the presentation name as the subject.
6. Add any optional notes in the message text.
7. Click Send.

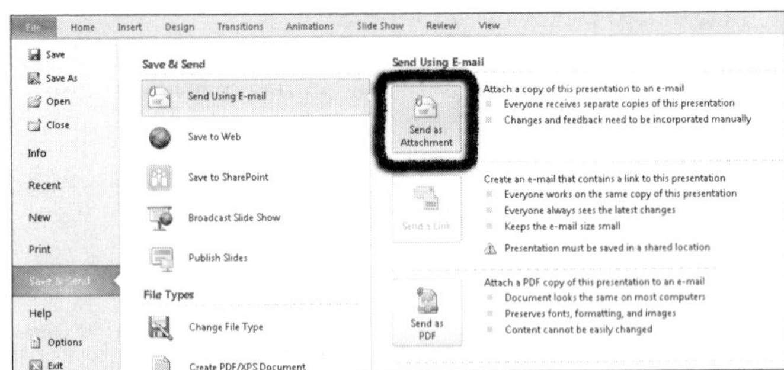

Figure 18-18

Presenting the Presentation

Chapter 19

Good speakers don't just stand up and move their lips. Good speakers add enrichment by making hand, face, or body gestures at key points during their talk. Sometimes their vocal tone changes to reflect importance. The changes help keep the audience focused on the speaker.

So it is with a slide show presentation. Adding movement to a slide keeps your audience paying attention to your presentation and can call special attention to information you want especially noticed. Movement from one slide to the next is a *transition;* movement during a slide is *animation*.

This chapter shows you how to prepare, start, and lead a presentation as well as give it your own comments in the form of annotations.

This chapter also shows how you can package a presentation so it can run repeatedly by itself at a kiosk or from a CD that you prepare.

Get ready to . . .

Set Up Your Show

1. Open or create a presentation in PowerPoint.
2. Choose Slide Show➪Set Up➪Set Up Slide Show. The Set Up Show dialog box appears (see Figure 19-1), with the following options:
   - *Show Type:* Specify how you want the audience to view the presentation. If you have a live audience, select the Presented by a Speaker (Full Screen) option.
   - *Show Options:* Specify whether you want the sound files and animations running continuously. You can also specify a pen color for annotations you make with the electronic felt-tip pen (see Figure 19-2).

The pen color option is available only if you select the Presented by a Speaker option. For easiest viewing by your audience, consider using red.

   - *Show Slides:* Specify which slides you want running during the presentation.
   - *Advance Slides:* Specify whether the presentation should run automatically using timings that you set up or assigned during rehearsal, or whether to advance the slides manually.
   - *Multiple Monitors:* If you're showing the presentation on a computer with multiple monitors, specify which monitor you want to use.
3. Choose the options you want and then click OK.

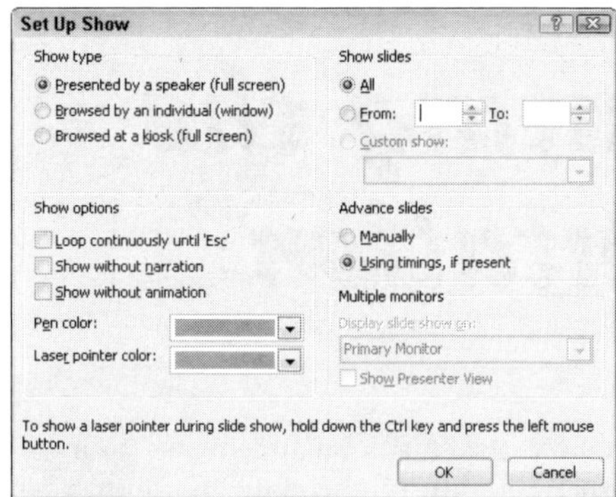

Figure 19-1

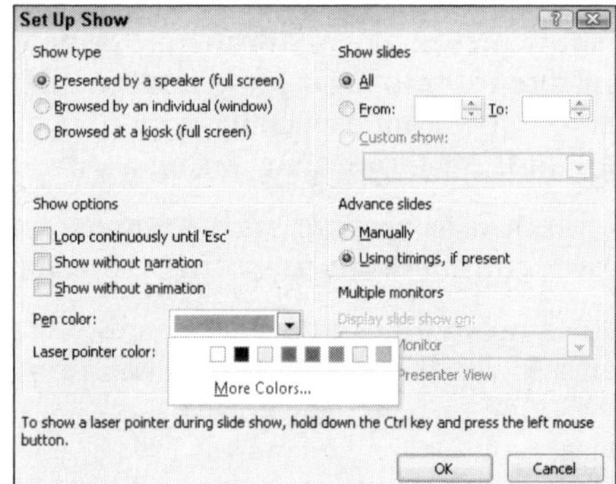

Figure 19-2

Set Slide Transitions

1. Open or create a PowerPoint presentation.

2. Choose View➪Presentation Views➪Slide Sorter, or click the Slide Sorter View button (on the status bar). You can apply transitions in Normal view, but working in Slide Sorter view is easier.

3. Select the slides to which you want to apply transition effects, choose Transitions➪Transition to This Slide, and then click the More button. A gallery of slide transitions appears, as shown in Figure 19-3.

4. Click the transition you want. The selected slides preview the transition, and a transition icon appears beside the slide.

5. Choose Transitions➪Transition to This Slide➪Effect Options and choose the effect you want.

6. If you want a sound want associated with the transition, choose Transitions➪Timing, open the Sound drop-down list, and choose a sound. If you want the sound repeated until the next slide, choose Transitions➪Timing. Open the Transition Sound drop-down list and then choose Loop Until Next Sound.

7. Choose Transitions➪Timing. From the Advance Slide section, select when you want the slide to advance to the next slide. Select one or both of the following options shown in Figure 19-4:

   - *On Mouse Click:* The transition occurs when you click the left mouse button.

   - *After:* The transition occurs automatically after a specified number of seconds. If you choose this option, specify the number of seconds in the After field that you want the slide displayed. In Slide Sorter view, slides with timed transitions display the number of seconds under the slide.

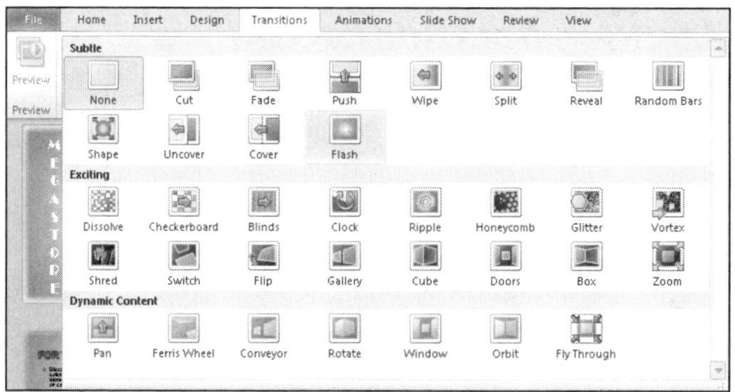

Figure 19-3

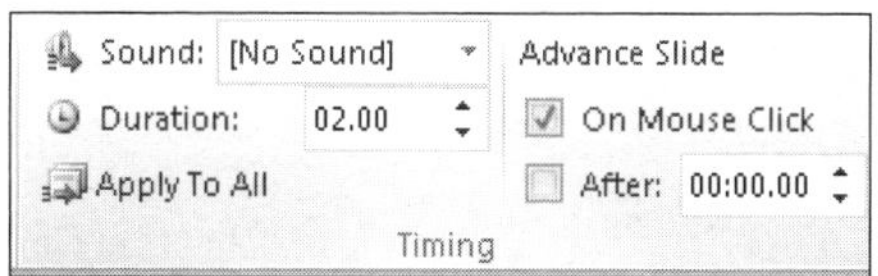

Figure 19-4

Apply Animation to Bullets

1. Open or create a PowerPoint presentation. In Normal view, with the bullet list placeholder you want to animate selected, choose Animations➪Animation and then click the More button to display a gallery of bullet animations (see Figure 19-5).
2. Choose the animation option that you want, *or* choose one of the More Effects options at the bottom of the gallery. A dialog box of more effects appears. From here, you can make a selection. Then click OK.
3. Choose Animations➪Animation➪Effect Options. From the resulting gallery, choose the effect option you want for the bullet list.

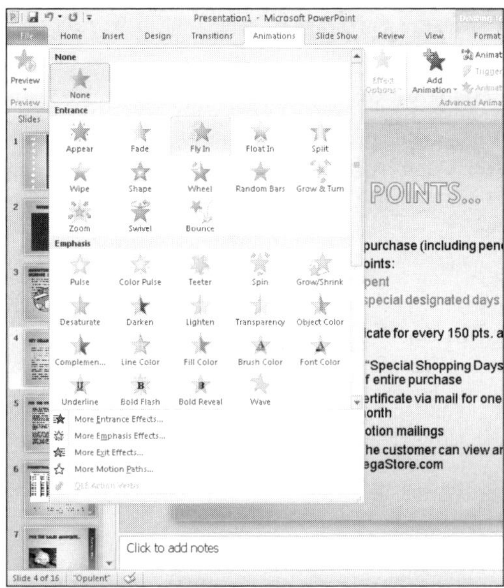

Figure 19-5

Animate a Chart by the Components

1. Open or create a PowerPoint presentation. In Normal view, select the chart you want to animate.
2. Choose Animations➪Animation and then click the More button to display a gallery of chart animation options. From here, choose the animation you want.
3. Choose Animations➪Animation➪Effect Options.
4. Hover your mouse over any option to preview its effect on the chart. Choose one of the available options. The options you see vary with the chart type you're modifying:
   - *As One Object:* Applies the animation to the entire chart.
   - *By Series:* Applies the animation to each data series, one at a time. See Figure 19-6.
   - *By Category*: Applies the animation to each chart category; one at a time.

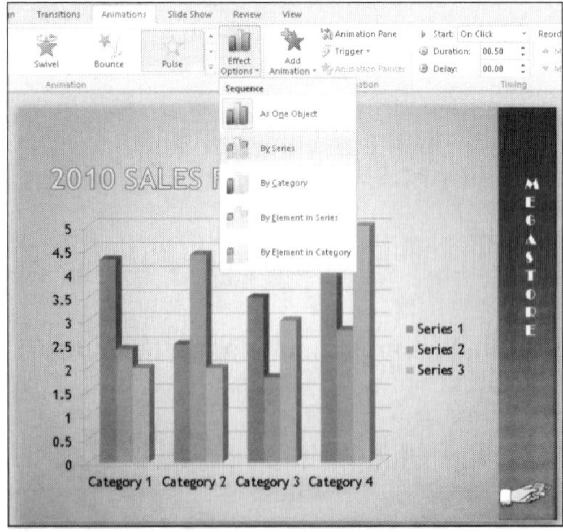

Figure 19-6

Apply Timing to Individual Slides

1. Open or create a presentation in PowerPoint.
2. Choose View➪Presentation Views➪Slide Sorter or click the Slide Sorter view icon.

You can also set timings by rehearsing the presentation. See the next task, "Rehearse Timings."

3. Select a slide. The selected slide has a border around it. Optionally, hold down the Ctrl key and select multiple slides. See Figure 19-7.
4. Choose Transitions➪Timing.
5. Beneath Advance Slide, select the After check box.
6. Use the spinner arrows or enter a timing (in seconds) that you want for the selected slides. As you enter a timing, the time appears beneath the selected slides (see Figure 19-8).

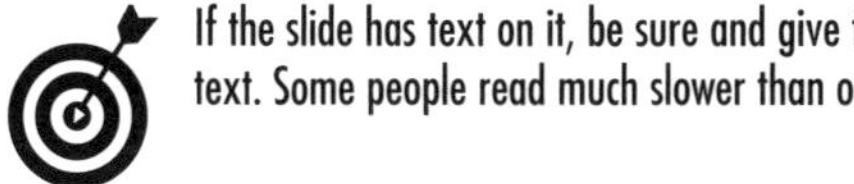

If the slide has text on it, be sure and give the audience plenty of time to read the text. Some people read much slower than others.

7. If you need to change a slide timing, select the slide again and modify the timing in the After timing field.

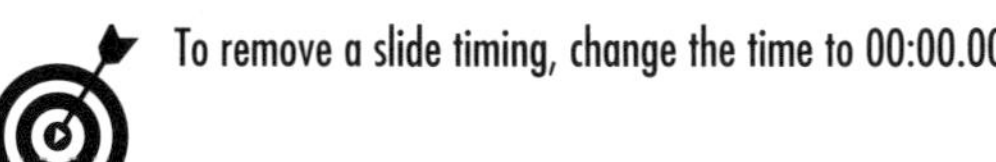

To remove a slide timing, change the time to 00:00.00.

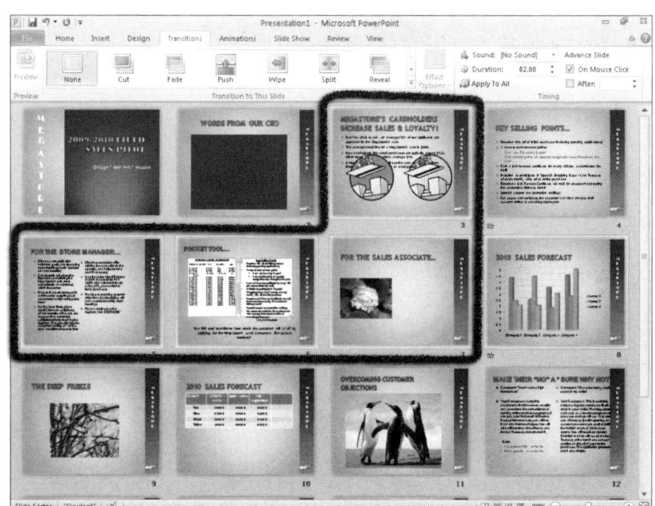

Figure 19-7

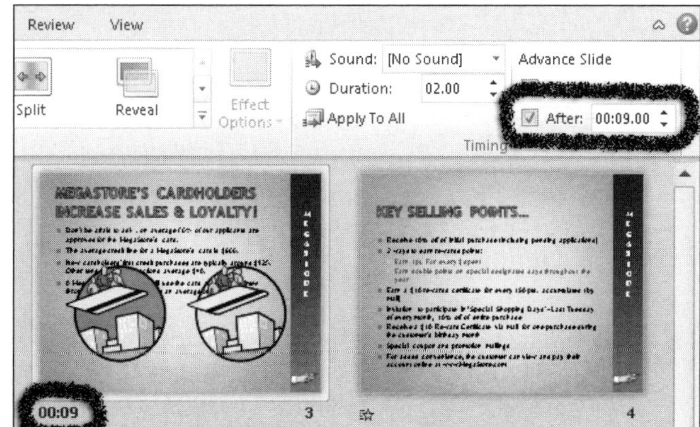

Figure 19-8

Rehearse Timings

1. Open or create a PowerPoint presentation.
2. Choose Slide Show➪Set Up➪Rehearse Timings. The presentation begins, and the Recording bar appears in the top left (see Figure 19-9). Timers on the Recording bar begin recording the time for each slide as well as for the overall presentation.

Before you begin your practice, have a copy of your speaker notes and any other tool you plan to use, such as a laser pointer.

3. Practice your presentation for the first slide and then click one of the following buttons on the Recording bar:
   - *Next:* Advance to the next slide. The Recording bar begins timing the next slide.

   Optionally, clicking anywhere on the slide progresses to the next presentation slide.

   - *Pause Recording:* Temporarily stop recording the slide timing. Click Resume Recording to restart the recording.
   - *Repeat:* Restart the timing and begin rehearsing the current slide again. Click Resume Recording to restart the recording.
4. After the last slide is displayed, a message dialog box appears, as shown in Figure 19-10. Click Yes if you're satisfied with the show timings, or click No to remove the timings. You can then rehearse the show again if desired.

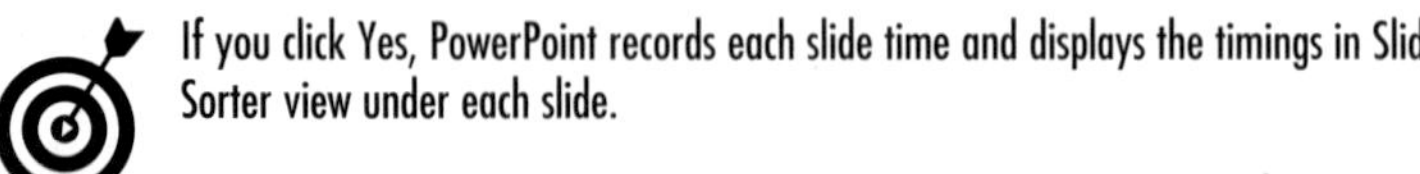

If you click Yes, PowerPoint records each slide time and displays the timings in Slide Sorter view under each slide.

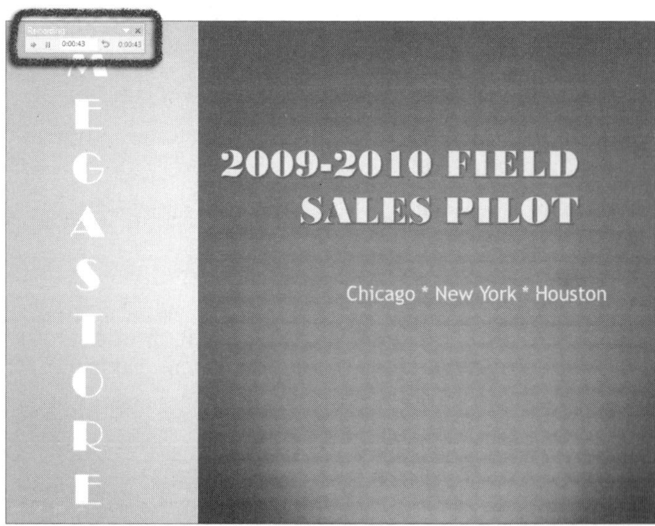

Figure 19-9

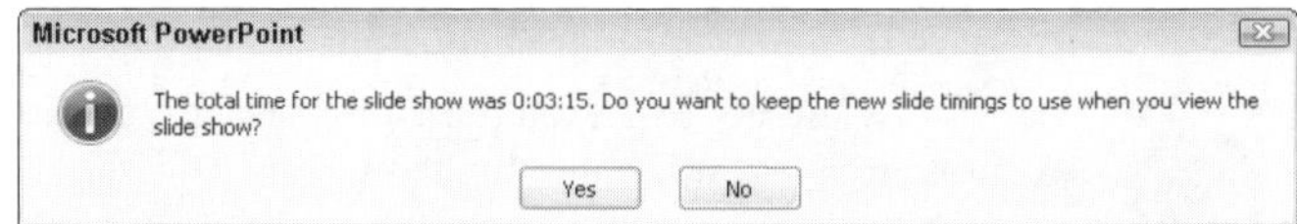

Figure 19-10

Start the Slide Show

1. Open or create a PowerPoint presentation.
2. Choose one of the following methods to launch your presentation. PowerPoint starts the presentation with the options you selected. Figure 19-11 illustrates a slide in full screen view.
   - Choose Slide Show⇨Start Slide Show⇨From Beginning.
   - Click the Slide Show View icon.
   - Press F5.
3. If your presentation isn't running on a timed display, continue the presentation with the controls located in the lower-left corner of the slide. See the task "Use Slide Show Controls," later in this chapter, for more information.

At any time, you can end a presentation by pressing the Esc key or by right-clicking a slide and choosing End Show from the contextual menu that appears.

Figure 19-11

Pause and Resume the Slide Show

1. From a PowerPoint slide show, right-click the mouse. A shortcut menu appears, as shown in Figure 19-12.
2. Choose Pause. The Pause option is available only if the presentation is running on timings. The presentation stops, and the current slide stays onscreen.
3. Right-click the mouse. A shortcut menu appears.
4. Choose Resume to restart the presentation.

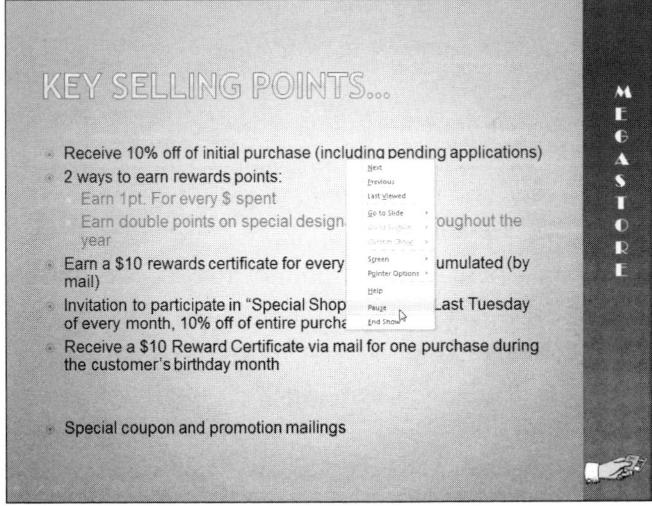

Figure 19-12

Use Slide Show Controls

1. From a PowerPoint slide show, position the mouse over the lower-left corner of the slide. A small group of icons appears, as shown in Figure 19-13.
2. Choose from one of the four available icons:
   - *Previous:* Display the previous slide.
   - *Pen:* Annotate your presentation. See the upcoming task, "Annotate Slides."
   - *Slides:* Display a particular slide.
   - *Next:* Display the next slide.

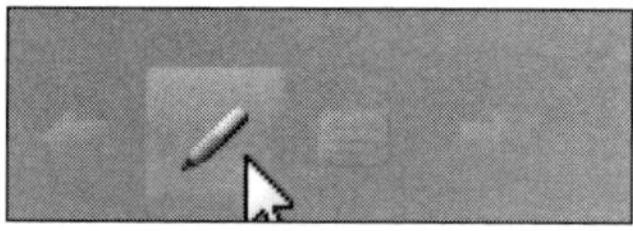

Figure 19-13

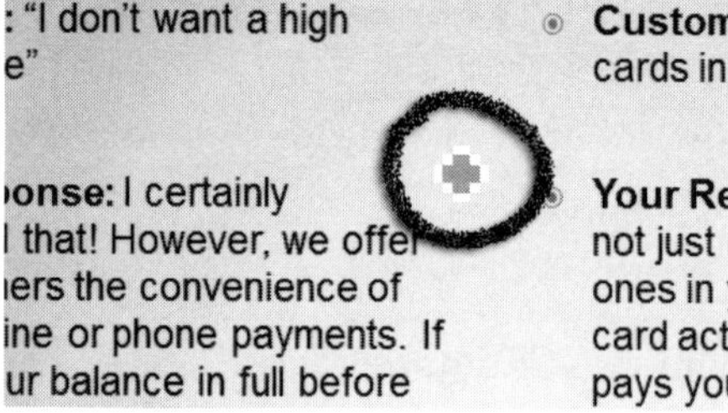

Figure 19-14

Navigate with the Keyboard

From a PowerPoint slide show, press any of the following keystrokes to perform an action:

- *N* or *spacebar:* Next animation, or next slide if no animations.
- *P:* Previous animation, or previous slide if no animations.
- *Ctrl+P:* Change the pointer to a pen for annotations (see Figure 19-14). Note: Your pointer will appear smaller than seen in this figure.
- *Ctrl+A:* Change the pointer from a pen to the regular mouse pointer.
- *S:* Pause. Press S again to resume.
- *B:* Pause show and display an all-black screen. Press B again to resume.
- *W:* Pause show and display an all-white screen. Press W again to resume.

Use Hidden Slides

1. Open or create a PowerPoint presentation. In Normal view or Slide Sorter view, select the slides that you don't want automatically displayed.
2. Choose Slide Show➪Set Up➪Hide Slide.
3. From the slide show, click the Slides button from the slide show controls. Choose Go to Slide, which displays a list of all slides. Hidden slides display with their number in parentheses (see Figure 19-15).
4. Choose the hidden slide that you want to display. The slide displays onscreen.

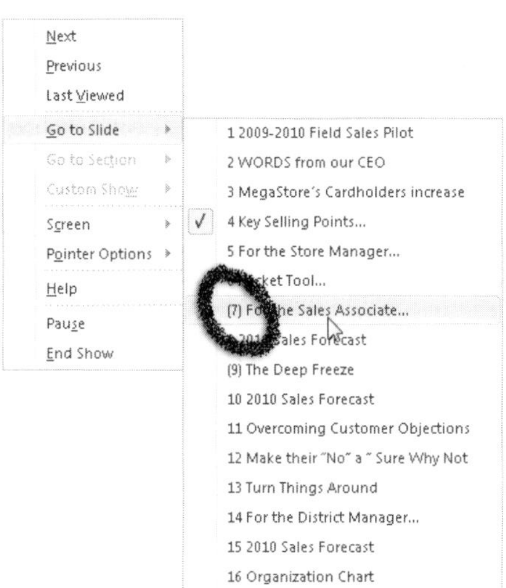

Figure 19-15

Annotate Slides

1. From a PowerPoint slide show, display the Pen by clicking the Pen icon from the slide show controls. A shortcut menu appears.
2. Choose a pen type and optional pen color.
3. Draw freely on your screen. Annotating marks appear in the color and pen style you selected (see Figure 19-16).
4. Cancel Pen mode by pressing Esc, pressing Ctrl+A, or clicking the Pen icon from the slide show controls and choosing Arrow.

You can quickly erase any annotations by clicking the Pen control icon and choosing Erase All Ink on Slide or by pressing E on the keyboard.

5. When the presentation ends, a message box appears. Click Keep if you want to keep your annotations with the presentation, or click Discard. Saved annotations appear as on the slide as objects.

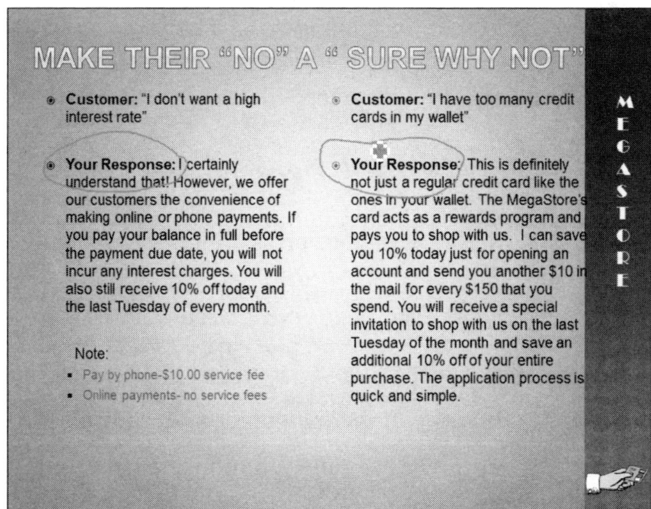

Figure 19-16

Package the Presentation

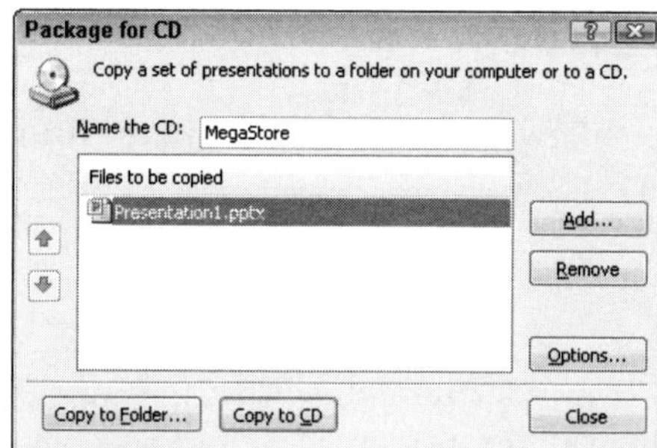

Figure 19-17

1. Open or create a presentation in PowerPoint. From the File tab, click Save & Send, and then choose Package Presentation for CD.
2. Click the Package for CD button. The Package for CD dialog box appears; see Figure 19-17. Perform one of the following steps:
   - *Copy to CD.* Give the CD a name and then click the Copy to CD button. Click Yes to the message that appears and then insert a blank recordable CD into the drive; the CD burn process begins. When finished, PowerPoint asks whether you want to burn another CD. Click Yes if you want another CD, or click No if you don't.
   - *Copy to Folder.* Click the Copy to Folder button. The Copy to Folder dialog box appears, prompting you for a folder name and folder location. If desired, change the folder name or location and then click OK. If prompted with a message about including linked files, click Yes. PowerPoint creates the folder and saves all the files.
3. Click Close if prompted.

Run a Packaged Presentation

Figure 19-18

1. Insert the CD with your presentation into a computer's CD or DVD drive.
2. From the AutoPlay dialog box that appears, choose Run PresentationPackage.html (see Figure 19-18). The actual options you see next depend on your version of Microsoft Windows.
3. Click the name of the presentation. A message box appears.
4. Click Open. The presentation immediately begins.

If you want to run the presentation from a folder, open the folder and double-click the Play file. The presentation immediately begins.

Part IV
Outlook

"Your mail program looks fine. I don't know why you're not receiving any personal e-mails. Have you explored the possibility that you may not have any friends?"

Getting Started with Outlook

Chapter 20

Outlook is one of the most widely used programs to send and receive e-mail messages, but Outlook is so much more than just an e-mail client. In addition to providing an address book where you can store information about the people with whom you correspond, Outlook also enables you to manage your calendar by storing meetings and tasks you need to accomplish. The appointment and task management functions available in Outlook are fairly advanced; if you work in an environment that uses a Microsoft Exchange server, you can even set up your calendar to make it available to others who can then set up meetings for you.

Before you dive in to using Outlook to exchange e-mail, manage your contacts, and handle your appointments and "to do" lists, you need to explore the Outlook window to better understand how to move around in Outlook. In this chapter, you

- Gain an understanding of the Outlook window
- Work with the Navigation pane, menus, toolbars, and the Ribbon
- Examine Outlook Today and the To-Do bar
- Set editing options while working in Outlook

Get ready to . . .

Open and Explore Outlook

1. Choose Start➪All Programs ➪Microsoft Office ➪Microsoft Outlook 2010. Outlook opens. Use the table and Figure 20-1 to help you identify the major parts of the Outlook window.

Location	Identifies
1	File tab
2	Quick Access Toolbar (QAT)
3	Navigation pane
4	Ribbon
5	"The right side"
6	Status bar

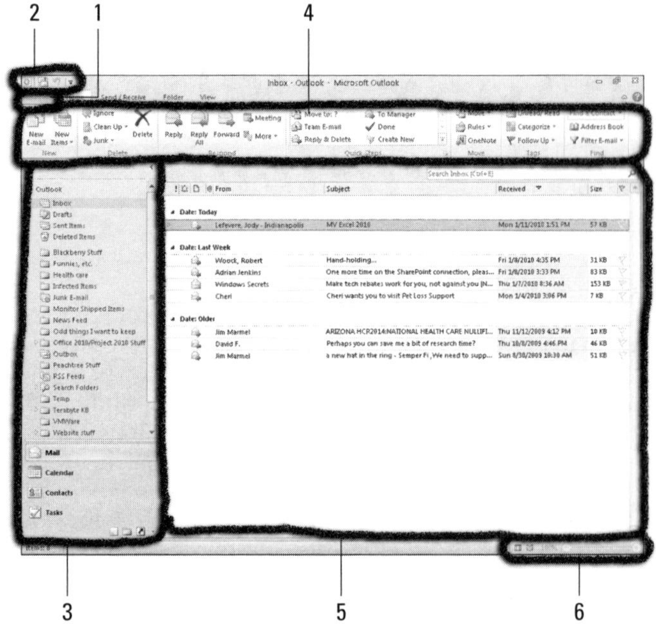

Figure 20-1

2. The Navigation pane contains buttons you click to switch among Outlook's various sections: Mail, Calendar, Contacts, Tasks, and so on.

3. The buttons on the Ribbon change, depending on the section of Outlook you're viewing.

4. I know of no official name for "the right side" of the Outlook window; in this area, you'll always find the contents of whatever button you select in the Navigation pane. In Figure 20-1, the right side shows the contents of the Inbox, which is selected in the Navigation pane. Because you can customize "the right side" of the window, you might see multiple panes.

You can change the appearance of the Ribbon, the Quick Access Toolbar, and the status bar; see Chapter 25 for details.

5. To close Outlook, click the X in the upper-right corner of the screen.

Work with the Navigation Pane

1. Click any button in the Navigation pane to display that section of Outlook. The Navigation pane buttons always appear at the bottom of the Navigation pane, while the information above and to the right of the buttons changes, depending on the button you select. In Figure 20-2, I clicked the Calendar button in the Navigation pane, and the Day view of the Calendar appears on the right side of the Outlook window, with a small calendar of the current month appearing above the Navigation pane buttons. You can read more about using the Calendar in Chapter 23.

2. To display more buttons in the Navigation pane, click the Configure Buttons button in the lower-right of the Navigation pane (see Figure 20-3). A menu appears that you can use to show more or fewer buttons.

3. To adjust the order in which the buttons appear, choose Navigation Pane Options from the Configure Buttons menu (see Figure 20-3) to display the Navigation Pane Options dialog box. Then, you can

   - Place a check beside a button to make it appear in the Navigation pane.
   - Use the Move Up and Move Down buttons to change the order of Navigation pane buttons.

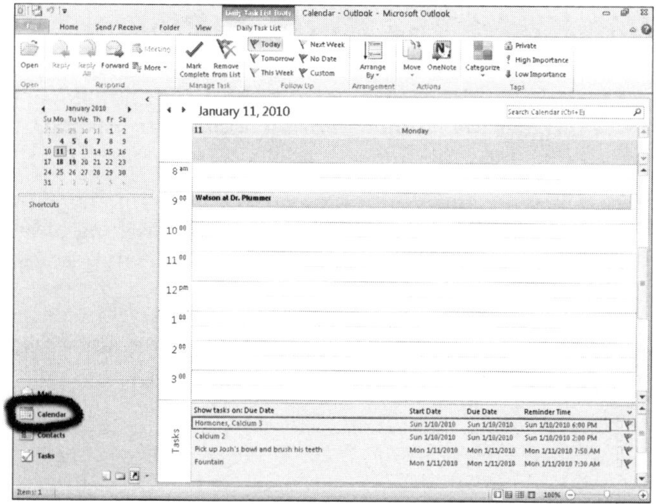

Figure 20-2

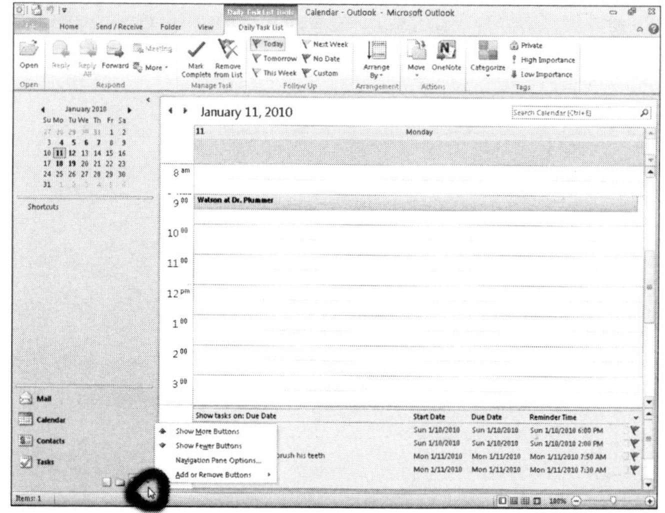

Figure 20-3

Work with the Outlook Ribbon

1. Click the Contacts button in the Navigation pane. Outlook displays the Home tab of the Ribbon, consisting of buttons related to working with contacts (see Figure 20-4).
2. Click the Tasks button in the Navigation pane. Outlook displays the Home tab of the Ribbon, consisting of buttons related to working with tasks and to-do items (see Figure 20-5).

The same five tabs appear on the Ribbon, regardless of the section of Outlook in which you work. But, the buttons on the tabs change to accommodate the tasks most commonly associated with the selected Outlook section.

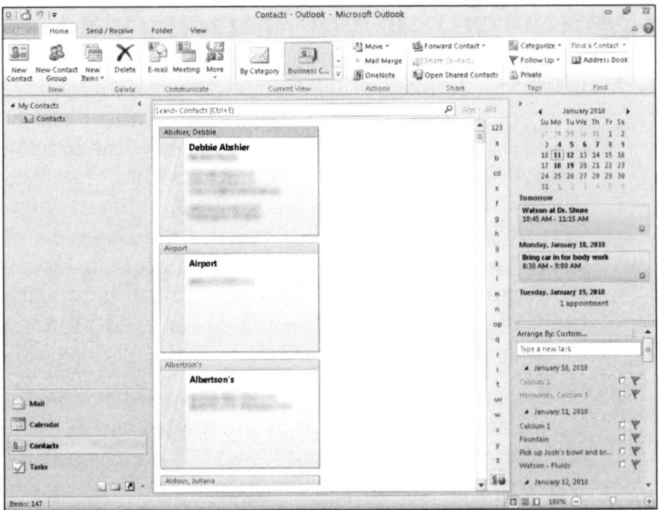

Figure 20-4

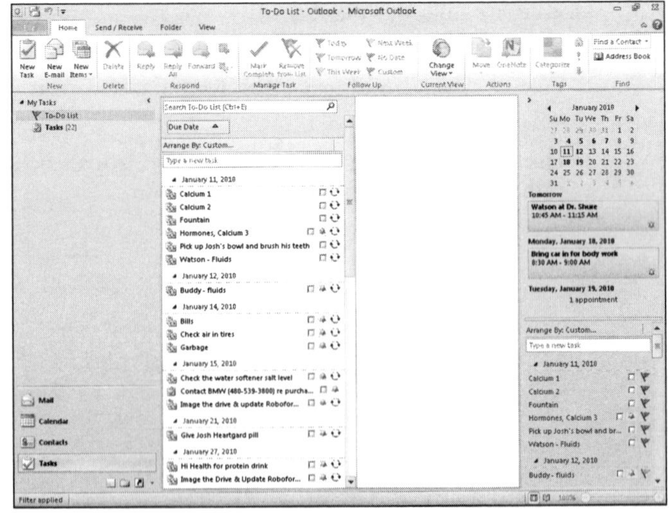

Figure 20-5

Use Outlook Today

1. Click the Mail button.
2. In the Navigation pane, click the name of your Outlook data file; in Figure 20-6, the Outlook data file name is, cleverly, "Outlook." Outlook Today appears on the right side of the Outlook window, summarizing your calendar, tasks, and e-mail.
3. Click the Customize Outlook Today button in the upper-right of the Outlook Today pane to display the Customize Outlook Today pane (see Figure 20-7). You can take any of the following actions:
   - *Always display Outlook Today when you open Outlook.* Select the When Starting, Go Directly to Outlook Today check box.
   - *Select folders to appear on the Outlook Today page.* Click the Choose Folders button. Figure 20-6 displays the Inbox, Drafts, and Outbox folders.
   - *Specify the number of calendar days you want Outlook Today to display.* Use the Calendar section.
   - *Identify the tasks you want Outlook Today to display as well as how you want the tasks sorted.* Use the Tasks section.
   - *Control the layout and appearance of the Outlook Today page.* Use the Styles section
4. Click Save Changes to see the effects of your changes.

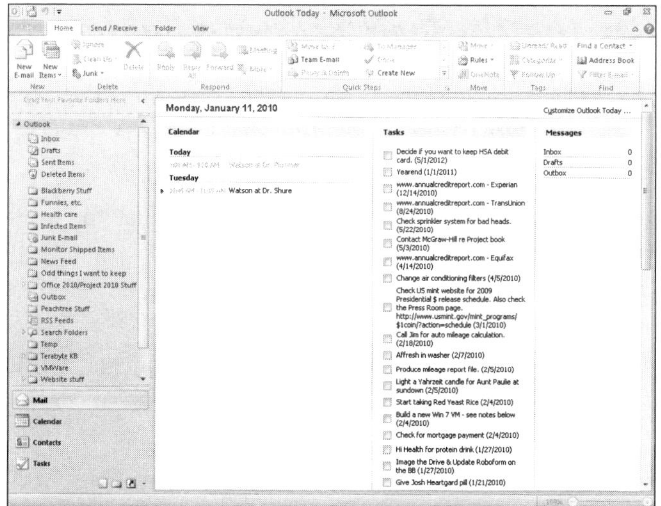

Figure 20-6

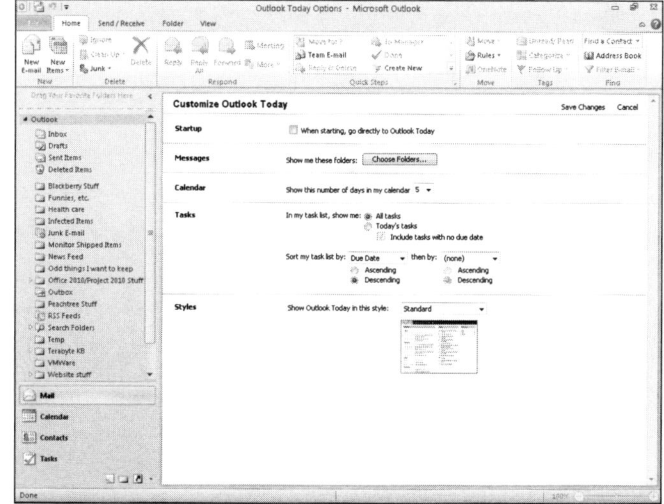

Figure 20-7

Set the Outlook Starting Folder

1. Click the File tab. From the Backstage view that appears, click Options. The Outlook Options dialog box appears.
2. On the left side, click Advanced (see Figure 20-8).
3. In the Outlook Start and Exit section, click the Browse button. The Select folder dialog box appears (see Figure 20-9).
4. Click the folder that you want to see each time you open Outlook.
5. Click OK twice. Each time you open Outlook, Outlook will display the folder that you selected.

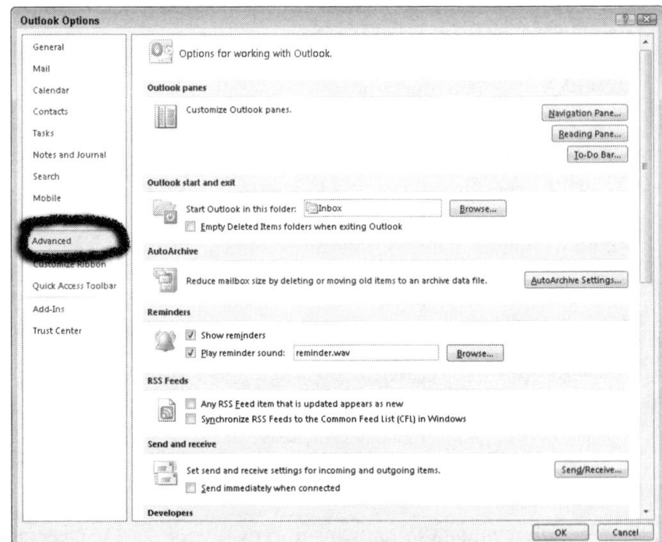

Figure 20-8

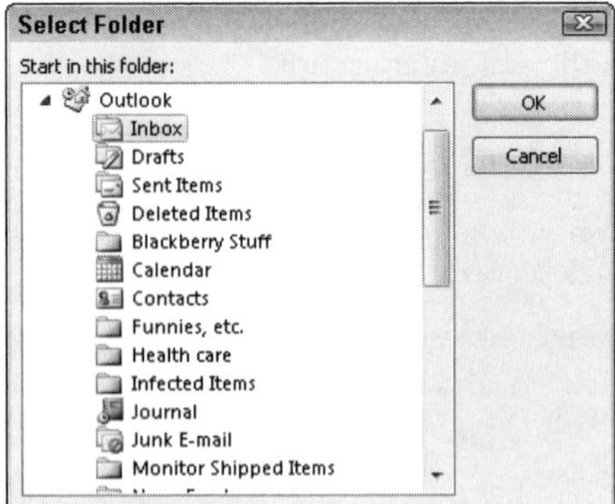

Figure 20-9

View the To-Do Bar

1. Click a button in the Navigation pane to select a section in Outlook to display the To-Do bar. For this example, I clicked the Tasks button.

The To-Do Bar can appear in any section of Outlook, and you can display it in multiple Outlook sections. By default, it appears minimized in the Tasks section.

2. Click the View tab.
3. In the Layout group, click the To-Do Bar button (see Figure 20-10).
4. From the drop-down menu that appears, click Normal. The To-Do bar appears on the right side of the selected section (see Figure 20-11), showing you today's agenda.

If the To-Do Bar was minimized, you can click the small carat at the top of the pane to display today's agenda. You can minimize the To-Do Bar again by clicking the carat.

5. You can add new tasks from the To-Do bar by clicking in the Type a New Task field in the middle of the To-Do bar and typing the task information. The Task Tools tab appears on the Ribbon, and the new task appears on both the To-Do bar and the Tasks list. You can read more about working with tasks in Chapter 24.
6. You can quickly minimize the screen real estate used by the To-Do bar; click the arrow in the upper left of the To-Do bar (refer to Figure 20-11). Click the arrow again to expand the To-Do bar.

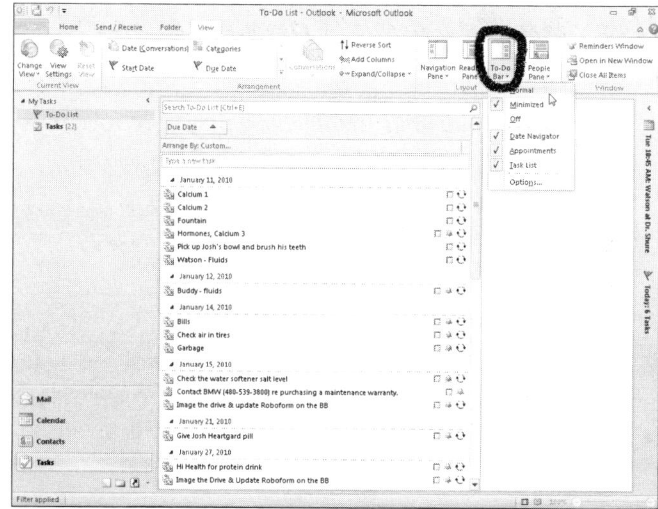

Figure 20-10

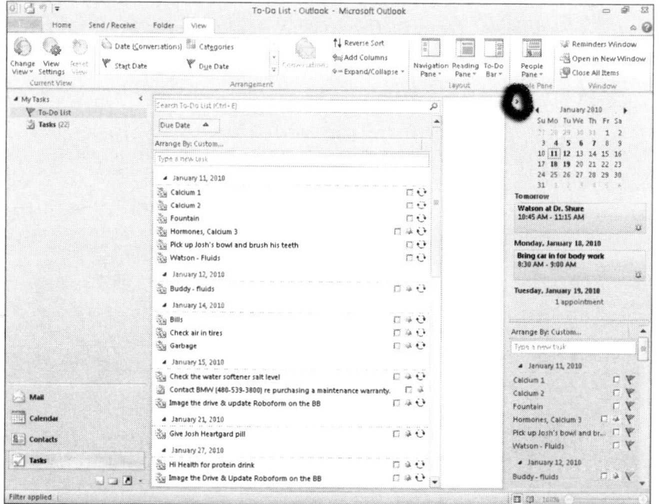

Figure 20-11

Use the Reading Pane

1. Click a button in the Navigation pane to select a section in Outlook to display the Reading pane. For this example, I clicked the Mail button and selected the Inbox.

By default, the Reading pane appears on the right side of the message list when you click the Mail button in the Navigation pane; these steps describe how to control the placement of the Reading pane.

2. Click the View tab and, in the Layout group, click the Reading Pane button.
3. From the drop-down menu, choose Bottom. Click a message, task, calendar event, or contact to view its details in the Reading pane (see Figure 20-12).

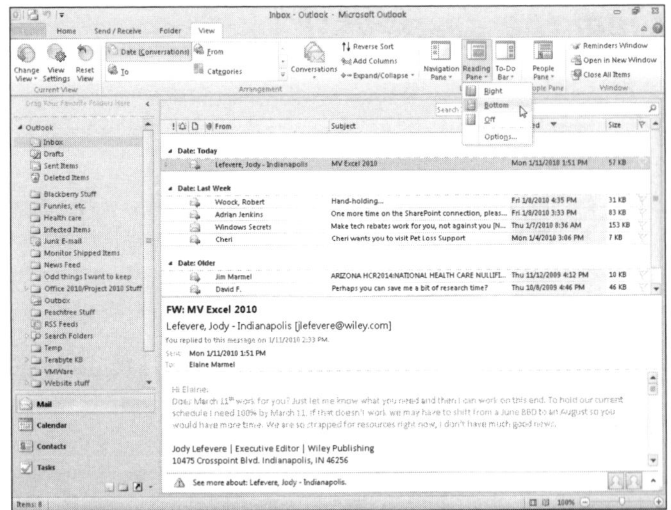

Figure 20-12

Set Outlook Options

1. Click the File tab. From the Backstage view that appears, choose Options to display the Outlook Options dialog box (see Figure 20-13).
2. Click a selection on the left to see the options available. You're mostly likely to use options on the following tabs:
   - When you click *General on the left, you see* groups of options that affect all of Outlook.
   - The *next five choices on the left display* options for each corresponding section in Outlook.
   - When you click *Advanced on the left,* you can control a variety of miscellaneous options.
   - You can click *Customize Ribbon* and *Quick Access Toolbar on the left* to tailor those elements. See Chapter 25 for details.
3. Click OK to save your selections.

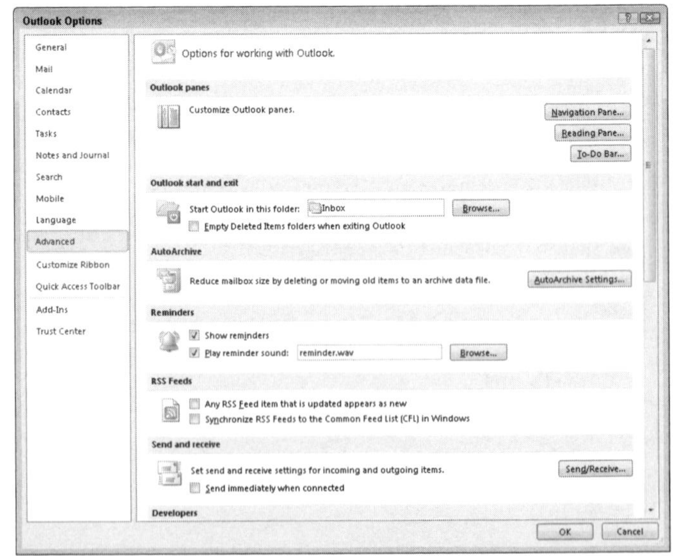

Figure 20-13

Clean Up Outlook Data

1. Click the File tab.
2. From the Backstage view that appears, click the Cleanup Tools button (see Figure 20-14).
3. Click Mailbox Cleanup, and the Mailbox Cleanup dialog box appears (see Figure 20-15). From this dialog box you can
   - *View the size of each Outlook folder* to help you identify the folders to clean.
   - *Search for items* by age or by size.
   - Click the AutoArchive button to *move old items to an archive file.* By default, every 14 days, Outlook moves dated items that are six months old to archive folders. To view all archived items, click the Mail button and then click the plus sign beside Archive Folders.
   - Click the Empty button to *permanently delete the contents of the Deleted Items folder* that appears when you click the Mail button in the Navigation pane. Outlook stores everything you delete — mail messages, contacts, and tasks — in the Deleted Items folder. To truly delete items stored in the Deleted Items folder, you must empty the folder.
4. Click Close when you finish cleaning up.

The other two commands visible on the Cleanup Tools button correspond to the AutoArchive button and the Empty button in the Mailbox Cleanup dialog box.

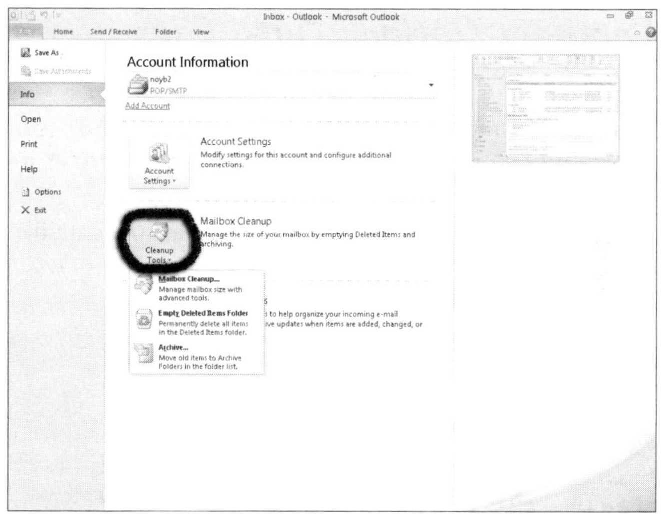

Figure 20-14

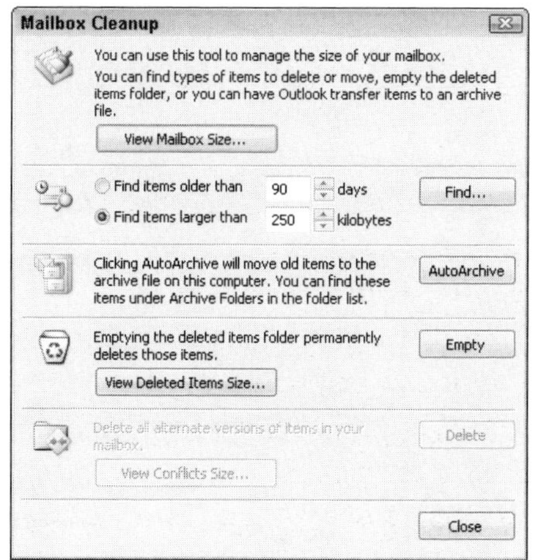

Figure 20-15

Compact Outlook Data Files

1. Click the File tab. From the Backstage view that appears, click the Account Settings button (see Figure 20-16). A drop-down menu appears; choose Account Settings to display the Account Settings dialog box.
2. Click the Data Files tab and then select the data file that you want to compact.
3. Click the Settings button above the list of data files. The Settings dialog box for the selected data file appears (see Figure 20-17).
4. Click the Compact Now button.

Deleting information (such as unwanted e-mail) doesn't reduce the size of your Outlook data file. To keep the data file to a manageable size, compact it occasionally by using these steps.

5. When Outlook finishes compacting, click OK and then click Close.

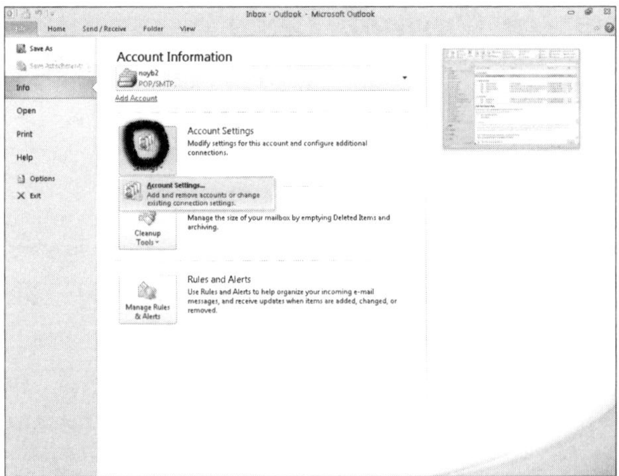

Figure 20-16

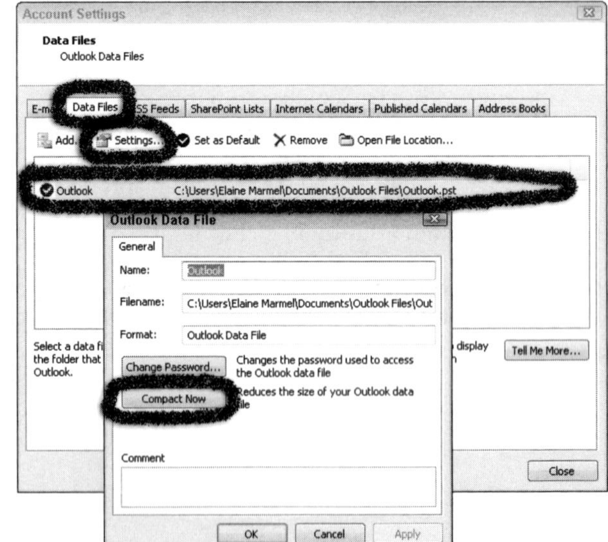

Figure 20-17

Working with E-Mail

E-mail is probably the single most widely used section of Outlook. From the Mail section of Outlook, you can perform the basics of sending, receiving, and reading e-mail, but Outlook goes far beyond those basics in providing you with features. In addition to forwarding e-mail to one or more recipients and sending and receiving attachments with e-mail messages, you can manage the mail you receive and make your life easier by storing contact information about the people with whom you exchange messages so that you can quickly and easily compose messages to people with whom you communicate frequently. In this chapter, you see how to

- Send, receive, read, respond to, and forward e-mail messages and attachments to single recipients or groups of recipients.
- Add the sender of a message to your list of contacts.
- Send a *blind copy* (a message sent to a recipient whose name isn't visible to other recipients of the same message).
- Manage e-mail messages by grouping and categorizing them and moving them into specific folders.
- Mark messages for follow-up.
- Work with out-of-office replies and e-mail message signatures.
- Manage junk mail.

Chapter

21

Get ready to . . .

Work with Conversation View

1. Click the Mail button in the Navigation pane; mail messages you have received appear on the right side of the Outlook window. By default, Outlooks displays messages organized by date in Conversation view (see Figure 21-1).

By default, Outlook displays the Reading pane to the right of the list of messages, but I prefer to place the Reading pane below the list of messages and have done so throughout this chapter.

2. To view all e-mail messages that are part of a particular conversation, click the message.

Conversation view is the new default view in Outlook 2010. If you prefer, you can use the View tab to order and view messages by date, sender, or recipient.

3. Click the small triangle that appears beside the message, and Outlook expands the conversation (see Figure 21-2).

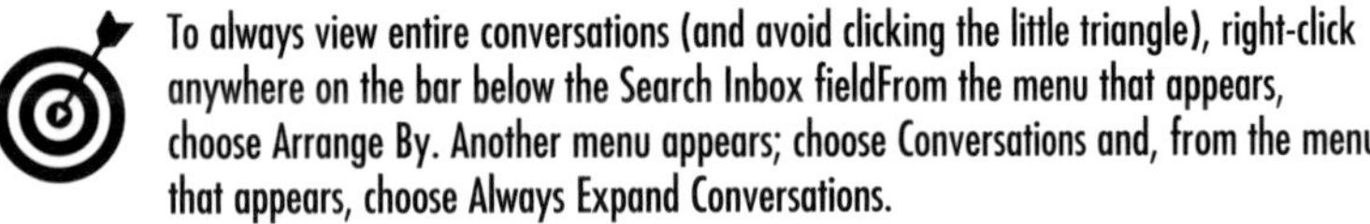

To always view entire conversations (and avoid clicking the little triangle), right-click anywhere on the bar below the Search Inbox fieldFrom the menu that appears, choose Arrange By. Another menu appears; choose Conversations and, from the menu that appears, choose Always Expand Conversations.

4. To read a mail message in the Reading pane, as shown in Figure 21-1, click it or double-click the message to open it.

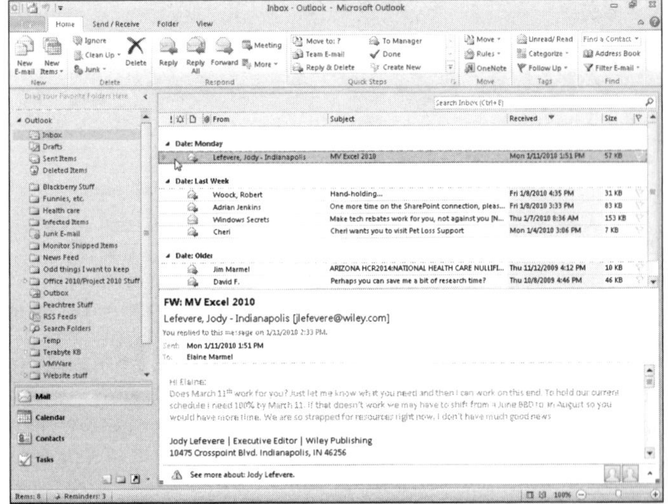

Figure 21-1

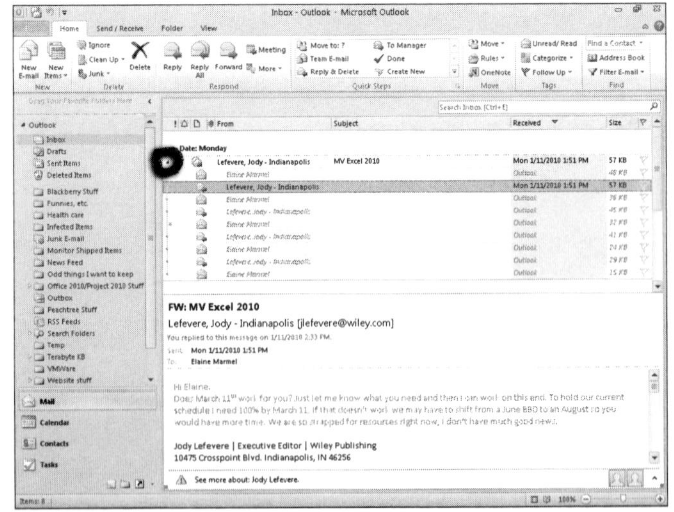

Figure 21-2

Create and Send an E-Mail

1. Click the Mail button in the Navigation pane.
2. On the Home tab, in the New group, click the New E-mail button (see Figure 21-3) to display a new e-mail message window (see Figure 21-4).
3. Click in the To field and type the e-mail address(es) of the recipient(s) of your message. Outlook automatically separates e-mail addresses with a semi-colon (;).

If you stored a contact in the Address Book and you previously sent an e-mail message to that contact, Outlook suggests contact names while you type the recipient's name or e-mail address. When Outlook suggests the correct name, press Tab to select it.

4. Click in the Subject field and type a subject for the message.
5. Click in the message body (the large empty field) and type your message.
6. Click Send to place the message in Outlook Outbox.

Outlook periodically sends messages from its Outbox, or you can click the Send/Receive All Folders button on the Quick Access Toolbar or press F9 to send the message immediately. On the Options tab of the message window, you can click the Delay Delivery button to set a date for Outlook to send the message.

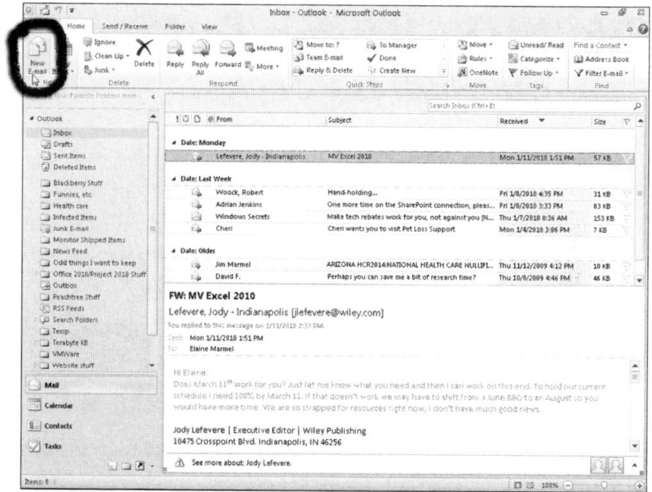

Figure 21-3

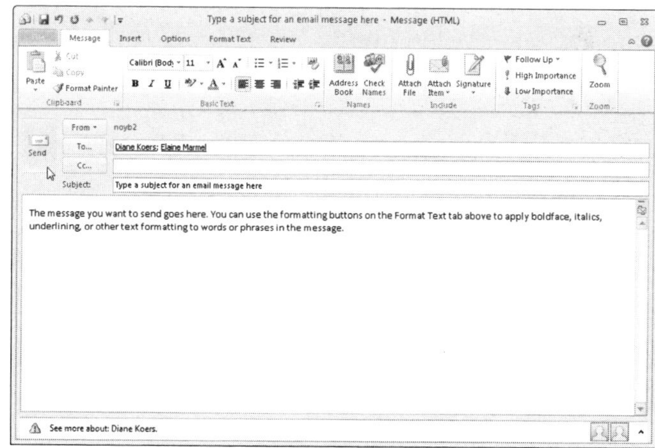

Figure 21-4

Select Mail Message Recipients from the Address Book

1. Perform Steps 1 and 2 in the earlier task, "Create and Send an E-Mail."
2. Click the To button beside the To field (where you can type mail recipient names or addresses). Outlook displays the Select Names dialog box (see Figure 21-5).
3. Highlight the recipient by typing a few letters of the recipient name or by clicking the recipient in the list.
4. Click the To button to add the recipient to the To field.
5. Repeat Steps 3 and 4 for each recipient to whom you want to send the message.
6. Click OK. Outlook redisplays the e-mail message window, and the selected recipients appear in the To field.

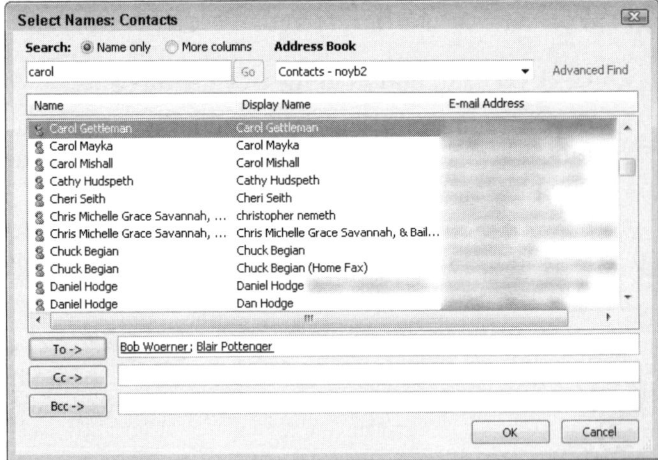

Figure 21-5

Reply to an E-Mail

1. Click the Mail button in the Navigation pane.
2. On the right hand side of the screen, click the message to which you want to reply.
3. Click the Reply button on the Home tab of the Ribbon. Outlook opens a new mail message and also fills in the e-mail address and the subject of the original message (see Figure 21-6).
4. Type the message and then click Send. Outlook stores the message in its Outbox.

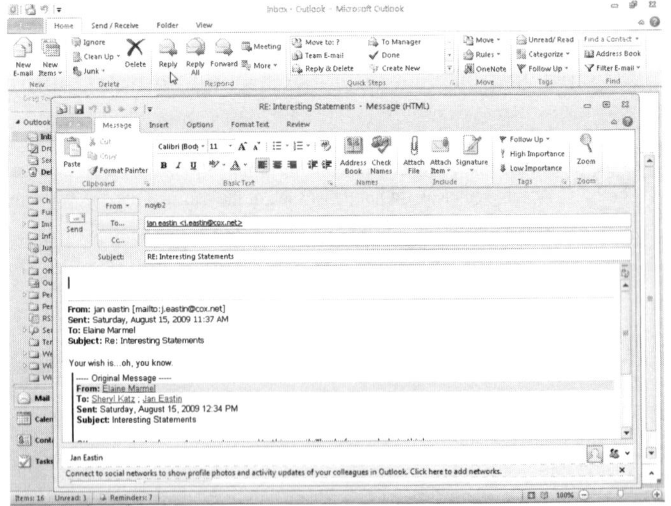

Figure 21-6

Forward an E-Mail

1. Click the Mail button in the Navigation pane.
2. On the right side of the screen, click the message you want to forward (see Figure 21-7).
3. On the Home tab, in the Respond group, click the Forward button, and Outlook displays the original message (see Figure 21-8).
4. In the To box, supply the addresses of the recipients to whom you want to forward the message.

You can click the To button and select contacts from the Address Book as described in the task, "Select Mail Message Recipients from the Address Book."

5. If appropriate, add text to the forwarded message.
6. Click Send. Outlook places the message in its Outbox, where it will remain until the next time Outlook sends messages, or until you click Send/Receive All Folders on the Quick Access Toolbar or press F9.

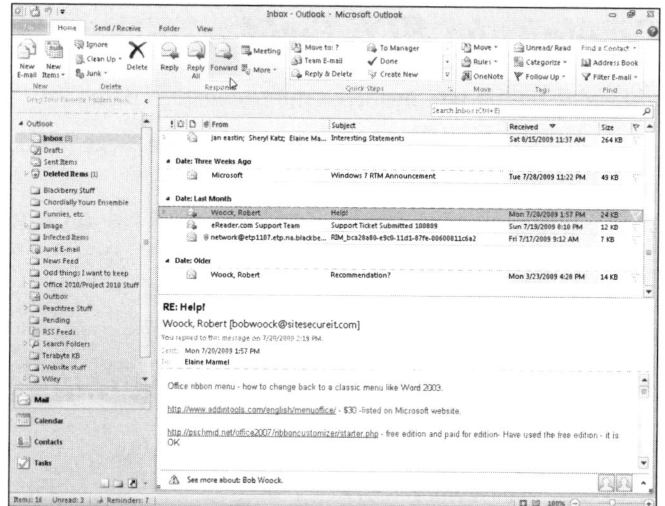

Figure 21-7

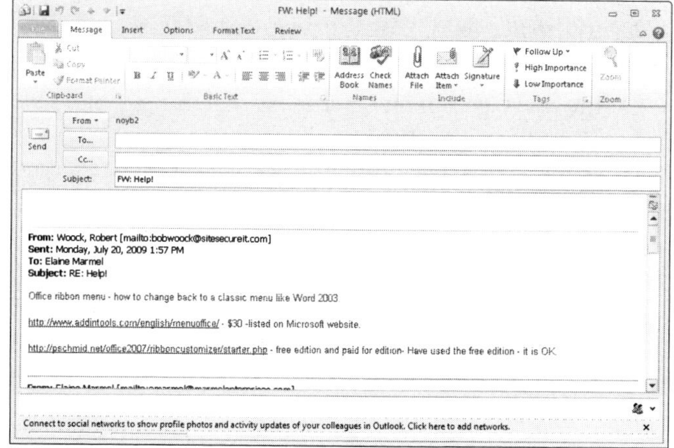

Figure 21-8

Display the BCC Field

1. Click the Mail button in the Navigation pane.
2. In a New, Reply To, or Forward Mail Message window, click the Options tab.
3. Click Show Bcc. Outlook adds the Bcc field to the message window (see Figure 21-9). Any recipients you include in the Bcc field will get the message, but their addresses will not be visible to other recipients.

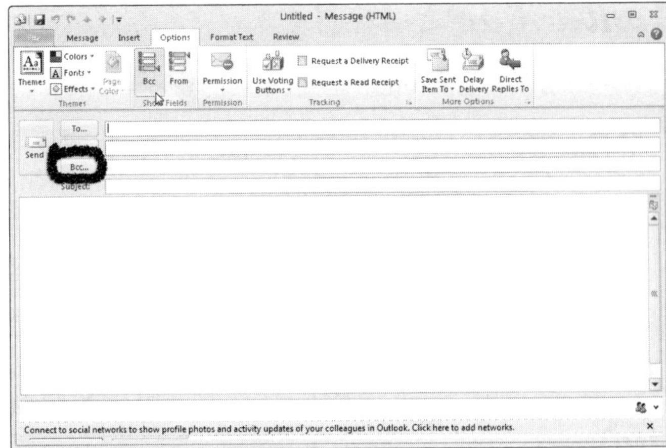

Figure 21-9

Send an E-mail without Displaying Recipient Names

1. Click the Mail button in the Navigation pane and then click the New E-mail button in the New group on the Home tab of the Ribbon.
2. In the Bcc field, type the recipient addresses.
3. In the To field, type the text that you want recipients to see as the message sender—perhaps something generic like **Message from Elaine Marmel**.
4. Following whatever you typed in Step 3, type your own e-mail address in brackets: **<emarmel@cox.net>** (see Figure 21-10).
5. Finish the e-mail message and send it. Each recipient gets a message whose sender matches what you typed in Step 3, but no recipient sees the names of any other recipient. You also receive a copy of the message.

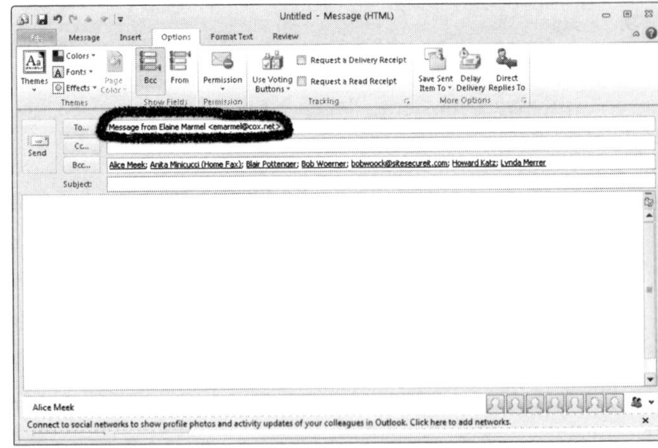

Figure 21-10

Control the Appearance of Original Message Text in Replies or Forwarded E-Mails

1. Click the File tab; the BackStage view appears (see Figure 21-11).
2. Click Options to display the Outlook Options dialog box.
3. Click Mail on the left and scroll down to the Replies and Forwards section (see Figure 21-12).
4. Open the When Replying to a Message list box and make a selection.
5. Open the When Forwarding a Message list box and make a selection.
6. Click OK.

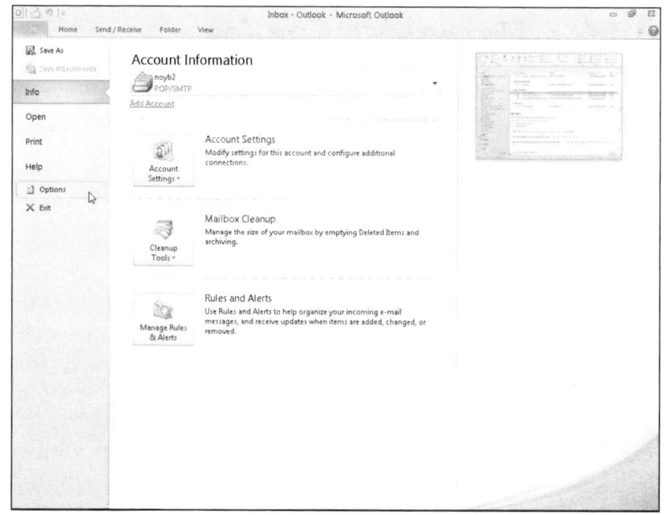

Figure 21-11

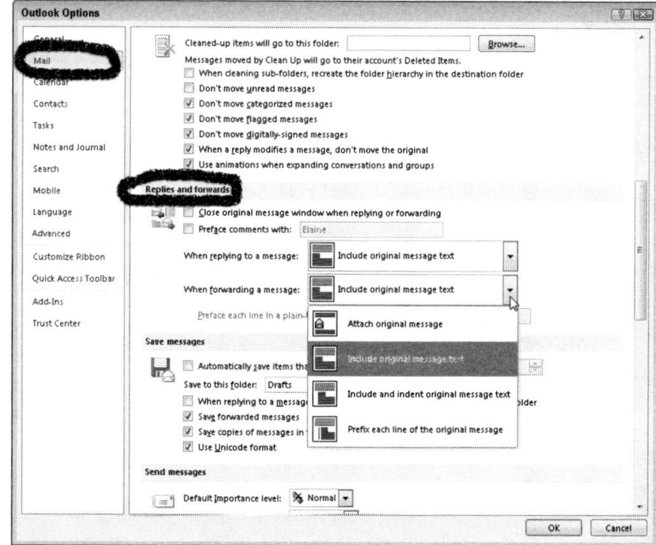

Figure 21-12

Add a Message's Sender to the Address Book

1. Click the Mail button in the Navigation pane.
2. Double-click the message from the sender whom you want to add to the Address Book.
3. Right-click the sender and choose Add to Outlook Contacts from the menu that appears (see Figure 21-13). The Contact window appears, with the sender's name and e-mail address filled in (see Figure 21-14).
4. Click the Save & Close button on the Ribbon.
5. Click the X in the upper right of the message window to close the message.

You can read creating a contact in Chapter 23.

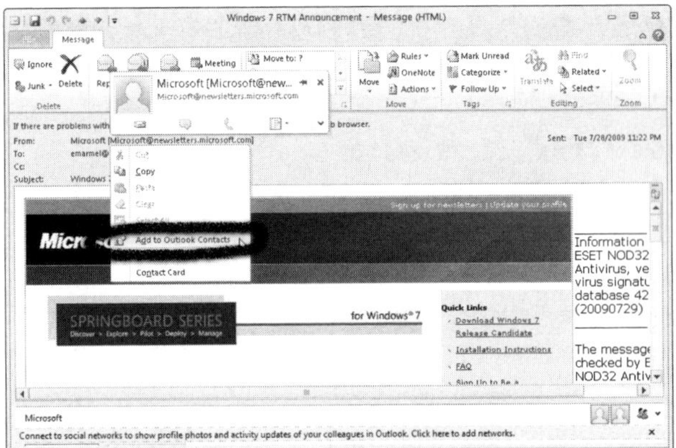

Figure 21-13

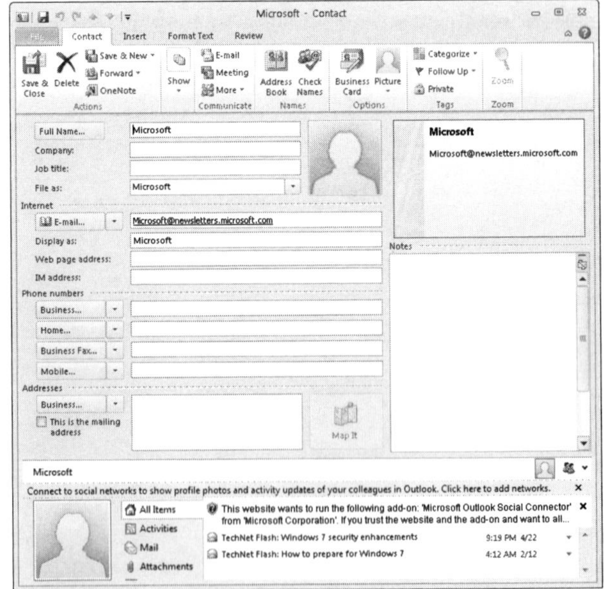

Figure 21-14

Attach a File to an E-Mail Message

1. Click the Mail button in the Navigation pane.
2. In a New, Reply To, or Forward Mail Message window, click the Message tab.
3. Click the Attach File button on the Ribbon (see Figure 21-15).
4. In the Insert File window that appears (see Figure 21-16), navigate to and select the folder where you stored the file you want to attach.
5. Click the Insert button (bottom right). The message window reappears, and a new field — the Attached field — appears below the subject of the message. In the Attached field, the file you selected in Step 4 appears.
6. Click Send. Outlook places the message in its Outbox, where it will remain until the next time Outlook sends messages, or until you click Send/Receive on the Quick Access Toolbar or press F9.

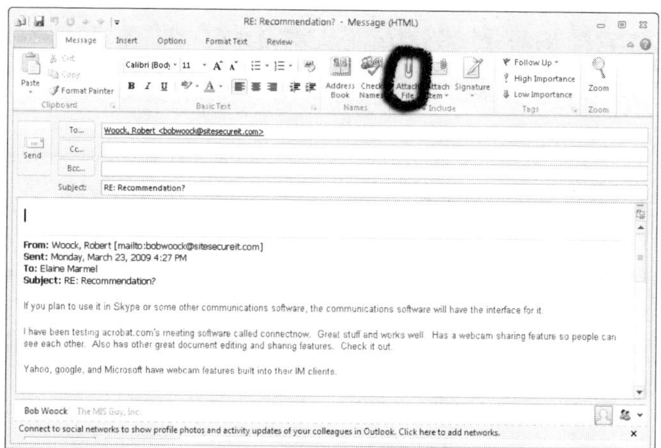

Figure 21-15

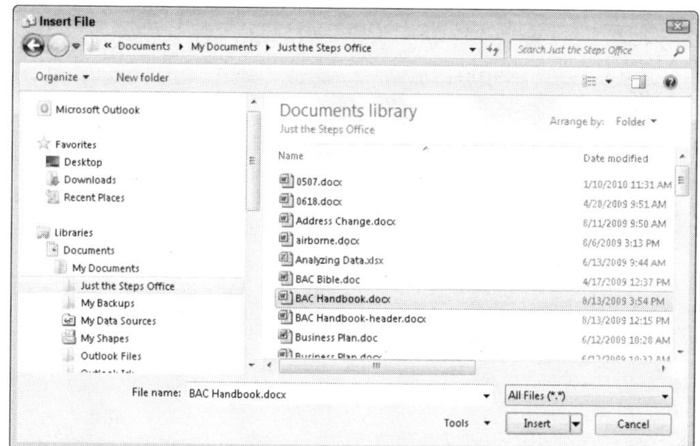

Figure 21-16

Send an E-Mail to a List of Contacts

1. Click the Mail button in the Navigation pane.

You must set up a Contact list before you can send e-mail to it. See Chapter 22 for details on setting up a Contact list.

2. In a New, Reply To, or Forward Mail Message window, click the To button.

3. In the Select Names dialog box, click or type the name of the Contact List and then click To (see Figure 21-17).

Contact List names appear in boldface type.

4. Click OK. Outlook redisplays the message window, and the To field displays the Contact List name, preceded by a plus sign (+), as shown in Figure 21-18.

You can click the plus sign to replace the Contact List name with the e-mail addresses included in the Contact List. You won't be able to "undo" this action, though.

5. Type a subject and the body of the message; then click Send.

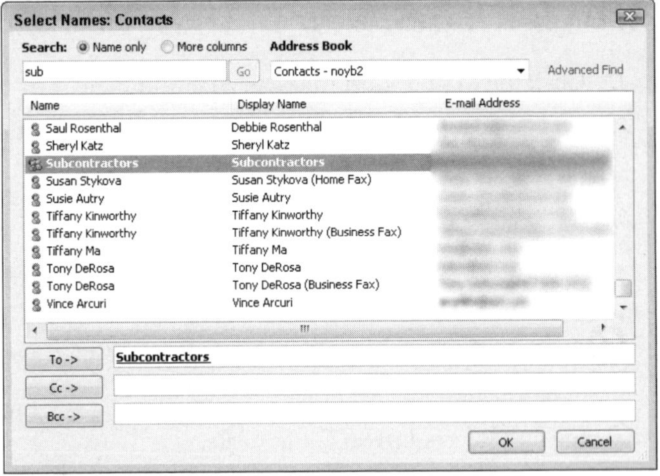

Figure 21-17

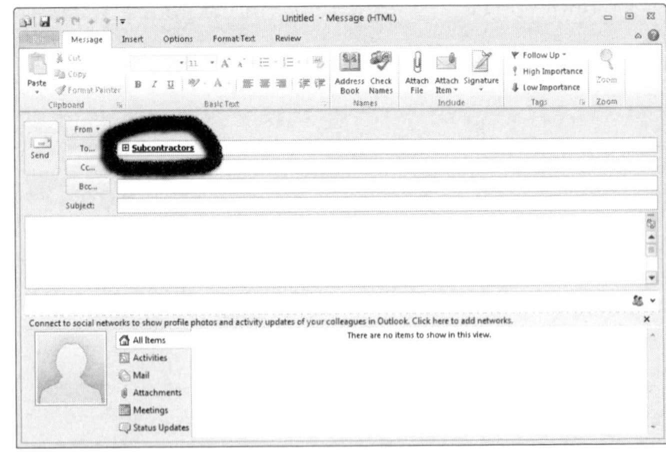

Figure 21-18

Use Quick Steps

1. Click the Mail button in the Navigation pane.
2. Click a message on the right side of the screen.
3. Click the Home tab on the Ribbon.
4. In the Quick Steps group, click an action you want to take. In Figure 21-19, I selected Reply & Delete.

Use Quick Steps to combine multiple actions into a single click.

5. Outlook performs the actions defined in the Quick Step you selected. In Figure 21-20, Outlook deletes the selected message and displays a reply e-mail message, which used the original e-mail's subject; all you need to do is type your message.

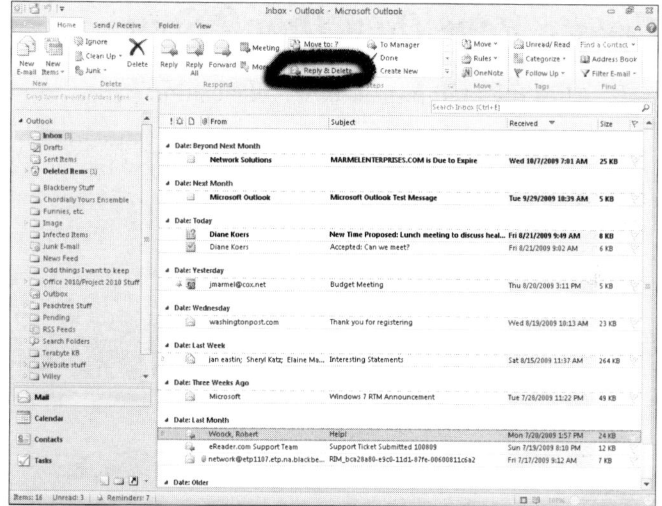

Figure 21-19

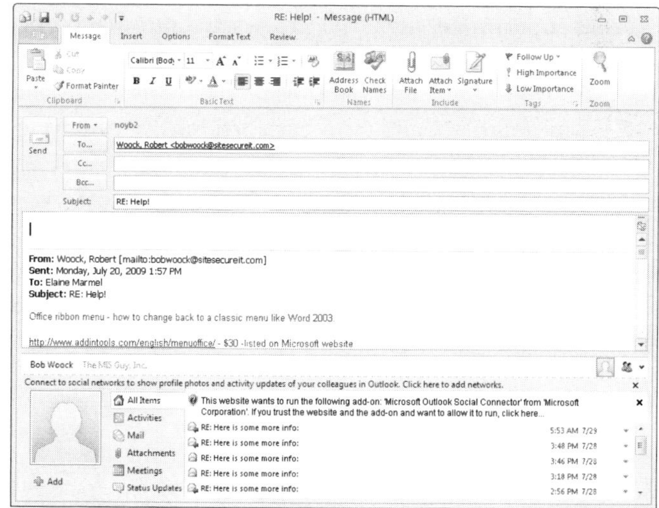

Figure 21-20

Create Your Own Quick Step

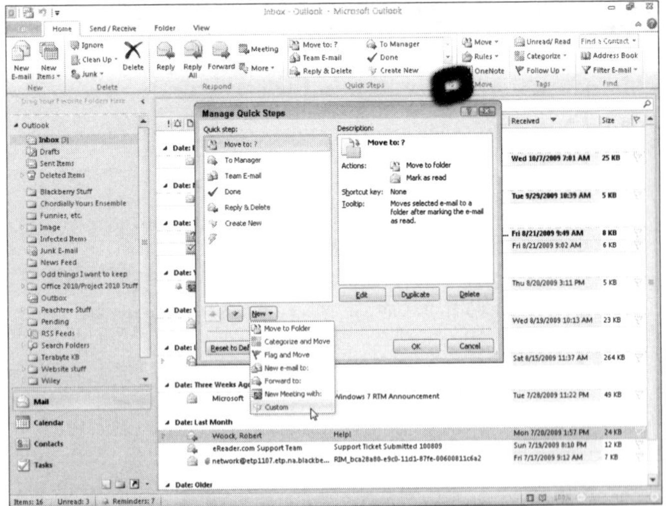

Figure 21-21

1. Click the Mail button in the Navigation pane.
2. On the Home tab, click the dialog box launcher for the Quick Steps group. Outlook displays the Manage Quick Steps dialog box (see Figure 21-21).
3. Click the New button and choose Custom. Outlook displays the My Quick Step dialog box (see Figure 21-22).
4. In the Name field, type a name for your Quick Step.
5. Open the Choose an Action list and select an action; for this example, I selected Forward in the Response section of the list.

Click the Show Options link to fill in any options you want Outlook to use each time you use this Quick Step.

6. If appropriate, click the Add Action button and open the new Choose an Action list that appears to select another action; for this example, I selected Move to Folder.
7. Repeat Steps 5 and 6 for each action you want to include in the Quick Step.
8. You can use the Shortcut Key list box to select a keyboard shortcut to assign, and you can type text you want to appear whenever you hover the mouse over the Quick Step.
9. Click Create, and then click Finish. Your Quick Step appears in the Quick Steps group on the Ribbon.

Figure 21-22

Create E-Mail Signatures

1. Click the File tab. From the Backstage view that appears, click Options to display the Outlook Options dialog box.
2. Click Mail on the left.
3. Click the Signatures button (see Figure 21-23).
4. In the Signatures and Stationery dialog box that appears (as shown in Figure 21-24), click the New button. In the New Signature dialog box that appears, type a title that describes the signature and then click OK.
5. From the upper right of the Signatures and Stationery dialog box, select a default e-mail account for the signature and a default signature for new messages and for message replies and forwards.
6. In the Edit Signature area, type the signature. You can select a font and font size; apply boldface, italics, underlining, and text color; set alignment; and insert a business card, graphic image, or hyperlink.

You can scan your signature, or take a digital photo of it and include it by clicking the Insert Picture button.

7. Click Save.
8. Repeat Steps 4–7 for each signature you want to create.
9. Click OK twice.

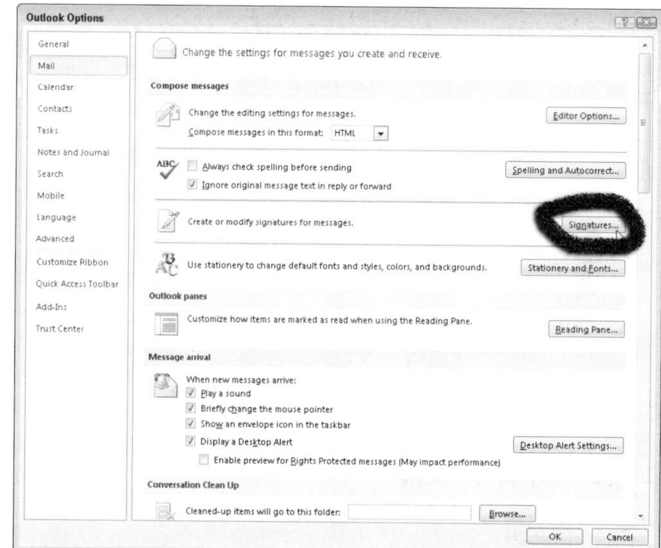

Figure 21-23

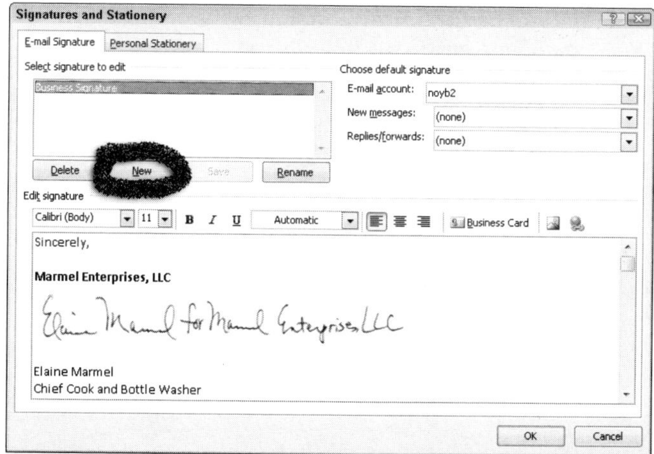

Figure 21-24

Select an Alternate Signature for an E-Mail Message

1. Click the Mail button in the Navigation pane.
2. In a New, Reply To, or Forward Mail Message window, click the Insert tab.
3. On the Ribbon, click the Signature button (see Figure 21-25).
4. From the drop-down list, select the signature that you want to include in the current e-mail message.
5. Complete the message and then click Send.

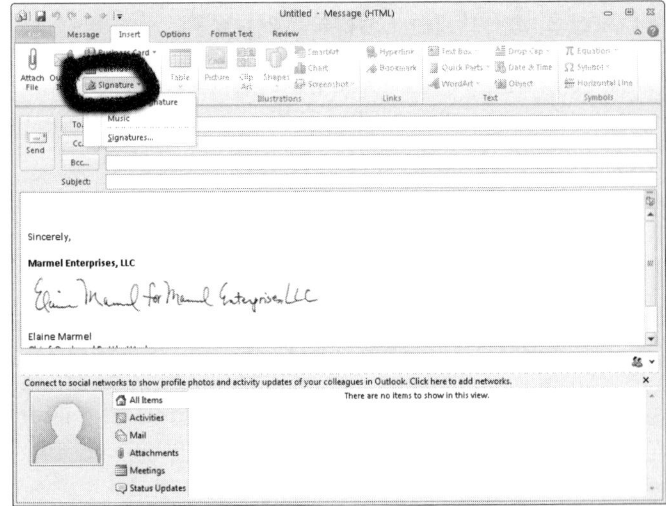

Figure 21-25

Search E-Mail

1. Click the Mail button in the Navigation pane, and then click the folder you want to search; for example, click the Inbox.
2. Click in the Search field on the right side of the screen, just below the Ribbon. To widen the search, use the buttons in the Scope group on the Ribbon.
3. Type the word or phrase for which you want to search; Outlook highlights the search phrase in yellow in either the subject or the body of all messages that contain the search phrase (see Figure 21-26). To redisplay all messages, delete the search word or phrase.

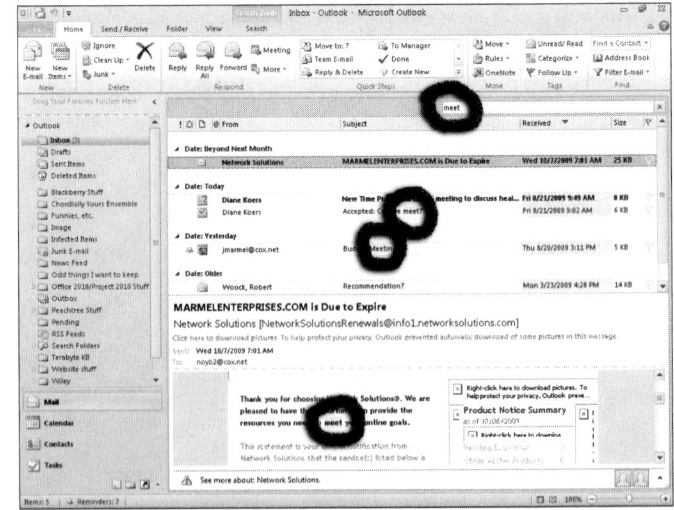

Figure 21-26

Sort and Group Messages

1. Click the Mail button in the Navigation pane.
2. Click the View tab; in the Arrangement group, select a method to sort messages. In Figure 21-27, messages are sorted by date but not in conversations or grouped, and the Reading pane doesn't appear.

You also can sort messages by clicking any column heading on the right side of the screen. And, by default, Outlook groups messages; these steps show you how to turn grouping on and off.

3. Click the More button in the Arrangement group (circled in Figure 21-27). From the drop-down menu that appears, click Show in Groups to make the grouping more obvious (see Figure 21-28).

Customize the arrangement of a view by choosing View Settings from the More drop-down menu. Use the buttons in the Advanced View Settings: dialog box that appears to select columns to display and methods to group, sort, and filter messages. You also can select fonts for the view, apply conditional formatting to messages that meet criteria you establish, and select formatting for each column in the view.

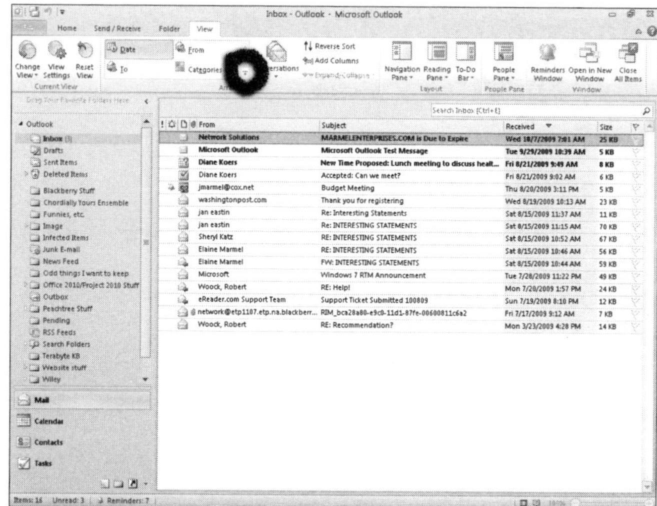

Figure 21-27

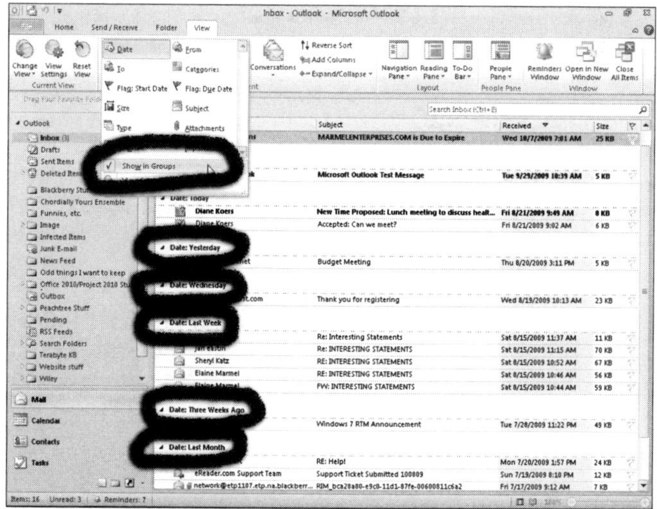

Figure 21-28

Automatically Move Messages to a Specific Folder

1. Click the Mail button in the Navigation pane and select a message upon which you can base a rule.

To move messages from a particular person, select a message from that person in the right-hand side of the window.

2. On the Home tab of the Ribbon, in the Move group, click the Rules button. From the list that appears, select Create Rule to display the Create Rule dialog box (see Figure 21-29).

3. In the When I Get E-mail with All of the Selected Conditions section, select the conditions that you want Outlook to match when moving a message to a specific folder.

4. In the Do the Following section, select the Move the Item to Folder check box. Outlook displays the Rules and Alerts dialog box (see Figure 21-30).

5. Select the folder where you want to store messages that match the criteria you set in Step 3.

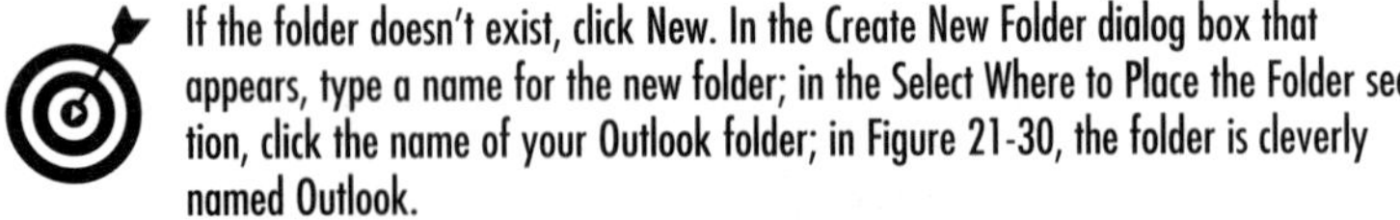

If the folder doesn't exist, click New. In the Create New Folder dialog box that appears, type a name for the new folder; in the Select Where to Place the Folder section, click the name of your Outlook folder; in Figure 21-30, the folder is cleverly named Outlook.

6. Click OK twice. Outlook displays a message indicating that you successfully created the rule, and Outlook offers you the opportunity to run the rule by selecting the Run This Rule Now on Messages Already in the Current Folder box.

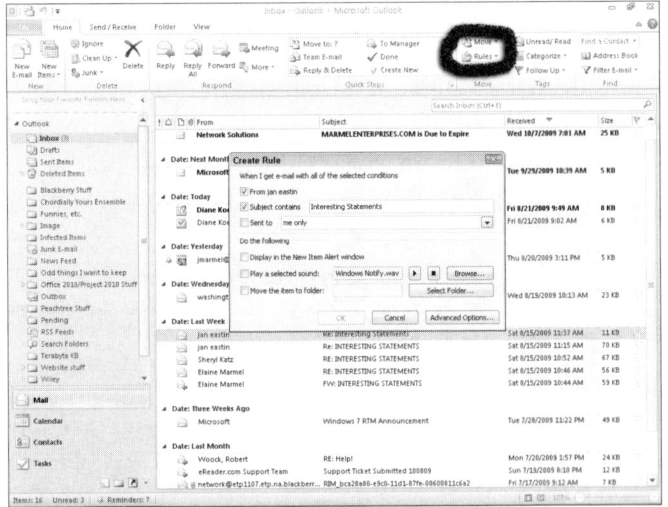

Figure 21-29

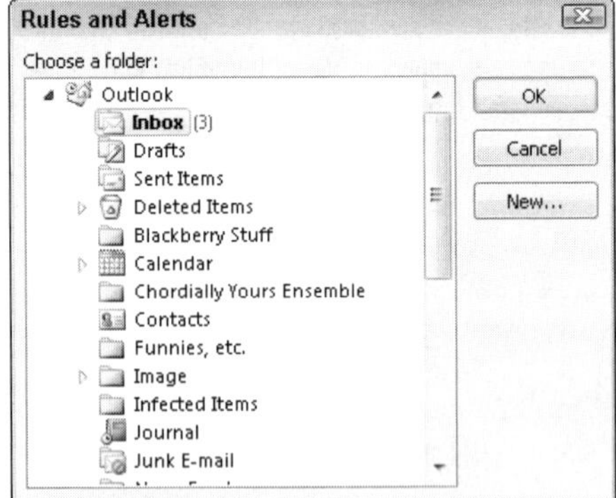

Figure 21-30

Categorize E-Mail

1. Click the Mail button in the Navigation pane.
2. Select a mail message on the right side of the Outlook window.
3. On the Home tab, click the Categorize button on the toolbar and then select a category to assign to the message (see Figure 21-31).

See Chapter 22 for details on creating categories.

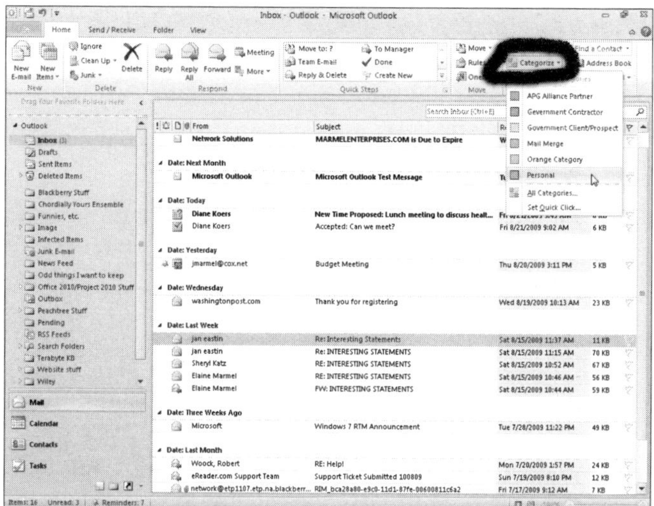

Figure 21-31

Follow Up on a Mail Message

1. Click the Mail button in the Navigation pane.
2. Select a mail message on the right side of the Outlook window.
3. On the Home tab, click the Follow Up button and then select a flag that represents when you want to follow up on the item (see Figure 21-32). Outlook displays a flag in the flag column beside the message and also creates a task that appears when you click Tasks in the Navigation pane.

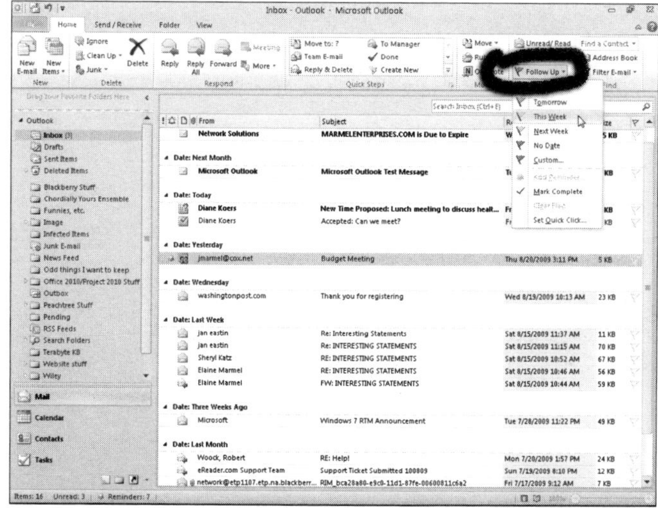

Figure 21-32

Create a Reminder

1. Click the Mail button in the Navigation pane.
2. Select a mail message on the right side of the Outlook window.
3. On the Home tab, click the Follow Up button and then choose Add Reminder from the drop-down list (see Figure 21-33).
4. In the Custom dialog box that appears, select the type of flag from the Flag To drop-down list (see Figure 21-34).
5. Set the Start Date and Due Date for the reminder.
6. Set a time for the reminder to appear. By default, Outlook plays a sound when the reminder appears, but you can shut off the sound by clicking the button to the right of the reminder time.
7. Click OK.

You set up reminders for e-mail messages, contacts, and tasks using these steps. To set a reminder on your Calendar, see Chapter 23.

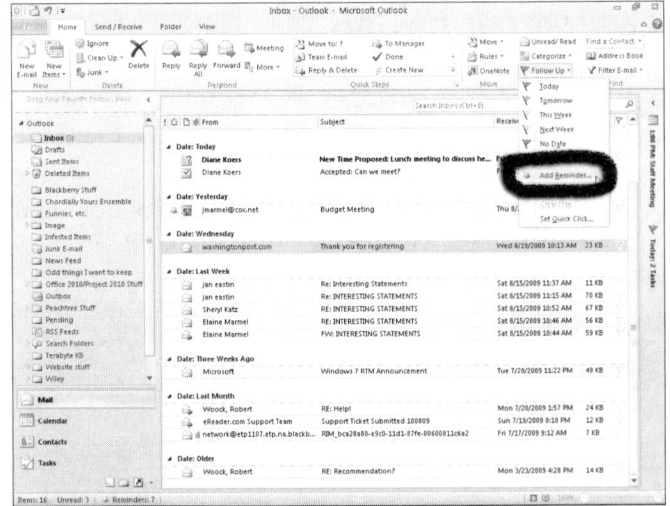

Figure 21-33

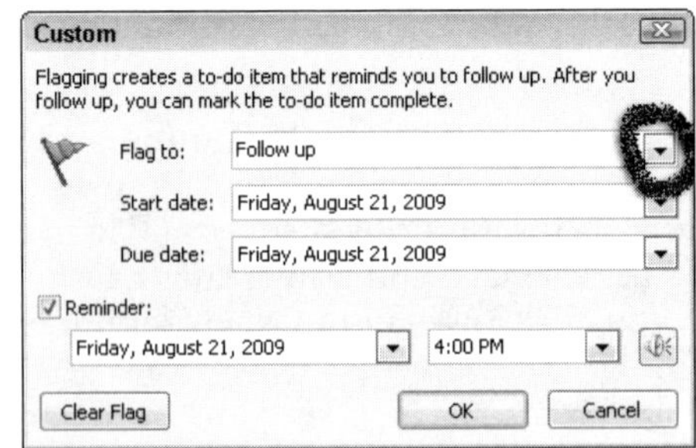

Figure 21-34

Set Up an Out-of-Office Reply Message

1. Click the Mail button in the Navigation pane.
2. Click the New E-mail button on the Home tab of the Ribbon.
3. Click the Format Text tab.
4. In the Format group, click Plain Text; if a message box appears, click Continue.
5. In the body of the message, type the message you want to send out as a reply to messages you receive while out of the office (see Figure 21-35).
6. In the message window, click the File tab. From the Backstage view that appears, choose Save As.
7. In the Save As dialog box that appears (shown in Figure 21-36), provide a filename.
8. Open the Save as Type list and choose Outlook Template (*.oft).
9. Navigate to C:\Users*user name*\AppData\Roaming\Microsoft\Templates.
10. Click Save.

You can close the e-mail message without saving or sending it. See the next task to turn on your out-of-office reply.

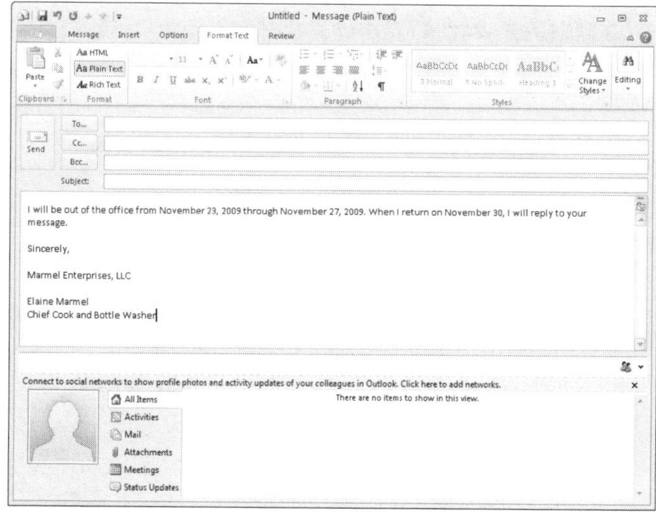

Figure 21-35

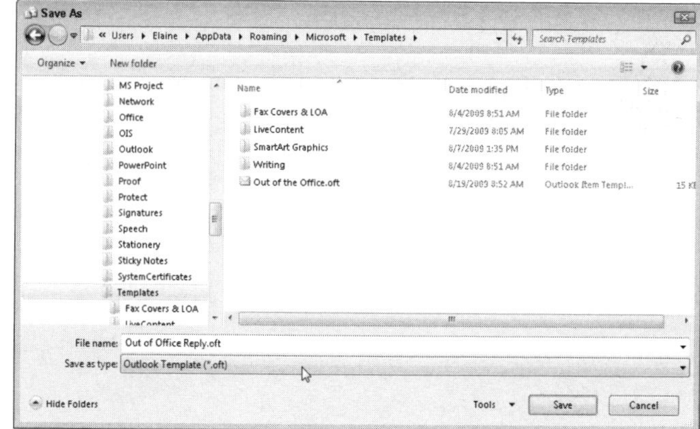

Figure 21-36

Turn On an Out-of-Office Reply Message

1. Click the Mail button in the Navigation pane.

These steps assume that you aren't using Microsoft Exchange Server. If you are using Microsoft Exchange Server, use the Automatic Replies button in Backstage view instead of using these steps.

2. On the Home tab, click the Rules button. From the drop-down menu, choose Manage Rules and Alerts.
3. In the Rules and Alerts dialog box shown in Figure 21-37, click the New Rule button to start the Rules Wizard.
4. In the Start from a Blank Rule section, click Apply Rule on Messages I Receive (see Figure 21-38).
5. Click Next.

Outlook must be running and checking for messages for the automatic reply to be sent. Outlook keeps track of the users to whom the automated reply is sent and sends the automated reply only once to each sender — that is, as long as you don't close Outlook and reopen it.

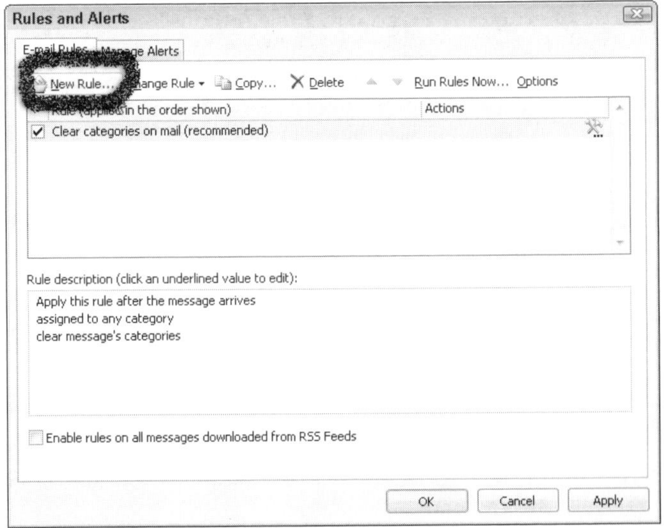

Figure 21-37

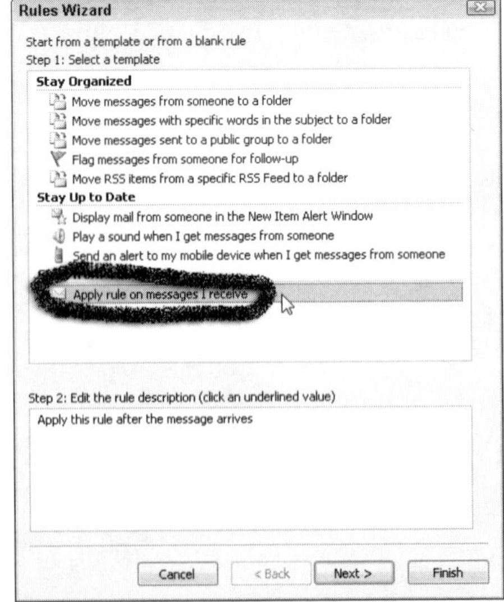

Figure 21-38

6. In the Which Condition(s) Do You Want to Check? section, select the Sent Only to Me check box (see Figure 21-39). If other criteria apply, select them as well. If a dialog box appears and informs you that Outlook will apply this rule to every message that you receive, click Yes.
7. Click Next.
8. In the What Do You Want to Do with the Message? Step 1: Select Action(s) section, select the Reply Using a Specific Template check box.
9. In the Step 2: Edit The Rule Description section, click the A Specific Template link (see Figure 21-40).

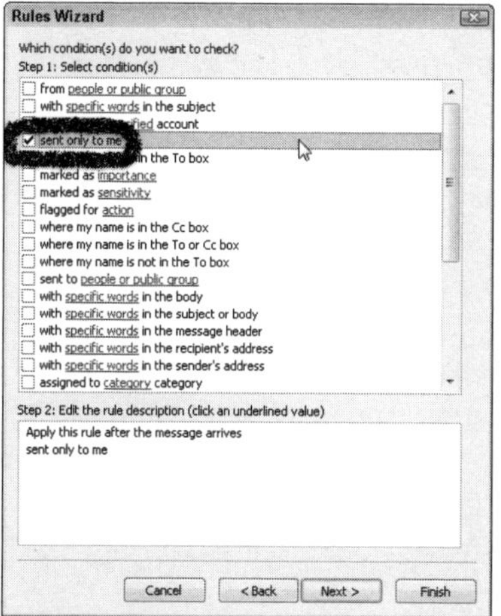

Figure 21-39

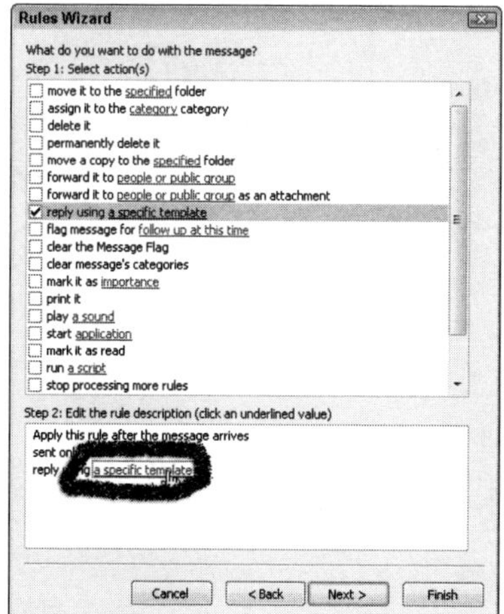

Figure 21-40

10. In the Select a Reply Template dialog box, open the Look In drop-down list and choose User Templates in File System (see Figure 21-41).
11. Select the template that you want to use for your out-of-office reply and then click Open to redisplay Figure 21-40. Outlook replaces the A Specific Template link with a link to your message template.
12. Click Next; if appropriate, select any exceptions that you want to apply to the rule. For example, you can avoid applying the rule to messages containing certain words in the subject.
13. Click Next.
14. Supply a name for the rule. If you want to start using it, select the Turn on This Rule check box (see Figure 21-42).
15. Click Finish to redisplay the Rules and Alerts dialog box shown earlier in Figure 21-37.
16. Click OK.

After you create a rule, the Rules and Alerts dialog box turns the out-of-office reply on and off. Complete Steps 1 and 2 in this task to redisplay the Rules and Alerts dialog box. Select or remove the check that appears beside the rule. Consider setting up a task or reminder to help you turn the rule on and off as appropriate.

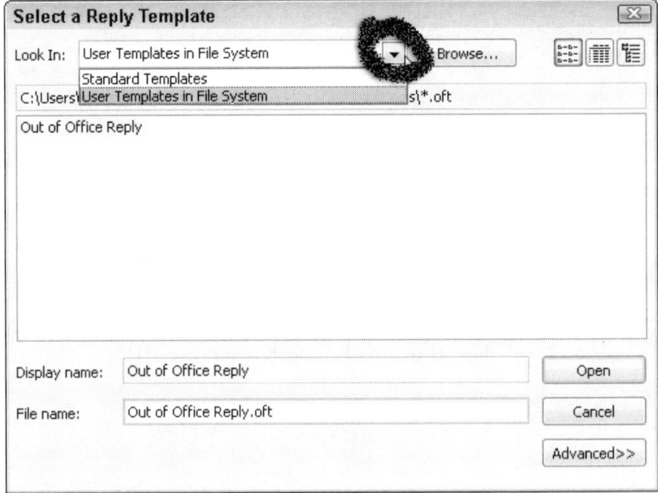

Figure 21-41

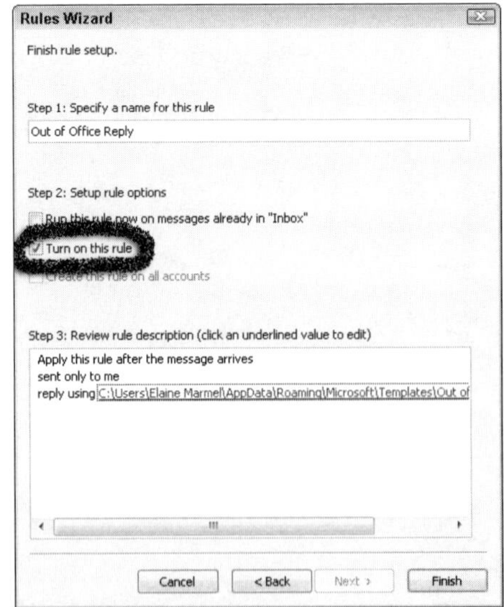

Figure 21-42

Manage Junk Mail

1. Click the Mail button in the Navigation pane.
2. On the Home tab, from the Delete group, click the Junk button. From the menu that appears, choose Junk E-mail Options (see Figure 21-43).
3. On the Options tab of the Junk E-mail Options dialog box, shown in Figure 21-44, you can set the level of junk mail protection that you want Outlook to apply.

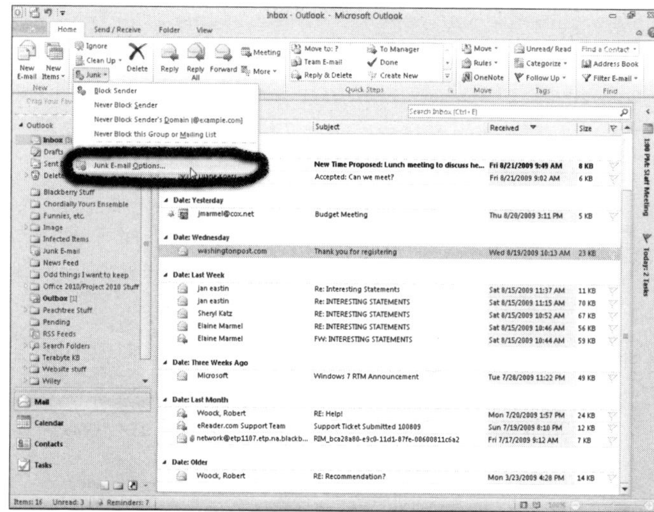

Figure 21-43

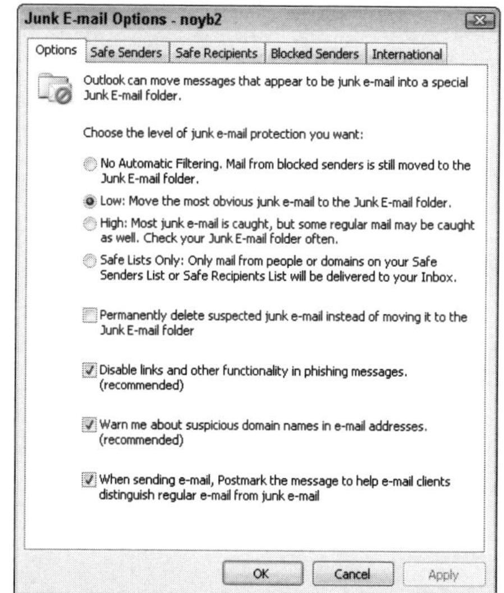

Figure 21-44

4. Click the Safe Senders tab (see Figure 21-45).
5. Click the Add button to add an e-mail address or domain name of someone from whom you always want to receive messages. Outlook will not treat e-mail as junk mail from anyone who appears on this list.

The Safe Recipients tab and the Blocked Senders tabs work the same way as the Safe Senders tab. On the Safe Recipients tab, you can add e-mail addresses or domain names for e-mail you send. On the Blocked Senders tab, you can add e-mail addresses or domains that you want Outlook to always treat as junk mail.

6. Click the International tab (see Figure 21-46).
7. Click the Blocked Top-Level Domain List button to select countries or regions from which you want to block e-mail.

You can click the Blocked Encodings List button to block e-mail messages in selected languages.

8. Click OK to close the Junk E-mail Options dialog box.

Figure 21-45

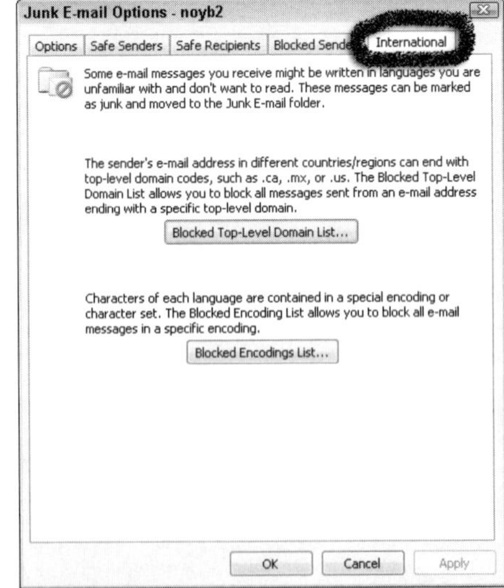

Figure 21-46

Managing Contacts

In Outlook, *contacts* are the people with whom you interact. You might send them e-mail, you might have meetings with them, or you might work with them on tasks. In the Contacts section of Outlook, you can store pertinent information about your contacts — including name, e-mail address, street address, and phone numbers — in your Address Book so that you always have that information at your fingertips. You also have room to store personal information about the contact, such as the contact's birthday and spouse's name. Outlook makes contact information readily available in other sections of Outlook. For example, if you store a contact's e-mail address, Outlook fills in the e-mail address automatically when you send an e-mail to the contact.

As your list of contacts grows, you might find it handy to organize your contacts by assigning them to color categories. You also can view your contact information in a variety of ways, including by category. In this chapter, you see how to

- Add a contact to the Outlook Address Book.
- Create a distribution list so that you can quickly send an e-mail to a group of people.
- View contacts in different ways.
- Manage contacts using categories.
- Print contact information.
- Share contact information.

Get ready to . . .

Add Contacts

1. Click the Contacts button in the Navigation pane.
2. Click the New Contact button on the Home tab of the Ribbon to display a new, untitled Contact window (see Figure 22-1).
3. Type a name in the Full Name field and provide other information for the contact. In the Display As field, type the name that you want Outlook to display in the To line of an e-mail message. Use the arrows beside various fields to store multiple e-mail and street addresses as well as phone numbers. You can categorize contacts to help manage them; see "Create Color Categories for Contacts" later in this chapter.
4. Click the Save & Close button.

To create another contact from the same company, click the Save & New button. Then, click the arrow beside the Save & New button and choose Contact from Same Company. Outlook displays a new Contact window that contains Company, Business Phone, and Business Address information. To create a contact from an e-mail message, see Chapter 21.

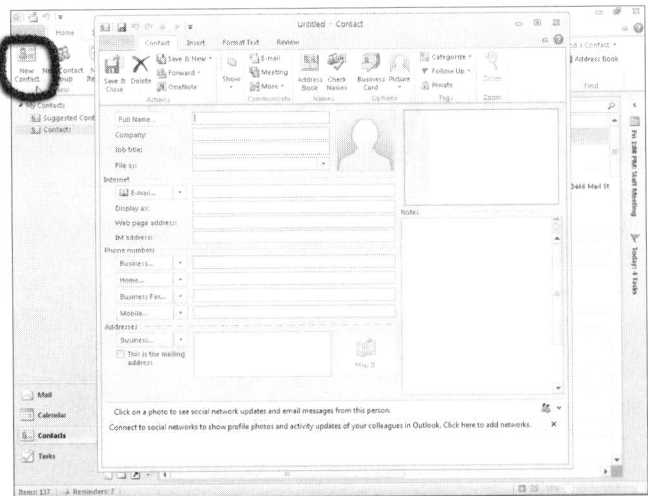

Figure 22-1

Search for a Contact

1. Click Contacts in the Navigation pane.
2. On the right side of the screen, click in the Search Contacts field that appears above your list of contacts.
3. Type some letters of a contact name; Outlook displays the closest matches (see Figure 22-2).

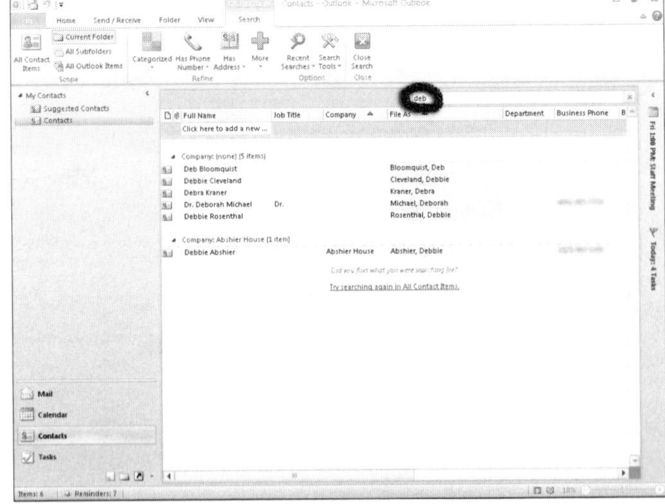

Figure 22-2

Create a Contact Group

1. Click the Contacts button in the Navigation pane.
2. On the Home tab, in the New group, click New Contact Group to display the Contact Group window (see Figure 22-3).

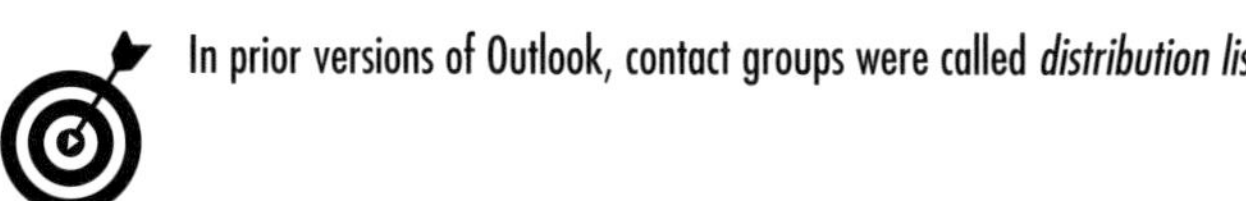

In prior versions of Outlook, contact groups were called *distribution lists.*

3. In the Name field, type a name that describes the contact group.
4. From the Members group, click Add Members and then select a source for the members you want to add. Outlook displays the Select Members window (see Figure 22-4).
5. Click a contact; or, in the Search field, type some letters of a name that you want to include in the group. Outlook highlights the first contact that matches the letters you typed.
6. When Outlook highlights the correct contact, click the Members button to add the contact to the contact group.
7. Repeat Steps 4 and 5 for each contact that you want to include in the contact group. Outlook separates contact names with a semi-colon (;).
8. Click OK to redisplay the Contact Group window shown in Figure 22-3; the window now contains a list of contacts included in the contact group.
9. Click the Save & Close button.

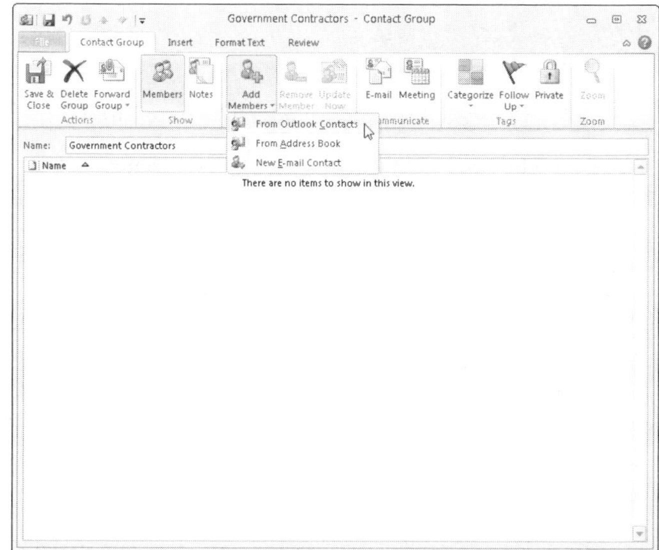

Figure 22-3

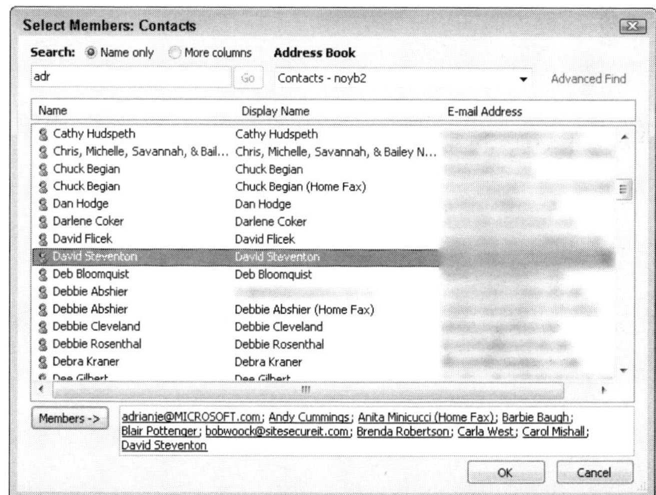

Figure 22-4

Work with Views

1. Click Contacts in the Navigation pane.
2. Click the View tab on the Ribbon.
3. From the Current View group, click the Change View button and select a view; Figure 22-5 shows Business Card view, and Figure 22-6 shows Phone view, which present contacts in a list format.
4. Click each view to explore the different ways how Outlook can display your contact information. Each view can help you focus on different types of contact information.

In list views, contact groups appear in bold letters.

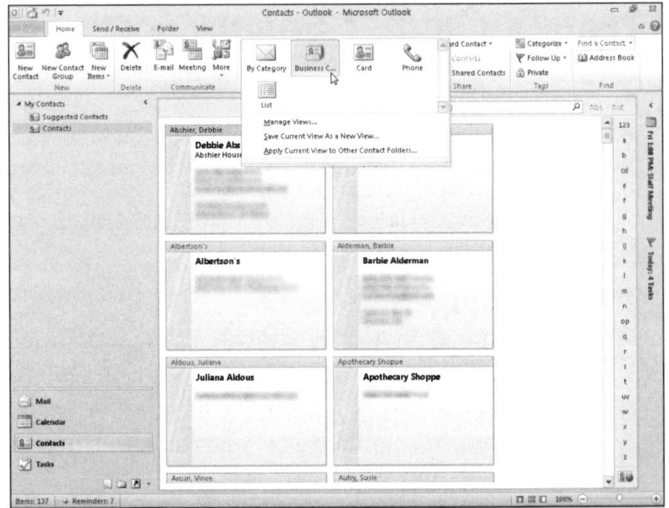

Figure 22-5

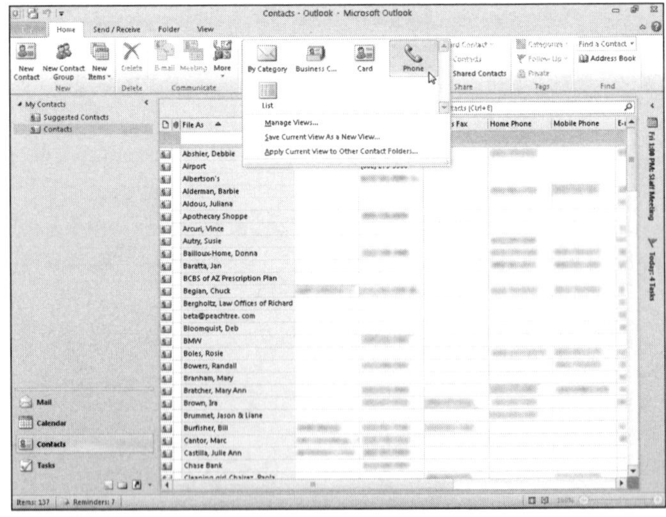

Figure 22-6

Create Color Categories for Contacts

1. Click Contacts in the Navigation pane.
2. Select any contact on the right side of the window.
3. On the Home tab, click the Categorize button and then choose All Categories to display the Color Categories dialog box shown in Figure 22-7.
4. To rename the existing categories, click a category; then click the Rename button and type a new name.
5. To add another category, click the New button to display the Add New Category dialog box shown in Figure 22-8.
6. Type a name for the category. If you don't like the color Outlook selected, open the Color list and select a different color.

You can assign keyboard shortcuts to categories so that you can quickly and easily assign a category to an Outlook item.

7. Click OK; Outlook assigns the new category to the contact you selected in Step 2 by placing a check beside the category in the Color Categories dialog box. Use the check boxes beside each category to assign categories to the selected contact. You can assign a contact to more than one category.
8. Click OK to save the categories you established.

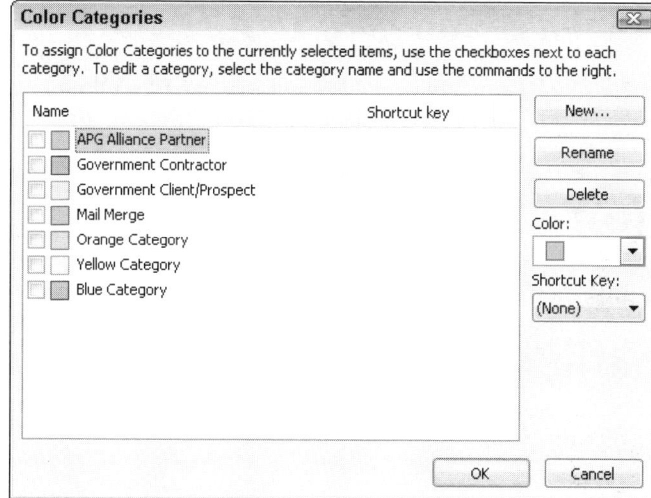

Figure 22-7

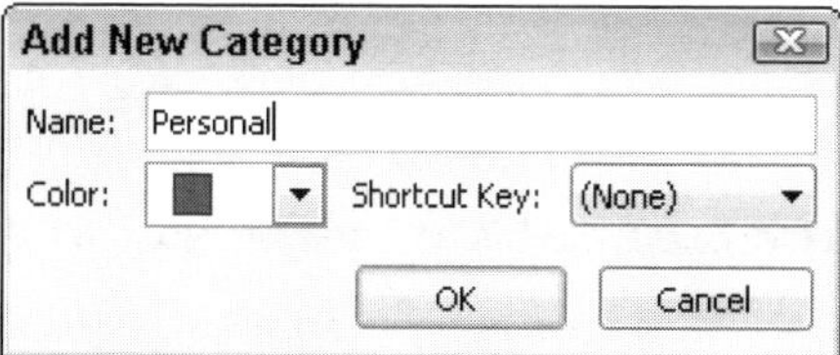

Figure 22-8

Assign a Category to a Contact

1. Click Contacts in the Navigation pane and then click the Home tab.

You can assign categories you create to any Outlook item: meetings or appointments on the Calendar, e-mail messages, tasks, contacts, notes, and so on.

2. Select any contact. Using List view or Phone view, you can simultaneously assign the same category to multiple contacts. To select a contiguous set of contacts, click the first contact, press and hold the Shift key, and then click the last contact. Select individual contacts by pressing and holding Ctrl while you click.
3. On the Home tab, in the Tags group, click the Categorize button; from the list that appears, select a category (see Figure 22-9). Outlook assigns that category to the selected contact(s).
4. To view contacts by category, click the View tab.
5. In the Arrangement group, click Categories (see Figure 22-10).

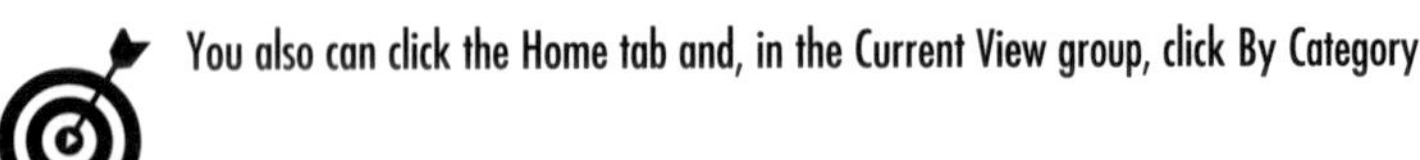

You also can click the Home tab and, in the Current View group, click By Category.

6. Double-click a category's heading to expand or contract your view of the contacts in that category.

You also can assign a category to a contact as you create the contact; in the Untitled – Contact window, the Categorize button appears on the Contact tab in the Tags group.

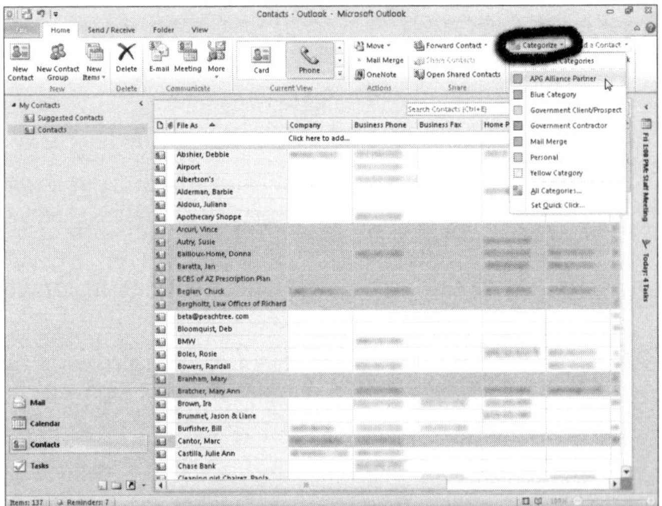

Figure 22-9

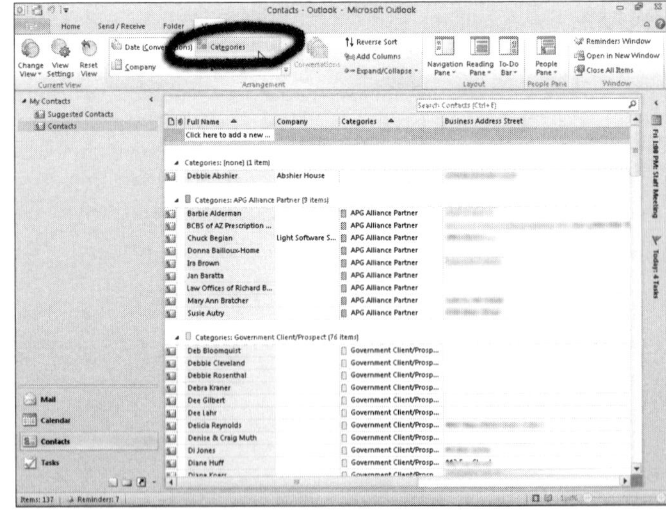

Figure 22-10

Print a View

1. Click Contacts in the Navigation pane.
2. Use the Current View group on the Home tab to select the view you want to print. In Figure 22-11, I selected Card view.
3. Click the File tab. In the Backstage view that appears, click Print (see Figure 22-12).
4. In the Printer section, click the button to select a printer.
5. You can click the Print Options button to display the Print dialog box, where you can opt to print selected pages, set up the number of copies you want to print, and change the page orientation from Portrait to Landscape.
6. In the Print What section, select a print style; the choices available depend upon the view you selected in Step 2. The preview on the far right changes to reflect the print style you select.
7. Click Print.

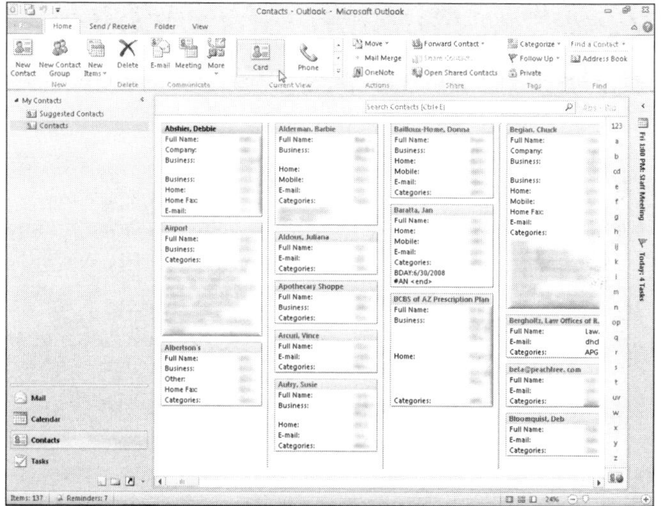

Figure 22-11

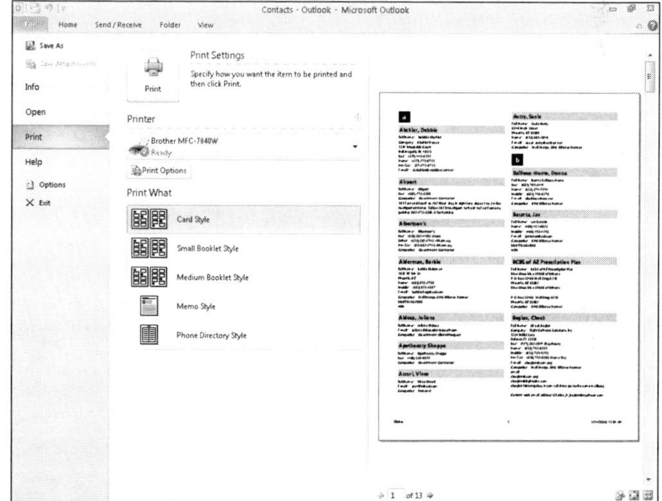

Figure 22-12

View One Category of Contacts in Any Contact View

1. Click Contacts in the Navigation pane.
2. Click the View tab.
3. In the Current View group, click the Change View button and select any view except By Category; for this example, use Business Card view.
4. In the Current View group, click the View Settings button (see Figure 22-13).
5. In the Advanced View Settings dialog box that appears, click the Filter button (see Figure 22-14).

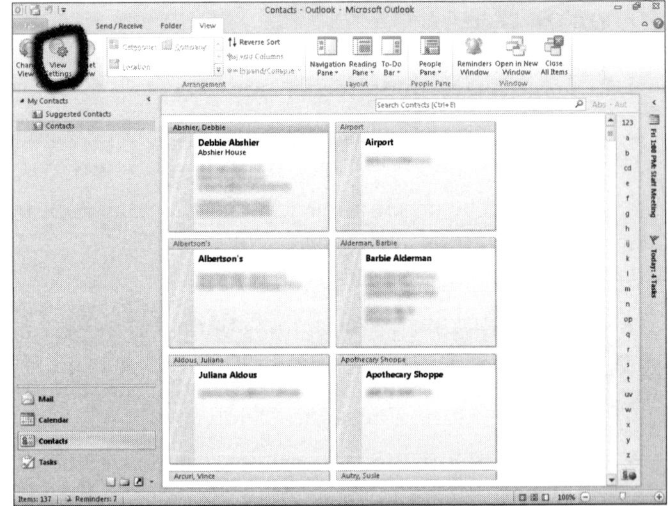

Figure 22-13

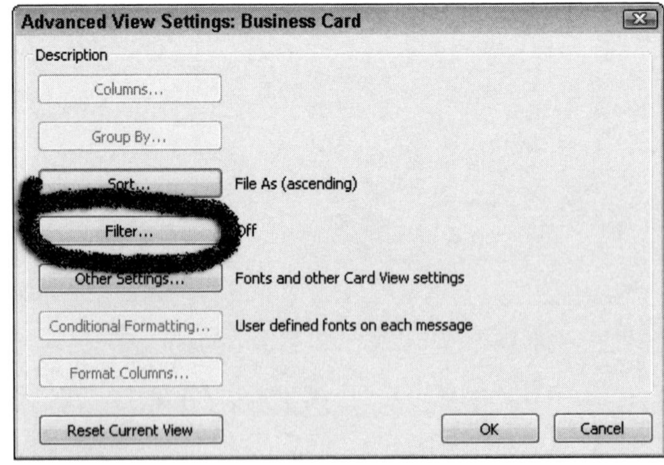

Figure 22-14

6. In the Filter dialog box that appears, click the More Choices tab (see Figure 22-15).
7. Click the Categories button.
8. In the Color Categories dialog box that appears, select the check box beside the category you want to display (see Figure 22-16).
9. Click OK three times. The view you selected in Step 2 — Business Card view, in this example — now displays only those contacts assigned to the selected category.

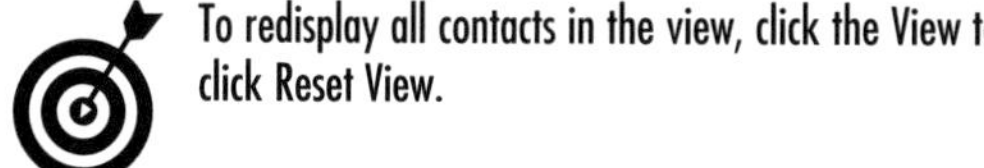

To redisplay all contacts in the view, click the View tab and, in the Current View group, click Reset View.

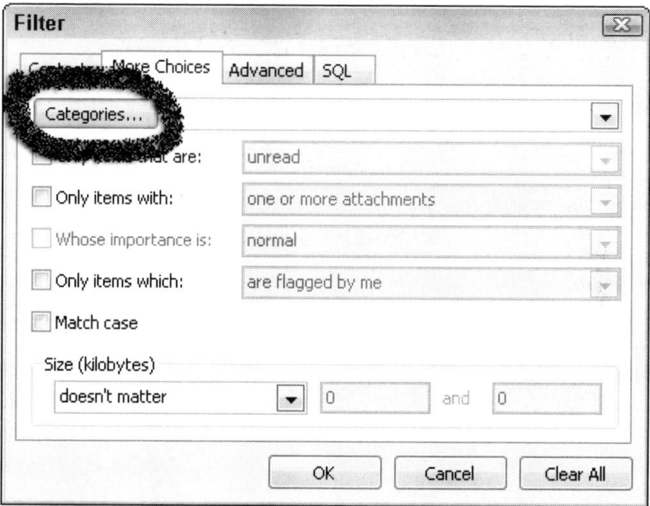

Figure 22-15

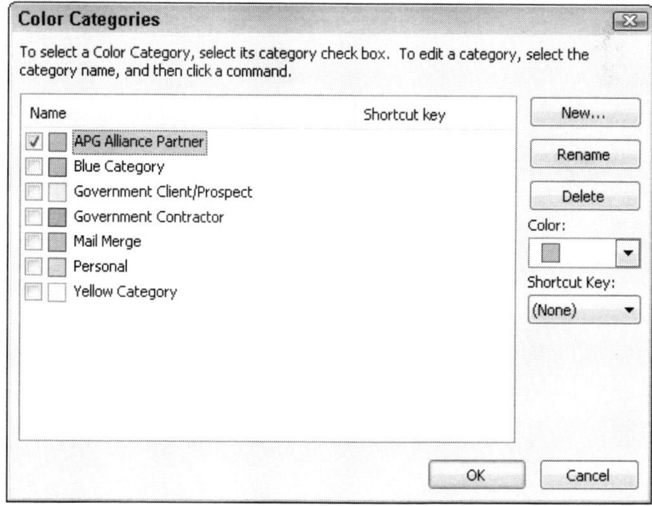

Figure 22-16

Print a Category of Contacts

1. Follow the steps in "View One Category of Contacts in Any Contact View" preceding this section to set up the category of contacts to print.

Outlook prints the information you have displayed on-screen when you opt to print. So, to print a selection of information, you first customize a view to display that information and then you print it.

2. Click the File tab to display the Back Stage view (see Figure 22-17).
3. Click Print to display printing options (see Figure 22-18).

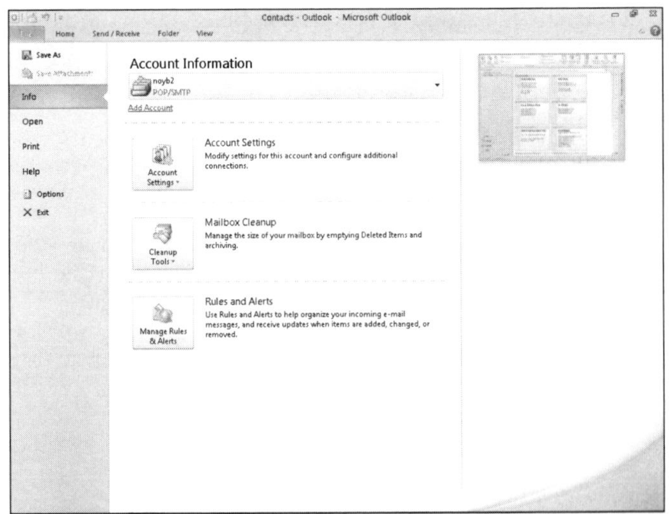

Figure 22-17

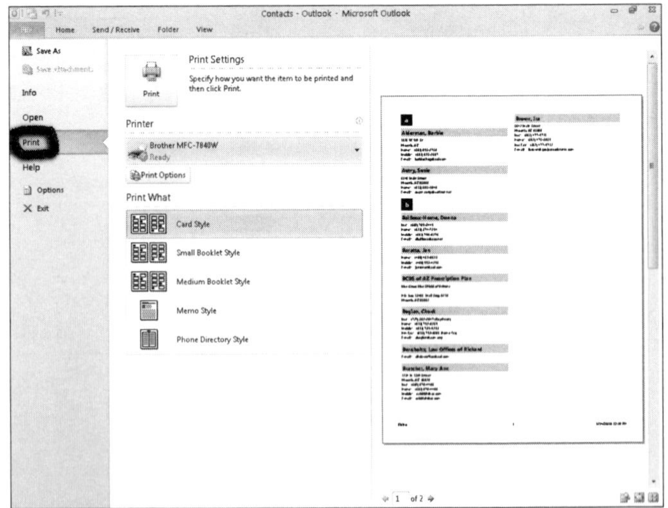

Figure 22-18

4. Click the first button in the Printer section to select a printer (see Figure 22-19).
5. You can click the Print Options button to display the Print dialog box, where you can opt to print selected pages, set how many copies you want to print, and change the page orientation from Portrait to Landscape.
6. In the Print What section, select a print style. Outlook displays a sample of what you'll get if you print. Figures 22-18 and 22-19 show the Card Style, Figure 22-20 shows the Phone Directory Style.

You can use the arrows below the preview to page through the document, and you can click the Preview area or use the buttons below it on the right to zoom in and out of the preview.

7. Click Print.

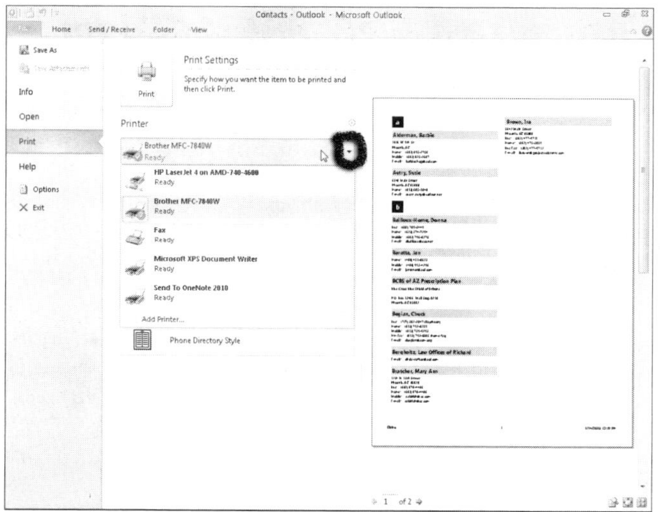

Figure 22-19

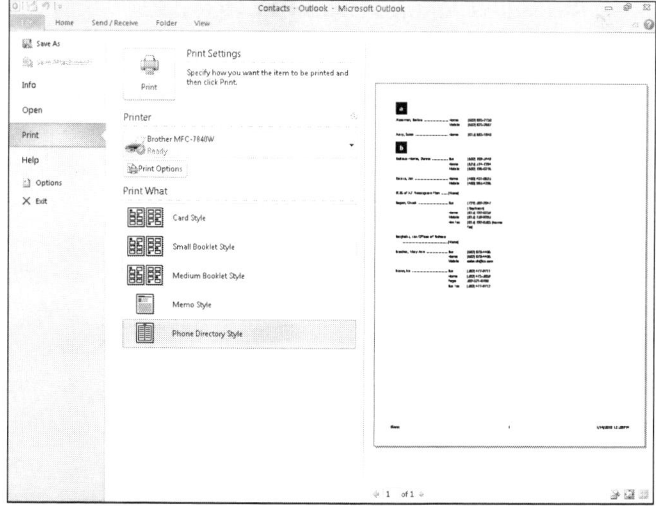

Figure 22-20

Customize a View to Display and Print Address Information

1. Click Contacts in the Navigation pane.
2. Click the View tab; in the Current View group, click the Change View button to select the view in which you want to display address information. For this example, I'm using Phone view.

Outlook prints address information only if it appears onscreen. To print address information for a particular category of contacts, select and customize By Category view. See "View One Category of Contacts in Any Contact View" earlier in this chapter.

3. On the View tab, from the Arrangement group, click Add Columns (see Figure 22-21).
4. In the Show Columns dialog box that appears, open the drop-down list box above the Available Columns list and then select Address Fields (see Figure 22-22).
5. In the Available Columns list, click a field to add.
6. In the Show These Columns in This Order list, click the field that you want to display to the right of the new field.
7. Click the Add button.
8. Repeat Steps 5–7 for each field.
9. Click OK.

You can use reorder fields in the view by using the Move Up and Move Down buttons, and you can remove a field by clicking it and then clicking Remove.

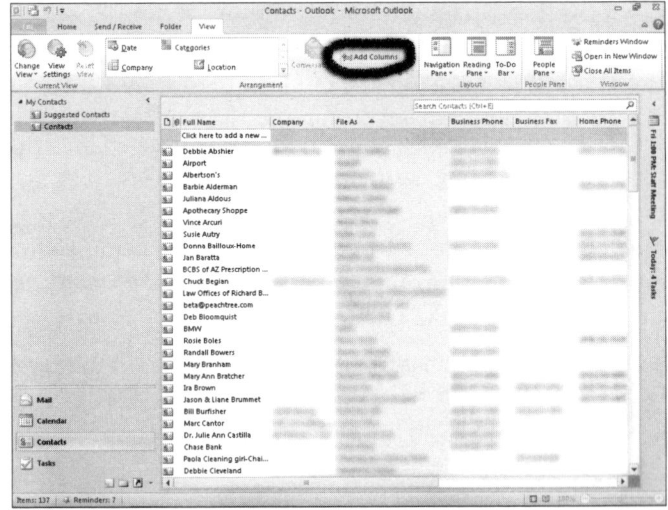

Figure 22-21

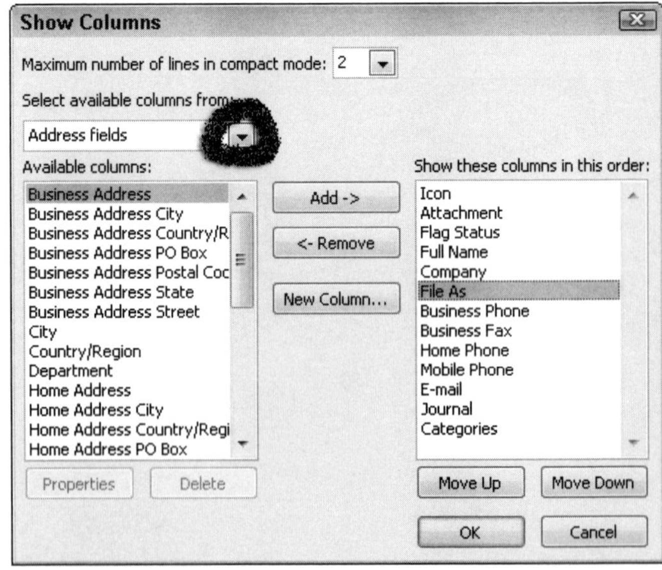

Figure 22-22

E-Mail a Contact's Information

1. Click Contacts in the Navigation pane.
2. Right-click a contact and choose Forward Contact from the menu that appears. From the submenu that appears, click As a Business Card (see Figure 22-23). Outlook opens an e-mail message. An *electronic business card* — nothing more than a paper business card in electronic form — appears in the body of the message. Outlook also includes a `.vcf` attachment that users of Outlook and other e-mail clients that support business cards can import into their own databases (see Figure 22-24).

If you want to send just the `.vcf` attachment, click Forward Contact and then select As an Outlook Contact.

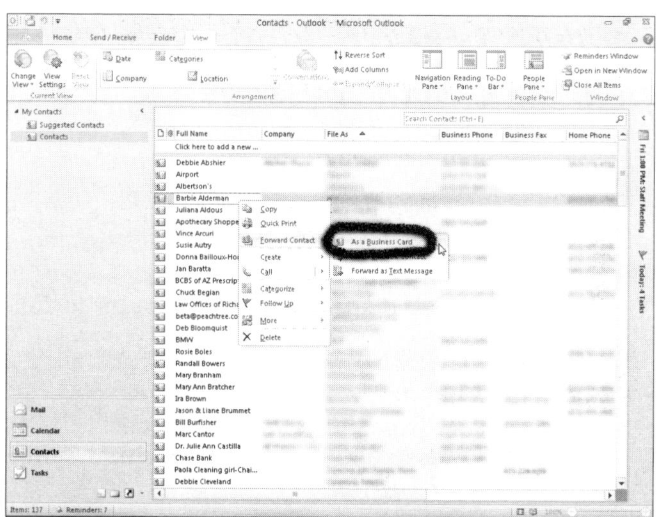

Figure 22-23

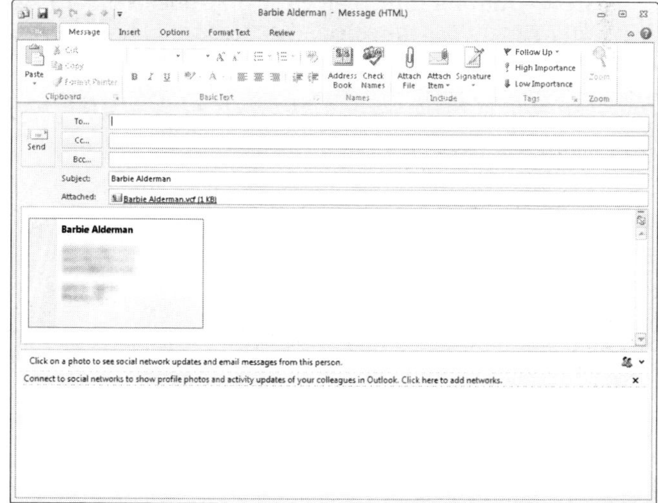

Figure 22-24

Forward Contact Information from an E-Mail Message

1. Click Mail in the Navigation pane.
2. On the Ribbon in the New group, click the New E-mail button to start a new mail message.
3. Place insertion point in To field or in the body of message and then click the Attach Item button in the Include group.
4. From the list that appears, click Business Card (see Figure 22-25).
5. Select a name from the list that appears or click Other Business Cards to display the Insert Business Card window (see Figure 22-26).
6. Highlight the contact whose contact information you want to forward and then click OK. In the body of the message window, Outlook inserts an electronic business card and a `.vcf` attachment for the selected contact.

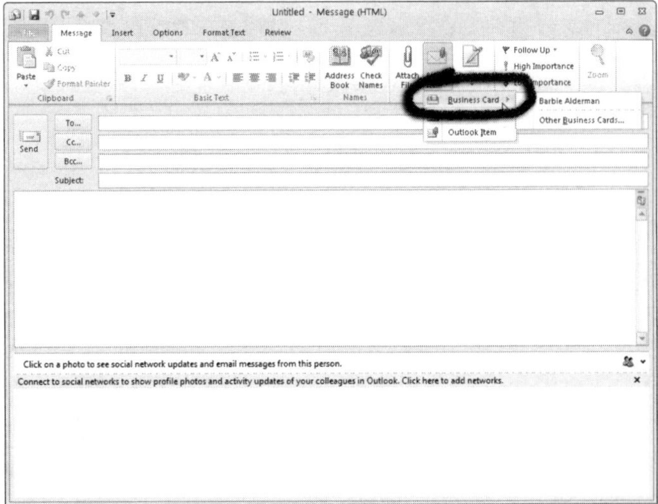

Figure 22-25

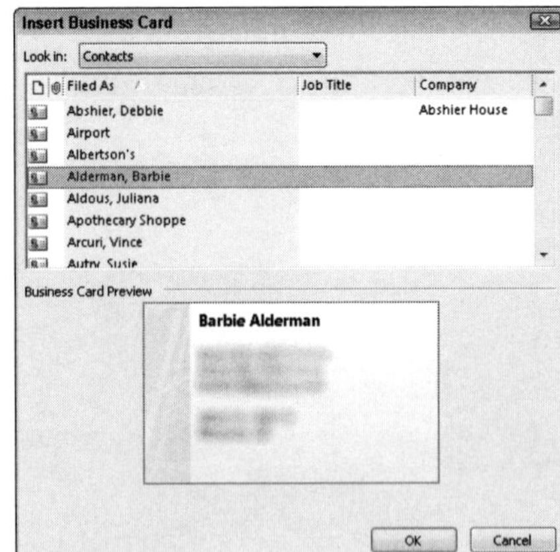

Figure 22-26

Include Your Electronic Business Card as Your Outlook E-Mail Signature

1. Click the file tab. From the Backstage view that appears, click Options to display the Outlook Options dialog box.
2. Click the Mail tab.
3. Click the Signatures button. Outlook displays the E-mail Signature tab of the Signatures and Stationery dialog box (see Figure 22-27).
4. In the Select Signature to Edit section, click the New button. Outlook displays the New Signature dialog box, where you type a name for the signature and then click OK to redisplay the Signatures and Stationery dialog box.
5. Click in the Edit Signature field, type any text that you want to include in the signature, and then click the Business Card button. Outlook displays the Insert Business Card dialog box (see Figure 22-28).

To format signature text, select the text and then use the style and formatting buttons to select options. You also can include an image, such as a scanned graphic of your signature, by clicking the Picture button.

6. Select your own contact information and then click OK. Outlook redisplays the Signatures and Stationery dialog box, which now displays your electronic business card in the Edit Signature field.
7. If you want to include your electronic business card on new e-mail messages and replies or forwarded messages, use the list boxes in the choose Default Signature section to select your e-mail account and the electronic business card signature.
8. Click OK twice.

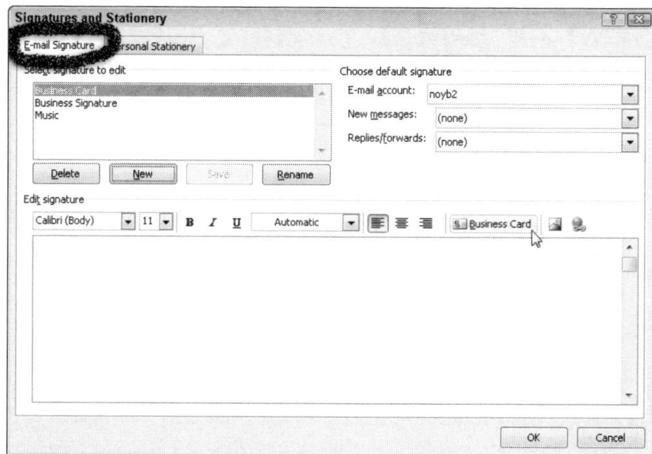

Figure 22-27

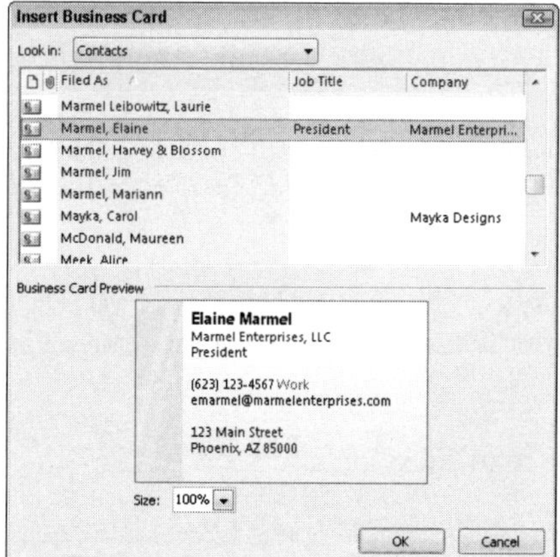

Figure 22-28

Send an E-Mail to All Contacts in a Category

1. Click Contacts in the Navigation pane.
2. On the Ribbon, click the View tab. From the Current View group, click the Change View button and then select By Category.
3. Click the heading of the category containing the contacts who should receive your e-mail to select that category.

If the heading of the category you want to use isn't visible, click the Expand/Collapse button in the Arrangement group and choose Collapse All Groups.

4. Click the Home tab. From the Communicate group, click E-mail (see Figure 22-29). Outlook displays a message indicating that the action will apply to all contacts in the selected category.
5. Click OK. Outlook opens an e-mail message with all the addresses for the category listed in the To field (see Figure 22-30).

If anybody in the selected category doesn't have an e-mail address, Outlook displays a warning, telling you that you should supply valid e-mail addresses before sending the message.

6. Complete the e-mail message and send it.

You can hide the recipient names; see "Send an E-Mail without Displaying Recipient Names" in Chapter 21 for details.

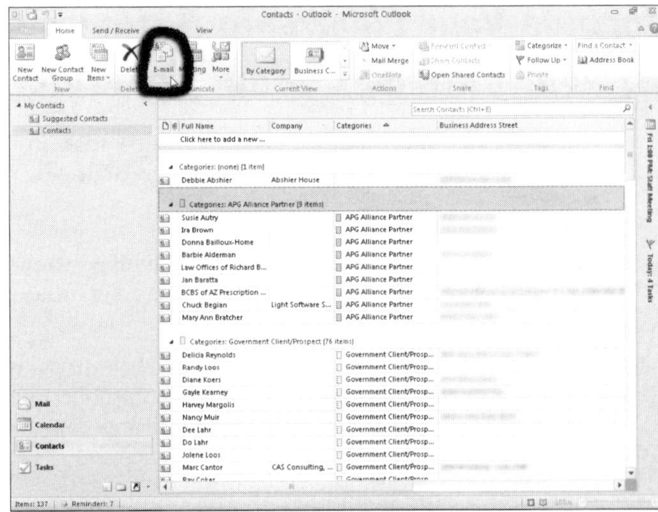

Figure 22-29

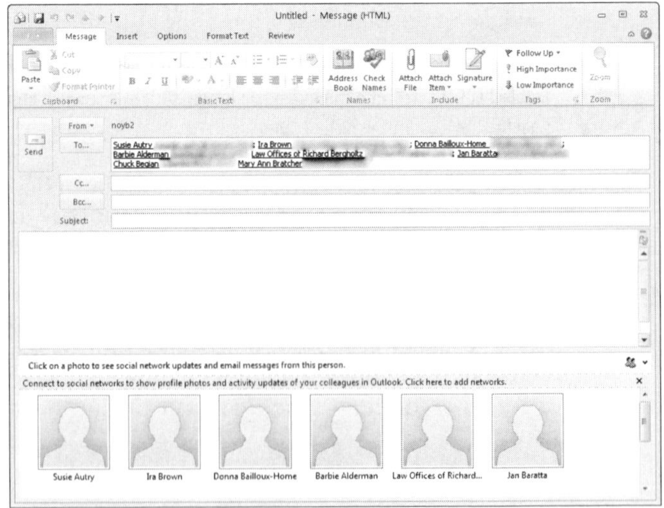

Figure 22-30

Using the Calendar

Many people swear that they live by their calendars and that they couldn't survive without them: They simply wouldn't know where to be at any given point without their calendars.

The Calendar in Outlook gives you lots of flexibility to plan. You can set up appointments and meetings and then easily move them around as dates or times change. *Appointments* are activities that don't involve inviting other people to attend, and *meetings* are activities that do involve inviting other people to attend. You can set up recurring appointments to record, for example, your weekly physical therapy appointments. And you can set up recurring meetings to handle your bi-monthly staff meetings. You also can set up reminders so that Outlook displays a window — and even plays a sound — to help you avoid accidentally missing appointments or meetings. In this chapter, you see how to

- Set up appointments and meetings.
- Create recurring appointments and meetings.
- Propose alternative meeting times.
- Accept and decline meeting invitations.
- Change meeting dates and times.
- Work with reminders.
- Manage the appearance of your calendar.

Get ready to . . .

Set Up an Appointment

1. Click the Calendar button in the Navigation pane.
2. In the mini calendar that appears in the upper left corner of the Navigation pane, click the date on which you want to schedule an appointment.

A red square appears around today's date. Days containing appointments appear in boldface type.

3. Click a time slot.
4. Type information that describes the appointment and then press Enter. Outlook establishes a 30-minute appointment.
5. To make an appointment last longer, move the mouse pointer over the handle — circled in Figure 23-1 — and drag the handle downward.

You can color-code appointments by using the Color button on the View tab.

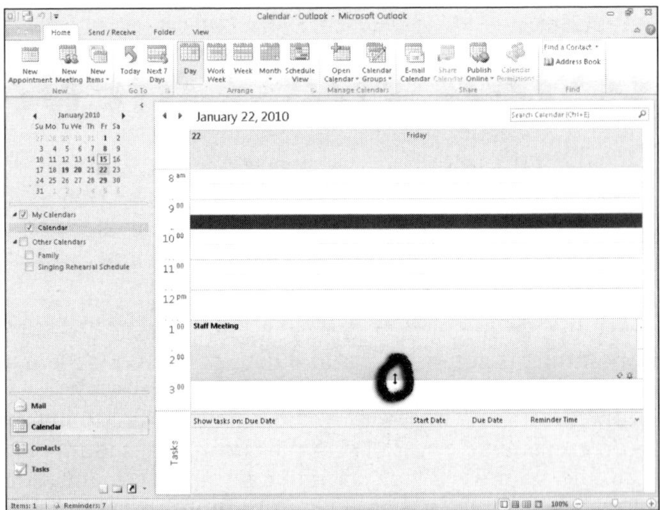

Figure 23-1

Set Up a Recurring Appointment

1. Click the Calendar button in the Navigation pane and use the mini calendar in the Navigation pane to click a day containing an existing appointment.
2. Click an existing appointment. The Calendar Tools Appointment tab appears on the Ribbon.
3. From the Options group, click the Recurrence button to display the Appointment Recurrence dialog box (see Figure 23-2).
4. In the Recurrence Pattern section, select a frequency option (such as Weekly) and then select the options for the frequency. Click OK to save the recurrence settings.

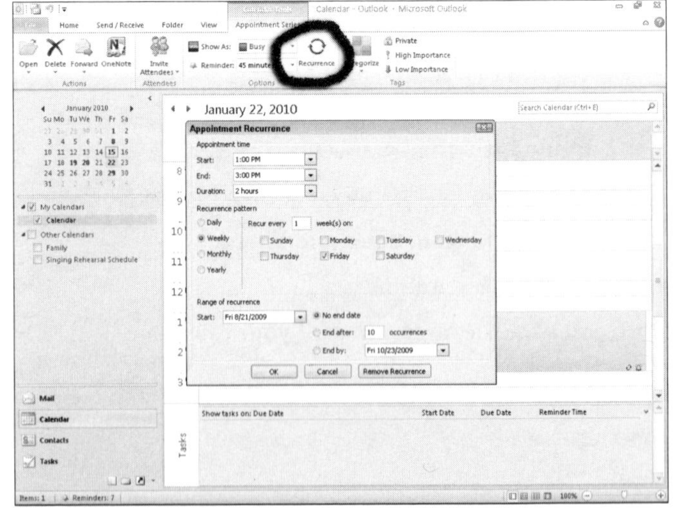

Figure 23-2

Change an Appointment Date or Time

1. Click the Calendar button in the Navigation pane.
2. In the mini calendar in the Navigation pane, click the date of the appointment.
3. Click the appointment and drag it to its new date, using the small calendar that appears in the Navigation pane (see Figure 23-3). The appearance of the mouse pointer changes while you drag the appointment; when you drop it on the new date, Outlook displays the appointment on the new date.

On the small navigation calendar, today's date is circled, and the date you're reviewing appears highlighted. Using buttons in the Arrange group on the Home tab, you can change the Calendar view on the right side of the window to display a day, week, or month at a time.

4. To change an appointment's time, drag it to the new time slot (see Figure 23-4). The appearance of the mouse pointer changes as you drag the appointment.

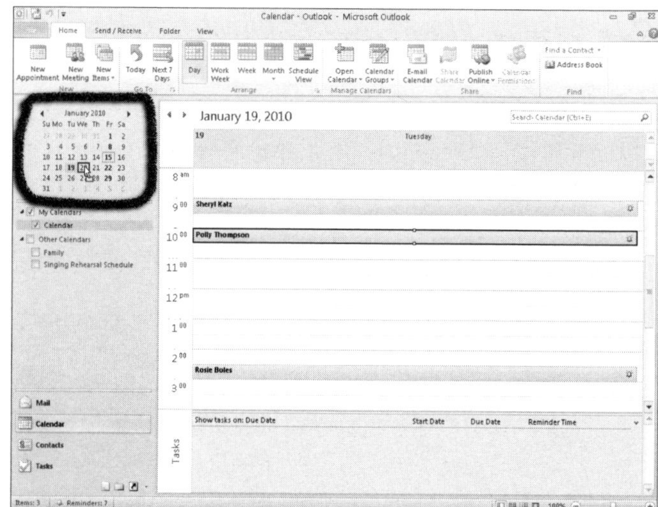

Figure 23-3

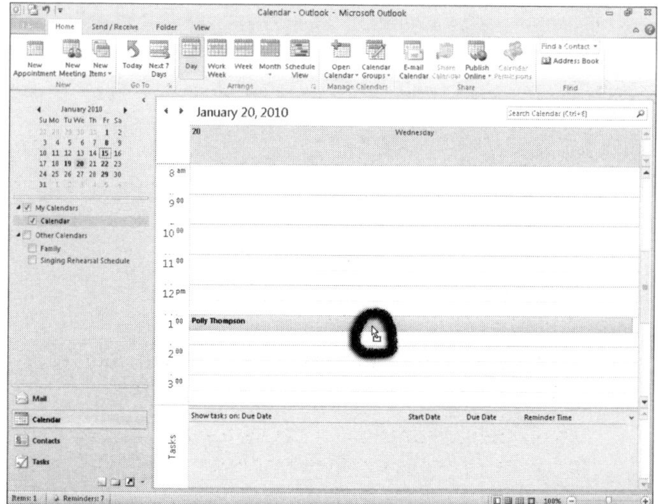

Figure 23-4

Set Up a Meeting

1. Click the Calendar button in the Navigation pane.
2. Use the mini calendar in the Navigation pane to select click the day; then click time slot that you want to use for the meeting.
3. On the Home tab, from the New group, click New Meeting (see Figure 23-5).
4. In the Meeting window that appears, as shown in Figure 23-6, supply a subject and a location for the meeting. If you need to attach a document to the meeting request, click the Insert tab and then click the Attach File button from the Include group.

If you're using Microsoft Exchange, you can click the Meeting Suggestions button on the Meeting tab to display the Meeting Suggestion pane, where you can make suggestions concerning the date, time, and place for the meeting.

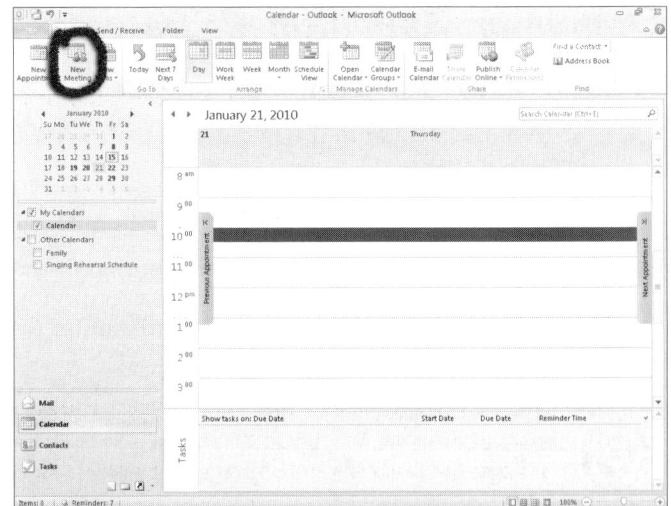

Figure 23-5

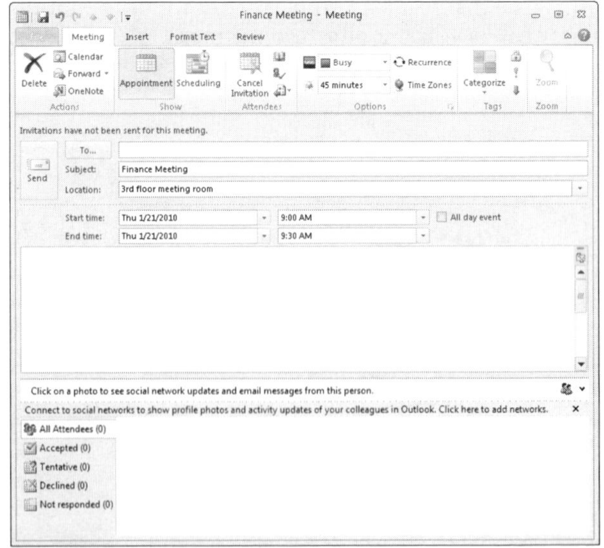

Figure 23-6

5. Click the To button to display the Select Attendees and Resources window (see Figure 23-7).
6. Highlight a contact and then click the Required or the Optional button, based on whether the person's presence determines whether the meeting can be conducted. Click OK when you finish selecting attendees, and Outlook redisplays the Meeting window shown in Figure 23-6.
7. If your organization stores Outlook calendars on a Microsoft Exchange Server and you have privileges to update those calendars, you can click the Scheduling button in the Show group to help you find the best time for a meeting and schedule the meeting on each attendee's calendar. In Figure 23-8, the hatch marks indicate no access to the calendars of the proposed attendees, and the meeting time is represented by the vertical block; in color, the left side of the meeting displays a green bar, indicating the beginning of the meeting, and the right side displays a red bar, indicating the end of the meeting.
8. Click the Send button above the list of attendees to send a meeting invitation to the selected recipients.

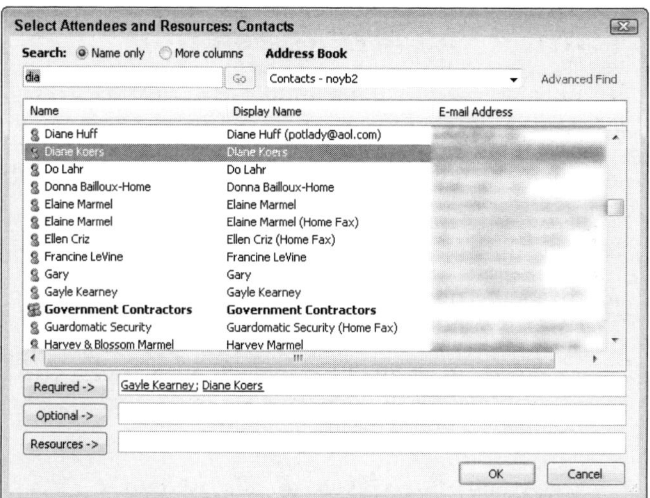

Figure 23-7

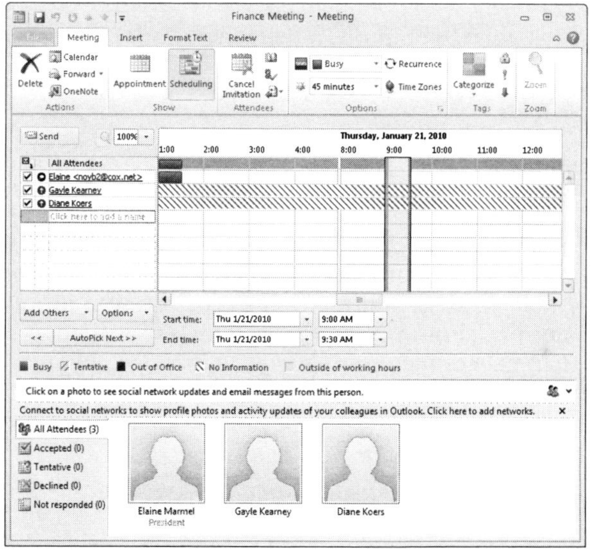

Figure 23-8

Create a Recurring Meeting

1. Perform Steps 1–7 described in the earlier task, "Set Up a Meeting."
2. Click the meeting to display the Calendar Tools tab.
3. From the Options group, click the Recurrence button to display the Appointment Recurrence dialog box (see Figure 23-9).
4. In the Recurrence Pattern section, select a frequency (such as Weekly) and then select options for the frequency. Click OK, and Outlook prompts you to send an update to meeting participants. Click the Save Change and Send Update button and then click OK.

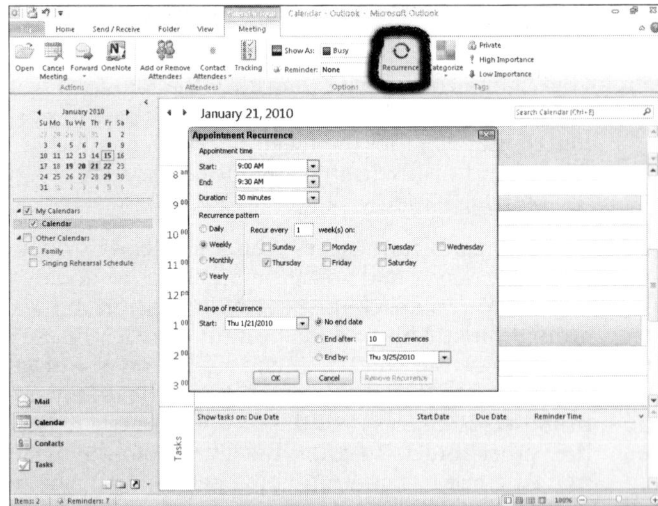

Figure 23-9

Accept or Decline a Proposed Meeting Time

1. Click the Mail button in the Navigation pane.
2. Double-click the e-mail message containing the meeting request.
3. From the Respond group on the Ribbon, click the Accept button, the Tentative button, or the Decline button (see Figure 23-10) and make a selection from the drop-down menu that appears. If you choose to send the response immediately or to edit the response before sending it, Outlook creates an e-mail message addressed to the person who proposed the meeting; above the To button, your response appears. Outlook then deletes the meeting request message. If you opt not to send a response, Outlook simply deletes the meeting request message.

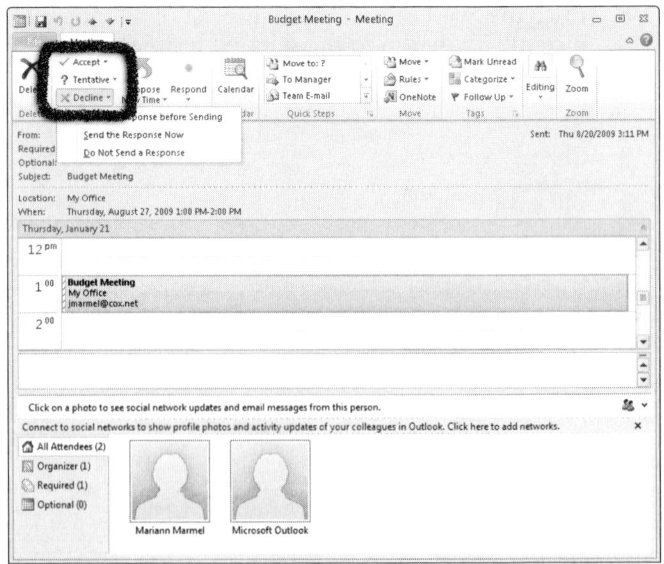

Figure 23-10

Propose a Different Meeting Time

1. Click the Mail button in the Navigation pane and then double-click the e-mail containing the meeting request.
2. From the Respond group, click Propose New Time. Outlook displays the Propose New Time window (see Figure 23-11).

If your organization uses Exchange Server to store and make calendars available, you can see available time for meeting participants.

3. Select a time and then click the Propose Time button. Outlook creates a Meeting Response e-mail addressed to the person who initially proposed the meeting. Below the subject, the original and proposed dates and times appear.
4. Click Send to place the message in your outbox.

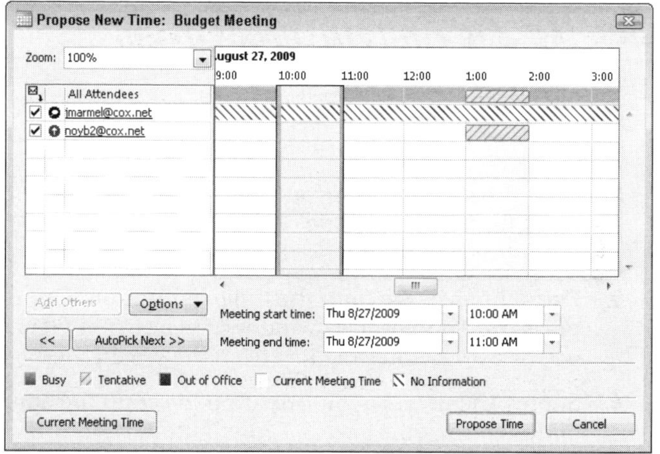

Figure 23-11

Change a Meeting Time or Date

1. Click the Calendar button in the Navigation pane.
2. Double-click the meeting you want to change.
3. Change the date, the time, or the location, as needed.
4. Click the Send Update button (see Figure 23-12).

If you need to cancel a meeting, open the meeting; from the Actions group on the Ribbon's Meeting tab, click the Cancel Meeting button. Outlook removes the meeting from your calendar and gives you the option to send cancellation messages to the other meeting attendees.

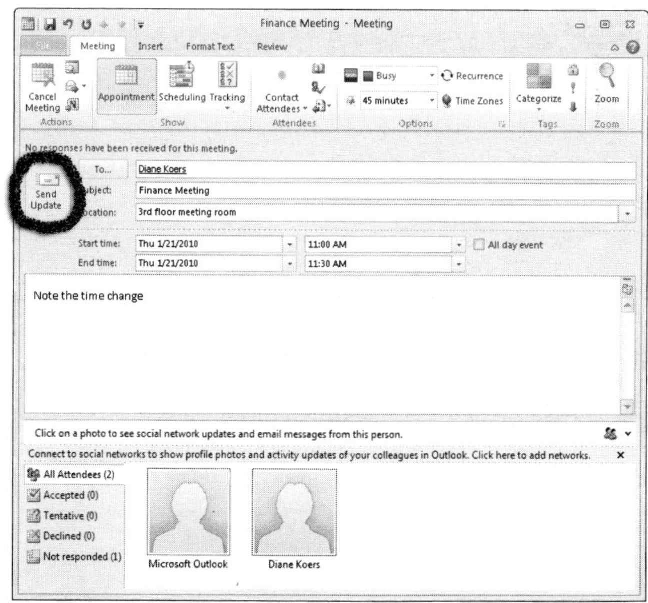

Figure 23-12

Set Up an Appointment from an E-mail Message

1. Click the Mail button in the Navigation pane.
2. Drag the message that you want to use to set up the appointment from the right side of the window to the Calendar button in the Navigation pane (see Figure 23-13).
3. Drop the message onto the Calendar button. Outlook displays the Appointment window, as shown in Figure 23-14, which incorporates the text from the e-mail message.
4. Supply the necessary information to set up the appointment and then click the Save & Close button.

For details on setting up an appointment, see the earlier task, "Set Up an Appointment."

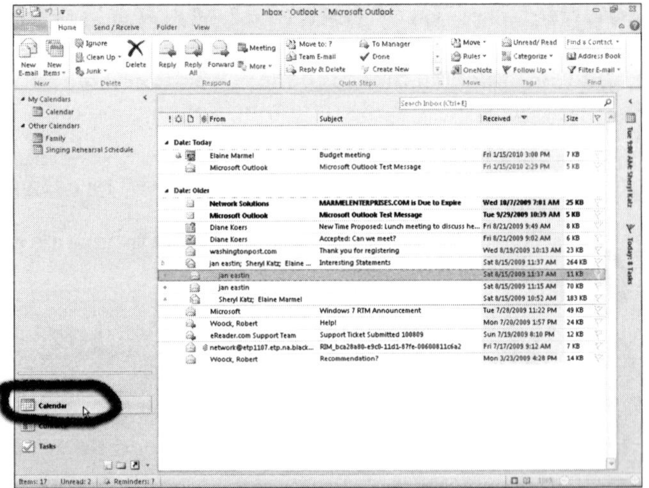

Figure 23-13

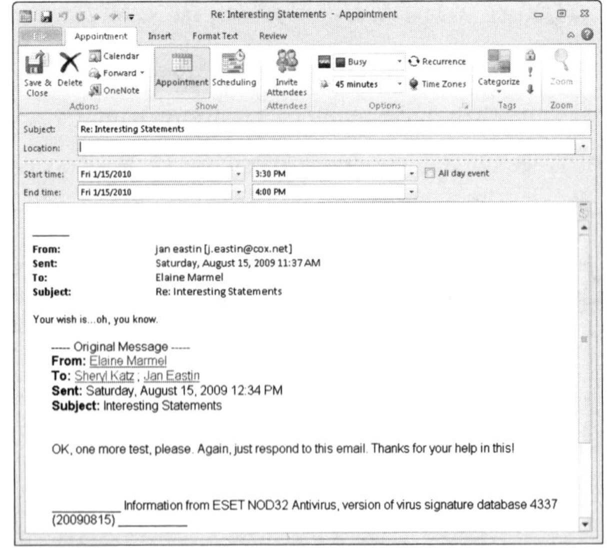

Figure 23-14

Create a Reminder for an Existing Appointment or Meeting

1. Click the Calendar button in the Navigation pane.
2. Click the appointment or meeting for which you want to set a reminder. The Calendar Tools Appointment tab or the Calendar Tools Meeting tab appears on the Ribbon.
3. From the Options group, open the Reminder list and select the amount of time prior to the appointment or meeting that you want Outlook to remind you (see Figure 23-15).

You can type an amount that doesn't appear in the list, such as 45 minutes.

4. When the reminder time occurs, Outlook displays a Reminder window (like the one shown in Figure 23-16) at the time interval you established before the meeting or appointment.

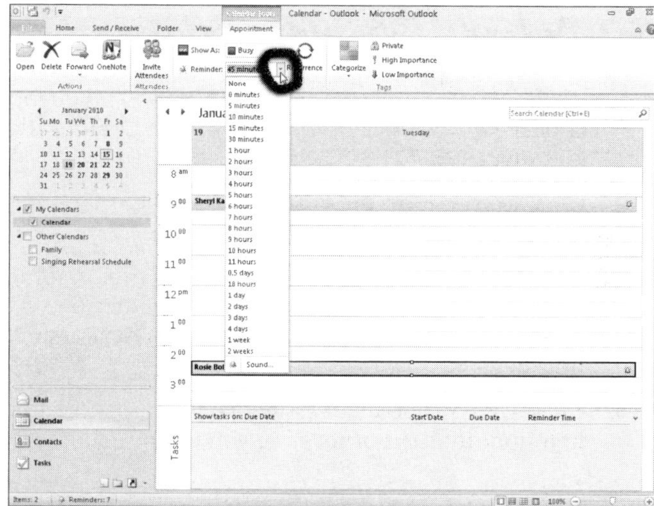

Figure 23-15

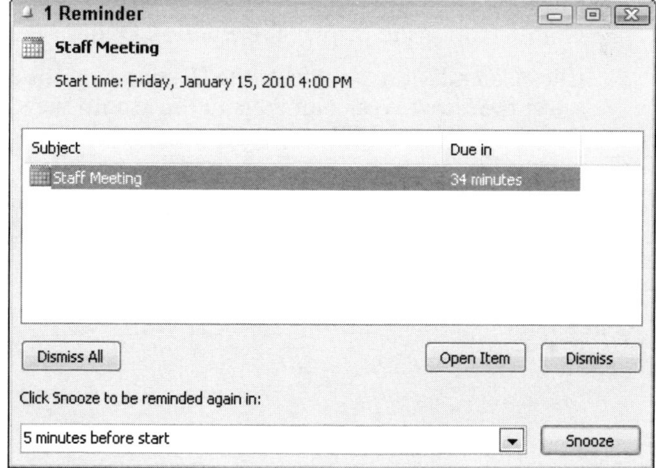

Figure 23-16

Set Default Reminder Information

1. Click the File tab. From the Backstage view that appears, choose Options to display the Outlook Options dialog box (see Figure 23-17).
2. Click Calendar on the left; in the Calendar Options section, select the Default Reminders check box.
3. Open the list and select the amount of time prior to a meeting or appointment that you want to be notified. You can type an amount that doesn't appear in the list, such as 45 minutes.
4. Click OK. Outlook will assign a default reminder to every new appointment or meeting you establish.

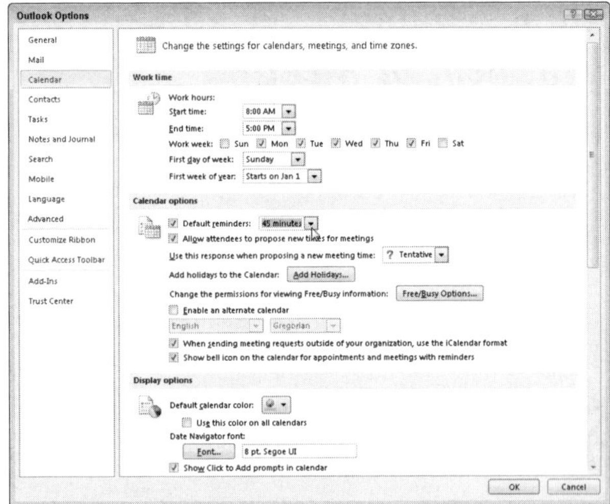

Figure 23-17

Show Week Numbers in the Month View

1. Click the File tab. From the Backstage view that appears, choose Options to display the Outlook Options dialog box.
2. Click Calendar on the left; in the Display Options section, select the Show Week Numbers in the Month View and in the Date Navigator check box (see Figure 23-18).
3. Click OK. When you switch to the Month view, Outlook displays week numbers at the left edge of each week in the view and in Date Navigator.

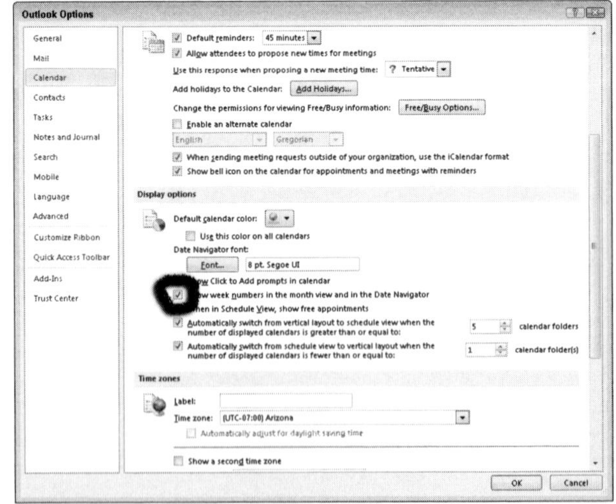

Figure 23-18

Display Two Time Zones

1. Click the File tab. From the Backstage view that appears, choose Options to display the Outlook Options dialog box.
2. Click Calendar on the left; in the Time Zones section, select the Show a Second Time Zone check box (see Figure 23-19).
3. Type a label for the additional time zone, and use the Time Zone drop-down list box to select the additional time zone. If appropriate, select the Adjust for Daylight Saving Time check box.

You also can provide a label for your primary time zone.

4. Click OK. When you view Day or Week view of the calendar, your default time zone and the additional time zone that you added appear (see Figure 23-20).

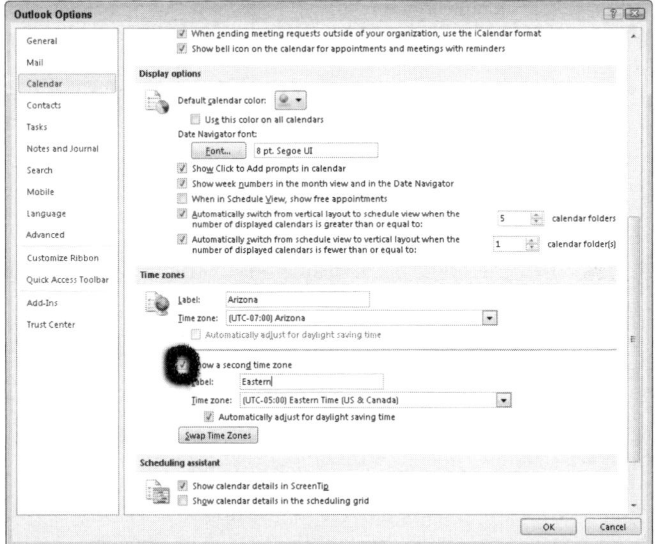

Figure 23-19

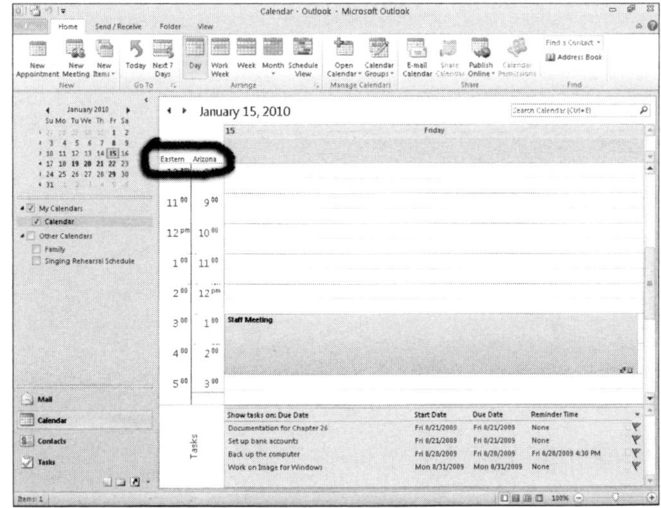

Figure 23-20

Add Holidays to the Calendar

1. Click the File tab. From the Backstage view that appears, choose Options to display the Outlook Options dialog box.
2. Click Calendar on the left; in the Calendar Options section, click the Add Holidays button to display the Add Holidays to Calendar dialog box shown in Figure 23-21.
3. Select the check box beside the country whose holidays you want to add.
4. Click OK twice. Outlook adds holidays to the calendar (see Figure 23-22).

Don't perform these steps twice for the same country; Outlook adds the holidays twice.

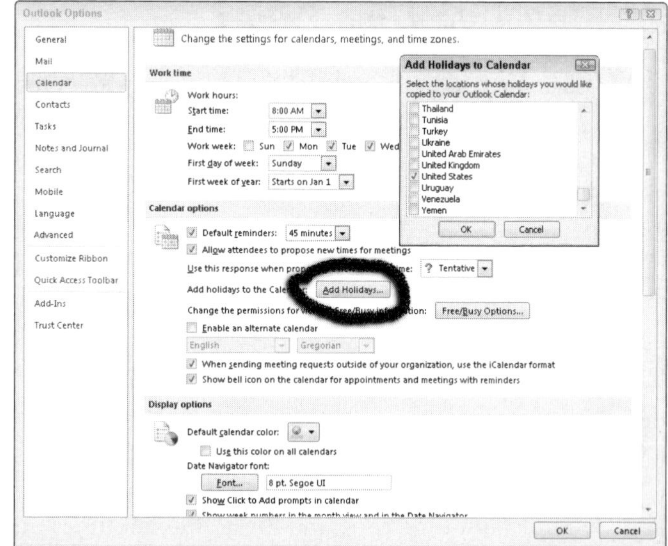

Figure 23-21

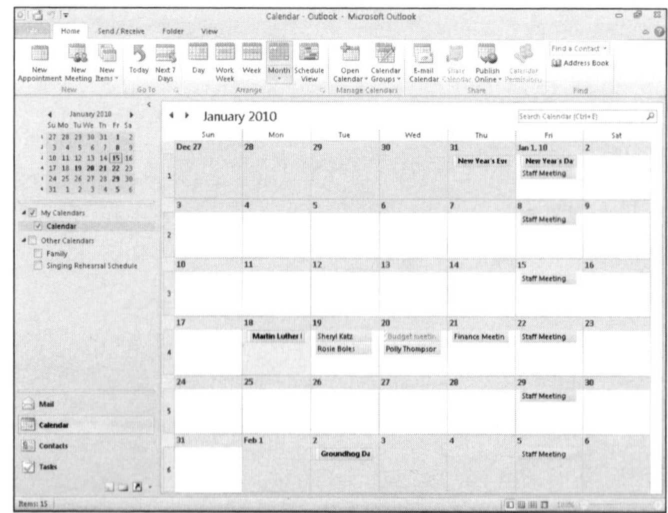

Figure 23-22

Using Tasks and To-Do Items to Manage Your Time

Get ready to . . .

Tasks are activities that can track in Outlook until they are complete. You can establish start and end dates, indicate progress on the task, and set reminders to complete a task. You can set recurring tasks to handle — for example, preparing for the weekly staff meeting. Tasks appear in the Tasks section, on the To-Do bar, and in the Calendar Daily Task List.

So what about those other types of things that you want to track for follow-up — like that e-mail from the boss, or that phone conversation you had last week with a contact. Is there an easy way to manage those items? You bet — you can flag those e-mails and contacts for follow-up. These to-do items with follow-up flags automatically appear in the Mail section, in the Tasks section, on the To-Do bar, and in the Calendar Daily Task List. *To-do items* aren't as robust as tasks in Outlook; you can't indicate progress or percentage of completeness for to-do items like you can for tasks.

Be aware that Outlook automatically flags all tasks you create for follow-up, but Outlook doesn't create a task for any e-mail or contact you for follow-up.

In this chapter, you see how to

- Create tasks, recurring tasks, and to-do items.
- Mark a task as complete and reinstate completed tasks if necessary.
- Hide and display completed tasks.
- Sort and reorder tasks.
- Link a task to a contact.
- Display only today's tasks on the To-Do bar.

Create a Task Using the Task Window

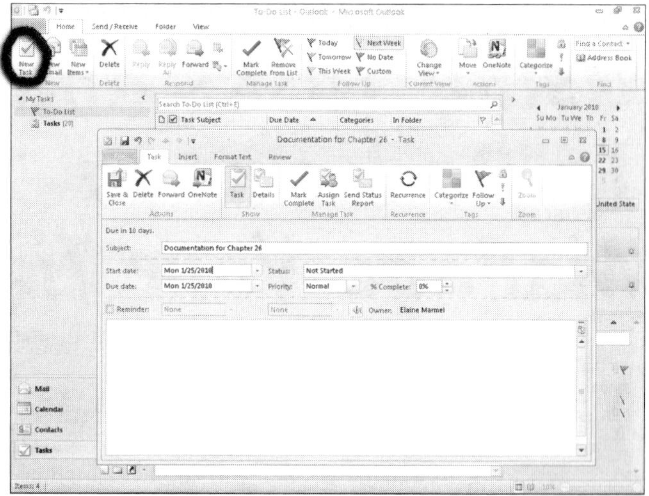

Figure 24-1

1. Click the Tasks button in the Navigation pane.
2. Click the New Task button on the Home tab of the Ribbon to display the Task window shown in Figure 24-1.
3. In the Subject field, type the task name.
4. (Optional) Set the Start Date and the Due Date, select a status that reflects progress, establish the task's priority, and set the percentage complete.
5. On the task's Ribbon Task tab in the Actions group, click the Save & Close button. The task appears in the Tasks section, on the To-Do bar, and in the Calendar Daily Task List.

Use the To-Do Bar to Create a Task

1. Click the Tasks button in the Navigation pane.

In the figure, the Reading pane doesn't appear and I expanded the To-Do Bar. See Chapter 20 for information on displaying the To-Do bar.

2. Click in the Type a New Task text box in the middle of the To-Do bar (see Figure 24-2).
3. Type a subject for the task and then press Enter. The task appears in the Tasks section, on the To-Do bar, and in the Calendar Daily Task List.

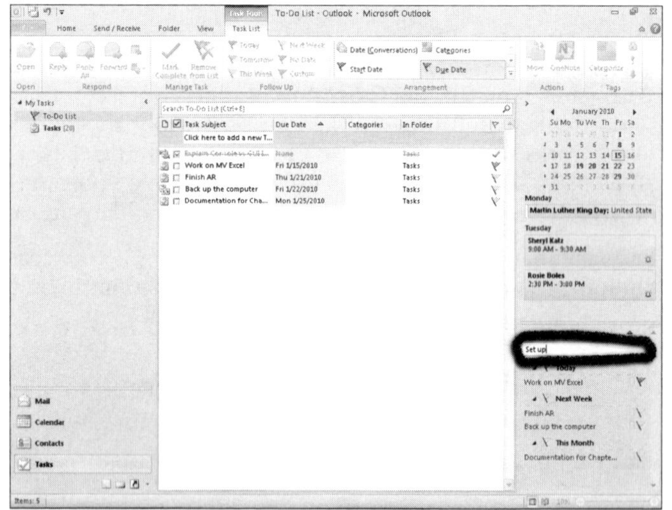

Figure 24-2

Create a Task in the Calendar Daily Task List

1. Click Calendar in the Navigation pane.
2. Click Day View or Week View from the Arrange group on the Home tab of the Ribbon.
3. Below the Calendar, click in the Calendar Daily Task List (see Figure 24-3).

If the Daily Task List isn't visible, click the up arrow in the lower right of the screen.

4. Type the Task subject and then press Enter. The task appears in the Tasks section, on the To-Do bar, and in the Calendar Daily Task List.

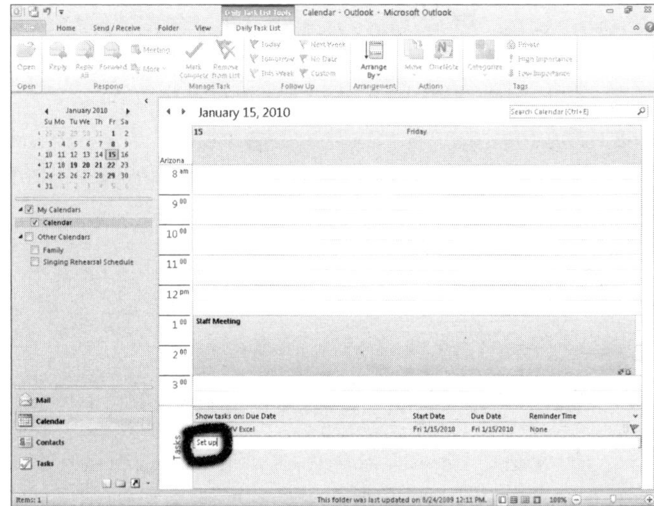

Figure 24-3

Create a To-Do Item

1. Click Mail or Contacts in the Navigation pane. If you click Mail, click the Inbox in the Navigation pane.
2. Click an e-mail message or a contact and then click the Follow Up button in the Tags group on the Home tab (see Figure 24-4).
3. From the menu that appears, choose a follow-up date. To assign a date that doesn't appear, click Custom. The to-do item appears in the Mail section, in the Tasks section, on the To-Do bar, and in the Calendar Daily Task List.

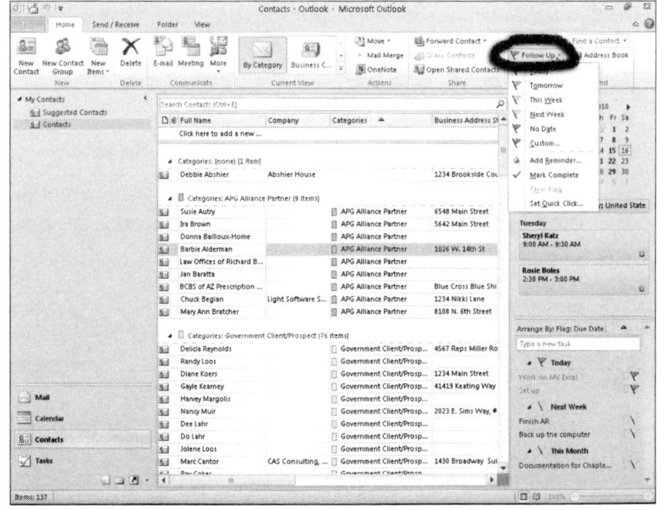

Figure 24-4

Create a Recurring Task

1. Click the Tasks button in the Navigation pane.
2. Double-click the task that you want to set up as recurring, or click the New button on the toolbar to start a new task. For a new task, fill in the subject and other task information.
3. Click the Recurrence button on the Task tab of the task window to display the Task Recurrence dialog box shown in Figure 24-5.
4. In the Recurrence Pattern section, select a frequency (such as Weekly) and then select the options for the frequency. Click OK to save the recurrence settings.

Select the Regenerate New Task option when the recurring pattern isn't absolute; instead, subsequent occurrences of the task depend on completing prior occurrences of the task.

5. Click the Save & Close button on the Ribbon.

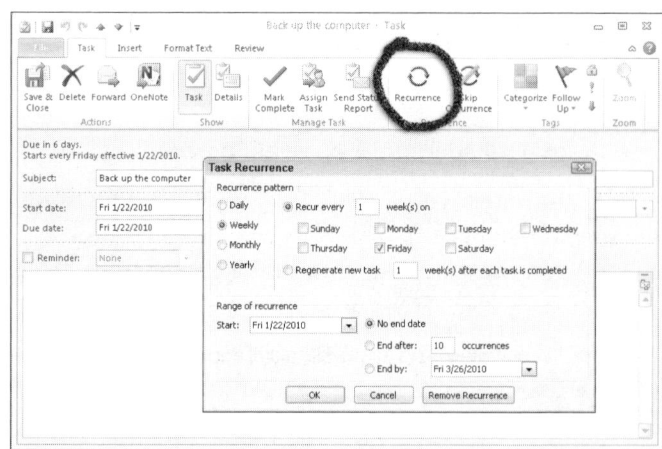

Figure 24-5

Complete a Task

1. Click the Tasks button in the Navigation pane.
2. Use the Change View button in the Current view group on the Home tab to select either the Detailed view or the Simple List view.

Other views will also work; for this example, I used the Simple List view.

3. In the Flag Status column, click the flag of the task that you want to mark complete. Outlook changes the flag to a check mark (✓) and draws a line through the task (see Figure 24-6).

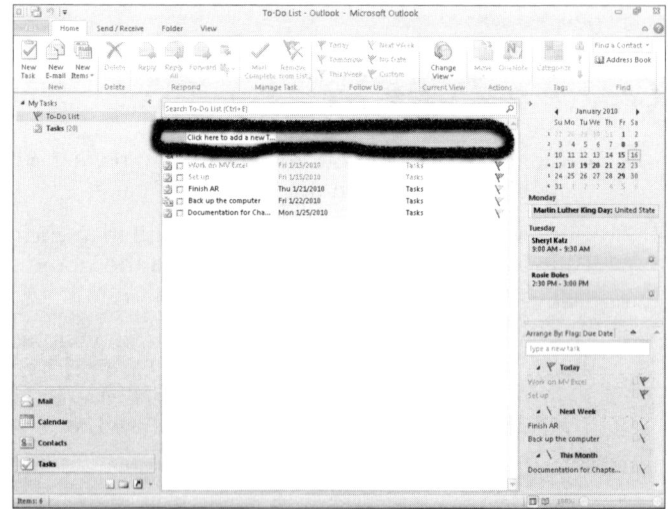

Figure 24-6

Display Completed Task in the To-Do Bar

1. Click the Tasks button in the Navigation pane.
2. On the To-Do bar, click Arrange By and choose View Settings from the menu that appears (see Figure 24-7).
3. In the Advanced View Settings: To-Do List dialog box that appears, click the Filter button.
4. In the Filter dialog box that appears, click the Advanced tab (see Figure 24-8).
5. Click the Clear All button to remove all criteria.
6. Click OK twice. Completed tasks now appear on the To-Do bar.

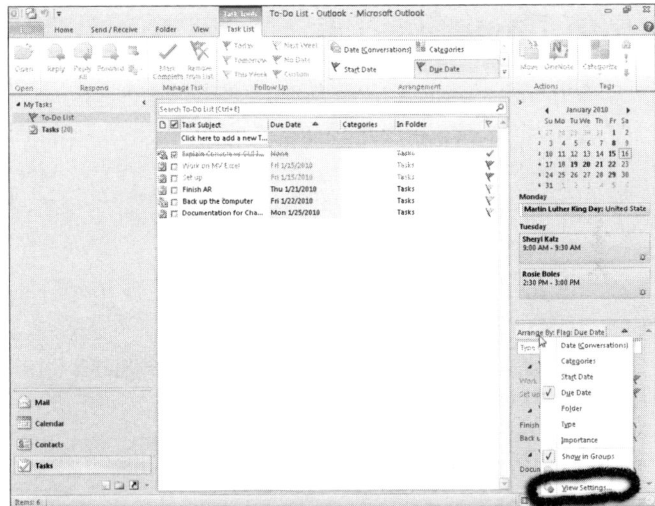

Figure 24-7

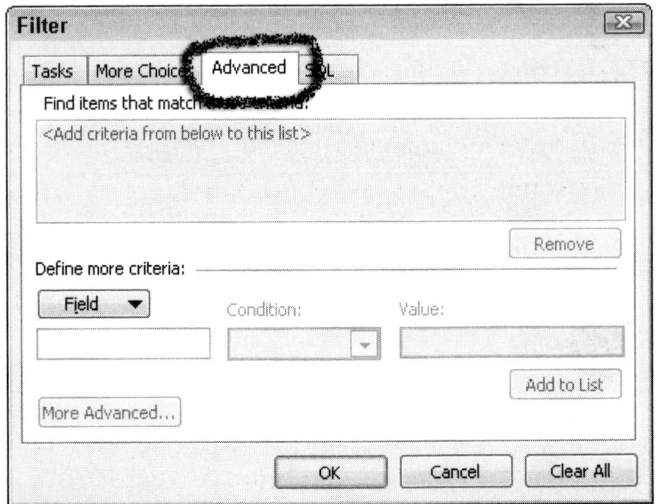

Figure 24-8

Hide Completed Tasks in the To-Do Bar

1. Click the Tasks button in the Navigation pane.
2. On the To-Do bar, right-click Arrange By and then choose View Settings from the menu that appears (see Figure 24-9).
3. In the Advanced View Settings: To-Do List dialog box that appears, click the Filter button.
4. In the Filter dialog box that appears, click the Advanced tab (see Figure 24-10).
5. Click the Field button, point to All Task Fields, and click Date Completed.
6. In the Condition list, click Does Not Exist, and then click the Add to List button.
7. Repeat Steps 5 and 6, making the following selections:

Field Set	Field	Condition	Value
All Task Fields	Date Completed	On or After	Today
All Mail Fields	Flag Completed Date	Does Not Exist	
All Mail Fields	Flag Completed Date	On or After	Today

8. Click OK twice.

In the Tasks section, use any view except the Simple List view or the Detailed view to see only uncompleted tasks.

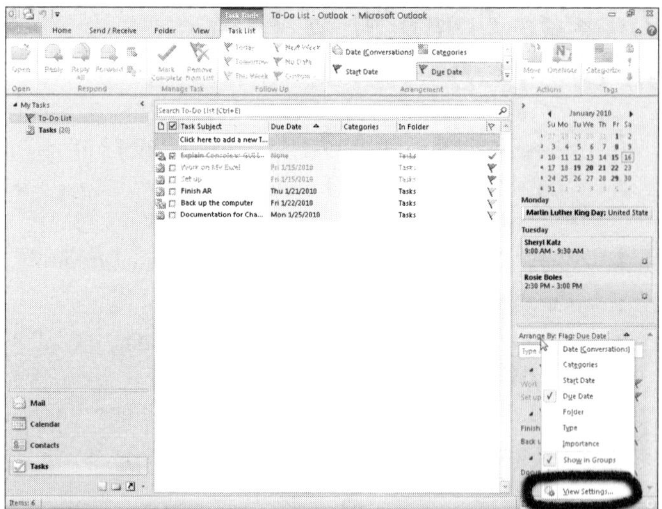

Figure 24-9

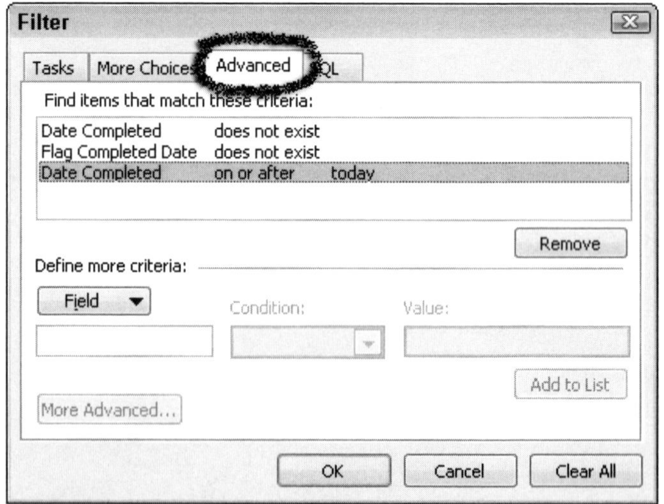

Figure 24-10

Hide or Display Completed Tasks in the Calendar's Daily Task List

1. Click the Calendar button in the Navigation pane.
2. If necessary, click the Day button in the Arrange group on the Home tab.
3. Right-click Show Tasks On and choose click Show Completed Tasks from the menu that appears (see Figure 24-11). When a check appears beside Show Completed Tasks, completed tasks appear in the Calendar Daily Task List. When no check appears, completed tasks don't appear.

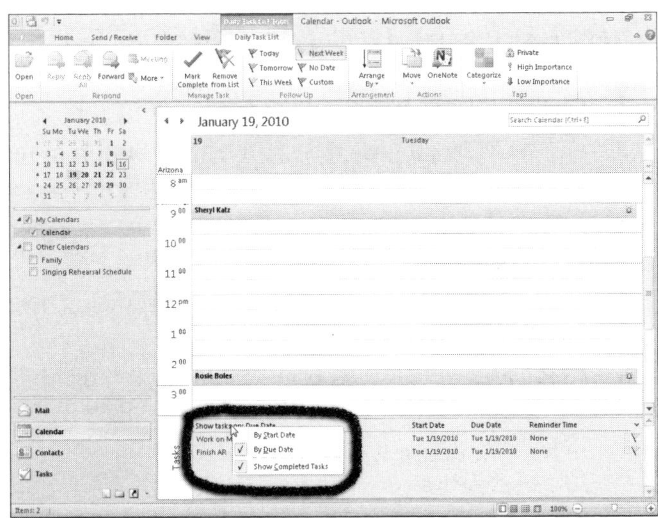

Figure 24-11

Reinstate a Completed Task

1. Click the Tasks button in the Navigation pane.
2. In the Current View section on the Home tab, click the Change View button and select Completed.
3. Double-click the completed task that you want to reinstate as active.
4. Change the Status to anything other than Completed (see Figure 24-12).

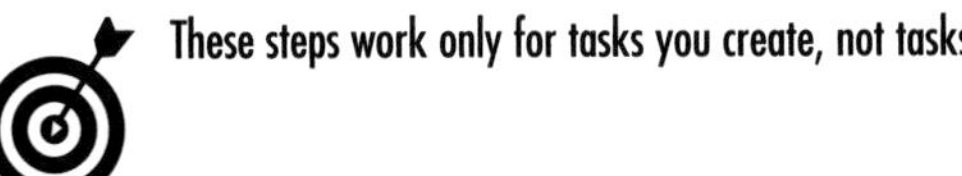

These steps work only for tasks you create, not tasks others assign to you.

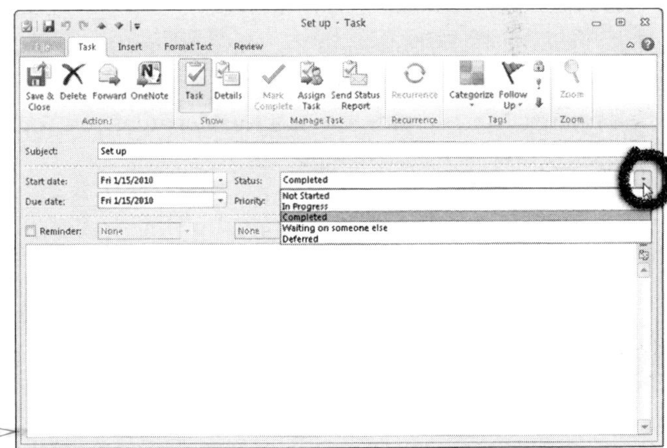

Figure 24-12

Sort Tasks in the Task List

1. Click the Tasks button in the Navigation pane.
2. On the View tab, use the Change View button in the Current View group to select the view you want to sort.
3. Click the View Settings button in the Current View group to display the Advanced View Settings dialog box.
4. Click the Sort button to display the Sort dialog box shown in Figure 24-13.
5. In the Sort Items By section, open the drop-down list and select a field. Repeat this process to set up additional sort fields.
6. Click OK twice.

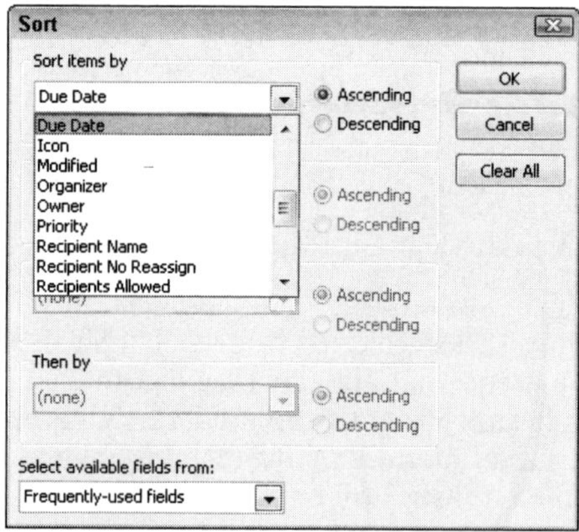

Figure 24-13

Reorder Tasks with the Same Due Date

1. Click the Tasks button in the Navigation pane.
2. From the Current View section of the View tab, click the Change View button to select the view that you want to use to reorder tasks.
3. Drag the tasks to new locations within the same due date. As you drag, Outlook displays a red line that indicates the task's current location in the list (see Figure 24-14).

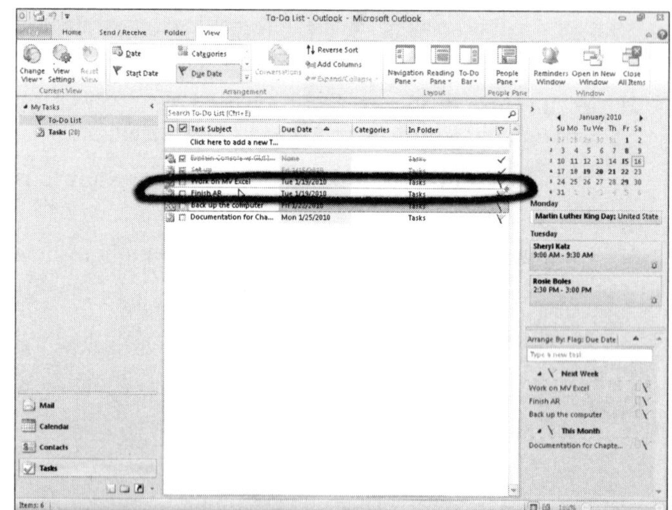

Figure 24-14

Link a Task to a Contact

1. Click the File tab. In the Backstage view that appears, click Options to open the Outlook Options dialog box.
2. Click Contacts on the left.
3. In the Linking section, select the Show Contacts Linked to the Current Item check box (see Figure 24-15).
4. Click OK.
5. Click the Tasks button in the Navigation pane.
6. Double-click the task that you want to link to a contact.
7. At the bottom of the window, click the Contacts button to display the Select Contacts window shown in Figure 24-16.
8. Click a contact and click OK. To select multiple contacts, click each and click the Apply button. Then click OK. Outlook displays the selected contacts in the text box beside the Contacts button in the task window.
9. Click Save & Close.

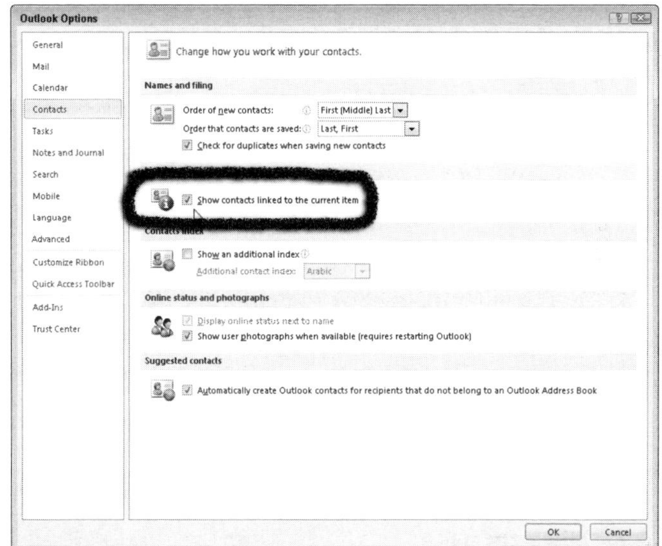

Figure 24-15

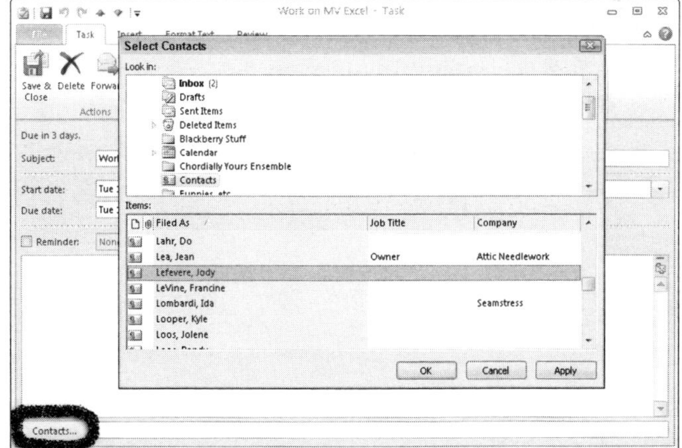

Figure 24-16

Display Only Today's Tasks in the To-Do Bar

1. On the To-Do bar, click Arrange By and choose View Settings from the menu that appears (see Figure 24-17).
2. In the Advanced View Settings: To-Do List dialog box that appears, click the Filter button.
3. In the Filter dialog box that appears, click the Advanced tab (see Figure 24-18).
4. Click the Clear All button to remove any current filters.
5. Click the Field button, point at Date/Time Fields, and click Due Date.
6. Open the Condition drop-down list and select Today.
7. Click OK twice.

To reset the To-Do bar to its default view, perform the steps in the earlier task, "Hide Completed Tasks in the To-Do Bar."

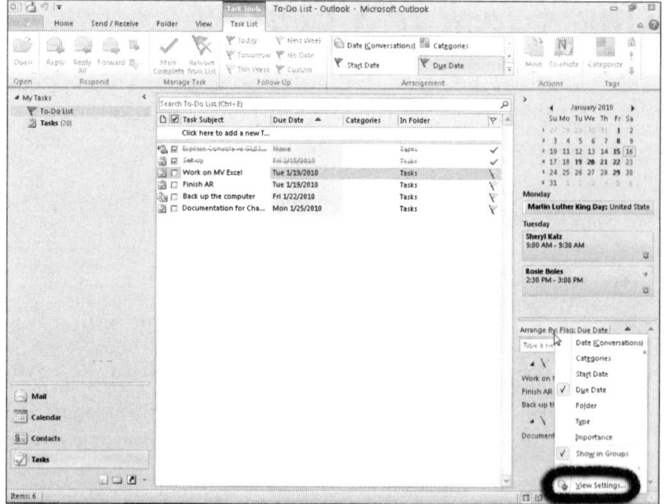

Figure 24-17

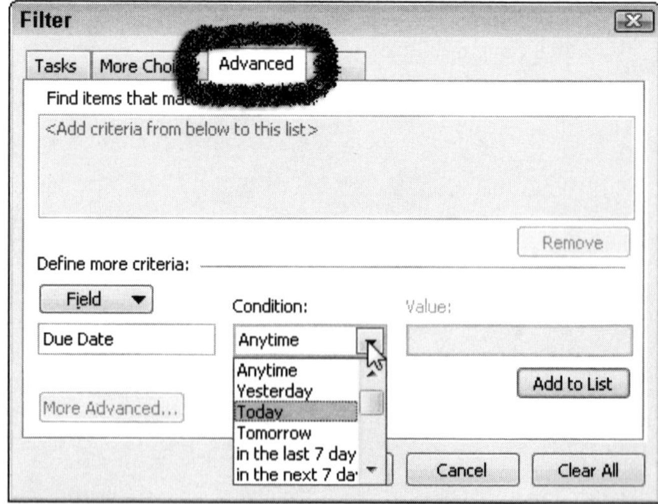

Figure 24-18

Part V
Using Office Products Together

"The odd thing is he always insists on using the latest version of Office."

Features Common to Office Programs

Chapter 25

All Microsoft Office 2010 programs share certain common features, and these features work the same way in each product. For example, all Office 2010 programs sport the Ribbon interface that uses tabs and buttons. The tabs on the Ribbon organize related groups of commands. On each tab, commands for related functions appear in the form of buttons.

The Quick Access Toolbar contains some of the more common commands you use, such as saving a document or undoing an action. You can add commands to the both the Ribbon and the Quick Access Toolbar, as you discover in this chapter.

This chapter helps you familiarize yourself with features that are common to all Office 2010 programs. In this chapter, you see how to

- Work with the Ribbon, in Backstage view, and with dialog boxes to choose commands.
- Work with the status bar to display document information.
- Customize the Ribbon and the Quick Access Toolbar.

Get ready to . . .

Select Commands from the Ribbon

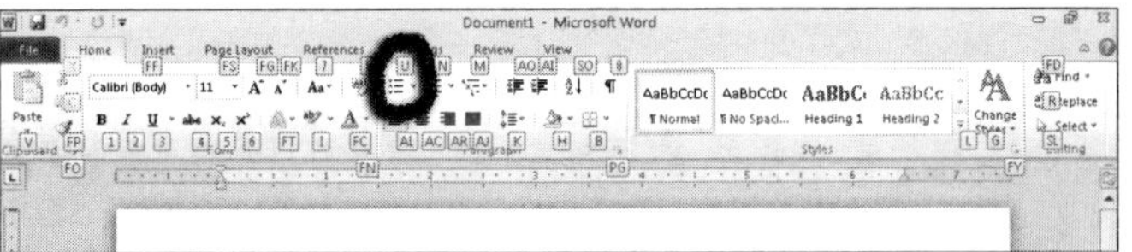

Figure 25-1

1. To select commands from the Ribbon using the mouse, click a tab and then click a button or a dialog box launcher.

Each Ribbon tab contains *groups* of commands; in Figure 25-1, you see the Clipboard, Font, Paragraph, Styles, and Editing groups.

2. To select commands from the Ribbon using the keyboard, press Alt to display keys to press to select a tab. For this example, press H for the Home tab.
3. Press a letter to select a command; for this example, press N in Word to begin a numbered list (see Figure 25-1).

Use Backstage View

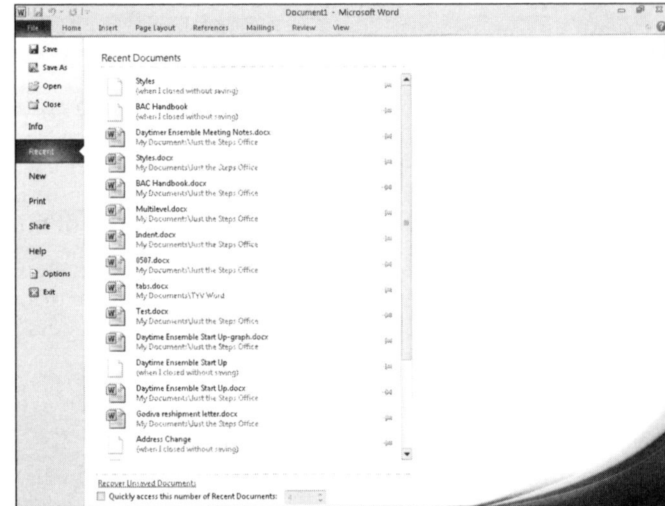

Figure 25-2

1. Click the File tab. Backstage view appears (see Figure 25-2).
2. From the column on the left, select a command or an option. If you select an option such as Recent or New, additional options that you can select appear to the right. If you select a command, typically, you'll see a dialog box, such as Save As or Open.

If you change your mind about selecting a Backstage view command or option, click the File tab or any other tab or press Esc.

Open a Dialog Box

1. On the Ribbon, in the lower-right corner of some groups, a dialog box launcher icon appears (see Figure 25-3).

In Figure 25-3, the Editing group does not have a dialog box launcher icon.

2. Click the dialog box launcher icon to display the dialog box associated with the group.
3. Select the option(s) you need and then click OK.

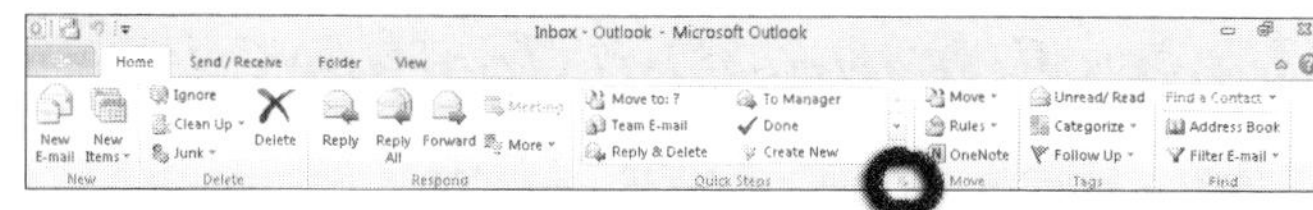

Figure 25-3

Use the Status Bar

1. Right-click the status bar to display a menu of options and their current settings (see Figure 25-4).

Use the status bar menu to get more information about your document and to add information to the status bar.

2. Options that already appear on the status bar have check marks beside them; click one to remove that option from the status bar.
3. To add an option to the status bar, click it.

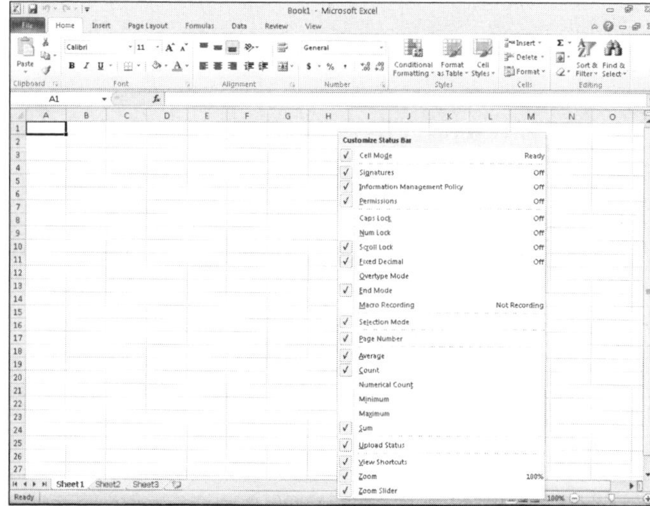

Figure 25-4

Work with the Mini Toolbar and the Contextual Menu

1. Select text and slide the mouse pointer upward slightly. The Mini Toolbar appears in the background (see Figure 25-5).
2. Position the mouse pointer over the Mini Toolbar to make it appear solidly.

> You can turn off the Mini Toolbar from the program's Options dialog box by deselecting the first option on the General Options page.

3. Right-click anywhere below the Ribbon in Word, Excel, or PowerPoint — or in any text field in Outlook — to display both the Mini Toolbar and its contextual menu (see Figure 25-6).

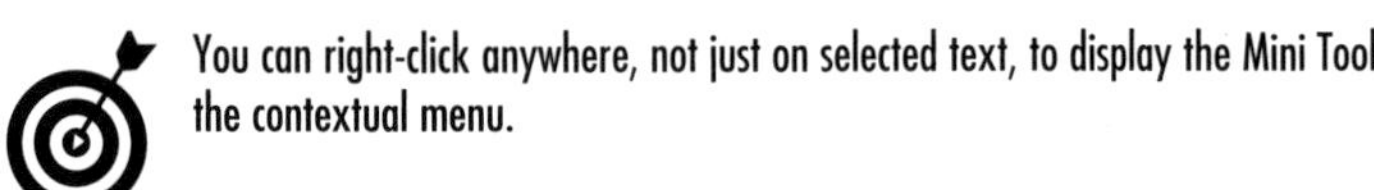

> You can right-click anywhere, not just on selected text, to display the Mini Toolbar and the contextual menu.

4. Click any command or button. The program performs the actions associated with the command or button.

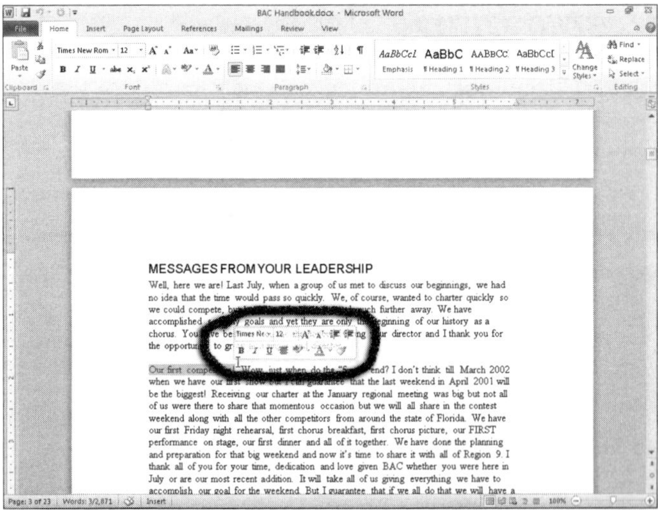

Figure 25-5

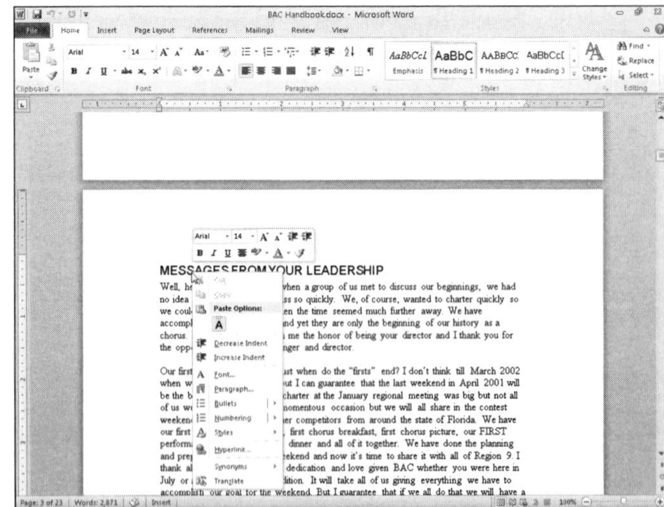

Figure 25-6

Customize the Ribbon

1. Click the File tab to display Backstage view (see Figure 25-7).
2. Click the Options command to display the program's Options window (see Figure 25-8).
3. On the left, click Customize Ribbon.
4. Because you cannot add commands to the original Ribbon groups or tabs, click New Group or New Tab below the Customize the Ribbon column on the right. If you click New Tab, the program automatically creates both a new tab and a new group.
5. Reposition any group or tab by using the Move Up or Move Down buttons beside the Customize the Ribbon column.
6. Click the new group or tab and then click the Rename button to assign a name to your group or tab.
7. In the Choose Commands From column on the left, click a command and then click the Add button to add the command to the new group on the right. Take any of the following actions as appropriate:
   - Add commands already displayed on the Ribbon.
   - Remove any group — an original, or one that you create — by selecting it and clicking the Remove button.
   - Hide any of the original tabs by deselecting the check beside them. To work with specialty tabs (such as the Table Tools tab), open the Customize the Ribbon above the right column and choose All Tabs.
8. Repeat Steps 4–7 until you finish customizing. Then click OK to save your choices.

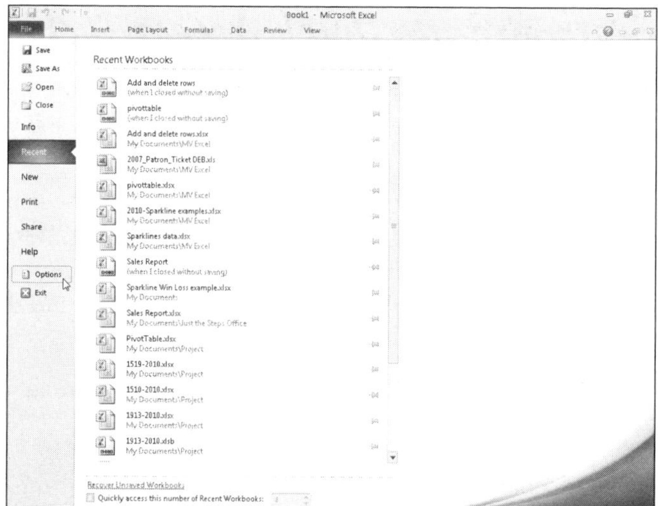

Figure 25-7

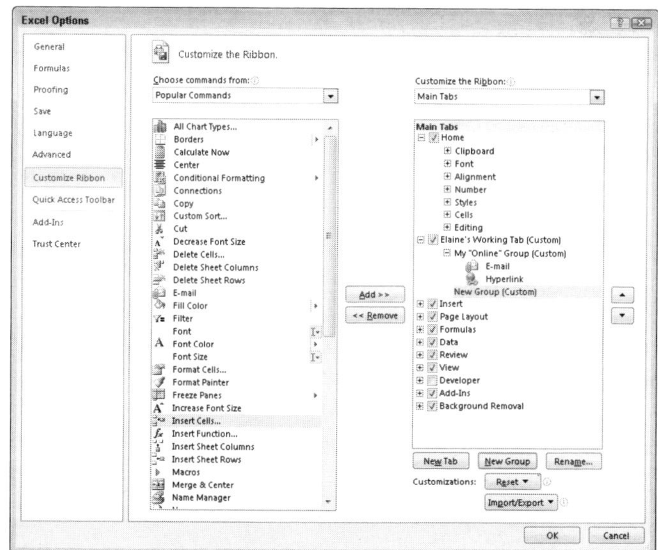

Figure 25-8

Customize the Quick Access Toolbar

1. Click the small button at the right edge of the Quick Access Toolbar to display some common commands that you can add to the Quick Access Toolbar (see Figure 25-9).
2. If the command you want doesn't appear in the list, click More Commands to display the program's Options window (see Figure 25-10).
3. In the list on the left, locate and click a command that you want to display on the Quick Access Toolbar.

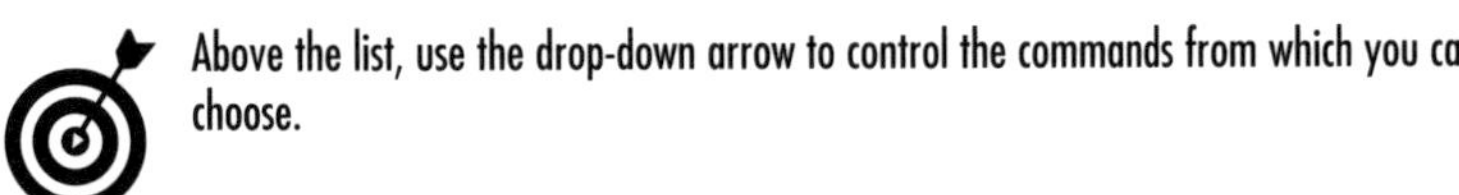

Above the list, use the drop-down arrow to control the commands from which you can choose.

4. Click the Add button to move the command from the left column to the right column.

To remove a command from the Quick Access Toolbar, click it in the right column and click the Remove button. To reposition a command, use the up and down arrows on the right side of the right-hand column.

5. Repeat Steps 3 and 4 for each command you want to add.
6. Click OK to save your selections.

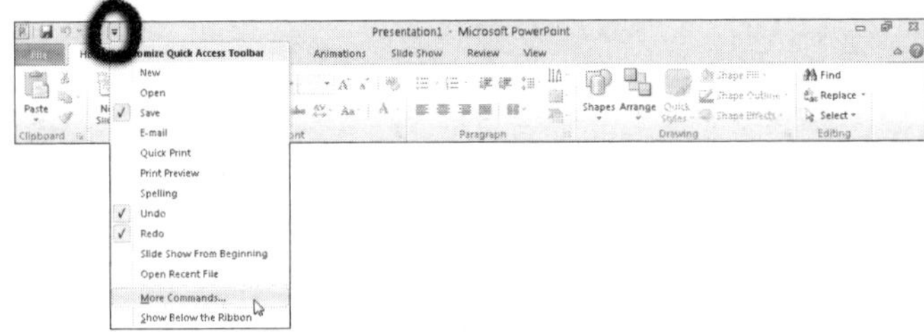

Figure 25-9

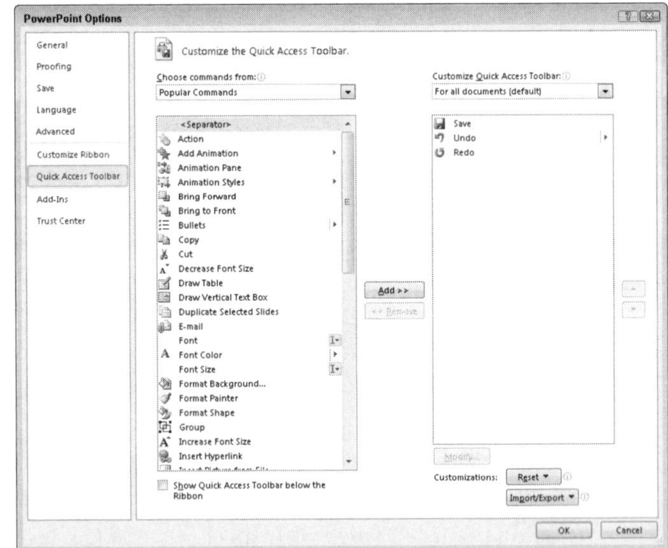

Figure 25-10

Using Information from One Office Program in Another

Chapter 26

Many people use more than one program that is considered part of Office. Office comes in several variations, and each variant includes some different software packages. Many people use Word, Excel, PowerPoint, and Outlook, so in this book, I focus on these four Office products.

When you're in one Office program, it's not uncommon to need information created and stored in another. For example, how do you get a mailing list stored in an Excel file into your Outlook contacts? Or, how do you use an outline created in Word to generate PowerPoint presentation slides? In this chapter, you see how to exchange information between

- Excel and PowerPoint
- Word and Excel
- Excel and Outlook
- Word and PowerPoint

Get ready to . . .

Transfer Excel Data into PowerPoint

1. Open the PowerPoint presentation in which you want the Excel data to appear.
2. Open the Excel workbook containing the information that you want to transfer to PowerPoint.

Don't want those Excel workbook lines on the PowerPoint slide? Click the Page Layout tab; from the Gridlines portion of the Sheet Options group, clear the mark check beside View.

3. Select the information and then click the Copy button in the Clipboard group of the Home tab (see Figure 26-1).
4. Switch to the appropriate the PowerPoint presentation using the Windows task bar.
5. Click the slide on which the Excel data should appear.

You can change the slide layout to a blank slide or delete any PowerPoint Click Here boxes to make the slide easier to see.

6. From the Clipboard group on the Home tab, click the arrow at the bottom of the Paste button and then choose Paste Special.
7. In the Paste Special dialog box that appears, choose Microsoft Office Excel Worksheet Object and then click OK to display the data on the PowerPoint slide (see Figure 26-2).

Drag a handle to resize the Excel data on the PowerPoint slide. To reposition the data on the slide, place the mouse over the data; when the pointer becomes four-headed, drag the data.

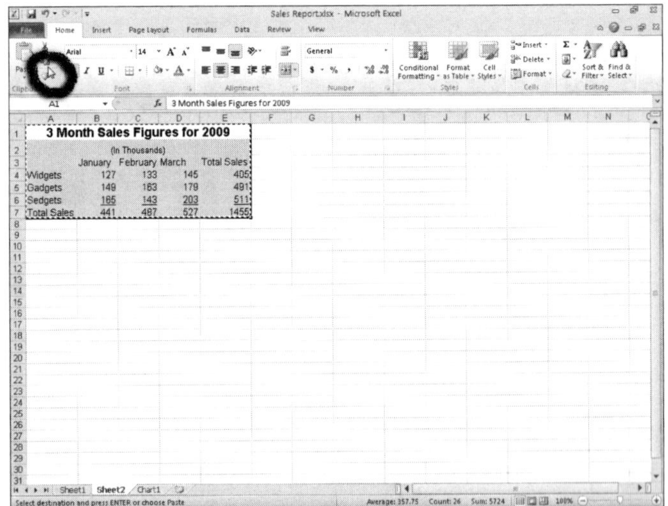

Figure 26-1

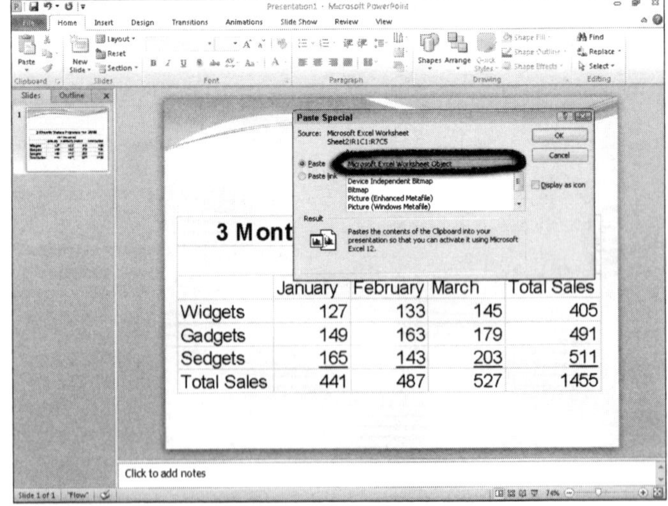

Figure 26-2

Transfer an Excel Chart to a PowerPoint Slide

1. Open the PowerPoint presentation in which you want the Excel chart to appear.
2. Open the Excel workbook containing the chart that you want to transfer to PowerPoint.
3. Click near the outside edge of the chart to select it.
4. On the Home tab, from the Clipboard group, click the Copy button (see Figure 26-3).
5. Switch to the appropriate PowerPoint presentation using the Windows task bar.
6. Click the slide on which the Excel chart should appear.

You can change the slide layout to a blank slide or delete any PowerPoint Click Here boxes to make the slide easier to see.

7. From the Clipboard group on the Home tab, click the Paste button to display the chart on the PowerPoint slide (see Figure 26-4).

You can connect the chart in PowerPoint to the Excel file so that updates in the Excel file appear in the PowerPoint chart. In Step 7, click the down-arrow portion of the Paste button and select Paste Special. On the left side of the Paste Special dialog box, select the Paste Link option; then, choose Microsoft Office Excel Chart Object and click OK.

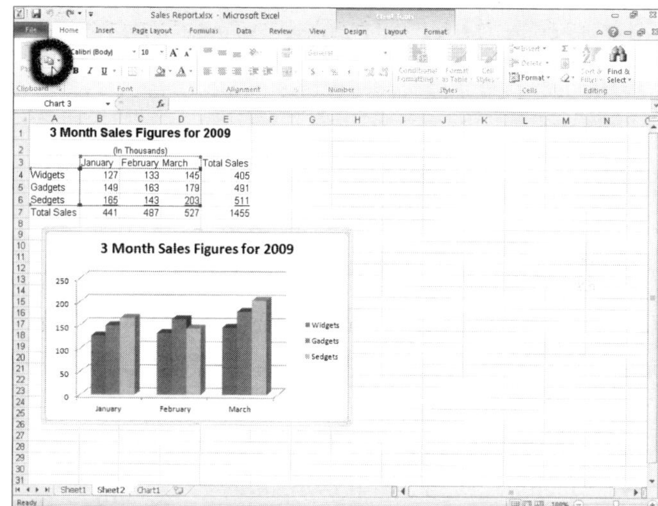

Figure 26-3

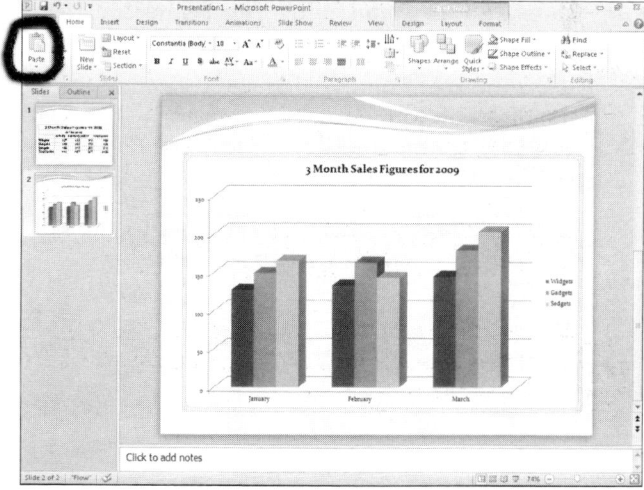

Figure 26-4

Create a PowerPoint Slide from a Word Outline

1. Open a Word document and create the outline information that you want to transfer to a single PowerPoint slide (see Figure 26-5). Click the Outline icon on the Word status bar to work in Outline view. Pressing Tab indents a heading; pressing Shift+Tab outdents a heading.

To create multiple PowerPoint slides, create separate Word documents.

2. Save and close the Word document.
3. Open a PowerPoint presentation.
4. On the Home tab, from the Slides group, click the bottom of the New Slide button. From the drop-down menu that opens, choose Slides from Outline (see Figure 26-6).
5. In the Insert Outline dialog box that appears, navigate to and select the Word outline that you created in Step 1; then click the Insert button. PowerPoint creates a slide containing the contents of the Word document; PowerPoint treats each heading in the Word document as a bullet.

If the contents appear to run over the edge of the slide, click the slide, and PowerPoint will adjust the font size to accommodate the text.

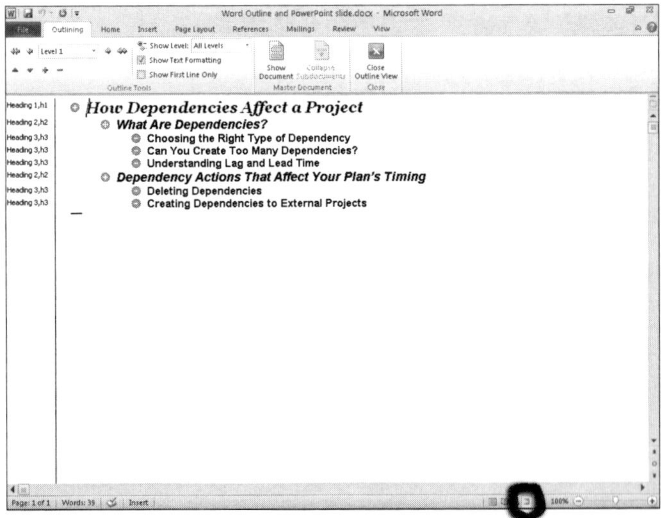

Figure 26-5

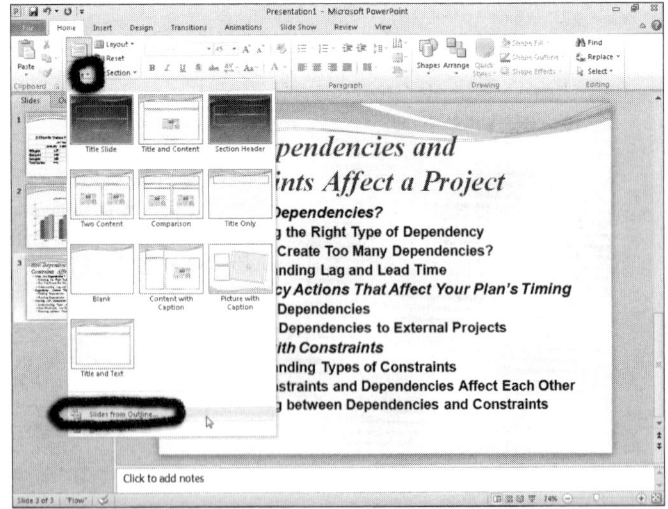

Figure 26-6

Place a Word Table in Excel

1. In Word, select the rows of a table that you want to place in Excel.

To copy the entire table, click the Select Table handle (upper left corner of the table).

2. On the Home tab, from the Clipboard group, click the Copy button (see Figure 26-7).
3. Open the Excel workbook in which you want to place the Word table and then select the cell that you want to set as the upper-left corner of the data.
4. On the Home tab, from the Clipboard group, click the Paste button. The Word data appears in Excel.
5. Click the Paste Options button that appears and select the formatting for the data you copied (see Figure 26-8).

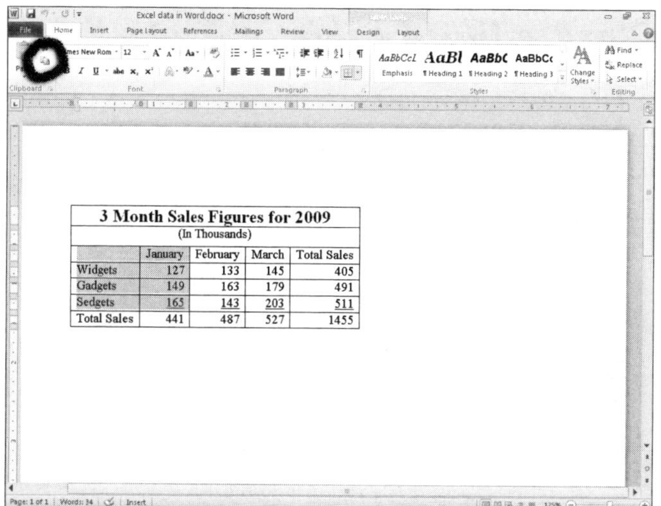

Figure 26-7

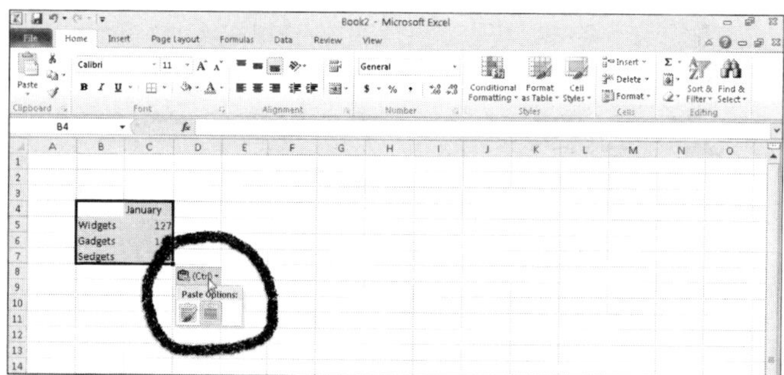

Figure 26-8

Place a Word Table in PowerPoint

1. In Word, select the rows of a table that you want to place on a PowerPoint slide.

To copy the entire table, click the Select Table handle that appears in the upper left of the table.

2. On the Home tab, from the Clipboard group, click the Copy button (see Figure 26-9).
3. Open the PowerPoint presentation in which you want to place the Word table and then select the slide on which the table should appear.

You can change the slide layout to a blank slide or delete any PowerPoint Click Here boxes to make the slide easier to see.

4. On the Home tab, from the Clipboard group, click the down arrow under the Paste button and then choose Paste Special to display the Paste Special dialog box shown in Figure 26-10.
5. Choose Microsoft Office Word Document Object and then click OK to display the Word table on the PowerPoint slide. You can drag a corner to enlarge the data on the slide.

By default, the Paste option is selected in the Paste Special dialog box. If you select Paste Link, the Word table appears on the PowerPoint slide, and any changes you make to the table in Word also appear on the PowerPoint slide.

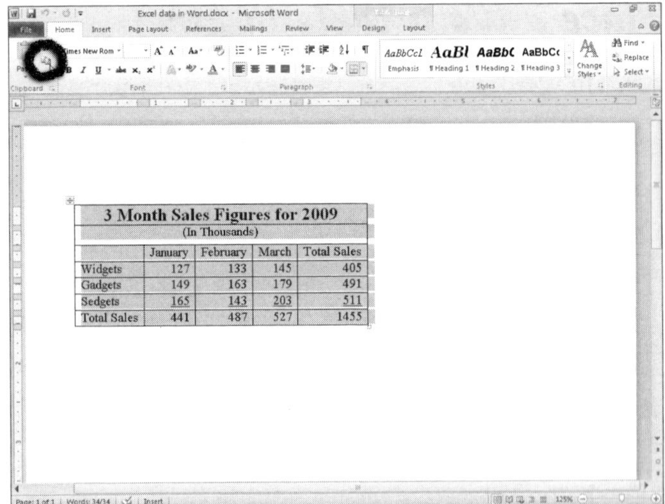

3 Month Sales Figures for 2009
(In Thousands)

	January	February	March	Total Sales
Widgets	127	133	145	405
Gadgets	149	163	179	491
Sedgets	165	143	203	511
Total Sales	441	487	527	1455

Figure 26-9

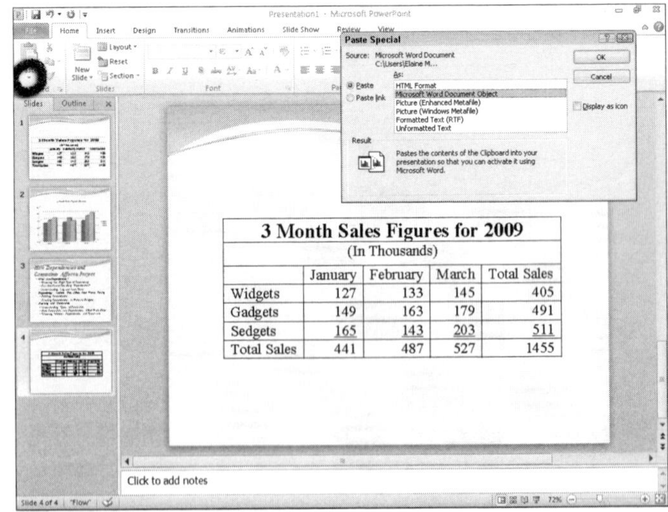

3 Month Sales Figures for 2009
(In Thousands)

	January	February	March	Total Sales
Widgets	127	133	145	405
Gadgets	149	163	179	491
Sedgets	165	143	203	511
Total Sales	441	487	527	1455

Figure 26-10

Place Excel Data in Word

1. In Excel, select the data you want to place in Word.
2. On the Home tab, from the Clipboard group, click the Copy button (see Figure 26-11).
3. Open the Word document in which you want to place the Excel data and then position the insertion point where you want the data to appear.
4. On the Home tab, from the Clipboard group, click the Paste button. The data appears in Word.
5. Click the Paste Options button that appears and select the formatting for the data you copied (see Figure 26-12).

If you choose either of the last two options on the Paste Options menu, any changes that you make to the data in Excel also appear in Word.

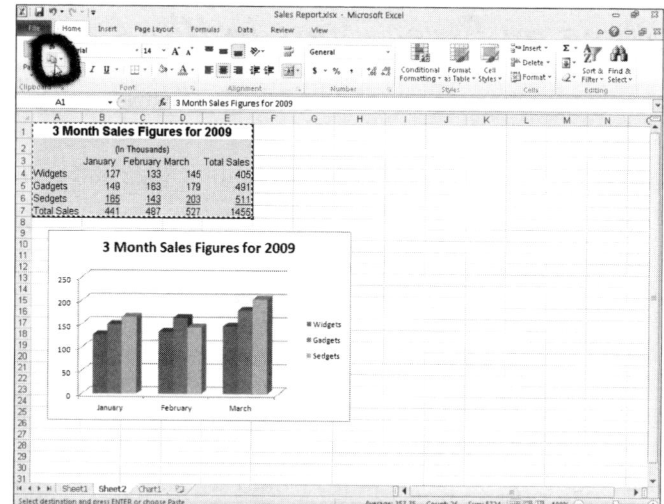

Figure 26-11

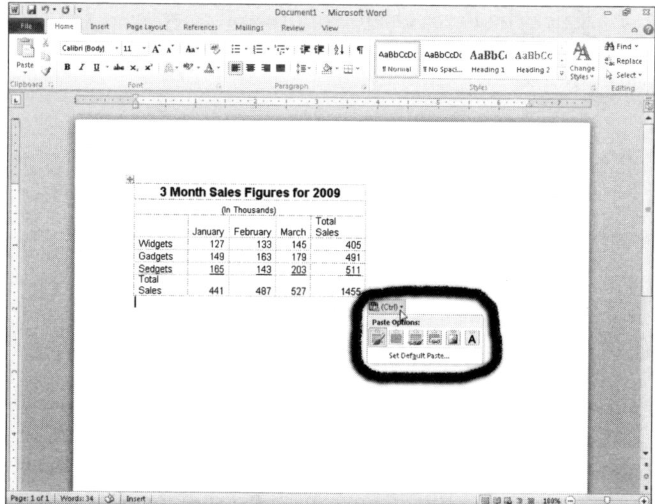

Figure 26-12

Place an Excel Chart in Word

1. Open the Word document in which you want the Excel chart to appear.
2. Open the Excel workbook containing the chart that you want to transfer to Word.
3. Click near the outside edge of the chart to select it.
4. On the Home tab, from the Clipboard group, click the Copy button (see Figure 26-13).
5. Click the Word document on the Windows task bar.
6. Click the location in the document where the Excel chart should appear.
7. On the Home tab, in the Clipboard group, click the Paste button to display the chart in the Word document (see Figure 26-14).
8. Click the Paste Options button that appears beside the chart and select the formatting for the chart and whether updates in Excel will update the chart in Word.

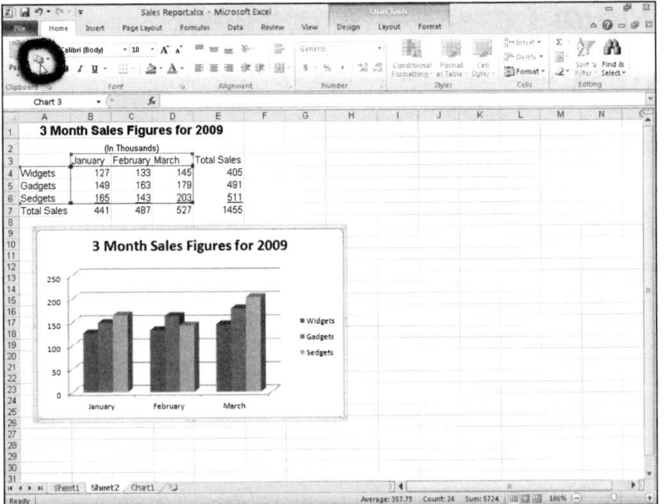

Figure 26-13

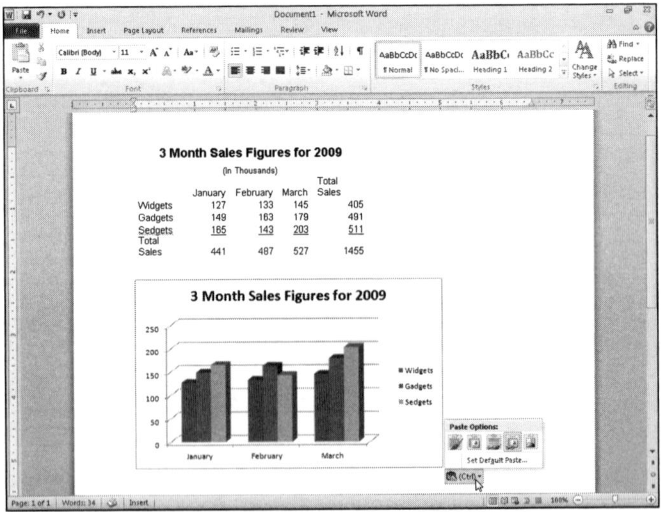

Figure 26-14

Import Contact Information from Excel into Outlook

1. In Excel, open the workbook containing the contact information that you want to import into Outlook and then establish a named range for the information. See Chapter 9 for details on naming a range.
2. Save the Excel workbook as an Excel 97–2003 workbook and close it. See Chapter 8 for details on saving an Excel workbook.
3. In Outlook, click the File tab. From Backstage view that appears, click Open (see Figure 26-15).
4. Click Import to start the Import and Export Wizard.
5. On the first screen, choose Import from Another Program or File; then click Next (see Figure 26-16).

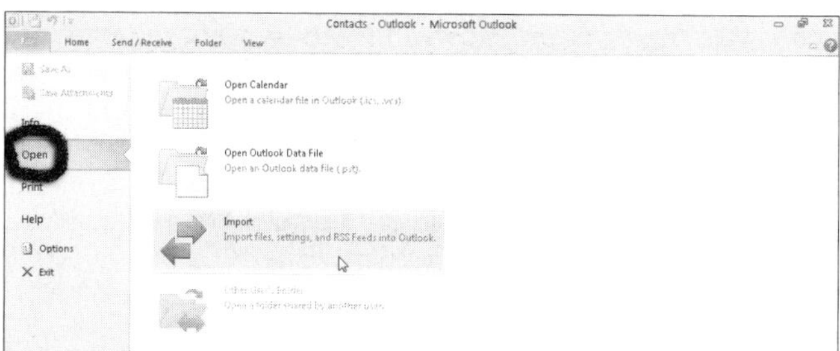

Figure 26-15

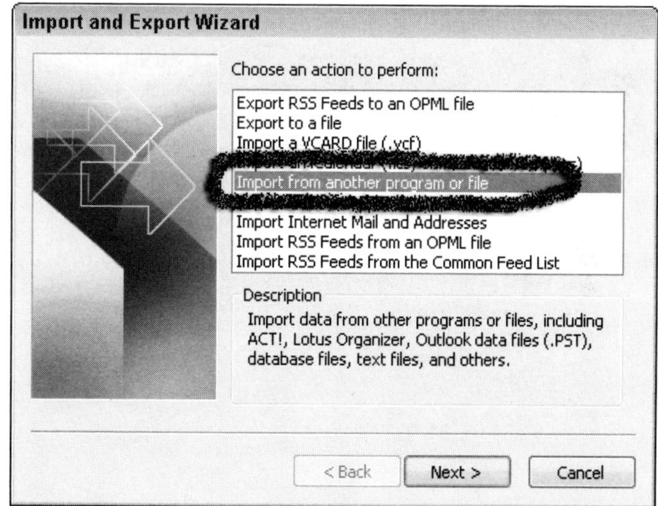

Figure 26-16

6. Use the next wizard window to identify the type of file containing the information you want to import into Outlook. In this example, choose Microsoft Excel 97–2003 then click Next (see Figure 26-17).

Note that, although you can import information from a wide variety of file types into Outlook, you cannot directly import an Excel 2007 or Excel 2010 file into Outlook. That's why, in Step 2, you saved the Excel workbook in Excel 97-2003 format.

7. In the next wizard window, as shown in Figure 26-18, select the Do Not Import Duplicate Items radio button and then click Browse.

Although you can allow duplicates to be created, you won't have any way of easily identifying which of a set of duplicates came from Outlook and which came from Excel. Only allow duplicates to be replaced with imported items if you are positive that the information in the file you are importing is more accurate than the information currently in Outlook.

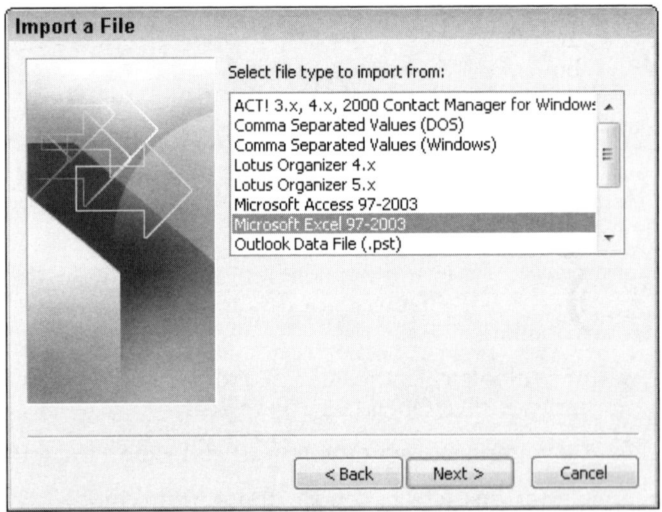

Figure 26-17

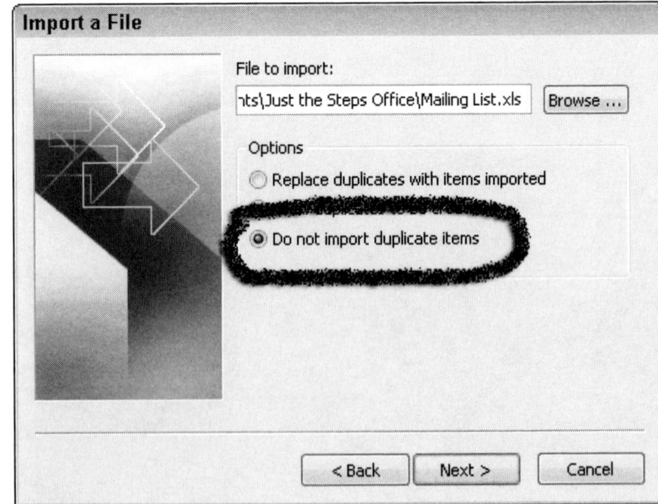

Figure 26-18

8. In the Browse dialog box that appears (shown in Figure 26-19), navigate to the folder that contains the Excel workbook that you opened in Step 1 and saved in Step 2. Click the workbook, and then click OK. The wizard dialog box shown in Figure 26-18 reappears; click Next.

9. In the next Import a File wizard window, choose Contacts (see Figure 26-20) and then click Next.

Although you can import the information into any folder in Outlook, when you are importing Contact information, placing the information in the Contacts folder ensures that the imported information will format properly in Outlook.

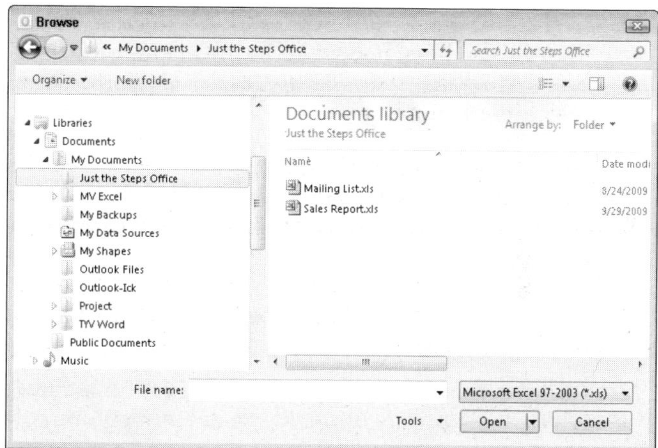

Figure 26-19

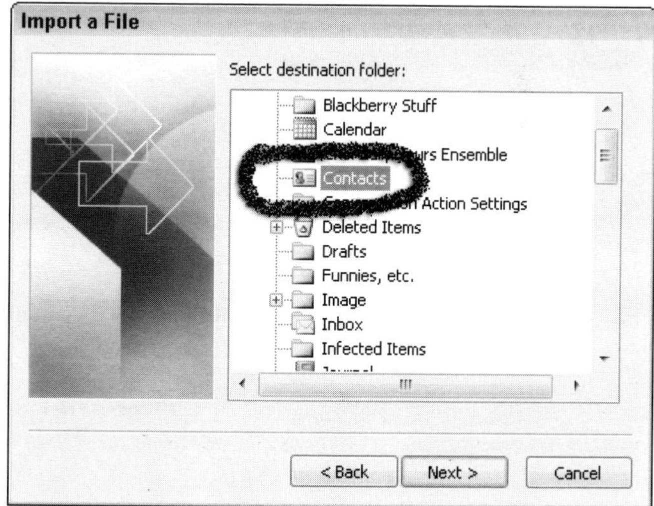

Figure 26-20

10. In the next wizard window (shown in Figure 26-21), click the Map Custom Fields button. In the Map Custom Fields dialog box that appears (see Figure 26-22), Outlook attempts to match fields in the Excel workbook (which appear on the left) with fields in Outlook (which appear on the right).

Outlook won't import any fields in the Excel workbook that don't match a field in Outlook, but the field names in Excel do *not* need to be the same as the Outlook field names.

11. On the right side of the dialog box, click each plus sign to display all fields. (The plus signs toggle to minus signs.)
12. Confirm that each field in the Value list on the left side of the dialog box appears in the Mapped From column of the right-hand list.

Count the fields in the Excel workbook and then count the fields in the Mapped From column of the right-hand list to get an idea of how many fields on the left remain unmapped.

13. If a field appears in the Excel workbook but not in the Mapped From column of Outlook fields, identify a field in Outlook that corresponds to the field you want to import. Then, drag the field from the Excel workbook list onto the appropriate field in the Field column of Outlook fields.
14. When you finish mapping, click OK.
15. Click Finish. Outlook imports uncategorized contacts. To categorize them, see Chapter 22.

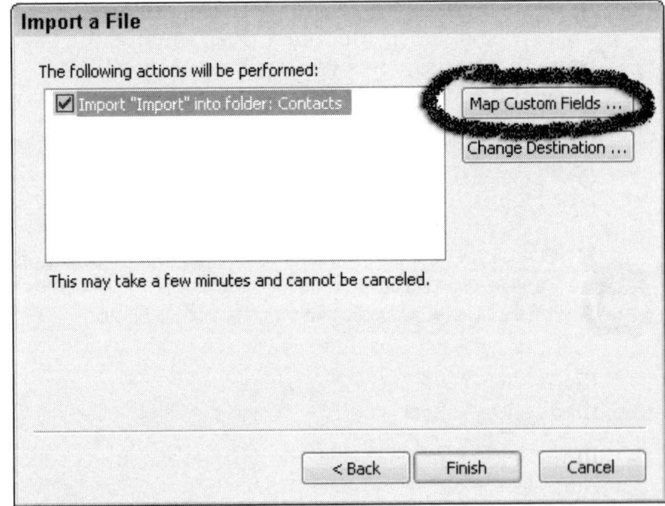

Figure 26-21

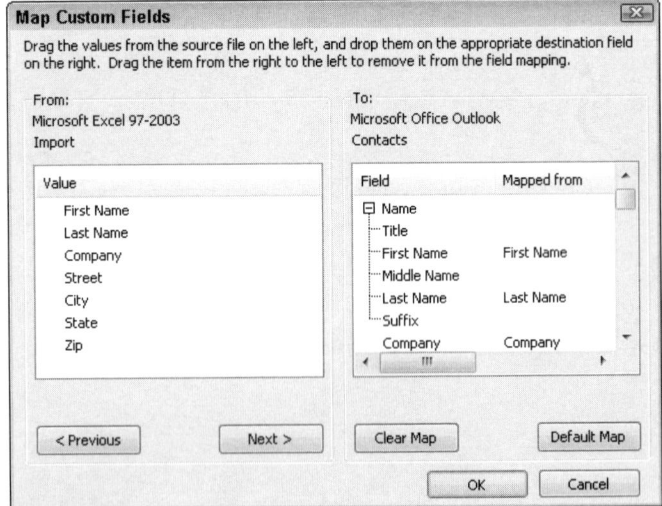

Figure 26-22

Export an Outlook Category of Contacts to Excel

1. In Outlook, click the Contacts button in the Navigation pane.
2. On the Home tab, from the Current View group, select By Category.

You need to display onscreen the address information for contacts that you plan to export to Excel.

3. Right-click any column heading in the view; from the menu that appears, choose Field Chooser (see Figure 26-23).
4. In the Field Chooser window, open the list and then click Address Fields (see Figure 26-24).
5. Drag and drop the address fields from the Field Chooser window onto the column headings of the view, selecting the address fields that match fields in the Excel workbook.

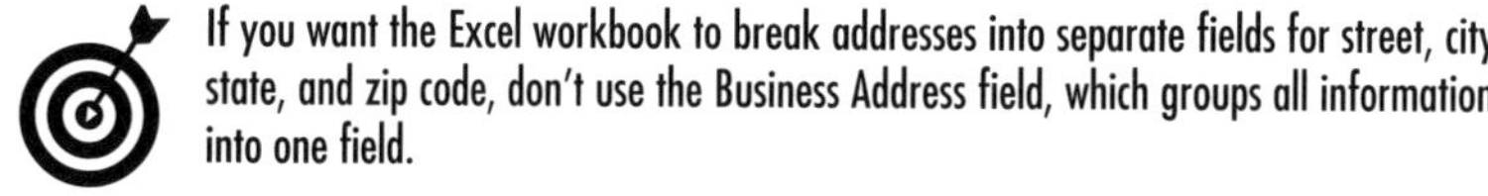

If you want the Excel workbook to break addresses into separate fields for street, city, state, and zip code, don't use the Business Address field, which groups all information into one field.

6. Click the X in the Field Chooser window to close it.

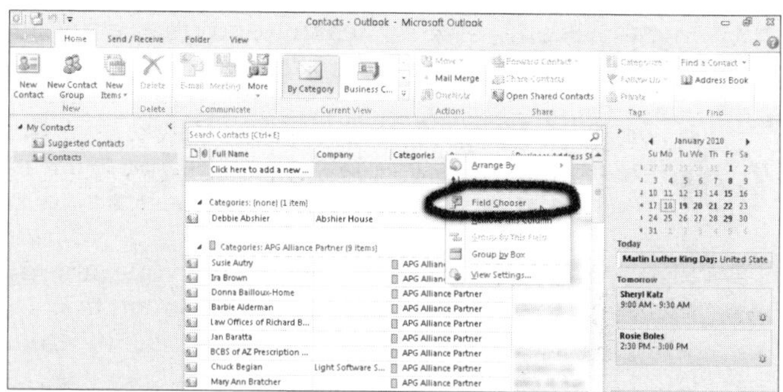

Figure 26-23

Figure 26-24

7. Right-click any category heading and choose Collapse All Groups from the menu that appears (see Figure 26-25).

Category headings typically contain a small colored square and, if you didn't rename your categories, you'll also see the color spelled out. If you did rename your categories, the names you supplied appear to the right of the small colored square.

8. Right-click the heading of the category you want to export to Excel and then choose Copy from the menu that appears. Outlook expands the category and selects all the names in it (see Figure 26-26).

Outlook exports only information that you select. When you right-click the heading of the category you want to export and choose Copy, Outlook understands that you want to export the Contact information for that particular category.

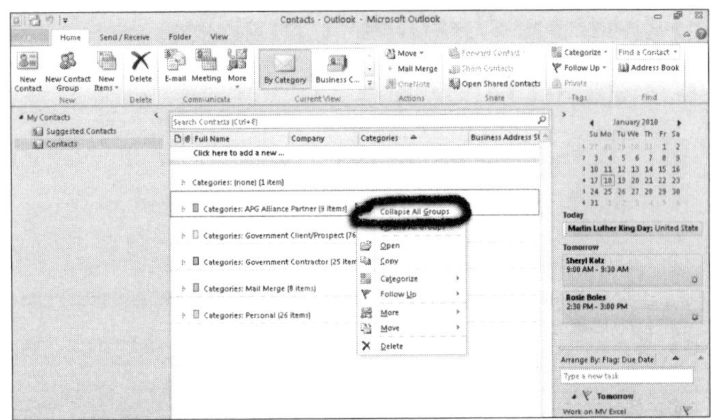

Figure 26-25

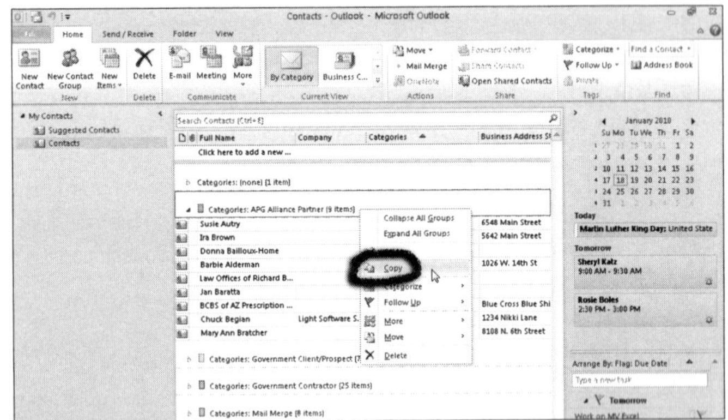

Figure 26-26

9. Open Excel.
10. With the cell pointer in cell A1, click the Paste button (see Figure 26-27). The names from the selected category appear in Excel, and they are all highlighted (see Figure 26-28).
11. Click the Select All button that appears above Row 1 and to the left of Column A to select the sheet.
12. Double-click the bar between Columns A and B. Excel expands all columns so that you can see all the information in each column.

The mouse pointer changes shapes when you have it positioned properly on the bar between Columns A and B.

13. Click the File tab; from Backstage view, click Save As and then choose Excel Workbook.
14. In the Save As dialog box that appears, navigate to a folder where you want to save the Excel workbook and then click Save.

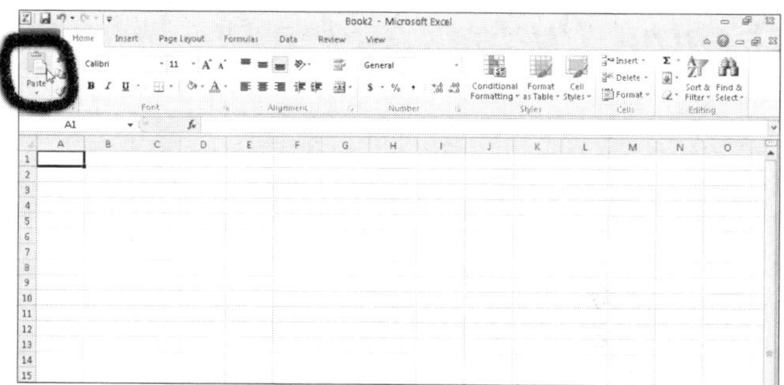

Figure 26-27

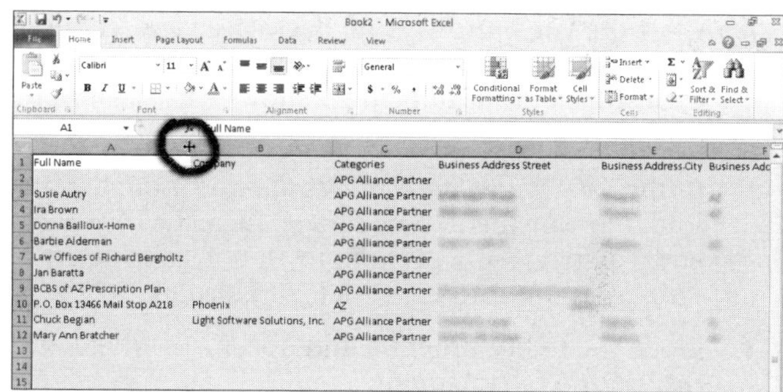

Figure 26-28

Display Outlook Calendar Information in Another Office Program

1. In Outlook, click the Calendar button in the Navigation pane. From the Arrange group, select the view that you want to use in another Office program.
2. In the Navigation pane, select the calendar containing information that you want to display in another Office program.
3. To save an appointment or meeting, open the item; otherwise, skip to Step 4.
4. Click the File button. From Backstage view, choose Save Calendar or, if you're saving an appointment or meeting, choose Save As. Figure 26-29 shows Backstage view for a calendar.
5. In the Save As dialog box that appears, note the name and folder in which you'll be saving; then click Save. To limit calendar information, click More Options and select a date range and the amount of detail to display.
6. Open the Office program and document where you want to display the calendar item.
7. Click the Insert tab. From the appropriate group (the Text group in Word), click the Object button. The Object dialog box appears (see Figure 26-30).
8. Click the Create from File tab.
9. Click the Browse button, navigate to the file you created in Step 4, select it, and then click Open to redisplay the Object dialog box.
10. Click OK to insert an icon in the document. Double-click the icon, and an Outlook calendar, meeting, or appointment window appears.

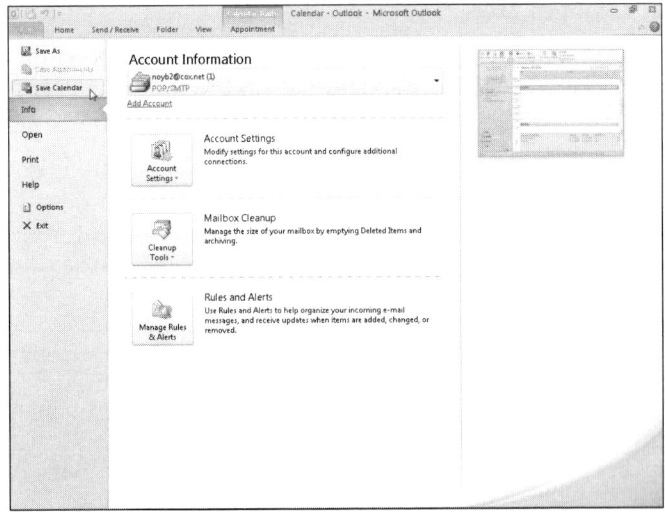

Figure 26-29

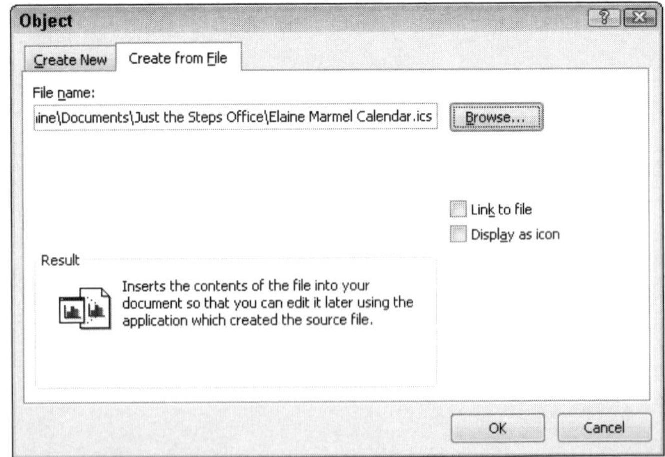

Figure 26-30

Handling Mail Merges

In most cases, you use a *mail merge* when you want to combine *dynamic* (changing) information (such as the recipient of a letter) with static (doesn't change) information (such as the body of the letter). However, you also can use a mail merge to prepare mailing labels and envelopes. If you're preparing a form letter to send to, say, your customer base, you need to write that form letter. Then, to incorporate mailing address information on the form letter and on mailing labels or envelopes, you need to set up a file that contains the mailing address information. You can set up that information in Word, in Excel, or you can use your Outlook Contact information. In this chapter, you see how to

- Create mailing lists in Word and Excel.
- Prepare a mail merge letter that incorporates changing recipient information.
- Prepare envelopes with data from an Excel file.
- Prepare mailing labels with data from an Excel file.
- Prepare mailing labels for all contacts in Outlook.
- Prepare mailing labels for a selected group of Outlook contacts.

Chapter

27

Get ready to . . .

Create a Mailing List in Excel

1. On a blank Excel worksheet, use row 1 to enter column headings to identify each field of a particular mailing address.
2. On subsequent rows, enter the appropriate information for each address you want to include in your mailing list (see Figure 27-1).
3. Save the Excel file.

Create an Address List in Word

1. In a blank Word document, click the Mailings tab.
2. Click the Select Recipients button from the Start Mail Merge group. From the drop-down menu that appears, choose Type New List to display the New Address List dialog box shown in Figure 27-2.
3. On each row, type mailing address information, pressing Tab to move across the row.
4. Click OK when you finish entering addresses. Word displays the Save Address List window, where you type a name for the list and then click Save.

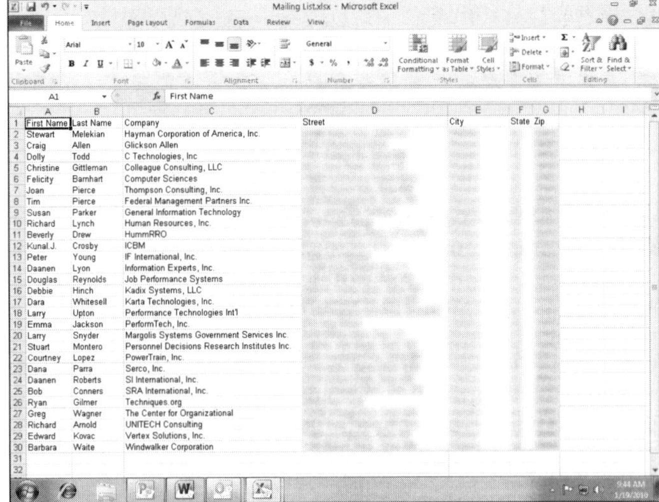

Figure 27-1

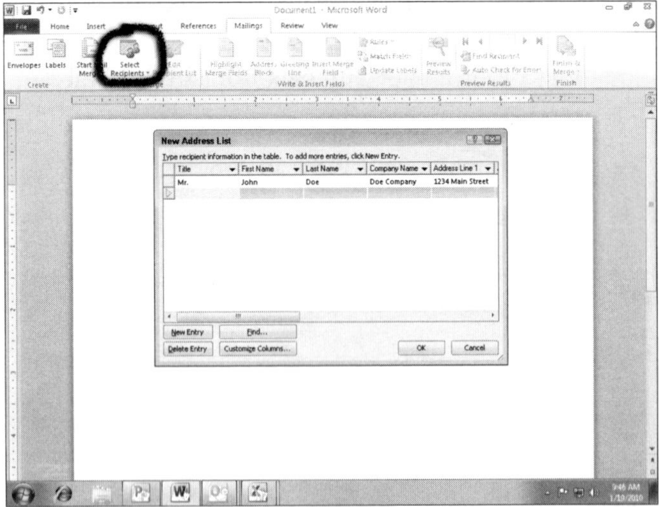

Figure 27-2

Create a Mail Merge Letter with Excel Data

1. Create a form letter but don't include any information that will change from letter to letter, such as the inside address.
2. Click the Mailings tab.
3. From the Start Mail Merge group, click the Start Mail Merge button and then choose Letters from the drop-down menu that appears (see Figure 27-3).
4. From the Start Mail Merge group, click Select Recipients and then choose Use Existing List from the drop-down menu that appears. The Select Data Source dialog box appears.

This example uses a mailing list stored in an Excel file. Make sure that the file containing mailing list information is not open.

5. Navigate to the folder containing the mailing list file, select the file, and then click Open. Word links with Excel, and the Select Table dialog box shown in Figure 27-4 appears. If the Excel workbook contains multiple sheets, select the sheet containing mailing list information and then click OK.

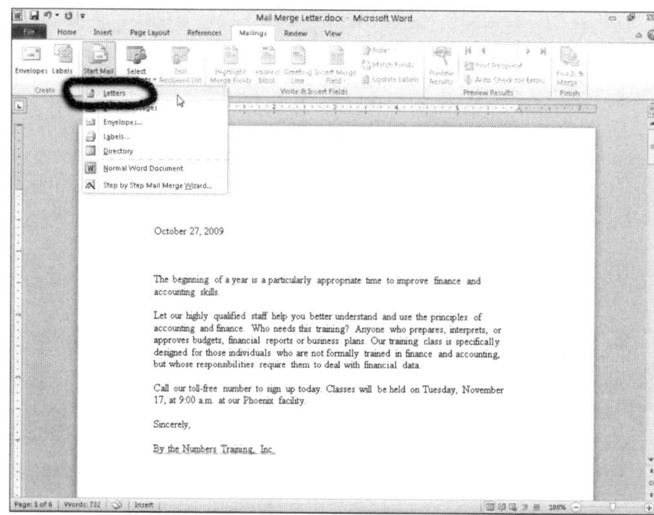

Figure 27-3

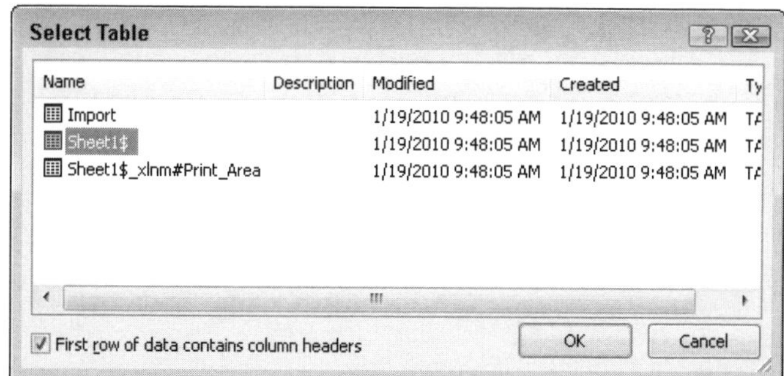

Figure 27-4

6. From the Start Mail Merge group, click the Edit Recipient List button to display the Mail Merge Recipients window shown in Figure 27-5. A check box appears beside each person's name, identifying the recipients of the form letter.

7. Remove the check beside any addressee to whom you do not want to mail a form letter. Then click OK to redisplay the form letter.

8. Place the insertion point at the location in the letter where you want the inside address to appear.

9. From the Write & Insert Fields group on the Ribbon, click the Address Block button to display the Insert Address Block dialog box (see Figure 27-6).

10. On the left side of the Address Block dialog box, select a format for recipient names; a preview of the format appears on the right side.

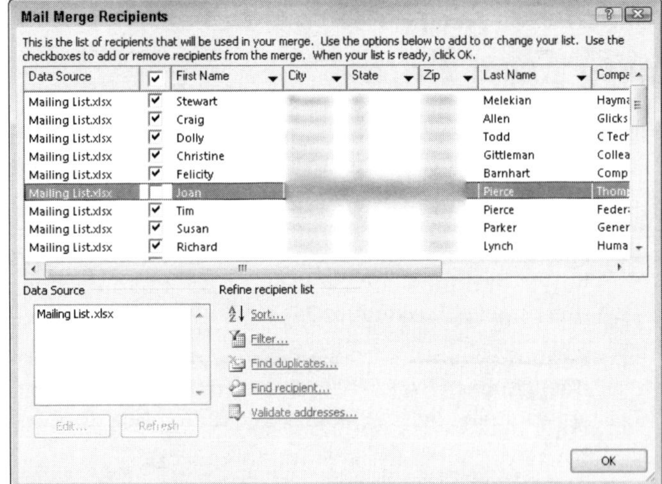

Figure 27-5

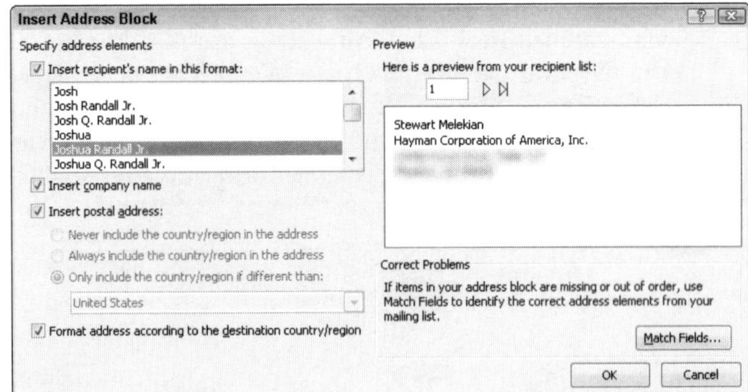

Figure 27-6

11. If information from the mailing list file doesn't appear correctly in the preview, click the Match Fields button to display the Match Fields dialog box (see Figure 27-7).

12. Open each list box that you want to include in your form letter and then select the corresponding field from the list. To avoid having to match fields for this mailing list in the future, select the Remember This Matching for This Set of Data Sources on This Computer check box and then click OK. Word redisplays the Insert Address Block dialog box (refer to Figure 27-6).

13. Click OK, and Word inserts the Address Block merge field in your document. When you merge the information, Word replaces the merge field with address information.

14. Place the insertion point at the location in your form letter where you want the greeting to appear.

15. From the Write & Insert Fields group on the Ribbon, click the Greeting Line button to display the Insert Greeting Line dialog box (see Figure 27-8). Use this dialog box to select a greeting line and to identify a universal greeting line for missing recipient names; then click OK. Word inserts a merge field representing the greeting line in the letter.

You might need to click the Match Fields button to make your greeting line appear how you want.

Figure 27-7

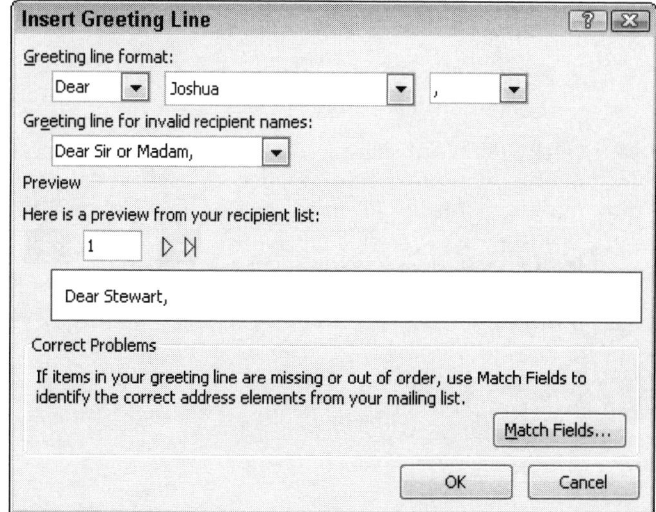

Figure 27-8

16. From the Preview Results group on the Ribbon, click the Preview Results button. Word displays a preview of the merged letter, using the unchanging content of the letter and the information from the mailing list file for the inside address and the greeting (see Figure 27-9). You can click the Next Record button and the Previous Record button in the Preview Results group to preview all letters.

17. Click the Preview Results button again to redisplay merge fields.

18. From the Finish group on the Ribbon, click the Finish & Merge button. From the drop-down menu that appears, choose Edit Individual Documents to display the Merge to New Document dialog box (see Figure 27-10).

19. Select an option to identify the recipients of the letter:

    - *All:* Creates letters for all entries on the mailing list.
    - *Current Record:* Creates only one letter for the recipient whose letter you're previewing.
    - *From* and *To:* Creates letters for recipients whom you specify by their record numbers.

20. Click OK. Word merges the form letter information with the mailing list information and places individual letters for each mailing list recipient in a new document named Letters1.

If you want, you can save Letters1 or you can simply close it.

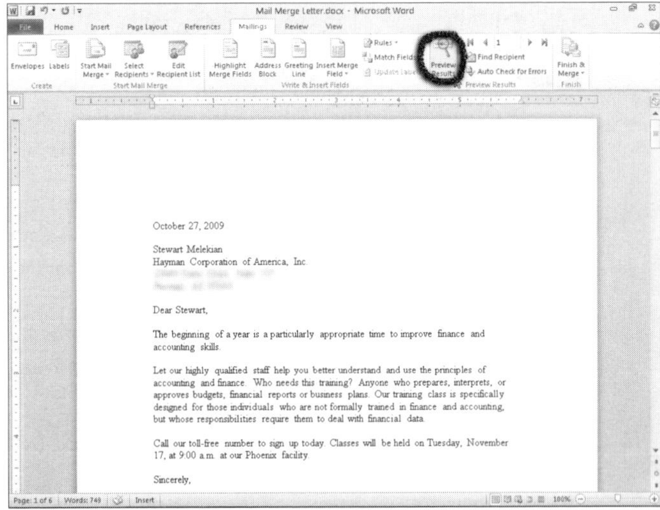

Figure 27-9

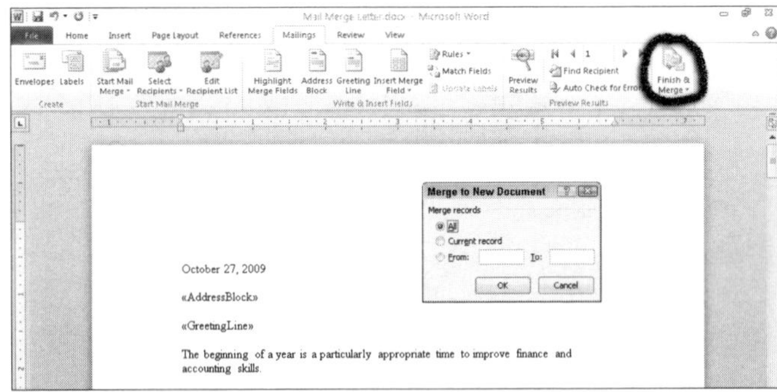

Figure 27-10

Create Mail Merge Envelopes in Word with Excel Data

1. In a new blank document, click the Mailings tab.
2. From the Start Mail Merge group on the Ribbon, click the Start Mail Merge button and then choose Envelopes from the drop-down menu that appears (see Figure 27-11).
3. In the Envelope Options dialog box that appears, select an envelope size and font (see Figure 27-12). You can use the Printing Options tab to select an envelope feeding method specific to your printer.
4. Click OK. Word sets up the document for envelopes.
5. From the Start Mail Merge group on the Ribbon, click the Select Recipients button and identify the type of recipient list that you plan to use. This example uses an existing list in an Excel file. The Select Data Source dialog box appears.

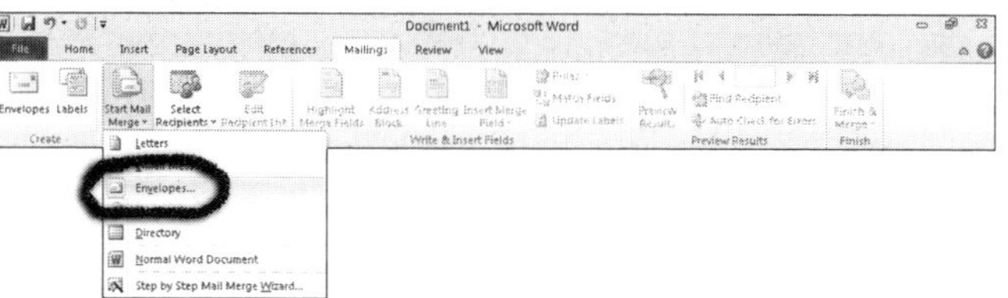

Figure 27-11

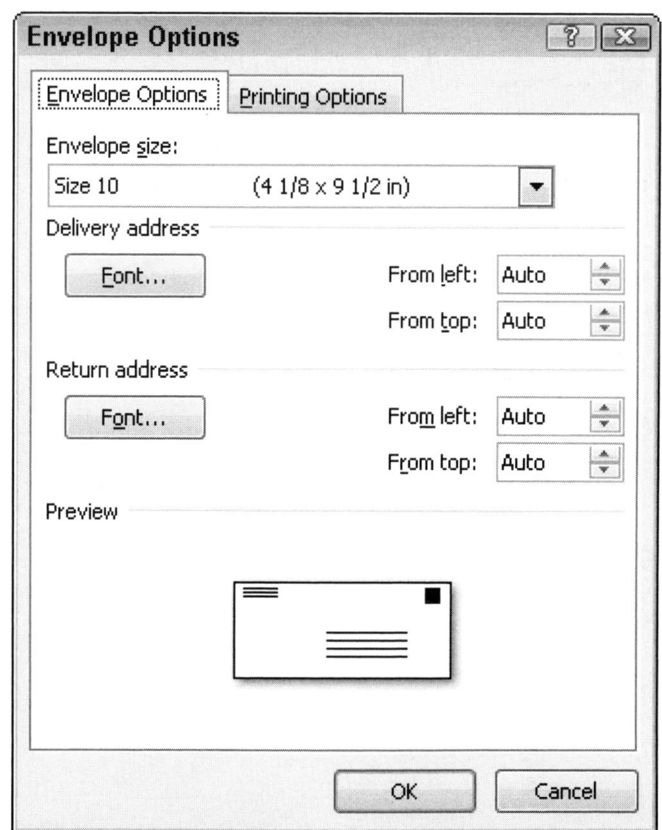

Figure 27-12

6. Navigate to the folder containing the mailing list file, select the file, and then click Open. Word links with Excel, and the Select Table dialog box appears (see Figure 27-13). If the Excel workbook contains multiple sheets, select the sheet containing the mailing list and then click OK.

7. Click in the area of the envelope where the recipient's name and address will appear.

You can click in the upper left of the envelope and type your return address, which requires no merge field because it will be the same on each envelope.

8. From the Write & Insert Fields group on the Ribbon, click the Address Block button to display the Insert Address Block dialog box (see Figure 27-14).

9. Click a format for recipient names; a preview of the format appears on the right side of the dialog box.

If the preview doesn't look right to you, click the Match Fields button and use the list boxes in the Match Fields dialog box that appears to match Word fields with the fields in your mailing list file. See "Create a Mail Merge Letter" earlier in this chapter for details.

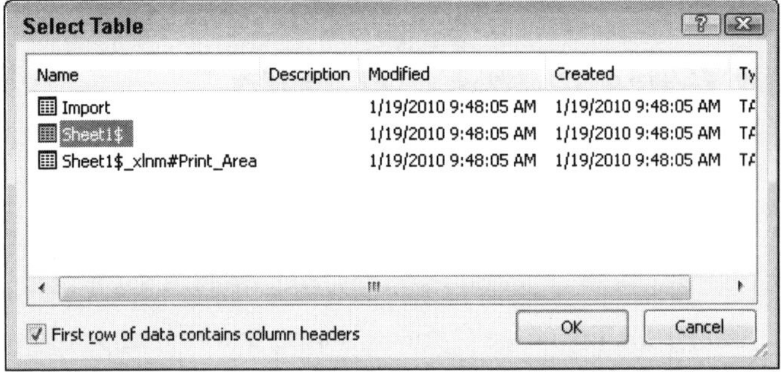

Figure 27-13

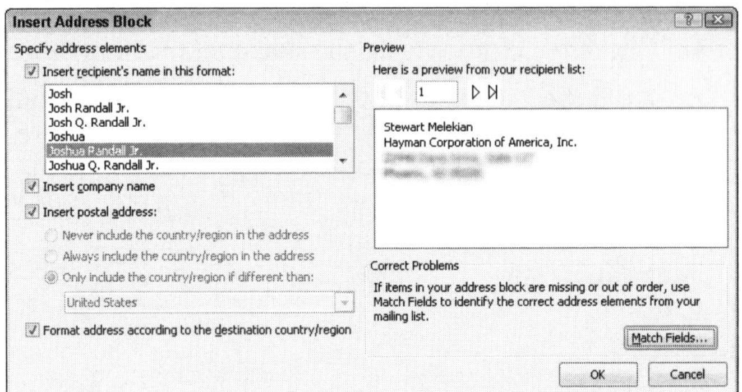

Figure 27-14

10. Click OK. Word adds the Address Block merge field to the envelope (see Figure 27-15). When you merge the information, Word replaces the merge field with information from the mailing list file.

11. From the Preview Results group, click the Preview Results button to see what your envelopes will look like. You can click the Next Record button and the Previous Record buttons in the Preview Results group to preview the all the envelopes.

12. Click the Preview Results button again to redisplay merge fields.

13. From the Finish group on the Ribbon, click the Finish & Merge button. From the drop-down menu that appears, choose Edit Individual Documents to display the Merge to New Document dialog box (see Figure 27-16).

14. Select an option to identify the recipients of the letter:

    - *All:* Creates an envelope for all entries on the mailing list.
    - *Current Record:* Creates only one envelope for the recipient you are previewing.
    - *From* and *To:* Creates envelopes for recipients whom you specify by their record numbers.

15. Click OK, and Word merges the mailing list information onto envelopes and places envelopes for each mailing list recipient in a new document named Envelopes1.

You can save Envelopes1 or you can simply close it.

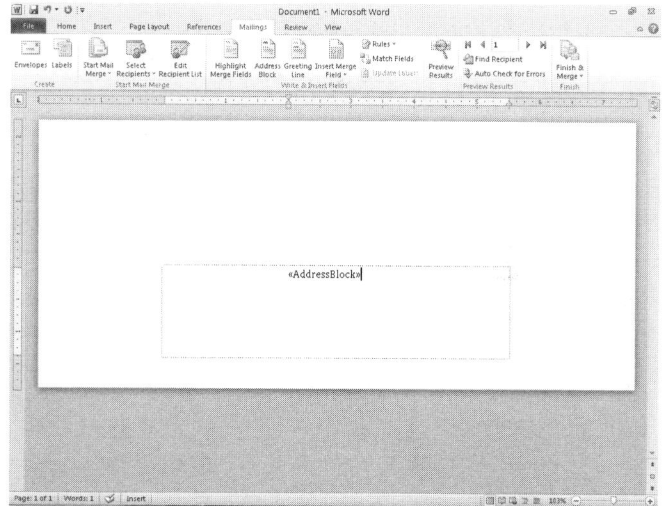

Figure 27-15

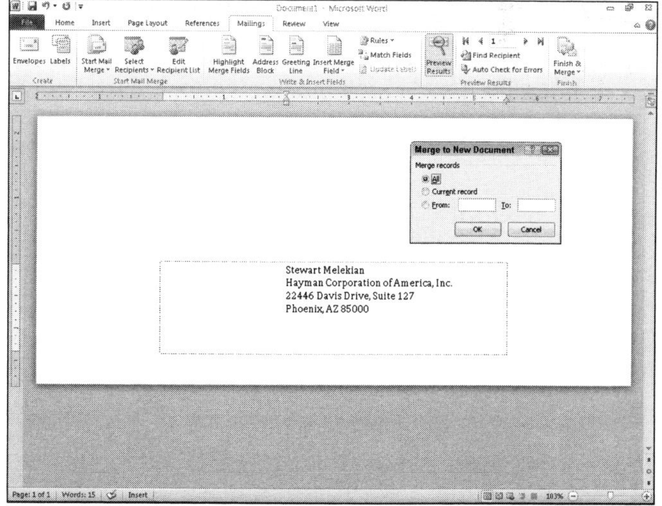

Figure 27-16

Create Mail Merge Labels in Word with Excel Data

1. In a new blank document, click the Mailings tab.
2. From the Start Mail Merge group on the Ribbon, click the Start Mail Merge button and choose Labels from the drop-down menu that appears (see Figure 27-17).
3. In the Label Options dialog box that appears, select an option to select the type of printer and a label vendor and product number (see Figure 27-18). Word displays information about the label you select.
4. Click OK. Word sets up the document for the labels you selected without gridlines to identify individual labels.

To display gridlines, click the Table Tools Layout tab on the Ribbon. From the Table group, click View Gridlines.

5. From the Start Mail Merge group on the Ribbon, click the Select Recipients button and identify the type of recipient list that you plan to use. This example uses an existing list in an Excel file. The Select Data Source dialog box appears.

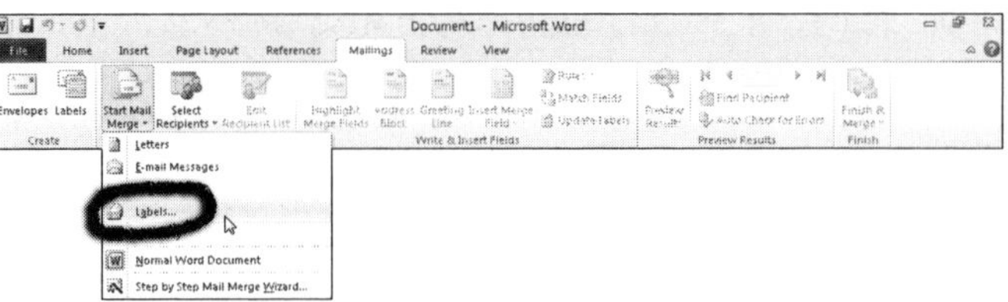

Figure 27-17

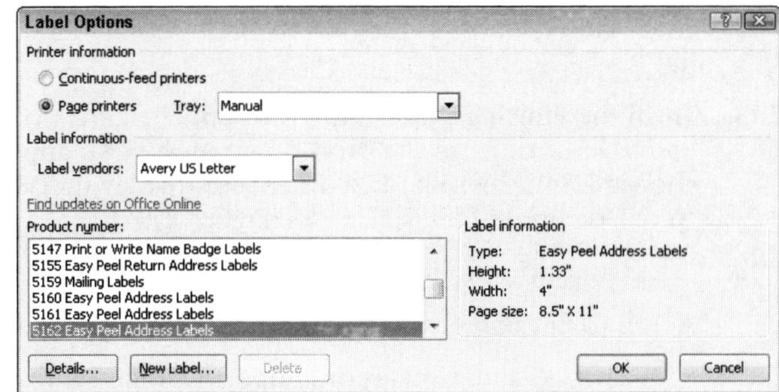

Figure 27-18

6. Navigate to the folder containing the mailing list file, select the file, and then click Open. Word links with Excel, and the Select Table dialog box appears (see Figure 27-19). If the Excel workbook contains multiple sheets, select the sheet containing the mailing list and then click OK.
7. Click in the first label.
8. From the Write & Insert Fields group of the Ribbon, click the Address Block button to display the Insert Address Block dialog box (see Figure 27-20).
9. Select a format for recipient names; a preview of the format appears on the right side of the dialog box.

If the preview doesn't look right to you, click the Match Fields button and use the list boxes in the Match Fields dialog box that appears to match Word fields with the fields in your mailing list file. See "Create a Mail Merge Letter with Excel Data" earlier in this chapter for details.

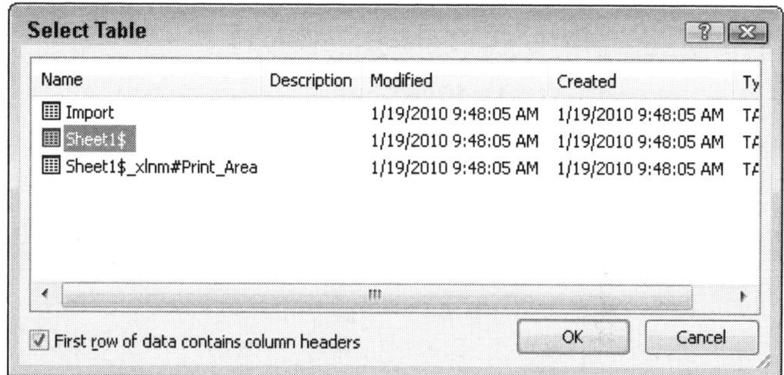

Figure 27-19

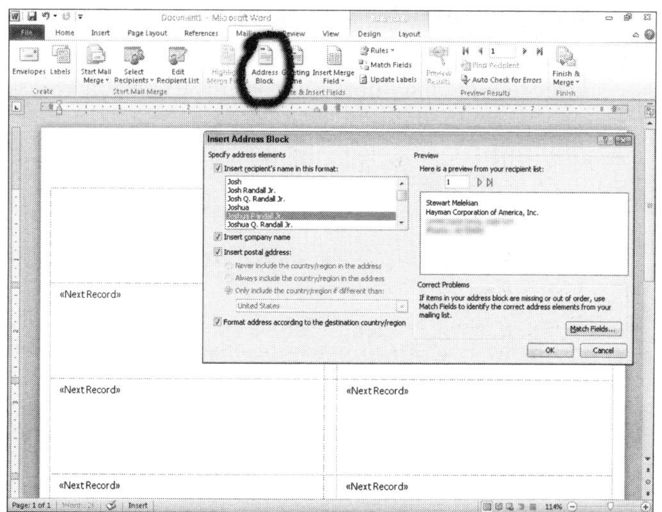

Figure 27-20

10. Click OK. Word adds the Address Block merge field to the first label. When you merge the information, Word replaces the merge field with information from the mailing address file.

11. From the Write & Insert Fields group on the Ribbon, click the Update Labels button to add the Address Block merge field to every label (see Figure 27-21).

12. From the Preview Results group, click the Preview Results button to see what your mailing labels will look like.

13. Click the Preview Results button again to redisplay merge fields.

14. From the Finish group on the Ribbon, click the Finish & Merge button. From the drop-down menu that appears, choose Edit Individual Documents to display the Merge to New Document dialog box (see Figure 27-22).

15. Click an option to identify the recipients of the letter:

   - *All:* Creates a label for each recipient on the mailing list.
   - *Current Record:* Creates only one label for the recipient you are previewing.
   - *From* and *To:* Creates labels for recipients whom you specify by their record numbers.

16. Click OK. Word merges the mailing list information onto the labels and places individual sheets of labels in a new document named Labels1.

You can save Labels1 or simply close it.

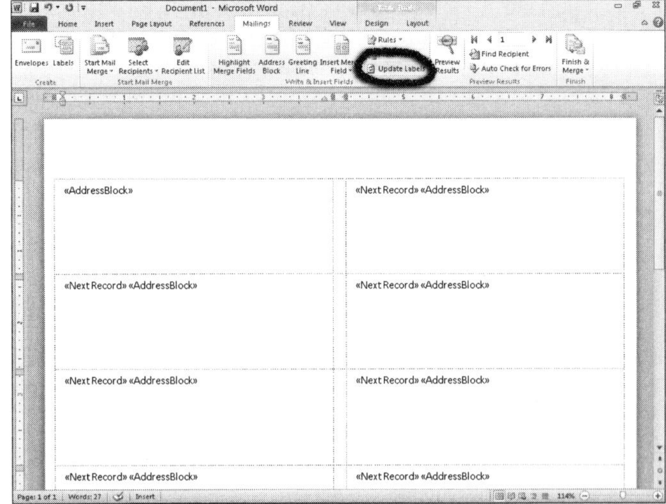

Figure 27-21

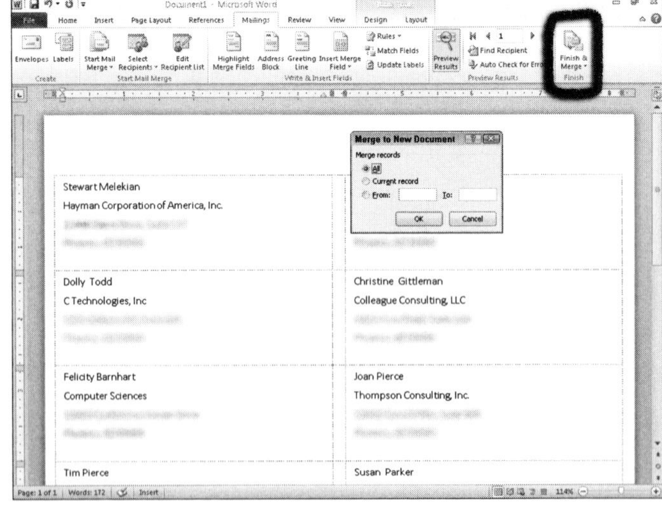

Figure 27-22

Create Mailing Labels with Outlook Contact Information

1. In a new blank document, click the Mailings tab.
2. From the Start Mail Merge group on the Ribbon, click the Start Mail Merge button and then choose Labels from the drop-down menu that appears (see Figure 27-23).
3. In the Label Options dialog box that appears, select an option to select the type of printer and a label vendor and product number (see Figure 27-24). Word displays information about the label you select.
4. Click OK. Word sets up the document for the labels you selected without gridlines to identify individual labels.

To display gridlines, click the Table Tools Layout tab on the Ribbon. From the Table group, click View Gridlines.

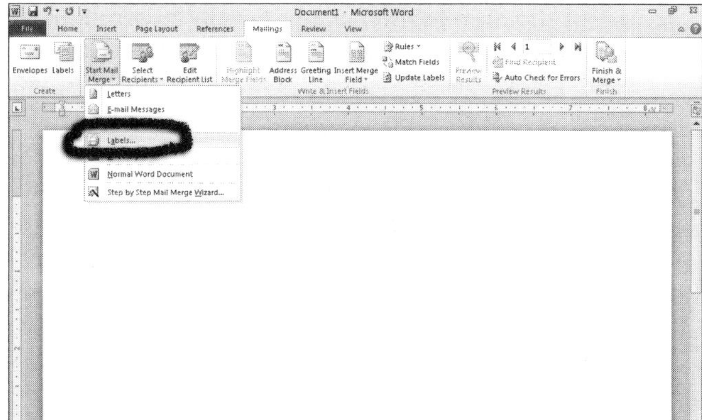

Figure 27-23

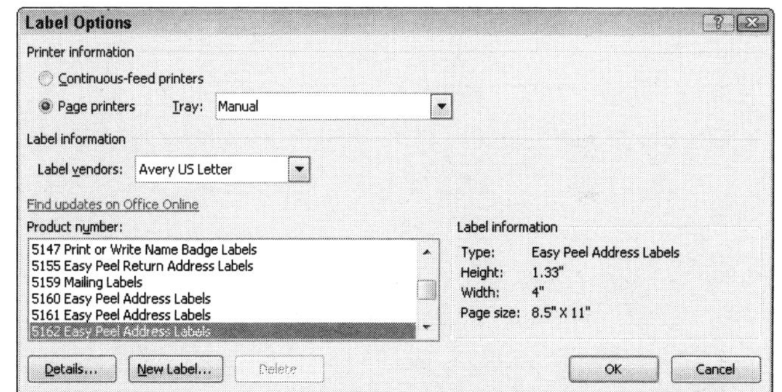

Figure 27-24

5. From the Start Mail Merge group on the Ribbon, click the Select Recipients button and then choose Select from Outlook Contacts from the menu that appears (see Figure 27-25).

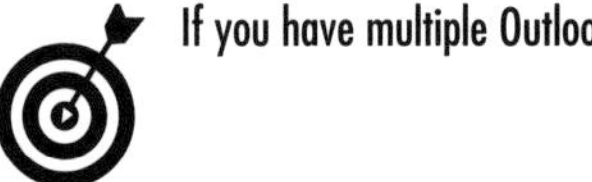

If you have multiple Outlook profiles, you'll be prompted to select one.

6. In the Select Contacts dialog box that appears, select the Contacts folder that you want to use and then click OK (see Figure 27-26).

You can have multiple Contacts folders, but most people have only one.

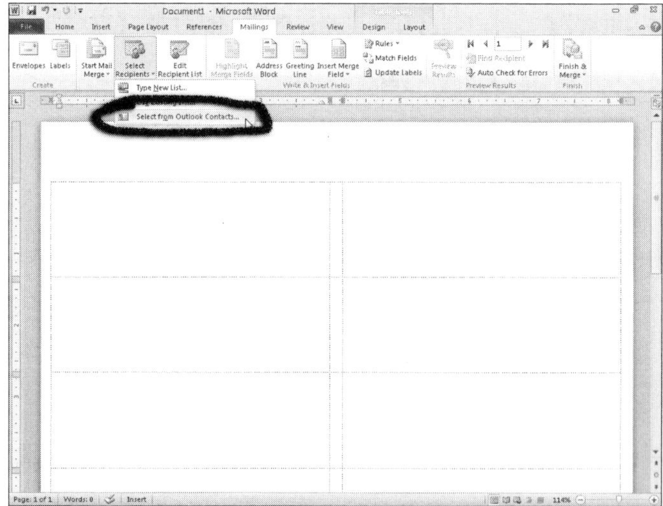

Figure 27-25

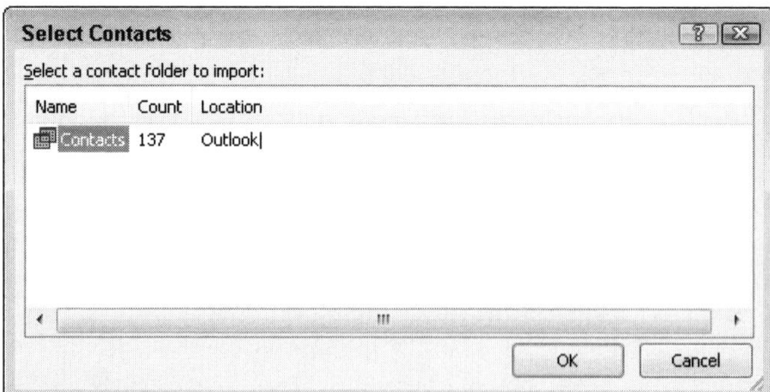

Figure 27-26

7. All the contacts stored in the Contacts folder that you select in Step 6 appear in the Mail Merge Recipients dialog box that appears (see Figure 27-27). Remove the check mark beside any addressee for whom you do not want to create a mailing label. Then click OK to redisplay the labels.

If you intend to limit the recipients, save time by assigning them to a category in Outlook as described in Chapter 22. Then, see "Using the Mail Merge Wizard with Selected Outlook Contact Information" later in this chapter.

8. Click in the first label.
9. From the Write & Insert Fields group on the Ribbon, click the Address Block button to display the Insert Address Block dialog box (see Figure 27-28).
10. Select a format for each recipient's name; a preview of the format appears on the right side of the dialog box.

If the preview doesn't look right to you, click the Match Fields button and use the list boxes in the Match Fields dialog box that appears to match Word fields with the fields in your mailing list file. See "Create a Mail Merge Letter" earlier in this chapter for details.

11. Click OK. Word adds the Address Block merge field to the first label. When you merge the information, Word replaces the merge field with information from the mailing address file.

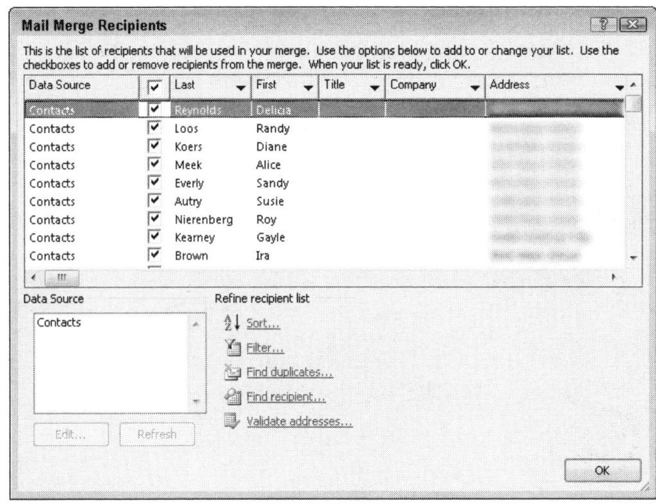

Figure 27-27

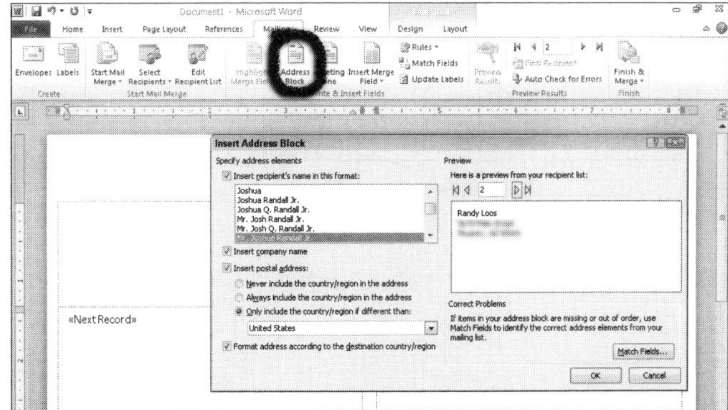

Figure 27-28

12. From the Write & Insert Fields group on the Ribbon, click the Update Labels button to add the Address Block merge field to every label (see Figure 27-29).

13. From the Preview Results group, click the Preview Results button to preview how your labels will look after you replace merge fields with Outlook Contact information.

14. Click the Preview Results button again to redisplay merge fields.

15. From the Finish group on the Ribbon, click the Finish & Merge button. From the drop-down menu that appears, choose Edit Individual Documents to display the Merge to New Document dialog box (see Figure 27-30).

16. Click an option to identify the recipients of the letter:

   - *All:* Creates a label for each recipient on the mailing list.
   - *Current Record:* Creates only one label for the recipient you are previewing.
   - *From* and *To:* Creates labels for recipients whom you specify by their record numbers.

17. Click OK, and Word merges the mailing list information onto the labels and places individual sheets of labels in a new document named Labels1.

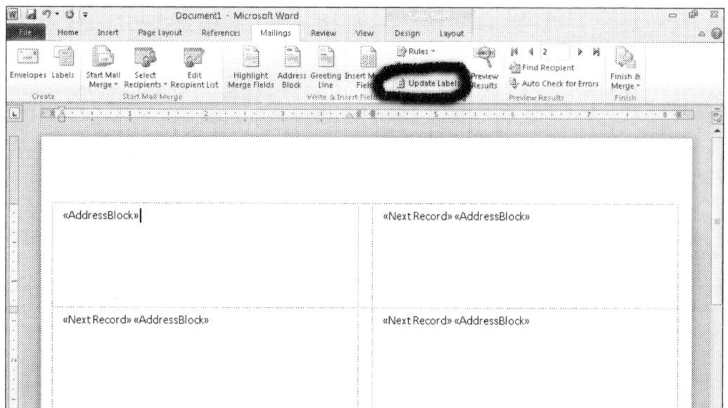

Figure 27-29

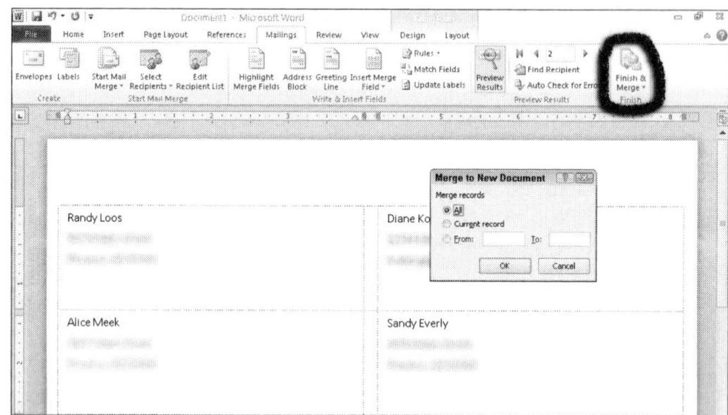

Figure 27-30

Using the Mail Merge Wizard with Selected Outlook Contact Information

1. In Outlook, assign all the contacts that you want to use in a single mail merge to one category. You can call the category "Mail Merge." See Chapter 23 for details on assigning contacts to categories.
2. Export the category of contacts to Excel as described in Chapter 26.
3. Open Word and click the Mailings tab. From the Start Mail Merge group, click the Start Mail Merge button and then choose Step by Step Mail Merge Wizard. Word displays the Mail Merge pane down the right side of the screen (see Figure 27-31).
4. Click the type of mail merge you want to create; for this example, use Labels.
5. At the bottom of the Mail Merge pane, click the Next: Starting Document button. On the subsequent Mail Merge pane, you can change the type of label you're using by clicking the Label Options link. At the bottom of the Mail Merge pane, click Next: Select Recipients. If the Label Options dialog box appears, click OK.
6. In the Mail Merge pane, select the Use an Existing List radio button and then click Browse (see Figure 27-32).

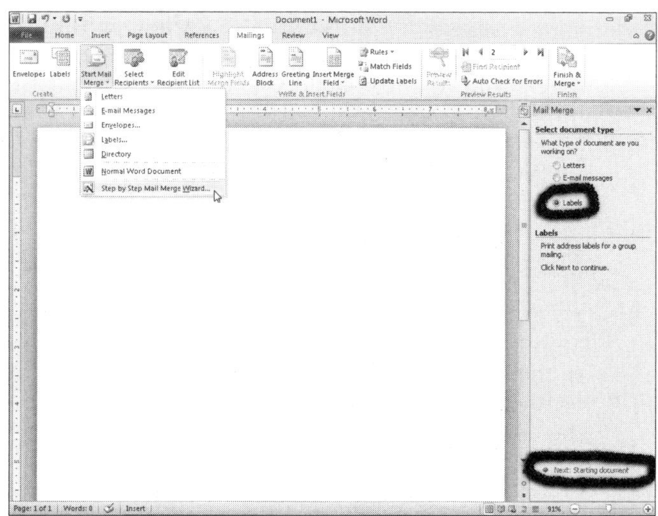

Figure 27-31

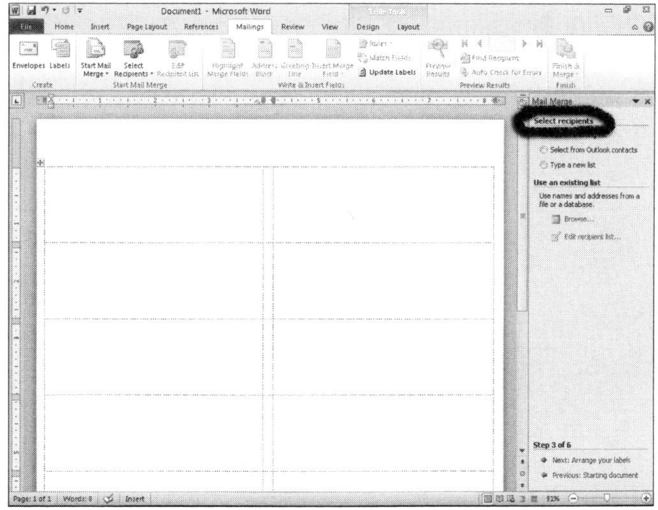

Figure 27-32

7. In the Select Data Source dialog box that appears, navigate to the folder in which you stored the Excel file containing mailing list information, select the file, then click Open. Word links with Excel, and the Select Table dialog box appears (see Figure 27-33). If the Excel workbook contains multiple sheets, select the sheet containing the mailing list and then click OK.

A check should appear in the First Row of Data Contains Column Headers check box.

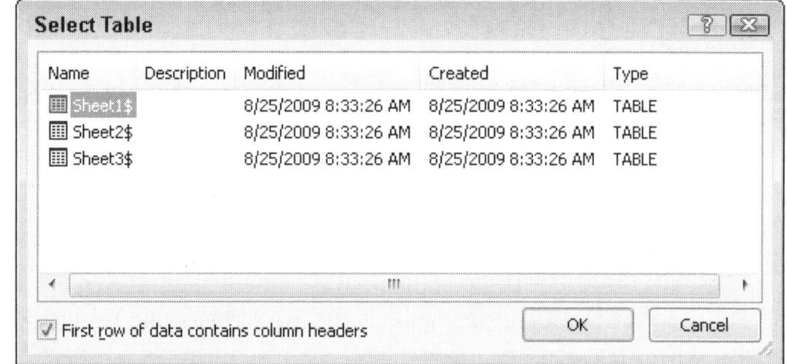

Figure 27-33

8. In the Mail Merge Recipients dialog box that appears (see Figure 27-34), you can sort the labels by any column; click the title of the column. You can optionally exclude a recipient by removing the check beside the recipient name. Click OK to redisplay Word and the Mail Merge pane.

9. At the bottom of the Mail Merge pane, click Next: Arrange Your Labels.

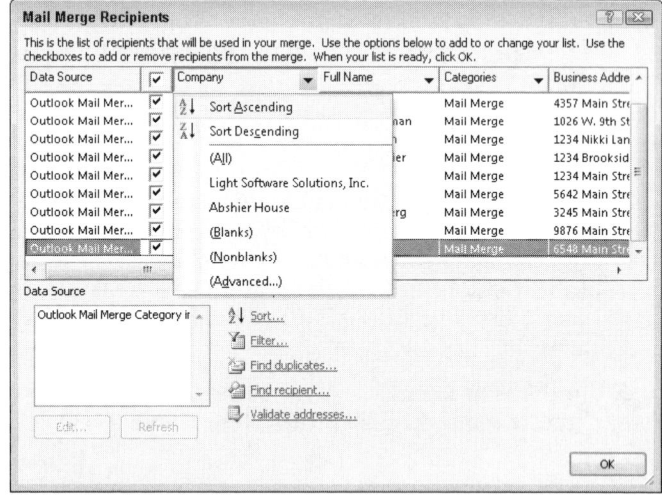

Figure 27-34

10. Click in the first label.

11. In the Mail Merge pane, click Address Block (see Figure 27-35).

Figure 27-35 shows you the Word document after completing Steps 10–15.

12. On the left side of the Address Block dialog box that appears, select a format for each recipient's name; a preview of the format appears on the right side (see Figure 27-36).

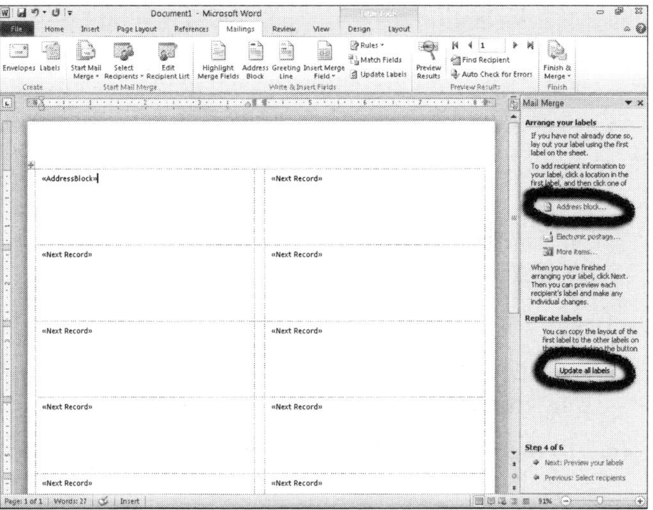

Figure 27-35

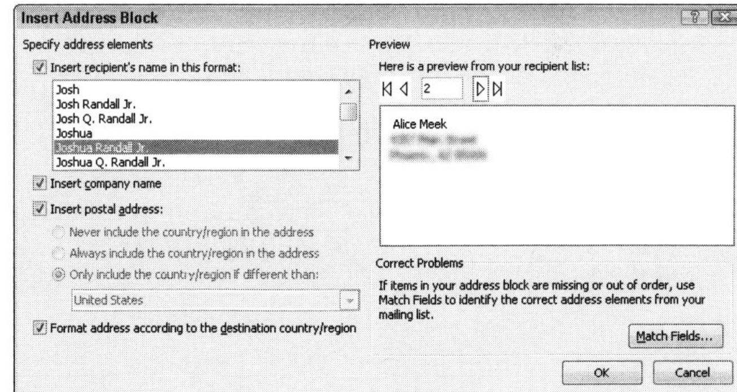

Figure 27-36

13. If information from the mailing list file doesn't appear correctly in the preview, click the Match Fields button to display the Match Fields dialog box (see Figure 27-37).

14. Open the list box for each field that you want to include in your form letter and then select the corresponding field from the list. To avoid having to match fields for this mailing list in the future, select the Remember This Matching for This Set of Data Sources on This Computer check box and then click OK. Word redisplays the Insert Address Block dialog box; refer to Figure 27-36.

15. Click OK. Word inserts the Address Block merge field in your document. When you merge the information, Word replaces the merge field with address information.

16. In the Mail Merge pane, click the Update Labels button. Word adds <<AddressBlock>> to each label (refer to Figure 27-35).

17. At the bottom of the Mail Merge pane, click Next: Preview Your Labels. Word displays your labels as they will print (see Figure 27-38). You can use the buttons at the top of the Mail Merge pane scroll through the labels.

18. At the bottom of the Mail Merge pane, click Next: Complete The Merge.

19. In the Mail Merge pane, click Print to immediately print the labels, or click Edit Individual Labels to merge to a document called Labels1.

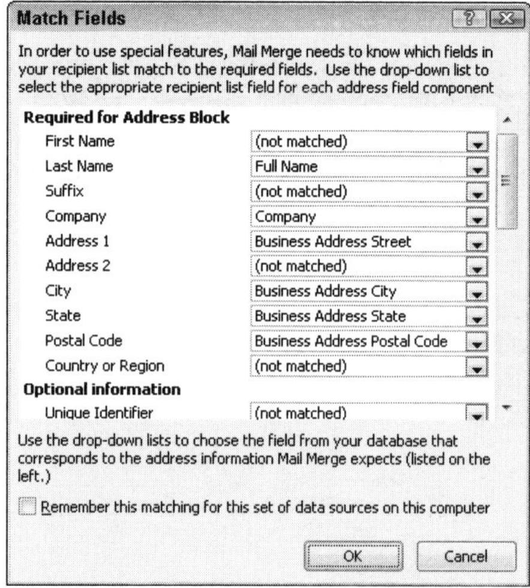

Figure 27-37

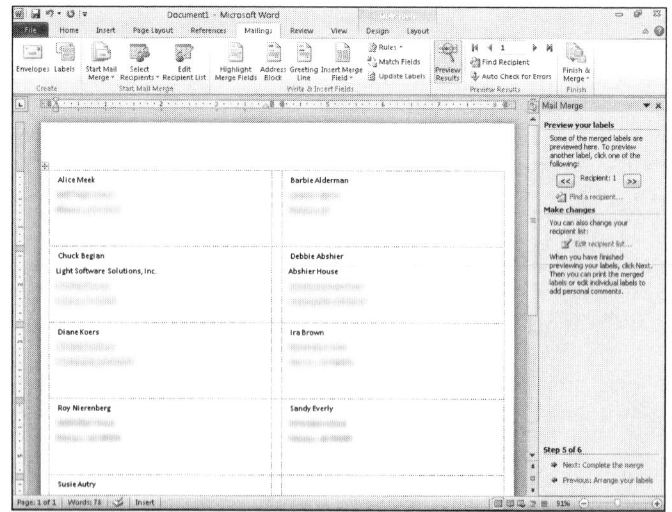

Figure 27-38

Working in Groups with Office Programs

Chapter

28

Often, you create a Word document, an Excel spreadsheet, or a PowerPoint presentation, and then you want other people to review it, make comments and corrections, and offer suggestions. You can use the Track Changes features in Word and Excel to view suggested changes that you can accept or reject; the feature also identifies who made each suggested change.

In all three programs, you can use the Comment feature to make suggestions for changes or corrections. You also can use the Comment feature to incorporate important information that falls outside the mainstream purpose of the document; for example, you might include a comment in an Excel workbook to explain the source of a number in the workbook. In this chapter, you see how to:

- Add, edit, delete, and print comments in Word, Excel, and PowerPoint.
- Set up a Word document and an Excel workbook to track reviewer changes.
- Review suggested changes and incorporate or reject them.

Get ready to . . .

Add a Comment to a Word Document

1. On the status bar, click the Print Layout icon.

You can insert comments in any view, but the appearance of the comment changes dramatically when viewed in Outline view or Draft view.

2. Select the text about which you want to comment.
3. Click the Review tab.
4. From the Comments group, click the New Comment button (see Figure 28-1). Word displays a comment balloon like the one shown in Figure 28-2. The comment balloon appears in the markup area on the right side of the document and is attached to the text that you selected.

In the comment, Word inserts the initials stored in the Personalize section of Word Options, followed by the comment number.

5. Type the comment text.
6. Click outside the comment balloon to save your comment.

To edit a comment, click inside the balloon and make changes. To delete a comment, click inside the comment; then, on the Review tab, from the Comments group, click the Delete button.

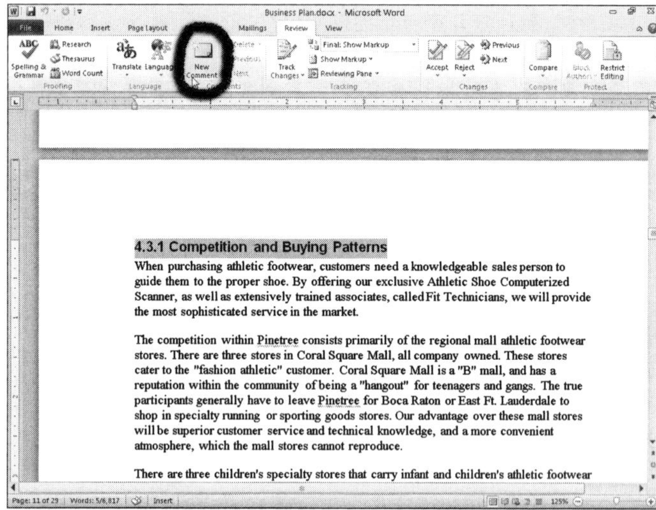

Figure 28-1

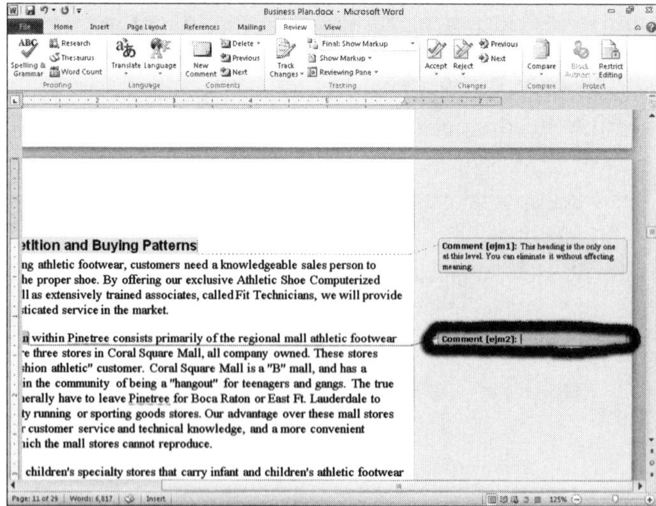

Figure 28-2

Track Changes to a Word Document

1. On the status bar, click the Print Layout icon (refer to Figure 28-1).
2. Click the Review tab.
3. From the Tracking group, click the top portion of the Track Changes button (see Figure 28-3). Word begins to monitor changes that you that make to the document.
4. Open the Display for Review list and choose Final: Show Markup.
5. Make changes to the document as needed (see Figure 28-4).
   - *Lines containing changes:* A vertical bar appears in the left margin beside these.
   - *Deleted text:* These changes appear with strikethrough formatting.
   - *Added text:* These changes appear underlined and in a color other than black.

To stop (toggle) tracking changes, repeat Steps 2 and 3. To review changes and accept or reject them, see the upcoming task, "Review Tracked Changes in a Word Document."

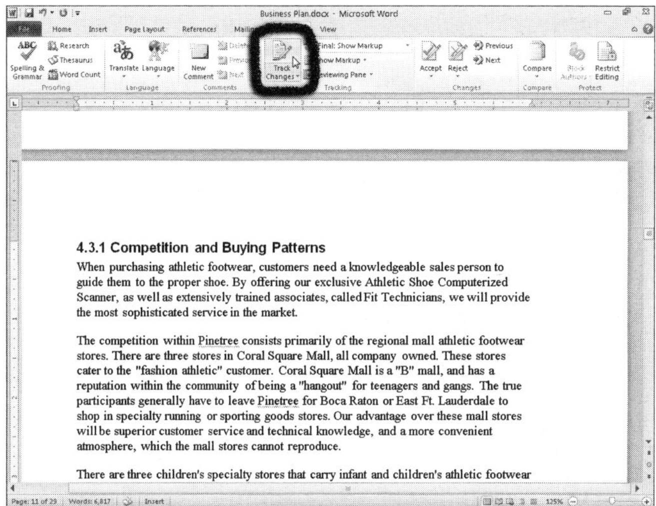

Figure 28-3

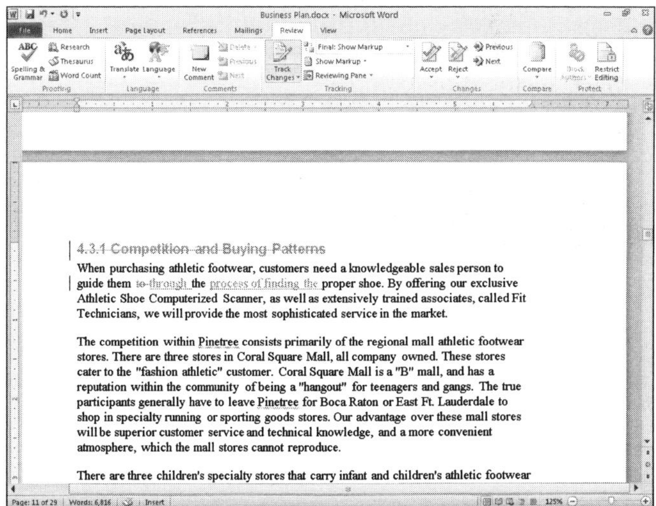

Figure 28-4

Review Tracked Changes in a Word Document

1. Open a document in which changes were tracked.
2. Click the Review tab.
3. From the Changes group, click the Next button to find the first tracked change, which Word highlights (see Figure 28-5).
4. Click Accept to incorporate the change into the document, or click Reject to revert the text to its original state. Word accepts or rejects the change, removes the revision marks, and highlights the next change (see Figure 28-6).

You can click Next to skip the change without accepting or rejecting it.

5. Repeat Step 4 to review each revision.

If you need to move backward to a change you skipped, click Previous.

6. After you review all changes, a message appears that no more tracked changes appear in the document. Click OK.

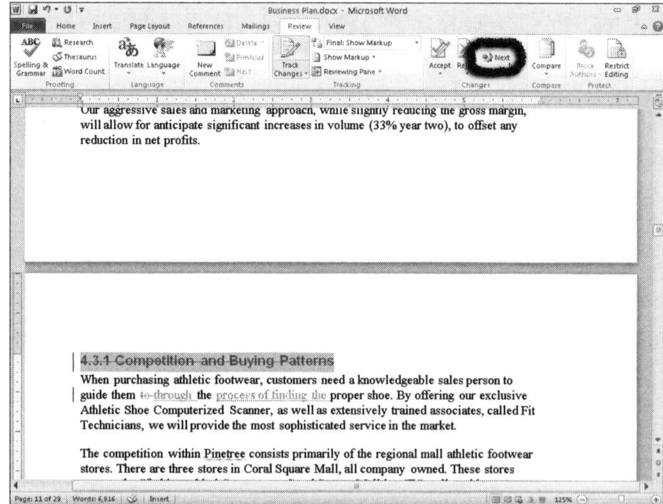

Figure 28-5

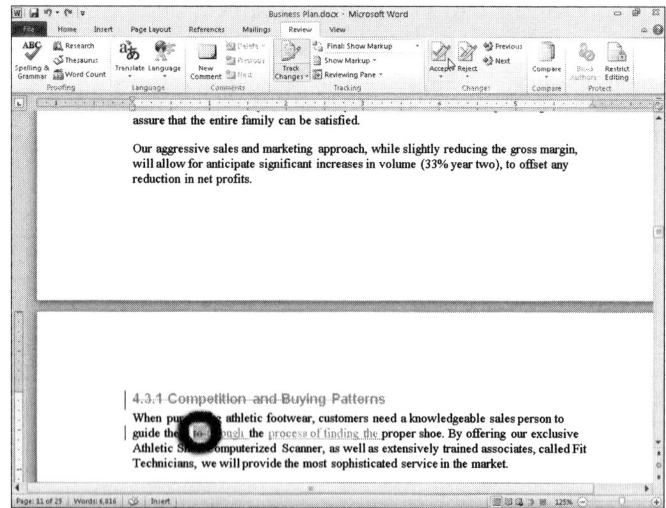

Figure 28-6

Combine Tracked Changes from Versions of a Word Document

1. With no documents open, click the Review tab. From the Compare group, click Compare. From the drop-down list that appears, choose Combine to display the Combine Documents dialog box (see Figure 28-7).
2. Click the Open icon in the Original Document section to navigate to and select the original document you want to combine. Then click Open.
3. When the Combine Documents dialog box reappears, repeat Step 3, clicking the Open icon in the Revised Document section.
4. Click OK. Word switches to Web Layout view and displays four panes (see Figure 28-8):
   - Left: Contains a summary of the revisions made by combining the documents.
   - Middle: Contains the results of combining the original document and the reviewed document.
   - Top right: Displays the original document.
   - Bottom right: Displays the reviewed document.
5. Use the steps in "Review Tracked Changes in a Word Document" to deal with revisions in the combined document. You can save the combined document and repeat these steps to incorporate comments from other revised versions of the document.

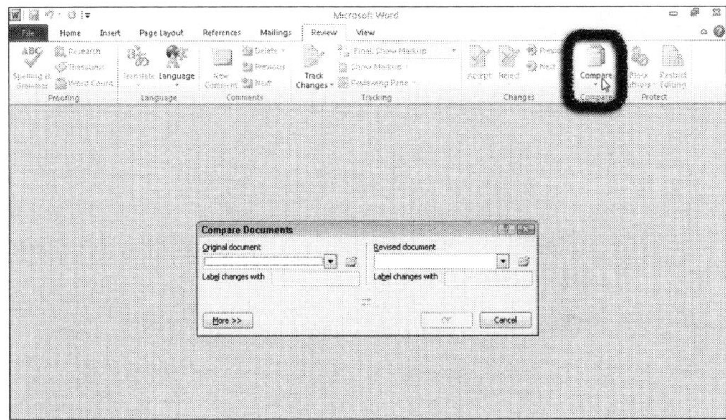

Figure 28-7

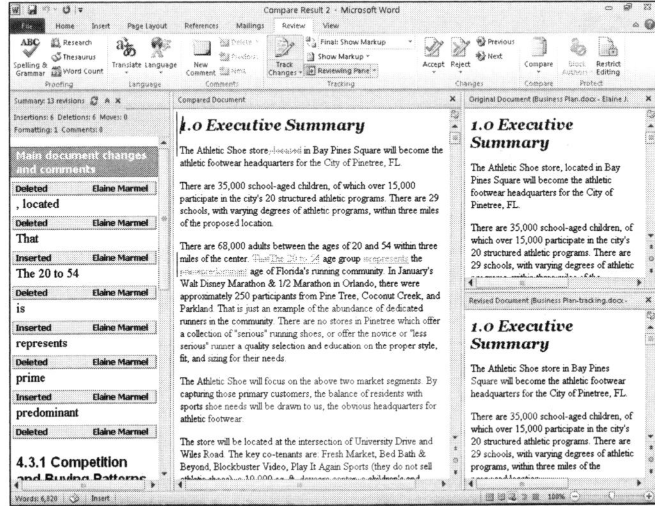

Figure 28-8

Add Comments to Excel Workbook Cells

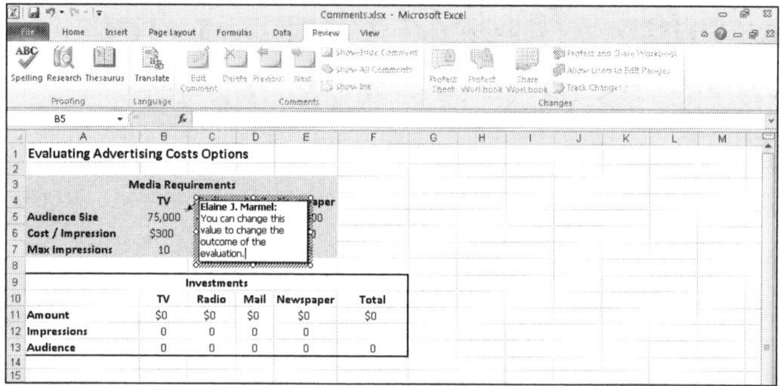

Figure 28-9

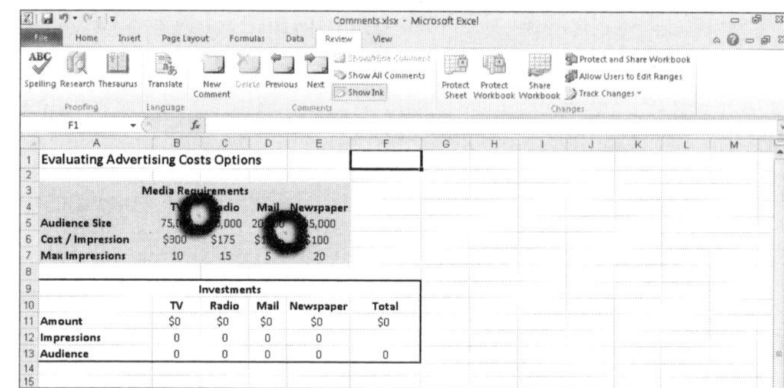

Figure 28-10

1. Click the cell to which you want to add a comment.
2. Click the Review tab.
3. From the Comments group, click the New Comment button. Excel displays a comment box containing your name or initials (see Figure 28-9).
4. Type the comment information.
5. Click outside the comment box. Excel stores the comment; a small, red triangle appears in the upper right of cells containing comments (see Figure 28-10).

To edit or delete an existing comment, click the cell containing the comment. Then, on the Review tab, from the Comments group, click the Edit Comment button or the Delete button.

Display a Cell Comment in an Excel Workbook

1. Select a cell containing a comment.
2. Click the Review tab.
3. From the Comments group, click the Show/Hide Comment button (see Figure 28-11). Excel displays the comment, and it remains visible even when you select another cell.

The Show/Hide Comment button is grayed out because I deliberately selected a cell containing no comment.

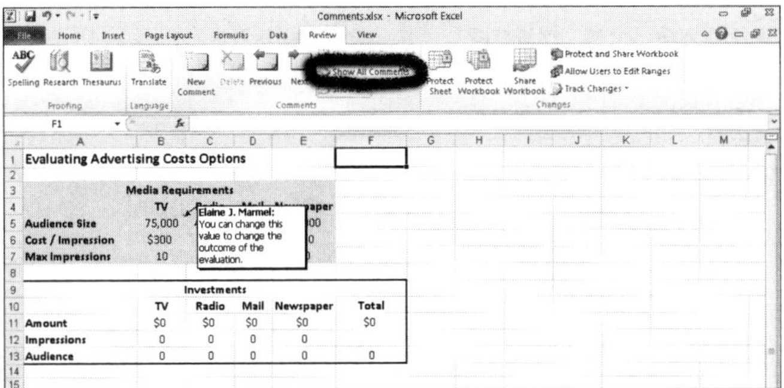

Figure 28-11

Display All Comments in an Excel Workbook

1. Click the Review tab.
2. From the Comments group, click the Show All Comments button (see Figure 28-12). Excel displays all comments in the workbook, and they remain visible.

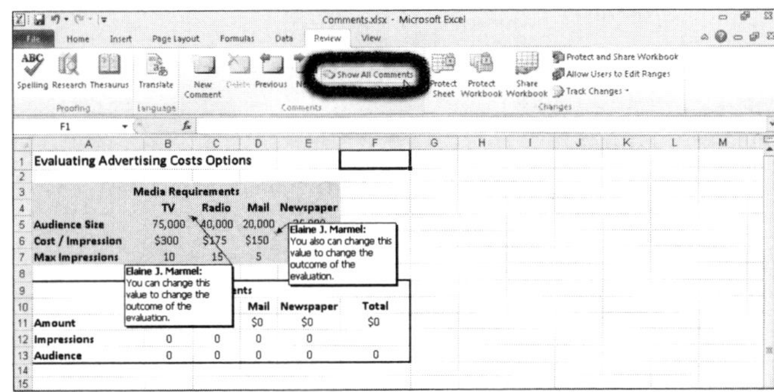

Figure 28-12

Share an Excel Workbook

1. Click the Review tab.
2. From the Changes group, click Share Workbook. The Share Workbook dialog box appears (see Figure 28-13).
3. Select the Allow Changes check box at the top of the Editing tab.
4. Click the Advanced tab and then select sharing options (see Figure 28-14):
   - *Track Changes:* Specify how long Excel keeps change history.
   - *Update Changes:* Specify when you receive updates from other users.
   - *Conflicting Changes between Users:* Specify how Excel resolves conflicts caused by two users changing the same data.
   - *Include in Personal View:* Select options to enable your local print and filter settings.
5. Click OK to share the file. Excel displays a message explaining that it will save the workbook and your changes. Click OK again.

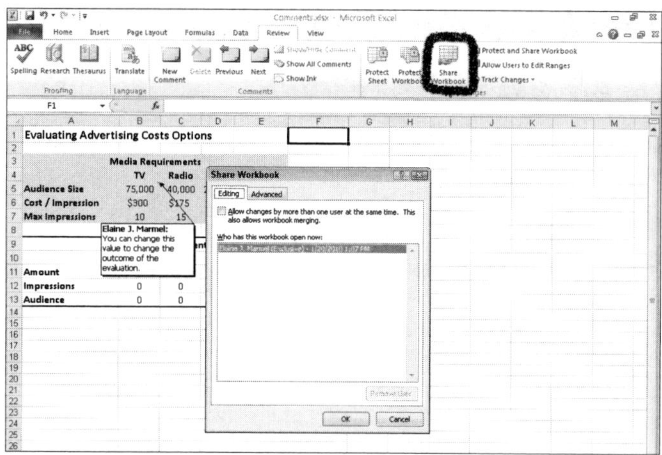

Figure 28-13

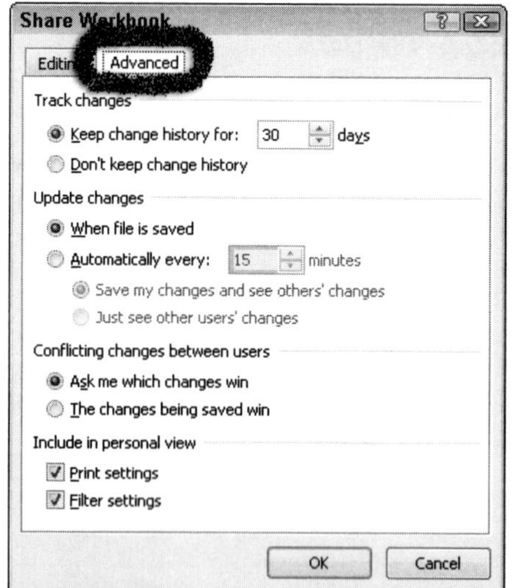

Figure 28-14

Track Changes in an Excel Workbook

1. Click the Review tab.
2. From the Changes group, click the Track Changes button.
3. From the menu that appears, choose Highlight Changes (see Figure 28-15). Excel displays the Highlight Changes dialog box (see Figure 28-16).
4. Select the Track Changes While Editing check box. Additional tracking options become available.
5. In the Highlight Which Changes section, select check boxes to identify the changes you want Excel to highlight.

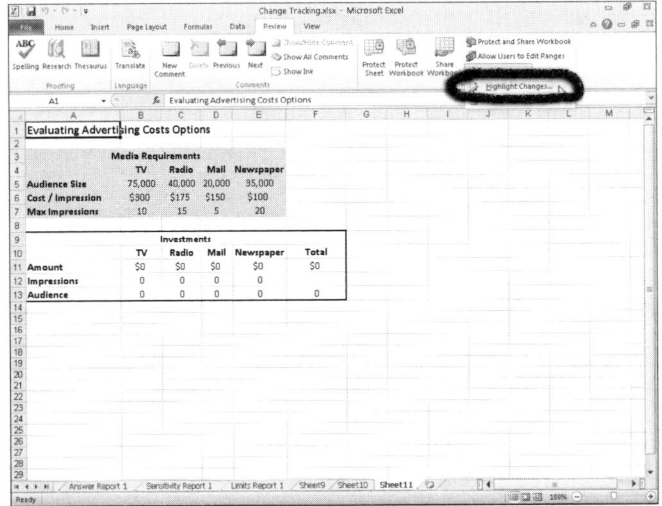

Figure 28-15

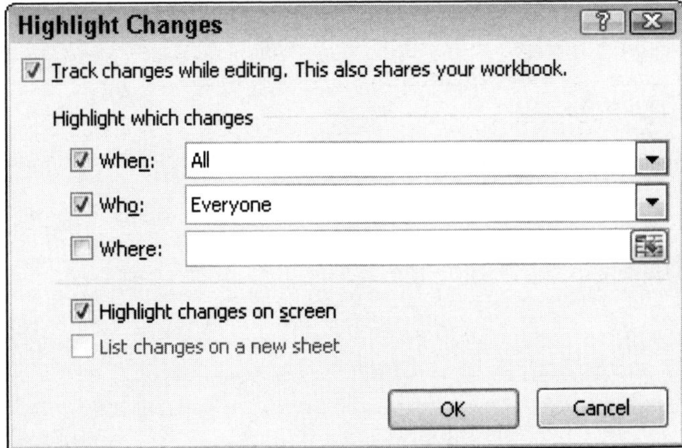

Figure 28-16

6. Click OK. When a message appears, telling you that Excel will save the workbook, click OK. Excel enables change tracking and shares the workbook.

7. Make changes in the workbook, such as changing values or adding or deleting rows or columns. Excel adds a dark-blue triangle to the upper left of every cell you change (see Figure 28-17).

8. Move the mouse pointer over a cell containing a dark-blue triangle. Excel displays a comment that describes the change (see Figure 28-18).

When you insert a row or column, Excel extends a dark-blue line along the edges of the row or column.

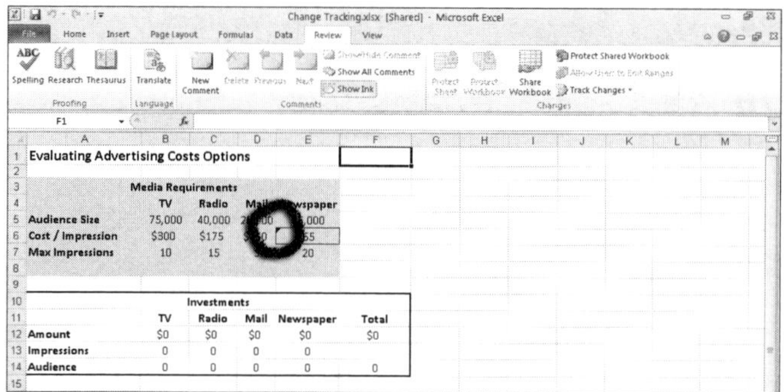

Figure 28-17

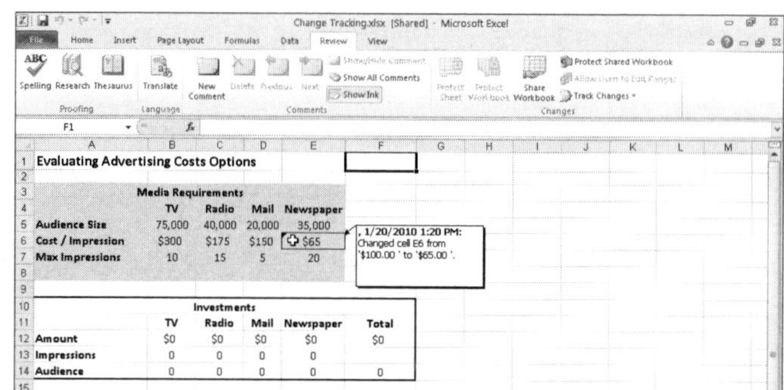

Figure 28-18

Review Tracked Changes in an Excel Workbook

1. Click the Review tab.
2. From the Changes group, click the Track Changes button. From the menu that appears, choose Accept/Reject Changes. At the prompt, click OK to save the workbook. Excel displays the Select Changes to Accept or Reject dialog box.
3. Specify the changes to review and then click OK. Excel highlights the first change and displays the Accept or Reject Changes dialog box (see Figure 28-19).
4. Click the Accept button or the Reject button. Excel makes the change or ignores it and selects the next changed cell.

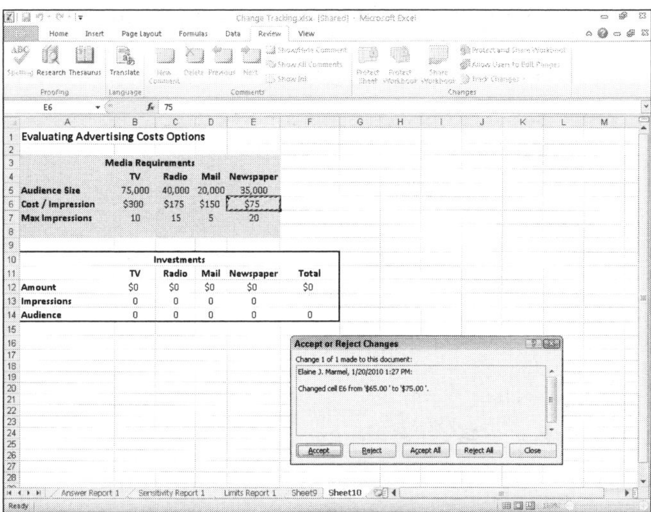

Figure 28-19

Print Comments in an Excel Workbook

1. Display all comments in the workbook as described earlier in this chapter in the task, "Display All Comments in an Excel Workbook."
2. Click the Page Layout tab.
3. From the Page Setup group, click the dialog box launcher button to display the Page Setup dialog box. Click the Sheet tab (see Figure 28-20).
4. Open the Comments drop-down list box and select an option.
5. Click OK and print the worksheet. Excel prints comments according to the setting you selected.

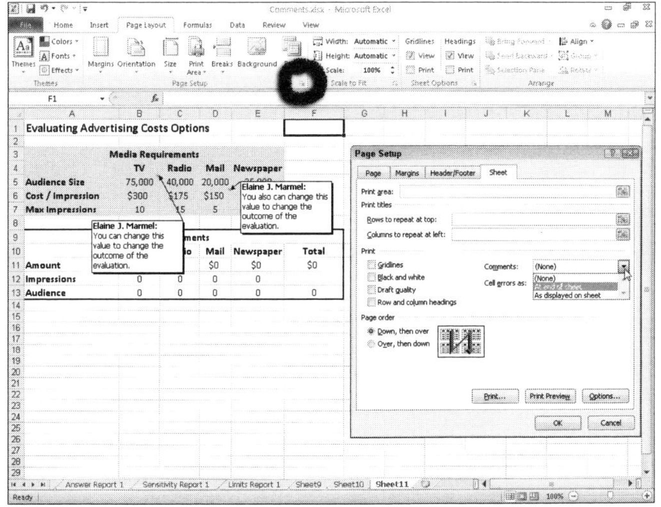

Figure 28-20

Add a Comment to a PowerPoint Slide

1. To add a comment *about a slide,* click anywhere on the slide; to comment *on an element on the slide,* select the item.
2. Click the Review tab.
3. From the Comments group, click the New Comment button. In the comment box that appears, type the comment (see Figure 28-21).
4. Click outside the comment box. PowerPoint adds a comment thumbnail containing your initials to the slide.

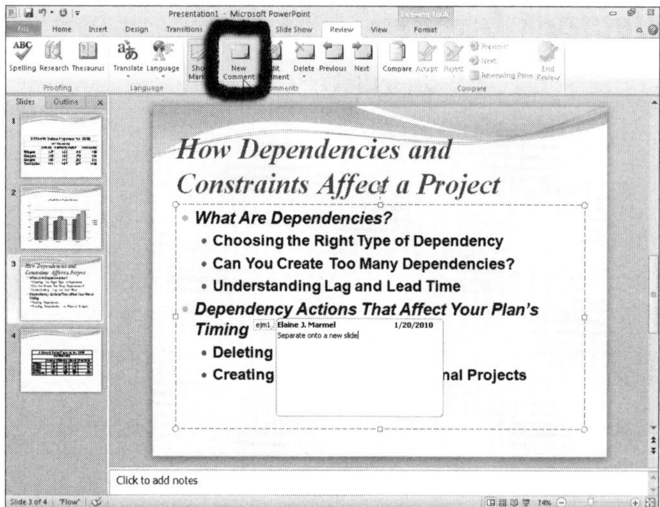

Figure 28-21

Edit a PowerPoint Slide Comment

1. Click the comment thumbnail to reveal its content (see Figure 28-22). If you don't see the comment thumbnail, click the Show Markup button on the Review tab in the Comments group.
2. Click the Review tab.
3. From the Comments group, click the Edit Comment button. In the box that appears, make changes to the comment.
4. Click outside the comment box to save your changes.

If one reviewer edits the comment of another reviewer, PowerPoint changes the initials in the comment to the last reviewer's initials.

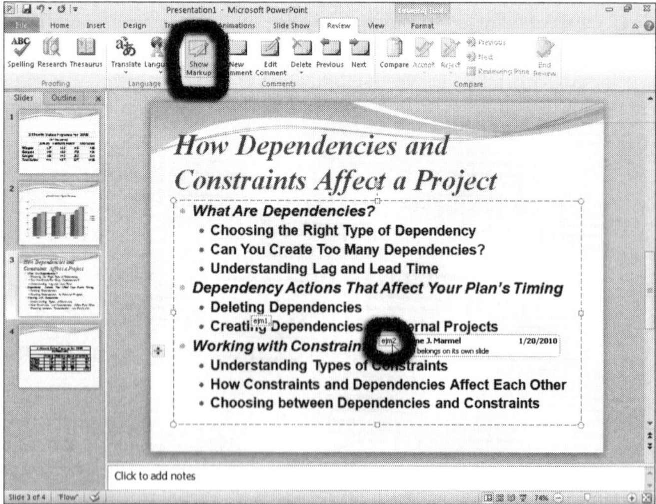

Figure 28-22

Delete a PowerPoint Slide Comment

1. Click the thumbnail of the comment that you want to delete.
2. Click the Review tab.
3. From the Comments group, click the arrow below the Delete button.
4. From the menu that appears, choose Delete (see Figure 28-23).

If one reviewer deletes another's comment, PowerPoint changes the initials of the comment to those of the reviewer who deleted the comment.

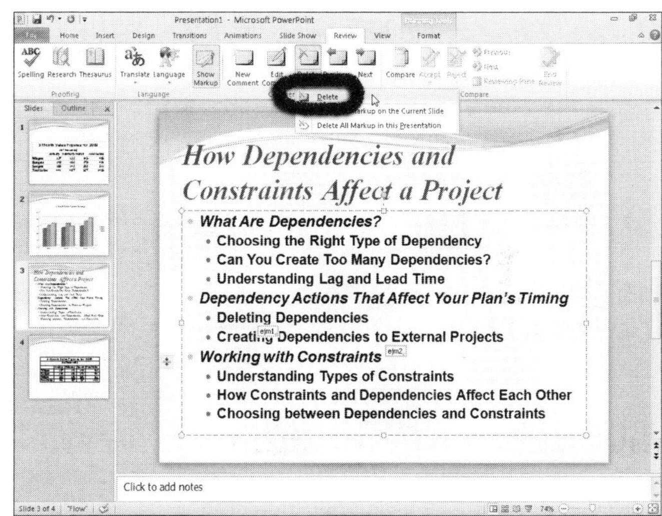

Figure 28-23

Review PowerPoint Slide Comments

1. Click the Review tab.
2. From the Comments group, make sure that the Show Markup button is selected (see Figure 28-24).
3. Click the Next and Previous buttons to display the next or previous comment in the presentation.

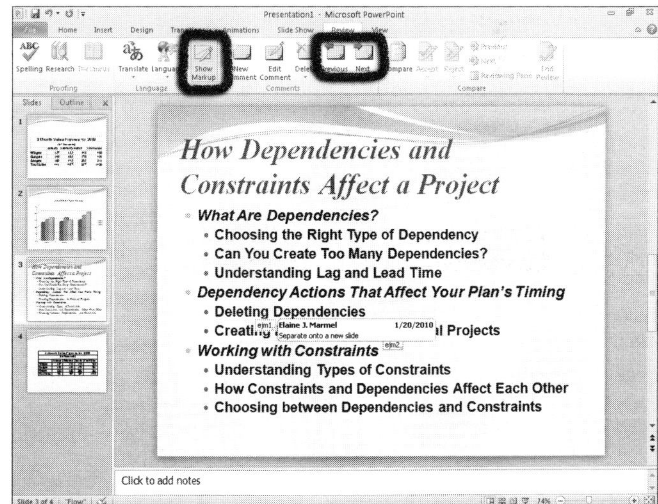

Figure 28-24

Print PowerPoint Slide Comments

1. Click the File tab. From Backstage view that appears, click Print (see Figure 28-25).
2. In the Settings section, click the Full Page Slides button.
3. Make sure that a check appears beside Print Comments and Ink Markup (see Figure 28-26).
4. Click the Print button at the top of the screen. PowerPoint prints the presentation, including its comments.

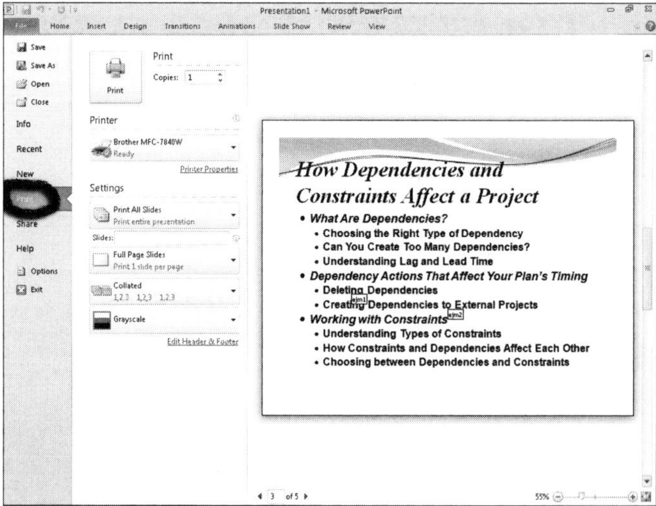

Figure 28-25

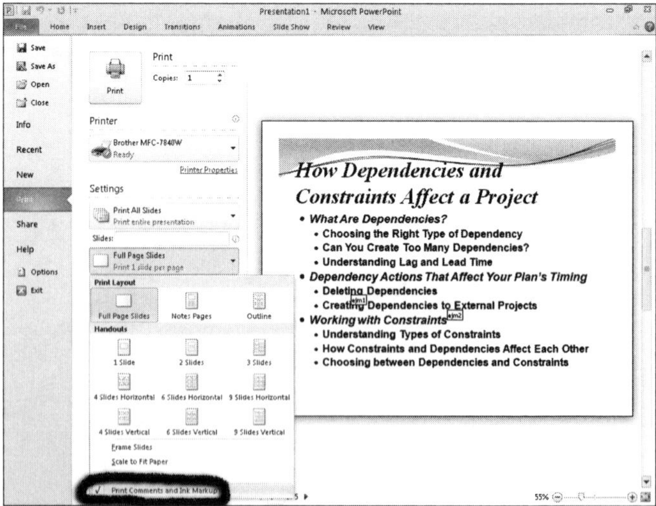

Figure 28-26

Index

• D •

• E •

• G •

• H •

• I •

• J •

• L •

• M •

• N •

• O •

• P •

• Q •

• S •

• T •

usiness/Accounting Bookkeeping
ookkeeping For Dummies
'8-0-7645-9848-7

Bay Business
l-in-One For Dummies,
d Edition
'8-0-470-38536-4

b Interviews
r Dummies,
d Edition
'8-0-470-17748-8

sumes For Dummies,
h Edition
8-0-470-08037-5

ock Investing
r Dummies,
d Edition
8-0-470-40114-9

ccessful
me Management
r Dummies
8-0-470-29034-7

Computer Hardware
BlackBerry For Dummies,
3rd Edition
978-0-470-45762-7

Computers For Seniors
For Dummies
978-0-470-24055-7

iPhone For Dummies,
2nd Edition
978-0-470-42342-4

Laptops For Dummies,
3rd Edition
978-0-470-27759-1

Macs For Dummies,
10th Edition
978-0-470-27817-8

Cooking & Entertaining
Cooking Basics
For Dummies,
3rd Edition
978-0-7645-7206-7

Wine For Dummies,
4th Edition
978-0-470-04579-4

Diet & Nutrition
Dieting For Dummies,
2nd Edition
978-0-7645-4149-0

Nutrition For Dummies,
4th Edition
978-0-471-79868-2
Weight Training
For Dummies,
3rd Edition
978-0-471-76845-6

Digital Photography
Digital Photography
For Dummies,
6th Edition
978-0-470-25074-7

Photoshop Elements 7
For Dummies
978-0-470-39700-8

Gardening
Gardening Basics
For Dummies
978-0-470-03749-2

Organic Gardening
For Dummies,
2nd Edition
978-0-470-43067-5

Green/Sustainable
Green Building
& Remodeling
For Dummies
978-0-4710-17559-0

Green Cleaning
For Dummies
978-0-470-39106-8

Green IT For Dummies
978-0-470-38688-0

Health
Diabetes For Dummies,
3rd Edition
978-0-470-27086-8

Food Allergies
For Dummies
978-0-470-09584-3

Living Gluten-Free
For Dummies
978-0-471-77383-2

Hobbies/General
Chess For Dummies,
2nd Edition
978-0-7645-8404-6

Drawing For Dummies
978-0-7645-5476-6
Knitting For Dummies,
2nd Edition
978-0-470-28747-7

Organizing For Dummies
978-0-7645-5300-4

SuDoku For Dummies
978-0-470-01892-7

Home Improvement
Energy Efficient Homes
For Dummies
978-0-470-37602-7

Home Theater
For Dummies,
3rd Edition
978-0-470-41189-6

Living the Country Lifestyle
All-in-One For Dummies
978-0-470-43061-3

Solar Power Your Home
For Dummies
978-0-470-17569-9

Internet

Blogging For Dummies, 2nd Edition
978-0-470-23017-6

eBay For Dummies, 6th Edition
978-0-470-49741-8

Facebook For Dummies
978-0-470-26273-3

Google Blogger For Dummies
978-0-470-40742-4

Web Marketing For Dummies, 2nd Edition
978-0-470-37181-7

WordPress For Dummies, 2nd Edition
978-0-470-40296-2

Language & Foreign Language

French For Dummies
978-0-7645-5193-2

Italian Phrases For Dummies
978-0-7645-7203-6

Spanish For Dummies
978-0-7645-5194-9

Spanish For Dummies, Audio Set
978-0-470-09585-0

Macintosh

Mac OS X Snow Leopard For Dummies
978-0-470-43543-4

Math & Science

Algebra I For Dummies
978-0-7645-5325-7

Biology For Dummies
978-0-7645-5326-4

Calculus For Dummies
978-0-7645-2498-1

Chemistry For Dummies
978-0-7645-5430-8

Microsoft Office

Excel 2007 For Dummies
978-0-470-03737-9

Office 2007 All-in-One Desk Reference For Dummies
978-0-471-78279-7

Music

Guitar For Dummies, 2nd Edition
978-0-7645-9904-0

iPod & iTunes For Dummies, 6th Edition
978-0-470-39062-7

Piano Exercises For Dummies
978-0-470-38765-8

Parenting & Education

Parenting For Dummies, 2nd Edition
978-0-7645-5418-6

Type 1 Diabetes For Dummies
978-0-470-17811-9

Pets

Cats For Dummies, 2nd Edition
978-0-7645-5275-5

Dog Training For Dummies, 2nd Edition
978-0-7645-8418-3

Puppies For Dummies, 2nd Edition
978-0-470-03717-1

Religion & Inspiration

The Bible For Dummies
978-0-7645-5296-0

Catholicism For Dummies
978-0-7645-5391-2

Women in the Bible For Dummies
978-0-7645-8475-6

Self-Help & Relationship

Anger Management For Dummies
978-0-470-03715-7

Overcoming Anxiety For Dummies
978-0-7645-5447-6

Sports

Baseball For Dummies, 3rd Edition
978-0-7645-7537-2

Basketball For Dummies, 2nd Edition
978-0-7645-5248-9

Golf For Dummies, 3rd Edition
978-0-471-76871-5

Web Development

Web Design All-in-One For Dummies
978-0-470-41796-6

Windows Vista

Windows Vista For Dummies
978-0-471-75421-3